Watching M*A*S*H, Watching America

A Social History of the 1972–1983 Television Series

by JAMES H. WITTEBOLS

McFarland & Company, Inc., Publishers
Jefferson, North Carolina, and London

The present work is a reprint of the library bound edition of
Watching M*A*S*H*, Watching America: A Social History
of the 1972–1983 Television Series, *first published in 1998.*

LIBRARY OF CONGRESS CATALOGUING-IN-PUBLICATION DATA

Wittebols, James H.
     Watching M*A*S*H, watching America : a social history of the
1972–1983 television series / by James H. Wittebols.
          p.   cm.
     Includes bibliographical references and index.

     ISBN 0-7864-1701-3 (softcover binding : 50# alkaline paper)

     1. MASH (Television program)   I. Title.
PN1992.77.M2854W58   2003
791.45'72—dc21
                                                          98-10800

British Library cataloguing data are available

Cover image ©2003 PhotoDisc

Manufactured in the United States of America

McFarland & Company, Inc., Publishers
   Box 611, Jefferson, North Carolina 28640
      www.mcfarlandpub.com

Acknowledgments

No effort like this book is accomplished without a great deal of assistance and support. For the last four years, I have subjected many friends and loved ones to the elements of discovery, surprise and frustration as I conducted the research on which this book is based. I am indebted to many individuals who provided key work in accessing episodes of *M*A*S*H*, managing the database developed for this research, and compiling and documenting the social and political history of the *M*A*S*H* era. Sara Mangan provided early efforts at cataloging and database development for each *M*A*S*H* episode. John Adair, Lisa Johnson and Danielle Smith provided immense help in compiling materials, which took hours of time and patient persistence. Jennifer Bergin made the indexing of this book much easier. Lois Ringle of WUTV Fox 29 helped round out my collection of episodes by providing some that are rarely aired. The Niagara University Library staff, especially David Schoen, provided a great deal of research assistance. Also important to the project were manuscript readings by Monica Barner and Jennifer Certo, which led to significant revisions and, I hope, improvements in the final package. My colleagues Bob Crawford and Mark Barner provided moral support and managed to keep me from going too crazy at crucial moments.

I would like to thank Niagara University for its support of this project in several phases. Initial research was provided by a Niagara University Research Council Summer Grant in 1994. Support funds provided during 1995–96 and a sabbatical leave in the winter 1996 semester allowed me to focus on the writing phase.

Watching M*A*S*H, *Watching America*

Contents

Preface

Unlike the citizens of Dickens's England, Americans in the 1970s saw neither the best of times nor the worst of times. What they saw, in the words of the old Chinese proverb, were interesting times. And a lot of people marked at least some of that time by watching one of television's most popular and longest running situation comedies, *M*A*S*H*. This is a book about those times and that show. It is a book about the relationship between television programs and the times in which they are produced.

M*A*S*H has been described as a show set in the 1950s that reflected the values of the 1960s for audiences of the 1970s and early 1980s. It is generally regarded as innovative both in form (mixing comedy and tragedy) and in content (addressing war in a way no program had done before, and very few have since). But was the show truly provocative? Did it really challenge American society to reflect on what it means to be a superpower? Did it have a lasting impact on how Americans thought about war? Or did its premier and popularity near the end of the Vietnam War merely reflect a society that was weary and wary of military solutions to world problems?

As one of the longest running shows on United States television, *M*A*S*H* presents a unique example of how a television series reflects societal change. This book will describe and analyze the changes in American society during the period *M*A*S*H* was aired on network television. We will see that *M*A*S*H* did not so much lead people's thinking about significant issues of the day—war, bureaucracy, spying, women's rights, drinking and drugs—as it followed prevailing and changing sentiment about those issues.

In other words, the political space that allowed a situation comedy such as *M*A*S*H* to even be considered for television was shaped by shifting public opinion on the Vietnam War. By the time of the show's premier in 1972, public opinion was overwhelmingly in favor of withdrawing American troops from Vietnam. As we will see, however, *M*A*S*H* changed to reflect the changes American society experienced as it moved from the Vietnam era to the Reagan eighties.

By the time the show signed off in February 1983, it had retired its litany of sexual innuendoes and significantly decreased the drinking and debauchery that characterized the early years of the show. Other changes were also evident. In the early 1980s, as President Ronald Reagan introduced policies geared toward rehabilitating the military, *M*A*S*H*'s early ridicule of army bureaucracy was gradually displaced by the portrayal of the *M*A*S*H* unit as a competent, caring arm of the United States military. At the same time, the rise of the women's movement was reflected in the show's decreased reliance on sexist jokes and situations, as well as its emphasis on the transformation of Margaret Houlihan, whose experiences as a nurse, girlfriend and wife led her toward a more feminist view of the world.

The passage of forty years since the Korean War and twenty-five since the premiere of *M*A*S*H* on network television make it possible to take a fresh look at the meaning of the 4077's eleven-year history as it relates to the changes in American society during the 1970s and early 1980s. With the benefit of hindsight, we can better assess the relationship between television and society. Does TV lead the way in social change? Or does it simply follow the trends, presenting a vaguely familiar yet relatively sanitized view of contemporary society? By looking at *M*A*S*H* and the historical events which occurred during its lengthy run, perhaps we can better understand the relationship between the lessons of television and social change.

The pages that follow will show that *M*A*S*H* provides a way to understand television and its role in society. Television, when it addresses social issues, does not lead public opinion. Instead, it reflects a safe middle ground—never too controversial, yet not completely out of touch with the problems and issues of the real world. This book will serve to illustrate that idea. We will take a look at *M*A*S*H* and its history as it relates to the history of the period during which it was airing in prime time.

The fact that *M*A*S*H* endures as a syndicated sitcom is an indication that the themes and values reflected in the show still have some resonance with the public. As over 200 stations nationwide regularly carry the show in syndication, those who are now watching it for the first time can come to a better understanding of its historical significance—as television culture and history, and as part of larger American culture and politics in an era gone by.

This book is intended to help the reader understand the social significance of television as a mass medium. The first chapter presents a brief review of situation comedy as a genre and of how sitcoms represent a window into contemporary society. In the second chapter, we will look at the development of *M*A*S*H*—how it began as a novel that was then made into a film; how it drew from other innovative situation comedies of the late 1960s; and how it represented a distinct change from other military sitcoms.

The bulk of the book will discuss the trends and changes in the series and examine the *M*A*S*H* episodes year by year while also presenting a political and social history of the times in which *M*A*S*H* aired. This book describes the events of the day as they were represented by the widely read media of the period such as *Time* and *Newsweek*. The idea is not to provide an updated or revised version of history, but rather to define the political, social and cultural milieu in which the planning and development of *M*A*S*H* occurred. As the "first draft of history," journalistic accounts allow us to see what millions of Americans learned about events as they occurred and what kind of understanding they could glean from the mass media of those times.

To be sure, numerous versions of history are available through hindsight. But looking at contemporary American society as the *M*A*S*H* creative team and the audience for the show experienced it will allow us to see how news and cultural developments reflect the conventional wisdom of the day. That is, news and the way it shapes the public consciousness can be seen as the backdrop for the evolution of *M*A*S*H* as a television situation comedy. As has often been said, the media do not so much tell us what to think as what to think about. The descriptions of contemporary political and social trends provide mainstream perspectives on the events which transpired from 1972 to 1983.

Chapters 3 through 8, which cover the years of the show, will provide the reader with an understanding of how *M*A*S*H* and American society evolved throughout the 1970s and early 1980s. As an organizing device, this evolution is discussed in two-year segments, which may make the changes appear more discrete than continuing. History, however, is fluid, making it difficult to identify when trends start and stop. Readers should be sensitive to this fact as they read these chapters.

We should also keep in mind that the conceiving and writing of episodes is multifaceted, and changes in the producers and writers who worked for the show over its lifetime would necessarily result in changes to the show. On the other hand, the creative team swims in the same cultural tides that washed over the rest of America in the 1970s and early 1980s. Thus, this book will illustrate how the real events of the day played a role in the changes *M*A*S*H* underwent throughout its life on prime-time network television.

The book closes with two chapters that put the show in context. One chapter will take a look at the legacy of *M*A*S*H*—what its long run and unique standing in American television mean for the television industry and American society. The final chapter considers the "values" debate surrounding television and examines what the values projected by *M*A*S*H* say about television and social change.

The Situation
Comedy as Social History

The situation comedy is as American as apple pie. In the nearly fifty years since television was introduced into American homes, the sitcom has emerged as a popular form of programming by providing people with something to laugh at. But the sitcom also has helped shape the country's collective image of itself. It has provided a window on the times in which we live.[1] The prototypical American sitcom has given viewers a highly idealized view of American life, particularly those family sitcoms which were part of the early years of television. As time went on, the sitcom began to respond to changes occurring in American society both within and outside the family.

In some ways, the changes in American television are reflected in the roles of some of the actresses who were so much a part of situation comedies over the years. Mary Tyler Moore began her career as a pair of secretarial legs in *Richard Diamond, Private Detective* (1957–60).[2] Viewers would never know it was Moore as the character remained a disembodied voice and a pair of legs. Her second television role was more conventional. As Dick Van Dyke's wife, Mary, she was a traditional housewife looking after the concerns of a "typical" nuclear family in *The Dick Van Dyke Show* (1961–66). By the 1970s, Mary was a career woman, often facing the less-than-friendly, male-dominated business world in *The Mary Tyler Moore Show* (1970–77). More recently, Moore's character on the short-lived *New York News* (1995) had broken through the "glass ceiling" said to close women out of executive positions; Moore played the editor of a big city newspaper.

The queen of the early sitcom was Lucille Ball, whose television career likewise took some twists and turns that reflected the changes families and women were going through. Married to Desi Arnaz in *I Love Lucy* (1951–61), later she found herself a single mother with children in the suburbs in *The Lucy Show* (1962–68) and *Here's Lucy* (1968–74). These changes were part of television's imperative to remain contemporary, even if such portrayals were highly idealized rather than truly representative of society. As we will see, the television situation comedy generally lags behind changes in the real world. Not until the tumult of the late 1960s did television take note of rapid

1

cultural and political changes and move beyond a candy-coated, rose-colored-glasses view of American society.

THE SITCOM AS AMERICAN GENRE

The situation comedy generally presents viewers with a variation on something with which they are familiar, something they can relate to in some way. Early situation comedies focused on family life. Later variations were set in schools, the workplace or some other situation with which viewers could identify. The family sitcom has become such a staple of television that through its evolution one can almost track the history of the American family from the 1950s to the 1990s. One way to study how family situation comedies reflect different segments of society and are aimed at different audiences is to group the programs into demographic areas or blocks.[3] In the case of family sitcoms, we can find urban-oriented shows, programs set in the suburbs and those which reflect a rural or Southern character.

The urban comedy, typified in the 1950s by *I Love Lucy* (1951–61), *Make Room for Daddy* (1953–65), and *The Honeymooners* (1955–56), reflected the introduction of television in urban America. These shows focused on husbands and wives coping with everyday life, struggling to make ends meet. The urban sitcom tended to focus on urban whites in the 1950s and later focused on minorities such as Latinos and African Americans.

The growing suburban sprawl of the 1950s brought another variation on the family sitcom, emphasizing the safety of family life outside the sometimes harsh urban existence. The "classic" situation comedies—*Father Knows Best* (1954–63), *Leave It to Beaver* (1957–63), *The Adventures of Ozzie and Harriet* (1952–66) and *The Donna Reed Show* (1958–66)—typify the highly idealized life of the American nuclear family as portrayed on television in the 1950s and early 1960s. These suburban comedies captured the upward mobility of white America, which emphasized acquisitiveness. They were largely cut off from racial tensions, cold war worries, and a decaying urban life. Personal fulfillment and career concerns took a back seat to the family in these programs. Class differences measured through the father's job meant blue-collar dads like the one in *Life of Riley* (1949–50, 1953–58) were ridiculed as bumbling and dimwitted. Middle-class fathers, in sitcoms such as *Father Knows Best* and *Leave It to Beaver*, were seen as wise and capable of teaching valuable lessons to their sons and daughters. Gender relations and roles within these families were decidedly traditional. Marital discord was unheard of, though sometimes, such as in *I Love Lucy*, wives would test the limits set by their husbands. Unmarried adults were an oddity, relegated to sitcoms set in schools (*Our Miss Brooks*, 1952–56; *Mr. Peepers*, 1952–55) or to bachelor shows (*The Bob Cummings Show*, 1955–59; *Bachelor Father*, 1959–64).

A third family sitcom setting was rural in character. *The Andy Griffith Show* (1960–68) and *Mayberry RFD* (1968–71) both featured widowed fathers raising sons, but both series drove home the idea that in a small town everyone looked after each other. Other sitcoms in the genre, *The Real McCoys* (1957–63), *The Beverly Hillbillies* (1962–71), *Petticoat Junction* (1963–70) and *Green Acres* (1965–71), portrayed urban sophistication as something to escape from, or at least made it an object of humor. The Clampetts of *The Beverly Hillbillies*, though objects of curiosity and scorn for the wealthy, were also astute commentators on the absurdities of affluent America. *Green Acres* focused on the fish-out-of-water experiences of Oliver Wendell Douglas (Eddie Albert) and his wife, Lisa (Eva Gabor), two affluent city dwellers who retreat to rural America as an escape from the city. This show provided laughs at both the Douglases and the idiosyncratic group of characters in Hooterville from whom they tried to learn about farming and rural life.

While the 1950s and early 1960s were generally a period of postwar prosperity and social mobility in America, that prosperity did not reach all of American society. Absent from TV was social inequality; the civil rights movement was just beginning its struggle. At this point, television presented a largely slapstick view of black America through shows like *Amos 'n' Andy* (1951–53) and *Beulah* (1950–53). Television stereotyped African Americans as poor but content, hopelessly ignorant yet engagingly humorous. Racial justice organizations protested such portrayals. The result was not genuine change in roles for African American actors, but fewer roles for minorities as a way of avoiding the controversy. Racial themes more reflective of reality would eventually appear on prime-time television, but largely in the context of the social and racial upheavals of the late 1960s.

The development and general approach of situation comedies from television's inception through the mid–1960s were conditioned by the social milieu. However, by the early 1960s the rumbling of social discontent was evident in the burgeoning civil rights movement and the nascent antiwar movement. As these two issues claimed more and more notice throughout the decade and were joined onstage by the women's rights, gay rights, and environmental movements, network television somehow managed to move in two distinct directions at once, becoming both more "real world" and more escapist at the same time.

Changes in family structure forced TV to include families that were different from the Ozzie-and-Harriet (intact nuclear families, with a mother who stayed at home) type of arrangements. *Family Affair* (1966–71), *Julia* (1968–71), *My Three Sons* (1960–71) and *The Brady Bunch* (1969–74) showed both men and women raising children on their own, or families bringing children not related to each other under the same roof. The story lines showed how adults and children adjusted to these new situations. *Julia* represented the first starring role for a black actress as Diahann Carroll portrayed a single mother who worked for a white doctor and lived largely in the white world. These modest diversions from the stereotypical "normal" family arrangements did little, however, to raise awareness that all was not well in America.

Meanwhile, other sitcoms required total suspension of disbelief—the escapist comedies of the mid–1960s, such as *Mr. Ed* (1961–65), *My Favorite Martian* (1963–66), *Bewitched* (1964–72), *The Munsters* (1964–66), *The Addams Family* (1964–66), and *I Dream of Jeannie* (1965–70). These and others like them utilized some gimmick as a comic vehicle for a series: a talking horse, a witch or a Martian with uncanny powers, or an ensemble of Halloween characters. On the surface, this genre offered pure escapism, though at the same time it employed traditional gender roles in some shows, and in other shows it made use of its odd characters to indirectly address social issues of equality and acceptance. Both the Addams family and the Munsters violated the norms of their neighborhoods, setting up a situation in which "normal" Americans were shown reacting irrationally to those whom they perceived as a threat. These shows didn't address the real-world issues directly, but metaphorically they asked white Americans to question their fears of minorities.

While the escapism of some sitcoms offered metaphorical lessons for the times, the gradual shift in the television situation comedy—from a highly idealized view of American life to one that showed the influence of the social movements of the 1960s—would develop through another type of show, the variety/sketch comedy genre.

THE LATE SIXTIES AND EARLY SEVENTIES

Somewhere in the late 1960s and early 1970s, television's largely romanticized portrayal of American life began to change. Television began to respond to the social upheaval caused by an unpopular war and the civil disturbances from the Watts riots in 1965 through the aftermath of Martin Luther King's assassination in 1968. Television's candy-coated world, shaped by mainstream ideals of the 1950s, contrasted sharply with the realities of the 1960s. Pioneers like Norman Lear and the Smothers Brothers interjected elements of the real world by addressing in a forthright, frequently shocking way the issues raised by the politics of war and race in the 1960s.

That Was the Week That Was (*TW3*) was the progenitor of such innovative comedy shows such as *Laugh-In* (1968–73) and *Saturday Night Live* (1975–) and its more immediate successor, *The Smothers Brothers Comedy Hour* (1967–69). *TW3* was the first show to use satire and irony to comment on contemporary politics and social issues. Based on a show in England that featured host David Frost, it included musical numbers by the satirical songwriter Tom Lehrer, as well as news parodies. The series was the boldest political humor show to date. Many said it was ahead of its time, which probably explains why it failed to break into the top 25 shows and lasted only one and a half years.

Two years later, *The Smothers Brothers Comedy Hour* would begin its brief run, during which it probably generated the most controversy of any television program ever aired. After a short attempt at a sitcom, the brothers transformed the traditional variety hour made popular by *The Ed Sullivan Show* (1948–71), *The Jackie Gleason Show* (1962–66), and *Hollywood Palace* (1964–69) into a vehicle for provocative sketch comedy and musical entertainment with social relevance. Joan Baez appeared on the show to dedicate a song to her imprisoned husband, serving time for draft evasion. Pete Seeger broke a 17-year television boycott (stemming from his early work with the Weavers during the McCarthy era) to challenge the staid conventional wisdom of television by singing "Knee Deep in Big Muddy," a song highly critical of the war in Vietnam. This occurred only after his appearance had been cut from the season opener in September 1967. The Smothers Brothers contributed to the show's reputation for controversy with their own acerbic humor and a tendency to submit program scripts to network censors too late to make changes. The net result of all this risk-taking was a stormy relationship between the Smothers Brothers and CBS for the entire run of the show, which was canceled at the first hint of a ratings decline.

CBS would continue to take risks in developing new programming, however. The network's genteel mid–1960s schedule of rural situation comedies became suddenly behind the times in the later years of the decade. Advertisers pushing for new programs to reach younger, urban, and especially more affluent audiences created an opening for shows like *The Mary Tyler Moore Show* (1970–77) and *All in the Family* (1971–1983). All of these changes in the American situation comedy preceded the arrival of *M*A*S*H* on network television.

Norman Lear's premiere of *All in the Family*, whose star, Carroll O'Connor, played the role of a big-city bigot, tried to get America to laugh at itself. The conflict between Archie and his liberal son-in-law, Mike, reflected the generation gap between the World War II generation and the baby boomers. The large numbers of births in the postwar years had created the first generation shaped by a system of mass public education and the rise of modern youth culture—nearly every teenager in the country attended high school, and certainly television programming aimed at young people provided a means for fashion and cultural trendsetting. All of these influences made the baby boomers' experience of the world vastly different from their parents'. Riots and antiwar protests provided the background for *All in the Family* as it explored Archie's relationship with his black neighbors (who would eventually have their own show, *The Jeffersons*, 1975–86) as well as his daughter and son-in-law. In the first few years of the show, the American public tuned in to see what kind of groundbreaking theme would be explored each week or what element of bigotry would be ridiculed through the character of Archie Bunker. Archie hated everyone: blacks, Jews, Latinos, whites of other backgrounds besides his own—anyone different from himself. Many viewers may have had their consciousness raised through the antics of Archie, but the character himself only occasionally learned a lesson or realized the harm or ugliness of his bigotry.

The shock value of *All in the Family*, with Archie's prolific use of ethnic slurs, generated a fair amount of controversy among critics. Some saw it as shock for shock's sake, while others agreed with Norman Lear that it effectively lampooned the world view of bigots like Archie Bunker.[4] The potential for controversy was an ongoing concern in the program's development. TV's orientation toward "least objectionable programming" had kept it away from subjects like racism. Lear took a militant approach with network executives and censors and resisted attempts to take the edge off the show. CBS chose to make a special announcement about the show right before the pilot episode aired, and extra telephone operators were on hand to handle an expected deluge of calls. The pilot's audience was rather small, however, and little was heard from those who did watch. The press was divided on the quality and appropriateness of the program.

Eventually, research on the program's reception and its effects on its audience suggested that neither Lear nor his critics were completely on target in their ideas about how the show might affect the American viewing public. CBS's own study found that most people who tuned into the show did not find it offensive and generally found it funny. Psychologists Milton Rokeach and Neil Vidmar, in a study of the process by which viewers selectively perceive characters like Archie, found that those with bigoted views were more likely to find Archie likeable than those with less prejudiced views. Evidence was found in this and other studies[5] that most viewers thought Archie's son-in-law, Mike, made more sense and was correct more often than Archie. Research did show differences in how the show and Archie were perceived across cultures. American audiences, whether prejudiced or not, seemed to be more tolerant of Archie's views than the Dutch, though this difference may have been due to the Dutch viewers being measurably less prejudiced than the American audience. As hard as it is to definitively determine why people watch a program, it is even harder to measure why they don't watch—that is, why they selectively avoid things they perceive as threatening to their views or offensive to their sensibilities. African Americans enjoyed the show about as much as the whites who found Archie bigoted, but they tended to speculate that more white Americans agreed with Archie than samples of white people in these studies actually showed. Members of minority groups tended to see the show as beneficial to society because it openly discussed the issue of race in America.

The relative balance of positive and negative evaluations of Archie reveals the multiple perspectives audience members bring to the viewing situation. It also demonstrates that when program creators produce shows that attempt to make social statements, the creators' intent doesn't always translate into what audiences learn from a program. Taken together, these studies show that the effects of fictional television are more complex than creative teams and network executives generally imagine. *All in the Family* may have challenged the conventional wisdom about least objectionable programming, but its effects on society were mixed at best. The legacy of the show is not so much that it made its audience less or more bigoted, but that it broke a stale mold of network television programming and more genuinely reflected American society in the late 1960s and early 1970s. It was also a show that opened the door to more contemporary themes and outlooks.

Mary Tyler Moore's "independent woman" situation comedy brought another nascent social issue to the TV screens of the nation. The women's movement in the late 1960s and early 1970s was beginning to question the boundaries placed on women's life choices. *The Mary Tyler Moore Show* (1970–77) made the workplace a setting for a sitcom that could explore the changes occurring as women sought opportunities outside traditional roles. Mary was neither a mother nor a wife—two television roles to which women had more or less been confined for the previous two decades. Instead, her coworkers and her neighbors served as her family as they learned to get along and help each other through life's rough spots.

But just as in earlier "independent women" comedies such as *That Girl* (1966–71) and *The Doris Day Show* (1968–73), the star was hardly a feminist icon. Mary's feminism was at best an embryonic one. Her role in the newsroom was to be supportive of the men who had more responsibility and power than she did. So, while the fact that she was single and working was rather new for television, later "single woman" characters would bring more depth and substance in terms of a liberated consciousness. Perhaps the most significant breakthrough on the show was Mary's friendship with a married man at the TV station, Murray Slaughter (Gavin McLeod). Though Murray quite clearly fell in love with Mary, he remained faithful to his wife, and he and Mary were supportive of each other at work. The introduction of a platonic friendship between adults of the opposite sex was something that had not occurred in TV land before.

COMEDY AS SOCIAL CRITICISM

The emergence of situation comedies that addressed real-world issues and phenomena may have been a new development in television, but comedy as a form of social criticism may be as old as human civilization—or at least as old as the comic "method." As it often operates out of a sense of contradiction, or at least irony, comedy offers space for critique of social institutions and the powers that be. Such comedy is meant to challenge the prevailing value system and point out its contradictions and hypocrisies.

David Marc traces the roots of "social comedy" to fifth-century Greek dramatists, who accomplished social criticism through allegories of contemporary events.[6] Hal Himmelstein sees the roots of the television sitcom in sixteenth-century Italian comedy, which emphasized the use of stock characters who employed both satirical and slapstick humor. Shakespeare, in focusing on human complexities and contradictions, also used comedy to critique hypocrisy and pretentiousness. George Bernard Shaw's emphasis on conflicts between the individual and modern industrial capitalism was a twentieth-century expression of comedic social criticism.[7]

Himmelstein argues that "comedy is grounded in both time and place—it addresses the immediate life conditions of the society in which it is produced."[8] He also places programs like *The Mary Tyler Moore Show*, *All in the Family* and *M*A*S*H* in a special category of social comedy, seeing in them "a crying out for human improvement," and notes that such comedy "thrives during troubled times when it is possible for both the artist and the spectator to note the contradictions and value conflicts of society."[9]

At the same time, television has always placed boundaries on the degree of criticism allowed to reach audiences of millions. The emergence of television as a mass medium during the McCarthy era, which cast a suspicious eye on the whole entertainment industry, probably accounts for some of its timidness and conservatism. A more pervasive constraint on television content, both then and now, has been the commercial mission of the networks. Television's function to provide audiences for advertisers results in an economic conservatism that discourages provocative programming. Sponsors prefer that programs remain in safe territory so that no segment of the audience is unduly offended. The primary function of television is to sell products and produce profit for the network's stockholders. This "bottom line" often mitigates against the airing of social criticism or controversy across a range of mass media. The "least objectionable programming" approach that has characterized the system pushes television in the opposite direction—serving up mindless fluff about the oddities and misfits of society.

The changing face of the United States prompted a rare moment of experimentation with comedy that tried to respect the viewer's intelligence and to feed a search for meaning in a period of social upheaval. An attempt by CBS to reach younger, more affluent audiences with disposable income resulted in the development and introduction of *The Mary Tyler Moore Show*, *All in the Family*, and finally *M*A*S*H*, all through the opening provided by discontent in many sectors of society.

The convergence of "troubled times"—racism, war and mass movements for social change—provided the setting for the emergence of social sitcoms and "dramedies" like *M*A*S*H*. Though *M*A*S*H* was the last of the three just-named CBS sitcoms to break out of the safe conventions of network television, it differs from both *Mary Tyler Moore* and *All in the Family* in the subjects and objects of its humor. *Mary Tyler Moore* dealt with the emergence of professional women in the traditionally male professional world. *All in the Family* offered a critique of interpersonal intolerance and racism. The humor of *M*A*S*H* would take a different and perhaps even more daring course. While *Mary Tyler Moore* and *All in the Family* focused on critiquing individuals, *M*A*S*H*'s humor and plot lines were more politically volatile because they targeted institutions like the military and the government. And because it aired in a period of antiwar agitation, there was a chance the show might further inflame passions generated by opposition to the Vietnam War.

It is the notion of *M*A*S*H* as a provocative, boundary-challenging situation comedy that provides the impetus for the rest of this book. As an "out there" comedy that taxed network censors and executives, *M*A*S*H* is a perfect vehicle for studying the relationship between society and fictional television. The potential effects of television's portrayal of the fissures in society were widely discussed after the emergence of shows like *All in the Family*, *Mary Tyler Moore*, and *M*A*S*H*. Is it possible for situation comedies and television fiction in general to play a role in a society's critical self-examination? Most assessments have shown that television reflects rather than inspires periods of social ferment and change. It was the 1960s that changed television, rather than the other way around. And those changes were relatively small and short-lived. As we look into the development of *M*A*S*H*, we will see that the legacy of the program illustrates the inherent conservatism of television. In large part, it was *M*A*S*H*'s emphasis on universal values—helping others in need, recognizing the commonality of the human condition, and preferring peace and life over war and death—that characterized the show, rather than the far fewer critical moments that turned a sharp eye on the militarism and bureaucratic irrationality of an imperial superpower. In the final analysis, we will see that *M*A*S*H*, like most television, was better at getting people to feel than at making them think. Though *M*A*S*H* has been much acclaimed for its aesthetics and its relevance, those characteristics are often cast as more indicative of the show than they really deserve to be. Instead, *M*A*S*H* serves as an excellent example of the limitations on social expression in network television.

CHAPTER 2

From Novel
to Film to Television

Television since its inception has treated war and military issues both as serious subjects and as settings for comedy. *M*A*S*H*, however, is unique among both comedies and dramas for its use of humor to critique and ridicule the notion that war is a glorious enterprise. This use of humor was possible primarily because of the unique circumstances surrounding the development of the program toward the end of the Vietnam War. As we saw in the previous chapter, this was a time when television offered both relevance and escapism in its situation comedies. Other programs set in war during this period, however, did not engage in criticism of the military. *M*A*S*H*'s uniqueness among military sitcoms stems from both its emergence at the end of the antiwar era and the fact that it evolved from a novel and film of the same name.

CAN WAR BE FUNNY?

Military and war settings for situation comedies seem to crop up throughout American television history. Beginning with *The Phil Silvers Show/You'll Never Get Rich* (1955–59), war sitcoms until *M*A*S*H* largely avoided the ugly realities of war and did not offer comment on any war or military adventure being pursued by the Pentagon. Viewers of *Phil Silvers*, *McKeever and the Colonel* (1962–63), *McHale's Navy* (1962–66), *Mr. Roberts* (1965–66), *The Wackiest Ship in the Army* (1965–66), and *Gomer Pyle* (1964–78) heard no references to current United States military engagements (besides Indochina, troops were sent to the Dominican Republic in 1965, and there was a confrontation with North Korea over the seizing of the United States Navy ship *Pueblo* in 1968). Producers kept war at a distance from these sitcoms by setting them in locations where war did not intrude. Two other military sitcoms of the era, *Hogan's Heroes* (1965–71) and *F Troop* (1965–67), were set in the past (World War II and the post–Civil War West, respectively) and thus able to avoid any current military subjects in plot lines. Though *M*A*S*H* could have taken a similar tack, the creative team for that show made a conscious choice to bring the antiwar values of the 1960s to a show set in the 1950s.

More typical of how military sitcoms focused their plot lines was the longest-running military sitcom of the sixties, *Gomer Pyle, U.S.M.C.* (1964–70), a spin off of *The Andy Griffith Show*. Set on a base in California where no one ever "shipped out" or returned in body bags, this sitcom romanticized the role the military played in giving naive young recruits a sense of what it takes to be a man. Gomer was continually coached by his sergeant in the proper ways to be military and to earn the title of Marine. The premise of country bumpkin Pyle joining the military meshed well with the image of the military as a means of social mobility. The show illustrated how class differences in society, supposedly negated or diminished by military training, instead are reproduced in the form of military hierarchy. Sergeant Carter's ongoing "parenting" of Pyle reinforced the idea that even the toughest military men still had hearts.

MASH: THE NOVEL

M*A*S*H came to network television by way of a novel and film of the same name. *MASH* (no asterisks), the novel, was the brainchild of Dr. Richard Hornberger, who penned it under the name Richard Hooker. Hornberger was a doctor who served in a MASH unit in Korea. The book, which was based on the actual experiences of Hornberger, was rejected by seventeen publishers before being published in 1968 by William Morrow.

The novel never pretends to deal with the politics of the Korean War, or any war, for that matter. Throughout the novel there is an undercurrent of vague resentment among the doctors about being called up for duty. The doctors in the novel do display a lack of respect toward authority figures and are generally portrayed as hard-drinking, free-spirited, skirt-chasing, and apolitical.

The story is told through the eyes of Hawkeye Pierce, who arrives in Korea and is assigned to the 4077 with Duke Forest, a fellow surgeon. Hawkeye and Duke make sport of their commanding officer (CO), Col. Henry Blake. Though he is "regular army," as a doctor himself he realizes he can't treat the doctors as he would enlisted men. After arriving at the 4077, Hawkeye and Duke immediately have a run-in with their tentmate, Major Hobson, whose religiosity and disdain for alcohol conflict with the "anything goes" spirit of Hawkeye and Duke. Hobson eventually leaves the 4077, and his replacement, Trapper John McIntyre, arrives as a mystery man who is soon identified by Hawkeye as a former college football rival.

The doctors' tent, Tent Six, is christened "the Swamp" and serves as the location for the consumption of many martinis. The camp chaplain, Father John Patrick Mulcahy, is nicknamed "Dago Red" (he has red hair, but the origin of this name is not otherwise explained). The camp dentist, Captain Walter (the Painless Pole) Koskiusko Waldowski, who runs a nearly continuous game of poker, provides one subplot of the novel. A man with a reputation for being physically well endowed, he becomes concerned that he has lost his sexual ability. A mock suicide is staged, after which Waldowski is convinced that he will live to make love again.

Soon after, Captain Frank Burns arrives. Unlike the television series version, Burns in the novel is a surgeon with a good reputation. He and Hawkeye develop a rivalry as each is in charge of a surgical shift. Burns and Major Margaret (Hot Lips) Houlihan, who share a strict by-the-book orientation to their military and surgical responsibilities, are impressed with one another. They also develop an eye for each other. When Blake names Trapper John chief surgeon, both Burns and Houlihan resent such an important post going to a nonmilitary type like McIntyre. Hawkeye eventually goads Burns into a fight by teasing him about his affair with Hot Lips. The fight gets Burns transferred to another unit.

The Swamp's houseboy, Ho-Jon, is the focus of another subplot. Much to the consternation of the Swampmen, Ho-Jon (the only Korean in the novel) gets drafted by the South Korean army and returns six weeks later as a wounded soldier. Once he is repaired, the men conspire to send him to college at Hawkeye's alma mater. They creatively raise funds for tuition by developing a "Passion Play" in the sky featuring Trapper John as Jesus Christ on the cross suspended from a helicopter as Hawkeye sells autographed pictures of the Lord to GI's throughout Korea.

In another adventure, Trapper and Hawkeye fly to Tokyo to operate on an injured congressman's son. The two surgeons raise hell all over Tokyo—at the army hospital, on the golf course, and at the Finest Kind Pediatric Hospital and Whorehouse. They also defy military policy by taking a baby at the Finest Kind to the army hospital for treatment.

Next come the hijinks surrounding the challenge of a football game against the evacuation hospital staff. Hawkeye conspires to obtain the services of neurosurgeon Oliver Wendell Jones, otherwise known as Spearchucker Jones, an outstanding football player with whom Hawkeye once roomed. The 4077 recruits the ringer, who leads them to victory against the unwitting evac hospital. The remainder of the novel shows Hawkeye and Duke returning to the States.

The novel lacks a coherent plot; it is written as a series of slices of life showing doctors on the frontline. The humor in the novel focuses on sex and making fun of religion and those who are religious. These two elements were also the primary vehicles for humor in the film, which came out two years after the novel was published, and in the first year of the television series.

Sending Ho-Jon to college formed part of the plot of the pilot episode for the television series, though a subplot involving sex—raffling off a weekend with a nurse—was substituted for the religious heresy. Another brief episode in the novel, the 4077 treating some wounded British soldiers, also eventually appeared in the television series in 1978 as "Tea and Empathy," an episode in which Hawkeye criticizes the British tradition of giving wounded men tea, which can cause complications in surgery. Finally, the novel contains an incident in which Hawkeye plays poker as he waits for a patient to stabilize. For this he is criticized by a visiting surgeon. Hawkeye puts the surgeon in his place by successfully completing the surgery after the patient has been stabilized and given blood. The first-year television episode "Chief Surgeon Who?" contains a similar incident. Overall, however, the television series seems more like a distant cousin than a grandchild of the novel.

*M*A*S*H* ON THE BIG SCREEN

The movie rights to the novel were bought for $100,000 by Ingo Preminger, who assigned the task of writing the screenplay to Ring Lardner, Jr., an author blacklisted in the McCarthy era. The script was rejected by fifteen directors before Robert Altman made the film quickly and cheaply for release in the fall of 1970.

The film more or less follows the book in plot and tone. The novel's rather detailed discussions of operating room action and other medical aspects of MASH life are turned into bloody and gruesome operating room scenes. These scenes constitute the modest antiwar element of the film, which does not go out of its way to be antiwar. It does, however, exhibit an air of being anti-authority. As in the novel, Hawkeye Pierce, played by Donald Sutherland, arrives at the 4077 with Duke Forest (played by Tom Skeritt), who steals a jeep to get them to the camp. Both Duke and Hawkeye are quickly revealed to have an eye for the nurses in the camp, though each has his own approach to wooing them. Father Mulcahy (René Auberjonois), who as in the book is called Dago Red, serves as an object of religious humor and criticism. The character of Frank Burns (Robert Duvall) comes to the film as a combination of the novel's Major Hobson and Frank Burns. Very quickly in the film, Burns's religiosity is ridiculed when Hawkeye replaces the Bible Ho-Jon is using to learn English with a copy of a girlie magazine. In another scene, Frank is harassed while praying; the entire camp drowns out his prayer with a mocking version of "Onward Christian Soldiers."

Just as in the novel, Hawkeye and Duke set out to eject Burns—first from their tent and later from the camp entirely. Margaret (Sally Kellerman), whose surname in the film is O'Houlihan rather than Houlihan, arrives as a straight (though voluptuous) by-the-book head nurse. Walt Waldowski (John Judd), the Painless Pole, is given his due as the "best equipped" dentist in the army. Waldowski's suicide is in the film, but this time he is "cured" by an at first reluctant yet afterward satisfied Lieutenant Dish (Joanne Pflug). What's striking about the staging of the suicide scene is the use of the Last Supper as a metaphor for Waldowski's last meal. Altman presents a momentary recreation of Leonardo's "Last Supper" with meticulous detail.

A scene in the film reveals the reason for the nickname given to Margaret O'Houlihan—"Hot Lips." Radar O'Reilly (played by Gary Burghoff, the only film character who would reprise his role in the television series) manages to slip the camp microphone underneath the cot where Burns and O'Houlihan have their first encounter. "God meant us to find each other," they rationalize as they begin to disrobe. In the heat of passion, Margaret tells Frank Burns to "kiss my hot lips," thus setting into motion the use of her nickname.

The next morning, Hawkeye asks Burns to describe his sexual encounter with Margaret. The sanctimonious Burns remains silent for only so long in the face of ridicule before he jumps on Hawkeye in the mess tent—with Col. Blake (Roger Bowen) looking on. As a result, Burns soon departs camp in a straitjacket, prompting Duke to ask Blake, "If I nail Hot Lips and punch Hawkeye, can I go home?"

O'Houlihan is later humiliated in front of the whole camp when the doctors, to settle a bet on whether her hair is naturally blonde, arrange to have the tent flaps of the showers lifted while she bathes. The men cheer and whistle when her body suddenly is exposed to the outside. An angry O'Houlihan storms into Col. Blake's tent demanding she be transferred.

The film, which hit theaters during a time when antiwar protests were common, contains several drug references that seem more appropriate to the Vietnam era than to a Korean War story. Hawkeye and Trapper drug Ho-Jon before he goes for his army physical in the hope that he will be rejected for service as a result. Later in the film, the camp PA announces that marijuana has been declared a dangerous drug. At the football game, the 4077 manages to inject and sedate the star player for the other team, and another scene shows players passing a joint around as they sit on the bench.

As in the novel, Hawkeye and Trapper visit Tokyo to operate on a congressman's son and generally upstage the staff and administrator of the hospital, especially the hospital director, Col. Merrill. These scenes provide some of the anti-authority, anti-bureaucracy perspective that would become more apparent in the television series. But that perspective in the television show might more accurately be traced to a popular novel of the early 1970s, Joseph Heller's *Catch-22*. Thus, in many ways, the film and novel are more apolitical than the television show. While the situation comedy would draw upon the sexual hijinks and, to a lesser degree, the irreverence for religion that drive the novel and film, its own political humor would evolve in the second year of the show.

*M*A*S*H*: The Television Series

The film's commercial success ($36 million), popularity (14 million people saw it), and critical acclaim (it won Best Screenplay and received nominations for Best Director and Best Picture) quickly led to its development as a television series. William Self of 20th Century–Fox Television saw a potential situation comedy in the movie and recruited Gene Reynolds, a solidly credentialed producer, to organize and shoot a pilot episode.[1]

Most researchers agree that the translation from film to television was successful largely because Gene Reynolds persuaded Larry Gelbart to sign on as writer and producer. Gelbart was a longtime comedy writer who had worked with such celebrities as Danny Thomas, Bob Hope, Red Buttons, Neil Simon, Mel Brooks, and Woody Allen. His biggest commercial success before *M*A*S*H* was a book for the Broadway hit *A Funny Thing Happened on the Way to the Forum* in 1962.

Gelbart had chosen London for a self-imposed exile from Hollywood, which he had come to regard as a "schlock factory." He found working in London to be less constraining and more satisfying and was not easily enticed to join *M*A*S*H*. However, he was intrigued. He insisted on realistic operating room scenes—something the CBS executives fiercely resisted. He knew the success of a sitcom in a tragic setting depended on finding the main fault lines of conflict in society and bridging them.[2]

Gelbart's own perspective on Vietnam was a prime factor in his agreeing to do the show and provides further reasons for the show's unique identity vis-à-vis the novel and film. While the rest of Hollywood had not even considered addressing a war still close to American experience, the creative team at *M*A*S*H* saw ways to bring Vietnam-era themes and issues to television through a war comedy set in Korea. In essence, *M*A*S*H* used the setting of a war in the past as a means for commenting on the present. The show's central character, Hawkeye, also reflected this scrambling of wars, history, and politics. According to David Marc, Hawkeye Pierce was a "sixties hero in a seventies sitcom set in the fifties."[3]

The country's frustration with deceptive government bureaucrats and with a war that had become extremely unpopular helped transform the rather apolitical film and novel into something that at least hinted at criticism of the United States military and the government's imperialist attitude toward other countries. On the other hand, the realistic and gory operating room scenes from the film were replicated (albeit in milder forms) in the television show.

The series was also scrupulously faithful in its depictions of war as it was fought and medicine as it was practiced in the 1950s.[4] The 4077 was largely modeled after the 8055 in Korea. The 8055 was organized in July 1950, just six days after North Korea crossed the thirty-eighth parallel. The use of helicopters to transport wounded was a new development since World War II; eventually more than 17,000 badly wounded troops were moved in this way from the field to the hospital. The *M*A*S*H* set was as accurate as possible, though it was necessary to scale down the size of the camp, hospital, and staff for the sake of television. So, while the 8055 had 200 beds, 10 doctors, and 12 nurses and a total staff of 248, the 4077's operating room (OR) had about four operating tables (the OR at the 8055 was 168 feet versus the 27-foot 4077 OR), four doctors, and a total staff of about forty people, including extras.

"Bug-outs," instances in which a MASH unit moved to avoid becoming part of the battlefield, occurred much more frequently during the Korean War than on the program. The 8055 moved twenty-seven times in three years, while the 4077 moved just three times during nearly eleven years of episodes.

The television *M*A*S*H*'s frequent long OR sessions were true to life. Doctors in the Korean War typically worked eight- to twelve-hour shifts, though twenty-four-hour shifts were not unusual. And the success rate mentioned in many episodes is also accurate: The 8055 averaged 95 percent success in its medical care. Many medical innovations contributed to this success. For example, artery grafting resulted in a lower amputation rate than that of World War II.

More than 910 reserve doctors and 686 dentists served in Korea, most drafted after completing their residencies. Most were 25 to 28 years old; only a few had served in World War II. And while Hawkeye Pierce served for more than ten years on the television *M*A*S*H*, doctors were rotated out of real MASH duty after less than one year's service. Nurses portrayed on the television series were usually much younger than the career army nurses who served in Korea. The supply of young female characters enabled the creative team to make love and sex rather constant factors in the show. The television *M*A*S*H* also failed to reflect the actual racial composition of the unit: African Americans made up about 14 to 18 percent of medical units in Korea, but the show never approaches that figure. On the other hand, the use of Spearchucker Jones as a fourth doctor and member of the Swamp was dropped after the first year of the show because there is no record of African American doctors serving in Korea.

Beyond the reasonably realistic look and feel of the television *M*A*S*H*, meticulous research guided the efforts of Larry Gelbart and Gene Reynolds in coming up with plot lines and scripts. The first year's shows were based on general research by Gelbart—going through copies of *Time* from the early 1950s and finding and interviewing doctors who had served in Korea. In 1974, he and Reynolds went to Korea. Burt Metcalfe estimates that 60 percent of storylines came from research; the rest were arrived at by exploring how individual characters would react emotionally in certain situations. This was especially true in the later years of the show. Fans of the show sent in story ideas, and the program also purchased ideas from doctors—Dr. John Vester sold three stories to the program and had his name and a medical paper he wrote mentioned in an episode. CBS insisted on medical accuracy in the show. Dr. Walter Dishell served as a consultant for the series and eventually co-wrote an episode ("Life Time") with Alan Alda. The creative team fought CBS on the use of a laugh track, to which the team objected. CBS prevailed, but in the later years the laugh track was used less and less and at relatively low volumes.[5]

The creative team had other battles with network executives. Gelbart has noted that many of the disputes between the show's team and the network were presented metaphorically in the show as battles between the doctors and the army brass. The network, according to Gelbart, was not explicitly opposed to an "antiwar" comedy; the big problem for the creative team was the network's general resistance to the serious overtones of the show and how it broke from the usual sitcom form. Only one episode was completely rejected; it dealt with Hawkeye Pierce's simultaneous affairs with two nurses. One of the true stories that emerged from research was also too much for the network. It concerned an actual instance in which members of a MASH unit stood outside in the cold trying to get sick enough to be sent home. Such an antimilitary event was deemed too unpatriotic for mass audiences.[6]

Gelbart summed up the tension between network expectations and the desire to make points about war and politics:

> We wanted to say that war was futile, to represent it as a failure on everybody's part that people had to kill each other to make a point. We wanted to say that when you take people from home they do things they would never do. They drink. They whore. They steal. They become venal. They become asinine, in terms of power. They get the clap. They become alcoholics. They become rude. They become sweet. They become loving. They become tender. We wanted to make war the enemy without really saying who was fighting.
>
> ... routinizing an acceptance of war, year in and year out ... essentially defeats the original purpose of the series. I would almost hope that there would be a way to be even blacker about what war does to people, rather than just to say—and I'm afraid it always did, in the tenth year much more than the first—that listen: Given the right buddies, and the right CO, and the right kind of sense of humor, you can muddle through.[7]

Over its 10½-year run, *M*A*S*H* would win 14 Emmys and receive 99 nominations. The cost of a 30-second commercial would rise from $30,000 to $200,000. The final, 2½-hour episode, "Goodbye, Farewell and Amen," would garner $450,000 per half-minute and be one of the highest rated single programs in television history.

*M*A*S*H* AND CONTEMPORARY AMERICAN SOCIETY

The show's premiere in 1972 came as the Vietnam War, along with the protest and politics surrounding it, was seemingly winding down from the heights of the previous few years. In April of 1970, the Nixon administration announced that by early 1971, troops in Vietnam would be reduced by 150,000 from more than 500,000 at the height of United States involvement.[8] The draw-down in troop strength seemed to further indicate that American involvement in the war was coming to an end. *Newsweek* reported that these developments brought on difficulties for the military hierarchy in dealing with resistance and resentment among the troops sent to Vietnam.[9] Drugs and dissension had decidedly affected the ability and desire of the troops to perform their duties. No major operations had taken place since the May 1970 invasion of Cambodia, and the primary concern of the troops was avoiding American casualties. Only 10 percent of the 340,000 troops were combat units, and many of the frontline units were rife with drug abuse; 75 soldiers were reported to have died from heroin overdoses between August and mid–October of 1970. Racial tension and segregation were common and occasionally erupted into violence. Officers in Vietnam attributed these developments to the opposition to the war at home and the fact that unlike the enlisted men who had fought in the early years of the war, most of the troops now in Vietnam were drafted. Instances of "fragging," or trying to kill unpopular officers, were widely reported.

On the domestic front, the nation followed the outcome of William Calley's 1971 court-martial for his involvement in events at My Lai.[10] The March 1968 My Lai massacre of Vietnamese civilians—at least 175 persons, though estimates ranged as high as 400—was a low point in the war that probably helped turn public opinion decidedly against United States involvement. Calley was charged with 102 of the murders and was convicted of at least 22.[11] The conviction was greeted negatively by both pro- and antiwar groups. Supporters of the war maintained Calley should never have been prosecuted because such incidents are a part of all wars. War opponents saw Calley's conviction as a military attempt to scapegoat a minor officer while the architects of actions like My Lai went unpunished. The American public disapproved of the verdict by an eight-to-one margin. A poll showed that most of the public (71 percent of respondents) held others responsible and believed that Calley was a scapegoat (69 percent). One-half of those polled said they felt such incidents were common in the war. Several similar incidents from earlier in the war would get some press attention, but none would weigh as heavily on the American psyche as My Lai.[12] A second trial involving Captain Ernest Medina would find him not guilty, and the controversy over the involvement of higher-ups would wind down. Calley would be paroled in November 1974.[13] June 1971 would bring the publishing of the Pentagon Papers, a series of documents that further revealed the extent to which the government had deceived the citizens of the United States about the progress and prospects of the war.[14]

Meanwhile, the aftermath of the May 1970 killing of students at Kent State University in Ohio and Jackson State in Mississippi (the students, who were protesting the invasion and secret war in Cambodia, were killed by members of the National Guard) provided a lull which prompted *Time* in February 1971 to claim America was "cooling."[15] The article claimed the country was sick of violence and weary from a long war was therefore backing down from the confrontations that characterized the 1960s. Similarly, *Newsweek* reported that a poll of college students found that most of them just wanted to get on with their lives. Concerns about jobs and economic security were replacing outrage at the prosecution of a distant war.[16] Whether these reports were an attempt to project a change of mood in the country is debatable. But what is certain is that events quickly overtook such sentiment. The war and protests against it would reignite by mid–1971.

The issues surrounding the invasion of Cambodia in 1970 would resurface in 1971. United States assertions that North Vietnam was using Cambodia and Laos as sanctuaries to transport troops and materiel to be used against South Vietnam prompted bombing campaigns by the United States government. News accounts from early 1971 were often contradictory from week to week, praising the achievements of "Vietnamizing" during a South Vietnamese incursion into Laos one week while reporting retreats by South Vietnamese forces shortly thereafter.[17] The performance of the South Vietnamese forces who were beginning to take over the actual fighting from American combat troops was mixed at best. An assessment in August 1971 argued that after two years of "Vietnamization," South Vietnam was more vulnerable to attacks from the internal guerrilla forces of the Viet Cong and in some parts of the country the Viet Cong enjoyed significant support from the population.[18] The CIA-inspired Phoenix program, an attempt to win over the rural peasantry, had produced the opposite of the intended result.

Domestic protest over the war continued, even though American troops were gradually being withdrawn. The Capitol building in Washington was bombed in March 1971, causing damage to the building but no human injury. The bombings were attributed to the Weather Underground, a group that had decided to move from peaceful opposition to violent resistance against the war.[19] The war's spread to Laos also brought protesters back into the streets. Major demonstrations over the war occurred in April and May 1971. By this time, returning veterans were joining the antiwar movement, and in a dramatic demonstration on April 23, many threw their medals on the steps of the Capitol.[20] As protesters tried to shut down Washington, more than 13,400 were arrested and placed in stadiums and indoor arenas. Police arrested many illegally, including 23 newsmen. The war would drag on as the Nixon administration sought to disengage and withdraw from Vietnam with "honor." The Vietnamization of the war and the extensive use of United States air superiority in 1972 would only result in more calls for complete withdrawal.

This was the historical backdrop that led to the appearance of *M*A*S*H* on CBS in September 1972. *M*A*S*H*'s premiere in the wake of a tumultuous period in American and world history—a period that had left the public weary from an unpopular war—won it a space on network television, from which it would go forward to become one of the most unique programs in American television history. As we will see in the pages that follow, though set in the 1950s, the themes and plots of *M*A*S*H* bear a relationship with developments in the real world of the 1970s. While in many ways innovative at mixing comedy, drama and tragedy, *M*A*S*H* does not so much shape America's social consciousness as provide a politically palatable reflection of it. We will see that the program's long run serves as a marker for the changes American society went through in the aftermath of Vietnam. By the time the show signed off in 1983, it had done a complete about-face—critical and satirical of the American military in the early 1970s, by the Reagan 1980s, the 4077 had become a competent, much straighter and more conventional military unit. As if to underscore the changing times, less than a year after the show ended, United States military forces were again active in foreign lands—this time in Lebanon and Grenada.

Other social changes were reflected in the program as well. While drinking and sex were a primary feature of early shows, by the later years the program's treatment of these issues was much more tame, if not openly critical of the mores associated with the early 1970s. Essentially, the program became a much more conventional situation comedy in its last few years. As the Reagan era seemingly projected the values of the 1950s, *M*A*S*H* became a "family" sitcom, sharing themes with distant cousins like *Father Knows Best* and *Leave It to Beaver.*

*M*A*S*H,* then, was simultaneously new and familiar, risky and conventional. It was more contradictory than contrarian and more humorous than political as it addressed the human condition. We may never see a program like it, just as we may never live through a time like the ten years that took America from the antiwar early 1970s to the beginning of the Reagan years.

CHAPTER 3

It's a Man's War—
Year 1, 1972-73

Larry Gelbart wrote the pilot M*A*S*H episode in about two days in November 1971 and was paid $25,000 for his work. Probably nothing after that came as easy for him as far as M*A*S*H was concerned. Indeed, he was to discover many obstacles in creating a show that would blaze a new trail in television.[1]

Many thought M*A*S*H would be a gimmicky merging of two television staples: medical shows and war shows. Gelbart thought differently. In fact, he would have never consented to involvement with M*A*S*H if it was meant to be a typical sitcom. Looking back at year one (1972-73), it's quite clear he went slowly in introducing the serious themes in M*A*S*H. While addressing the ugly aspects of war would provoke network resistance, it was the network's concerns over sex and marital infidelity in the pilot episode that prompted changes. Hawkeye's part (Alan Alda as Benjamin Hawkeye Pierce) was originally written to include a wedding band on his ring finger. He was also to have a girlfriend in the unit named Lt. Dish, who was married as well. Frank Burns (Larry Linville) and Margaret Houlihan (Loretta Swit)—known as Hot Lips in the early years of the show—were already treading adulterous territory, and the network said one such couple was enough.[2]

Reflecting Gelbart's caution, the episodes from the first year are mostly conventional and relatively lighthearted. From the pilot episode, it is quite clear that hijinks are to be part of the not-very-military 4077. In that episode, a date with a nurse is offered as a prize in a raffle to raise money to send the Swamp's houseboy, Ho-Jon, to Hawkeye's alma mater. The first episode also establishes Frank and Margaret as an "item," though viewers get a sense of Margaret's appetite for powerful, macho men as she woos General Hammond over the phone while he fantasizes about their previous encounters. Margaret's attraction to army brass is further developed in such first-year episodes as "The Ringbanger," "Yankee Doodle Doctor," and "Cease Fire." "M*A*S*H— The Pilot" was nominated for two Emmys—Outstanding Directing (Gene Reynolds) and Writing (Larry Gelbart)—and an ACE "Eddie" for film editor Stanford Tischler. The pilot won a Directors Guild Award for Gene Reynolds.

Much of the first season consists of the kind of wacky comedy seen in the pilot. Some shows were embarrassing for those involved with the production: Many of the cast and the creative team cite "Major Fred C. Dobbs" as the worst. Starting with a tidbit of information about Korea being the fifth largest gold producer in the world, "Dobbs" revolves around a plot by Hawk and Trapper to convince Frank there are gold deposits near the 4077. The reason they want to do so is to make sure Frank and Margaret will not transfer out of the unit. By this twenty-second episode, however, it was quite clear to viewers that the animosity Hawkeye and Trapper felt toward Frank and Margaret would make this an unlikely scenario. The implausibility is explained by Hawk and Trapper's realization that they might get a far worse situation with two new superior officers.

Margaret and Frank's hypocrisy as straight by-the-book types who like to get out of uniform together is made apparent in the pilot and is highlighted throughout the first year in episodes such as "Chief Surgeon Who?," "Edwina," "Dear Dad," "Dear Dad...Again," "The Long John Flap," and "Cease Fire." In "Love Story," Frank and Margaret object when Radar (Gary Burghoff), recently jilted by a girlfriend back home via a Dear John record, falls in love with a newly arrived nurse who is an officer. Margaret and Frank attempt to split them up, but in the end Hawkeye and Trapper get Frank and Margaret to relent by humorously preventing their own frequent trysts.

Despite network pressures to go easy on sex, first-year episodes include a lot of sexually oriented humor, and the show manages to cover a lot of ground in at least suggesting sexual relationships between men and women—very often through Hawkeye hitting on and seducing nurses. Many episodes in the first year feature Hawk throwing off sexist one-liners at nurses and taunts at Margaret. In "Germ Warfare," Hawkeye is shown having an undressing fantasy as he sits across the table from a nurse in the mess hall. In "Edwina," Hawk draws the short straw for a date with a klutzy nurse in order to get the nurses to call off their sex "strike." The next-to-last episode of the year, "Cease Fire," finds Hawkeye in a bind in the midst of celebrating what is supposed to be the end of the war. There are three nurses expecting to continue their relationship with him back home. Hawk's solution is to tell them he's married—which works until the cease-fire is called off.

But Hawkeye isn't the only doctor who is getting to know the nurses. Commanding Officer Col. Henry Blake (McLean Stevenson) is frequently found in his tent with a nurse ("The Moose," "I Hate a Mystery," and "Cease Fire," for example), yet he worries in "Showtime" as his next child is about to be born back home. In "Requiem for a Heavyweight," Trapper "wins" a nurse through a valiant, if fixed, victory in a boxing match. That episode also features a rare salute from Hawk and Trap as a nurse accidentally loses her towel on the way back to her tent from the showers. Even Radar, who in later years would actually become *more* naive and virginlike in character, is shown taking advantage of a shelling episode to convince a nurse that the potential of dying deserves a sexual escapade in "The Army-Navy Game."

In "Bananas, Crackers and Nuts" (which won an ACE "Eddie" award for editor Fred W. Berger), guest star Stuart Margolin plays Capt. Sherman, an army psychiatrist brought to the 4077 by Frank and Margaret to investigate Hawk's sanity. Hawk and Trap convince him that Margaret desires him. After they set him up in her tent before she enters, his near assault on her is "discovered" by Hawk, Trapper, and eventually the whole camp, and he is forced to leave the camp in shame.

In retrospect, Gelbart has acknowledged that women were treated very poorly in the first few years. As he has put it, "We all got our consciousness raised over the years."[3] Indeed, things were afoot in American society that would begin to change some of the perceptions and treatment of women.

FROM BATTLEFIELD SEX TO THE BATTLEGROUND OF THE SEXES

When the show premiered, the sexual revolution was in full swing and the women's movement was beginning to receive serious attention. A cover story in *Time* chronicled how more open attitudes about sexuality were affecting teens.[4] Citing a survey on sexual practices, the article reported that in 1971, 46 percent of young women had lost their virginity by age 20. This trend was accompanied by a rise in venereal disease among high school and college students and an increase in illegitimate births among teenagers. Trying to account for these trends, the article cited sources who noted a general "erotization" of society and less onerous perspectives on sex among religious authorities.

Undoubtedly, some young women used sex to assert their independence as well. Among their options was the increasing acceptance of single motherhood. Homes originally set up to help "nice girls" who got pregnant were no longer serving that clientele as many women chose to have their children at home and bring them up themselves. Only a decade earlier, 10 percent of single mothers had brought up their children; now over 45 percent were choosing to do so.[5]

Women's reproductive rights also were coming under scrutiny, particularly with respect to abortion. By September 1971, seventeen states had liberalized their abortion laws. Colorado was the first in 1967, following the American Law Institute's suggested guidelines allowing abortions up to the sixteenth week of pregnancy. These laws were thought to help reduce the numbers of births to single women and prevent the harm women faced when they sought abortions illegally.[6] A *Newsweek* article presented a detailed discussion of the historical, scientific, and moral aspects of abortion and noted that the United

States Supreme Court had agreed to hear challenges to abortion laws in Texas and Georgia that would also nullify most anti-abortion laws in other states.[7] In a March 1972 decision, a three-judge federal court panel had determined a woman had the freedom and privacy of medical choice to decide to terminate pregnancy based on the ninth and fourteenth amendments. The Supreme Court would overturn abortion laws in all states by January 1973.[8]

Women's liberation was in the air, no doubt encouraged by the civil rights, antiwar and environmental movements that emerged in the 1960s. Actually, women's issues had begun to gain prominence in the late 1960s. The early period of the movement was characterized by consciousness-raising groups for women. Later, women began to challenge the laws and practices that constituted institutional sexism.

In 1971, the Supreme Court heard and upheld the first sex discrimination case brought under the Civil Rights Act of 1964. The decision upheld the equal hiring provisions of the act in a case involving a mother who was denied the right to serve as the administrator of her deceased son's estate. The law had said males must be preferred to females.[9]

In June 1971, the first National Women's Political Caucus met and attracted about 300 participants, who pledged to support female candidates as well as male candidates responsive to women's legislative concerns and issues—opposition to the Vietnam War, repeal of abortion laws, passage of an Equal Rights Amendment to the Constitution and redress of inequities in tax laws.[10] The group set a goal of tripling the number of women in Congress in the 1972 elections. By July of the following year, Jean Westwood was chosen as the first female chair of the Democratic National Committee.[11] The midterm elections of 1974 would find greater numbers of women pursuing and winning office at all levels—locally for mayorships, statewide for offices such as governor and at the federal level for House and Senate. Connecticut would elect Ella Grasso governor and New Jersey would put two women in the House of Representatives. Altogether there would be an increase of 27 percent in the number of women holding elected offices across the nation.[12]

Perhaps the most significant event for the women's movement in the early 1970s was the passing of the Equal Rights Amendment (ERA) by Congress on March 22, 1972. The event was heralded through a *Time* cover story and special issue dedicated to "The New Woman, 1972." The issue set out to examine "the question of women" in each department of the magazine.[13] By the end of the year, 22 states had ratified the ERA. (Later, however, the amendment was to founder, eventually failing to get the necessary approval from 38 states.[14] Women who opposed the amendment began to organize themselves as "Stop ERA." Phyllis Schlafly, long involved in conservative politics, used her experience and began to speak before women's, religious and political groups who felt the traditional roles of women were threatened by the ERA and asserted it would actually diminish the status of women in society.[15])

An essay by Ruth Byne in *Time* laid out the tasks and challenges women faced as they entered spheres of life that until then had been the province of men. The essay cited a poll showing 57 percent of American women under 25 agreeing that men treat women as sex objects. Women in the workplace were already a reality—43 percent of American women were in the labor force in the early 1970s, and they made up 37 percent of the total workforce. Seventy-five percent of working women worked full time to support themselves or their families. Married women made up 40 percent of the female labor force. Fifty percent of United States mothers who worked had school-aged children.[16]

Thus, regardless of whether men wanted women entering the workforce, it was happening. The movement of women into professional fields and their effect on previously male domains was exemplified in an issue of the *Yale Law Review* in the fall of 1971. The issue was devoted to the arguments and impact of the Equal Rights Amendment and was edited by three female law graduates and a male professor at Yale.[17] In December 1973, *Newsweek* touted women as the "new campus rebels." The article noted that women were not well represented in campus faculties but that women students were becoming more numerous and taking majors and roles once thought to be reserved for men.[18]

Women were on the move in religious circles as well. In June 1972, the first female rabbi was ordained in Cincinnati. The American Lutheran Church had decided to accept women as pastors in 1970, but the United States Episcopal Church and the Roman Catholic Church were still denying women the opportunity to become priests.[19]

Women were also becoming more visible in the media. An August 1971 special report in *Newsweek* profiled Gloria Steinem. In today's context, the article almost seems like a parody. The first paragraph consists largely of a description of Steinem in physical terms, and she is portrayed as a cheerleader for the women's movement: "in hip hugging raspberry Levi's, 2 inch wedgies and tight poor boy T-shirt, her long blond-streaked hair falls just so above each breast and her cheerleader-pretty face... Her cheekbones are broad and high, her teeth white and even...." Her commitment to the women's movement is met by comments from others quoted in the article that "what Gloria needs is a man."[20] In November, Steinem announced a new publication for the women's movement, a magazine that she would edit. *Ms.* magazine, completely controlled and operated by women, would begin publishing on July 1, 1972.[21]

As Steinem moved into publishing, other women were embarking on careers in television news. *Time* featured Barbara Walters on the occasion of her selection for the press entourage for Nixon's famous visit to China in February 1972.[22] The media section of *Newsweek* profiled several up-and-coming female reporters in August 1971. A 25-year-old Connie Chung, then a television news reporter in Washington, was quoted as saying, "I hate fashion stories! Give me a tear-gas, rock-throwing riot any time." The article went on to say how these reporters frequently felt like tokens—regarded as "house chicks" who were effective at getting a human angle on stories.[23]

The women's movement began to take on the television networks for the way women were portrayed in shows and the kinds of roles available to women. The sexism in television series was also evident in television news. In May 1972, women in New York targeted WABC for discrimination in programs and employment opportunities for women.[24]

No doubt many feminists of the early 1970s were disappointed with the treatment of women in *M*A*S*H*. If anything, *M*A*S*H* was behind the curve of social history in light of the changes women were forging around the time it premiered on CBS. The first year's episodes reflect the fact that decision-making was firmly in the grasp of male network executives. The sexist humor of the parent film and grandparent novel also influenced the first year of the television series. Furthermore, it is likely that despite the gains of the women's movement, the typical workplace of the early 1970s was not all that friendly for women, and in that respect MASH 4077 may have reflected reality with lots of sexual references, offers and innuendos, many of which would be considered sexual harassment today.

Along with the sexism, *M*A*S*H* was also prone to a lot of negative references to homosexuality in the first year. Gay bashing and jokes about homosexuality are a feature of several episodes. In some episodes, framing someone as gay is part of a plot twist. In "The Ringbanger," Hawkeye and Trapper want to keep a particular colonel, Buzz Brighton (Leslie Nielsen), out of action because his aggressive actions have resulted in a high casualty rate in his unit. To keep anyone from discovering that Brighton is not seriously injured, Hawk has to keep Frank Burns from examining him. Hawkeye accomplishes this by telling Brighton that Frank is gay and looking for company, which makes Brighton avoid all Frank's attempts at an examination. In "Bananas, Crackers and Nuts," Hawkeye is desperate for R and R and begins to act crazy to convince temporary CO Frank Burns that he needs a break. When Margaret and Frank bring in an army psychiatrist, Hawkeye tells him that he is secretly in love with Frank. At that point, the psychiatrist becomes convinced Hawk is sick and in need of psychiatric treatment.

Ironically, it was in 1971 that gays disrupted the American Psychiatric Association meeting in Washington and denounced the organization for its labeling of gays as mentally disordered.[25] At the same time, articles on the gay rights movement were beginning to appear in *Time* and *Newsweek*.[26] *Newsweek* presented a special report headlined "The Militant Homosexual," which was probably the first inkling for most Americans that another rights movement was taking hold. It pointed out recent events in which gays were coming out of the closet. Gay men who had kept quiet and felt shame or guilt were being encouraged to come out in the open. The Stonewall Rebellion, which erupted as the first resistance to a gay bar raid by New York City police in June 1969, is generally regarded as the "first shot" in a war for dignity and respect for gays and lesbians. Cities where large numbers of gays lived became focal points for organizing politically; Los Angeles and San Francisco were places where politicians found they needed to pay attention to the growing political savvy of gays.[27]

But gays faced an uphill battle as they experienced rejection even in the other liberation movements of the day. Black males expressed deep hostility toward gays, and homosexuals trying to get involved in the antiwar movement were usually rebuffed. Betty Friedan, founder of the National Organization for Women, is quoted as blaming lesbians for marginalizing the women's movement: "Women's lib is being distorted by the attention paid to a small minority. Lesbianism within the movement will divide women and play into their worst fears."[28]

In this context, *M*A*S*H*'s homophobia is "mainstream" and illustrates the show wasn't always breaking new ground. Some of this homophobia played a role in shaping the character of Corporal Max Klinger, as played by Jamie Farr. Farr was not a regular cast member in the first few years of the show and only appeared in six episodes in year one. And though he is dressed as a woman from the beginning, his character changed even before audiences saw his first fashion statement. His first appearance in "Chief Surgeon Who?" (which won a Writers Guild Award for Larry Gelbart) was originally written to have him play the character as an effeminate gay. The creative team thought it through and decided to keep the dresses but make Klinger a heterosexual trying to get out on a "Section 8" or psychological discharge. Eventually, Klinger would be challenged to come up with more convincing schemes, and his appearances would serve as comic subplots in various episodes.

MEANWHILE, BACK AT THE FRONT...

While the comedy of *M*A*S*H* in the first year focused on sex and the 4077 persisted in getting itself involved in all kinds of hijinks, there were a few serious moments as well. After all, the Vietnam War was continuing, even if "Vietnamization" was taking place.

The war's impact on American society was quite evident, even as Nixon adopted policies designed to get American troops home. Public opinion was squarely against further loss of American life, and the war had led many to question basic elements of the country's political leadership. A Gallup poll indicated large numbers of Americans had come to believe the country had slipped backward for the last five years, and nearly half believed the national tensions were serious enough to lead to a real leadership breakdown. A clear majority wanted the United States out of Vietnam even if it meant a "Communist takeover."[29]

These sentiments probably had their roots in the release of the Pentagon Papers in June 1971. This historic act by Daniel Ellsberg brought out even
more public cynicism as the secret history of the war, written by the men who
prosecuted it, revealed how the public had been deceived for many years. The
papers revealed, for instance, that the United States had sponsored a coup
against South Vietnamese president Ngo Dinh Diem in November 1963. General William Westmoreland had clearly misrepresented the situation throughout. He had continually raised the estimate of the number of troops needed,
from 175,000 to 275,000 in July 1965; by January 1966 there were 542,000
soldiers pursuing "the light at the end of the tunnel," and Westmoreland was
predicting that within two years, the United States would win the war. Such
rosy scenarios became a thing of the past as the Pentagon Papers were published in papers throughout the country.[30]

Public opinion on the politics of the Pentagon Papers clearly went against
political leaders. A Gallup poll revealed that 48 percent disapproved of the
government's attempt to suppress release of the secret history; 56 percent said
they thought the government tried to keep too much information secret from
the public.[31] These developments led the Senate in late June 1971 to urge
Nixon to set a date for a complete United States withdrawal from Vietnam.[32]
Public sentiment and weariness with war even changed the character of how
some celebrated the Fourth of July. *Time* reported that antiwar rallies and
peace picnics were conducted to show that "peace is patriotic," and military
parades were downplayed.[33]

Inevitably, 1972 presidential politics would come into consideration as
Nixon tried to decide how best to extricate the United States from Vietnam.
His gambit to China and trip there in 1972 had many speculating he might
be using that move to help his reelection chances with a foreign policy success.[34] There also was concern on the Republican president's part that the 18-
to 21-year-old voters who would participate for the first time would swing the
election to a Democrat. The ratification of the twenty-sixth Amendment on
June 20, 1971, meant 11.4 million new voters were enfranchised. Early regis-
trations by young adults indicated a 3-to-1 Democratic advantage, and in
August 1971 *Time* speculated that the new voters could swing nine states—
including California, New Jersey and Ohio—to the Democratic candidate and
thereby make Nixon's reelection very difficult.[35] Yet, most of the new voters
were not college students (thought to be the primary source of opposition to
Nixon), and most new voters asserted more independence from both Democ-
rats and Republicans than those over 21.[36]

Nixon's dilemma was one of "saving face"—how to accomplish the disen-
gagement and withdrawal from Vietnam without actually losing the war in
the process. "Vietnamization" and bombing campaigns would be his solution.
Vietnamization was the process of turning the ground war over to the South
Vietnamese forces and withdrawing United States combat forces as the South

Vietnamese proved they could go it alone. Nixon would support this effort by continuing to use United States aircraft to bomb North Vietnam. The rationale behind the late 1971 bombing campaign, which was described as the longest and largest American attack on North Vietnam since Lyndon Johnson had halted the bombing campaign in 1968, was the protection of the remaining 160,000 United States troops. But the military situation was deteriorating, and doubts were growing even among military officials about the effectiveness of the Vietnamization process.[37] By the end of January 1971, fighting in Laos and Cambodia had turned to the favor of the North Vietnamese, and a new Tet-style offensive was thought imminent by United States sources. The South Vietnamese army was plagued by draft-dodging and desertions, and soldiers were perishing at high rates. The "air support" provided by the United States was helping to the keep the ground forces from further decimation.[38]

The bombing campaign to get the North to reach an agreement at the peace talks was not without a domestic reaction. The Vietnam Veterans Against the War staged a dramatic protest at the Statue of Liberty, unfurling an upside-down United States flag as a symbol of distress. The vets called it "Operation Peace on Earth," and it was designed to get Nixon to set a definite date for withdrawal of United States forces. There were antiwar actions throughout the country, at an air force base in California and in cities such as Boston, San Francisco, Philadelphia, and Washington, D.C.[39]

Bombing deep into North Vietnam began in late April 1972 and reignited concerns that the United States would never really get out. Nixon responded that the protests were only aiding the North Vietnamese. These bombing raids, which were launched in response to a North Vietnamese offensive designed to test the staying power of the United States–trained South Vietnamese forces, eventually reached as far as Hanoi and the key port city of Haiphong. Many of the South Vietnamese forces retreated or fled when the North Vietnamese began to penetrate the South. Meanwhile, Nixon was trying to get a settlement with Vietnam by election day and used the bombing to counteract the offensive without losing a lot of American lives.[40]

The president's actions only served to polarize the Congress and the country. Former vice-president Hubert Humphrey, who had once supported Johnson's effort in Vietnam and who probably lost the 1968 presidential election because of it, was now an advocate for withdrawal. George Wallace, longtime conservative and segregationist and a presidential candidate in 1968 and 1972, declared in *Time* he was "for gettin' out." The Senate began to consider legislation designed to restrict Nixon's ability to expand and continue the war; this would be the seed that would grow into the War Powers Act. The bombing would increase the number of American POWs as the downing of planes resulted in 69 airmen killed, wounded, or missing. The military actions in Vietnam produced the largest demonstrations on United

States college campuses since the invasion of Cambodia in May 1970. Fifty thousand marched in the rain in New York against the bombing campaign.[41]

With their offensive in May 1972, the North Vietnamese made it clear that they were prepared to outlast the American presence, which prompted a renewal of peace talks. The national newsmagazines began to speculate about why the American effort to withdraw and leave the fighting to the South Vietnamese was failing. American concerns about POWs would become a priority in the peace talks as they stretched into the fall.[42]

The key in the peace talks for the United States was the early release of Americans captured by the North Vietnamese and Viet Cong. As the talks gathered momentum in the lead-up to the presidential election in the United States, it became obvious that Nixon was willing to forego "peace with honor," a line he had used for years, in favor of the safe withdrawal of remaining United States forces and release of the American POWs. While Secretary of State Henry Kissinger declared "peace at hand" one week before the election, the actual agreement would not be achieved until early 1973.[43]

Looking at the deal prompted many to speculate that such an agreement could have been forged much earlier. What had changed, evidently, was that the United States was now willing to allow North Vietnamese troops in the South to remain while a political settlement was worked out. Kissinger had apparently given up on saving face by resisting a coalition government in South Vietnam. It seemed clear that the willingness to forego a political settlement resulted in an agreement whose primary objective was to facilitate the withdrawal of remaining United States forces and attain the release of the POWs. The jockeying by both sides after the election and in early 1973 was due primarily to South Vietnamese president Thieu's resistance to the agreement.[44]

A report in *Time* one year after the peace agreement confirmed much of the earlier speculation.[45] Summarizing an article by Ted Szulc appearing in the academic journal *Foreign Policy*, the piece asserted that the United States elections were the primary factor in the timing and the negotiation of the agreement. Key concessions by the United States on the role of the Viet Cong in the future of the south had created movement. Indeed, Kissinger had kept Thieu in the dark, presenting the October 1972 agreement to him as a *fait accompli*. The agreement was not signed until much later because Thieu objected to anything that diminished his power.

The agreement would not be finalized without yet another bombing campaign by Nixon, an apparent effort to squeeze the North Vietnamese into more concessions and to thwart them from acquiring more territory on the ground in South Vietnam. The reaction domestically and internationally was outrage, for the peace agreement had been touted for months. NATO allies and the pope were among the critics of Nixon's duplicitous moves toward peace.[46]

The final agreement was signed January 22, 1973, in Paris. Whether there ever was a true cease-fire is debatable, since both the South and North Vietnamese continued military operations in trying to gain the upper hand.[47] The war would not really end until 1975; once the POWs were returned, the United States would continue to help the South Vietnamese with air support and bombing in an attempt to stave off the North.

Beyond the actual fighting, the United States began to struggle with the aftermath of the war. As the war wound down, discussion of what to do about the many men who left the armed forces or evaded the draft by moving to Canada and Europe was beginning. In January of 1970, the Pentagon revealed that 1,403 service personnel had deserted since July 1966. It was estimated that over 70,000 more had evaded the draft. Amnesty became an issue in the 1972 elections; public opinion was opposed to full amnesty, but 63 percent in a Gallup poll favored some kind of pardon conditioned on public service back in the United States. The signing of the peace agreement prompted further discussion, but it would be some time before a program would be adopted under President Gerald Ford.[48]

A lengthy analysis by Seymour Hersh, who won a Pulitzer Prize for breaking the story on the My Lai massacre, concluded that a primary beneficiary of the decision to get out of Vietnam was the United States military. His argument was that United States forces, wracked by internal violence, disregard and abuse of the Vietnamese people, and use of indiscriminate bombing, were best off cutting their losses in Vietnam. He related communication from an army psychiatrist who claimed that the army was on the verge of collapse due to rampant drug use, breakdown of authority, and violence. Fragging (blowing up an officer or adversary with a fragmentation grenade) had become a way of resolving differences between officers and their conscripts. There were five instances of fragging in a two-month period at one base alone. Taught that Vietnamese society was ignorant and superstitious, GIs regarded "gooks" as expendable, and a bureaucracy measuring success by body counts encouraged men to kill civilians, dig up bodies long dead, and otherwise pump up the numbers. The behavior of the United States military in Vietnam as a force that abused and destroyed the very people and society it was sent to "save" was for Hersh, the biggest factor in the demoralization of American forces. He concluded, somewhat ironically, that the antiwar movement in essence had saved the military from itself.[49]

United States troops would eventually be withdrawn, and the American people would finally begin to see less carnage on the nation's television news. But the public would not quickly forget the debacle that the war became, and would continue to be skeptical about Vietnam as well as future interventions.

WAR CAN MAKE COMEDY
A SERIOUS MATTER

It was the real war, the one on television newscasts, that rumbled in the back of network executives' minds when the creative team tried to bring serious themes about war to a sitcom format. Given the reality of the Vietnam War, Gelbart has said he began to "work in reverse" when it came to addressing serious issues like war on *M*A*S*H*.[50] This helped him tone down some of his ideas to make them more palatable for the network. He found the network was opposed not so much to antiwar messages as to seriousness or "heaviness" in general. From the beginning, Gelbart and company were told not to have too many OR scenes or show much blood.

The most serious attempt at an antiwar statement in the first year came in January 1973 when "Sometimes You Hear the Bullet" was broadcast. In this episode, Tommy Gillis, an old friend of Hawkeye's, arrives at the 4077 when his unit is nearby. Gillis is a writer who has come to Korea as a soldier to write from a soldier's perspective. Near the end of the episode, Hawk is taken aback when Gillis is brought in and put on his operating table. Hawk gets upset with himself for being upset by Gillis's death. Blake responds that there are only two rules about war. Rule 1: Young men die. Rule 2: Doctors can't change Rule 1.

Also in "Bullet," Ron Howard plays a sixteen-year-old who has forged his way into the army to win back a girlfriend back home. Early in the episode, Hawkeye promises not to turn him in, but Gillis's death later compels him to do otherwise.

Many associated with the show cite "Bullet" as indicative of the powerful emotions and potential of the show's noncomedic element. Gene Reynolds says that one of the network's henchmen warned him that such episodes would lose audience for the show. "Someday I'll tell you how you guys screwed up *M*A*S*H*," Reynolds was told. Alan Alda says "Bullet" represented the kind of television he wanted to do and that it was the beginning of mixing the dark and the light.[51] Larry Linville has cited "Bullet" as the finest example of what the show could accomplish.[52] Carl Kleinschmitt's teleplay was nominated for a Writers Guild Award.

Several other first-year episodes also showed *M*A*S*H*'s potential to challenge the conventional sitcom format. In many ways, "Yankee Doodle Doctor" and "Dear Dad" bring out the "war is hell" perspective in the show. "Yankee Doodle Doctor" is about using the 4077 success rate to make an army propaganda film about saving lives in Korea. Ed Flanders plays Lt. Bricker, an egotistical film director who chooses Hawkeye as his star for the film. After hearing Frank and Margaret's jingoistic script and realizing Bricker only wants to lionize doctors in Korea, Hawk destroys the film that has been shot, leading

Bricker to leave the 4077 in disgust. Hawk and company shoot their own film and play it for the camp. Most of it is a hilarious parody of the previous script, but the film ends with a strong antiwar statement that reveals Hawkeye's feelings about the futility of his job.

"Dear Dad" is another episode that effectively blends the lighthearted and serious elements in what would be the first of many Christmas episodes. This episode finds Hawkeye writing a letter to his father at Christmastime. "Letter" episodes would become regular features of the show over its run. Starting with a character (most often Hawkeye but also Radar, Father Mulcahy and later, Col. Potter, B.J. and Charles) writing a letter to someone back home, these episodes usually lack a cohesive plot, instead providing slices of life and character revelations as the letter writer describes life at the 4077 and some of the people stationed there. "Dear Dad" concerns the camp's holiday activities, such as preparing for the party with kids from the local orphanage. Viewers see the compassion of Trapper as he vaccinates local Korean children, while Radar is shown sending a jeep back home part by part. Frank Burns gives Klinger a hard time, and Klinger threatens to "frag" him, only to be talked out of it by Father Mulcahy. Margaret and Frank are seen in one of their trysts, worrying that peace might break them up. In the latter part of the episode, Hawk is getting dressed up to play Santa for the orphans when Blake comes in and sends him out into the battlefield, where a badly injured soldier needs Hawk's chest-cutting specialty. Soldiers in a foxhole look on in amazement as "Santa" is delivered by helicopter to take care of the man. The mix of irony and light comedy in this episode illustrated how *M*A*S*H* could break out of the sitcom mold.

Other episodes, such as "The Army-Navy Game," provide a first critique of military bureaucracy and CIA propaganda. Such critiques would appear occasionally over the life of the show. "The Army-Navy Game" concerns a shell landing in camp but not exploding. After dealing with both the army and navy bureaucrats, who are more interested in listening to the army-navy football game than in helping the 4077, the unit is told the bomb belongs to the CIA. Hawk and Trap go out to disarm the bomb, only to discover it's a propaganda weapon—its "shrapnel" consists of a leaflet advising, "Give yourselves up—you can't win. Douglas MacArthur."

Other first-year episodes poking fun at army bureaucracy include "To Market, to Market," which tracks Hawk and Trap's attempts to get hydrocortisone for their patients through the black market, and "The Long John Flap," which revolves around supply fiascoes—the army delivering warm-weather supplies in the dead of winter.

As mentioned earlier, "The Ringbanger" is an episode in which Hawk and Trap conspire to keep a gung-ho colonel (a "ringbanger," or military academy graduate) from creating more casualties. Over the years, the show would criticize the "no guts, no glory" attitude of field commanders. Pointing out the excesses of a few glory-seeking officers would be a way of critiquing militarism without taking on the reason for the war.

A March 1973 episode titled "Cease Fire" would air the same week a cease-fire was declared in Vietnam. In this episode, the unit begins to celebrate the war's ending based on a cease-fire and a "sure bet" rumor. A skeptical Trapper doesn't believe it and is eventually proved right. And no sooner is the cease-fire called off than the 4077 is deluged with casualties. The episode must have seemed like a warning not to believe in the announced end of the fighting in Vietnam. Indeed, it would be over two years before the United States would finally withdraw from what was still a shooting war.

The first year of *M*A*S*H* only began to scratch the surface in terms of more provocative themes. The unit's relationship with Koreans would develop beyond that explored in the "Dear Dad" or "Tuttle" episodes. "Tuttle," which was nominated for a Writers Guild Award, focuses on the creation of a fictional captain as a cover for Hawkeye and Trapper's generosity in helping Korean children orphaned by the war. The humor of this episode comes from the rest of the unit trying to figure out just who Tuttle is. Hawkeye's hilarious eulogy of Tuttle is one of the more ingenious elements of humor in the first year.

When one looks at the whole first season, it is quite clear *M*A*S*H* did not have enough security to venture too far into serious issues, much less politically volatile fare. The show ended the year forty-seventh in the ratings, a ranking that today would probably result in cancellation. Some sources say that the wife of CBS head William Paley liked the show and cite her preference as one reason *M*A*S*H* was given a second season. It certainly had tough Sunday night competition—Walt Disney on NBC and *The FBI* on ABC.[53]

M*A*S*H received mixed reviews from critics. *Life*'s review was the most positive, calling it the class of the new season's sitcoms, pointing to Alan Alda's presence as the primary reason. *Life* also noted that the rapid-fire humor allowed viewers not to brood on its more serious elements. Yet the quick one-liners that would characterize the early years of the show were seen by more critical reviewers as clichés. A brief review in the October 16, 1972, edition of *Time* described *M*A*S*H* as one of the season's biggest disappointments. Blaming the impossibility of bringing the film's "savage satire" to commercial television, the review claimed that the tension between comedy and horror had become as "bleached out" as *Hogan's Heroes*.[54] A review by Allene Tamey in *Vogue* in March 1973 offered praise for *M*A*S*H*'s "street smarts," seeing it and *Hogan's Heroes* as "reality relievers."[55]

In April 1973, *Newsweek* offered a column by "Cyclops" which, while decrying *M*A*S*H*'s move to Saturday night for the second season, offered much praise for the show as a crutch for the "hobbled human spirit." This review compared the show favorably to the film, asserting that Alan Alda and Wayne Rogers outdo their movie counterparts Donald Sutherland and Elliott

Gould as they exemplify friendship and fraternity. "Cyclops" cited the potential of the show, in episodes like "Yankee Doodle Doctor," as irony raised to its most abrasive.[56]

Other discussions of M*A*S*H during the first season focused more on the sexual mores and themes of the show. Harry Waters of *Newsweek* suggested the whole new television season be rated PG and specifically cited M*A*S*H, a show where "two Army surgeons endlessly try to operate their way into nurses' sleeping bags."[57]

Clearly, M*A*S*H had captured attention as television that was traversing new territory. The show received five Emmy nominations—Outstanding Comedy Series, Outstanding New Series, Outstanding Achievement in Editing, Outstanding Performance in a Leading Role (Alan Alda), and Outstanding Performance in supporting roles (McLean Stevenson and Gary Burghoff). It also got two Golden Globe Award nominations—Best Comedy Show and Best Actor in a Comedy (Alda).

As the show went on, characters would further develop. Father Mulcahy (who was called "Red" a few times during the first season as a carryover from the novel and film) would begin to be less a vehicle for religious humor and more a compassionate priest who experiences self-doubt. Margaret and Klinger would become less and less like cartoon characters and develop as more complex human beings.

This kind of critical acclaim and character development would help keep the show alive. As we shall see, as M*A*S*H acquired a loyal and large audience, it began to get more gutsy about showing the darker side of war and the ugliness of militarism.

CHAPTER 4

War Is Hell,
But Life's a Party—
Years 2-3, 1973-75

M*A*S*H began year two (1973-74) on Saturday evenings in the time slot right after *All in the Family*, CBS's biggest and, to that point, most socially provocative show. By the end of the year, *M*A*S*H* would be rated as the fourth most popular show on television, with a 28 rating (28 percent of all television households were tuning into the show on a regular basis). In year three (1974-75), it would be moved again, this time to Tuesday nights opposite weekly movies on ABC and NBC, and it would garner a 27 rating. Together, years two and three attracted the largest audiences over the life of the show. They were also the most provocative years of the show in its eleven-year lifetime.

A writer's strike in year two presented some difficulties but also probably helped facilitate a group process that many involved with the show have said contributed to its success. This "group therapy," as Larry Gelbart called it, allowed the cast to make suggestions about their character's roles in various situations. Gelbart says that although such an approach meant that emotions sometimes ran high, the giant suggestion box it generated was a real contribution to the character growth of the main cast.[1]

Furthermore, a trip by Gelbart and producer Gene Reynolds to Korea between years two and three helped to expand the storylines and incorporate actual incidents from the Korean War into the show. Gelbart had already been interviewing doctors in the United States who had served in Korea, but he says the trip to Korea and the 22 hours of taped conversation he brought back helped him to really value the experiences of those who were there. Gelbart contends such practices helped the show reach its zenith in these years and also helped it to develop enough clout to get away with more provocative storylines.[2] There would be less trouble with network censors, as the loyal audience the show acquired was drawn to the program precisely because of the mix of serious issues and comedy. Besides achieving success and acclaim, in these two years the show found its bearings, took a few more risks, and generally became a staple on American television.

Because the show had had a relatively small audience in the first year, Gelbart used the first episode of the second season as a second pilot to introduce new viewers to the show. "Divided We Stand" concerns General Clayton's dispatching of an army psychiatrist to assess the unit's psyche and determine if the 4077 should be disbanded. The captain's visit stirs concern in the unit, which tries to act as normal as is possible for the 4077. Nevertheless, the captain is witness to the shenanigans of Klinger, the trysts of Margaret and Frank, Hawkeye and Trapper's practical jokes, Blake's midday drinking, and the generally unmilitary decorum of the unit. Then the casualties pour in and the unit goes to work. The captain observes the gruesome OR action and almost passes out. When the general arrives to check on the investigation, he finds the captain drunk in the Swamp. The captain tells the general he has seen textbook lunacy in many situations but that such lunacy is expected at places like the 4077 where they do the impossible on a regular basis. He tells the general breaking the unit up would itself be crazy.

In this episode, Gelbart captures the essence of *M*A*S*H*. The zaniness of the unit contrasts with the bloody reality of the war. The crazy antics serve as a human response to ongoing human tragedy. Though no "message" is imparted in this episode, it does serve as an archetype for the mix of comedy and tragedy that would make the show famous and propel it to the top echelon of programs for the next decade. Indeed, many episodes from years two and three reflect a similar structure. Many open with OR scenes or have a number of OR sessions and incorporate a silly or comic relief element. Perhaps the prototype is an episode titled "O.R." Chaos in the OR amid shelling taxes the medical staff. Hawkeye takes the loss of a patient particularly hard, while Frank's incompetence provides some comic relief. The long OR session concludes with Hawkeye and Trapper passing out on operating tables.

WHICH WAR IS THIS: KOREA OR VIETNAM?

M*A*S*H's second season featured more episodes dealing with the ugly nature of war. Perhaps the most critical episode of the whole series can be found in "For the Good of the Outfit." It opens in the OR as the doctors are working on wounded civilians. Hawkeye and Trapper determine that the shrapnel has an American signature. The mention of napalm—an incendiary gel that saw heavy use in Vietnam—was one of several occasional linkages the show made between the Korean war of the past and the winding-down Vietnam War of the present.

Hawkeye and Trapper press the case and get an investigator to look into the situation. General Clayton arrives at the 4077 to persuade them to call off the inquiry. A letter to Hawkeye's father asking for a senator to get involved is intercepted by headquarters. Hawkeye, furious about the spying, is pressured by General Clayton to back off for his own good and "for the good of the outfit." But this time even Frank proves helpful, coming to the rescue with additional fragments and x-rays after the original evidence and investigator are "transferred."

This program brought the creative team tremendous network criticism as it evoked some of the worst aspects of United States military conduct—firing on civilians, covering it up, and generally acting as an imperial military power.[3] Despite this criticism, friendly fire incidents would surface in later episodes such as "As You Were" in year two and "Bombed" in year three. In these episodes, the 4077 is receiving misdirected artillery and has to go through several layers of military bureaucracy to get it stopped.

Some episodes effectively mix serious antiwar statements with a humorous spin. Year two's "Dr. Pierce and Mr. Hyde" concerns an overworked Hawkeye who has been operating for 24 hours. Though ordered to bed, Hawk proceeds to walk around like a zombie. He has Radar send a telegram to Harry Truman, reading simply, "Who's responsible? Signed, a dissatisfied customer." He approaches a chopper pilot and tells him not to go up anymore because he always leaves with an empty helicopter and comes back with wounded. He walks into a lecture by Frank about godless communists and asks "Why are we here?" Frank says the enemy is jealous of United States hygiene, and Hawk decides to send them a latrine to make peace. General Clayton hears about the telegram to Truman and comes to see who wrote it. Unfortunately for him, he chooses to use the latrine Hawkeye has attached to a jeep for delivery to the North.

The ugliness of war and the absurdity of army bureaucracy also come through clearly in such episodes as "Carry On Hawkeye," "The Incubator," "Iron Guts Kelly," "The Consultant," "Aid Station," and "Payday." In "Carry On Hawkeye," the PA announces the French anticipate a swift end to their involvement in the Vietnam War while Hawkeye valiantly battles the flu and Margaret's authority to get the unit through a heavy session of casualties. In "The Incubator," Hawk and Trap's search for an incubator to speed up diagnoses is rebuffed by army bureaucracy. Though Henry can get a barbecue or a pizza oven, the bureaucracy will not permit an incubator. As they defy the bureaucracy, they encounter an enterprising officer whose "business" dealings rival those of Milo Minderbender in Joseph Heller's novel *Catch–22*.[4] In the end, Radar's ingenuity and deal-making result in an incubator for the 4077. This episode garnered an Emmy for director Jackie Cooper and a Writers Guild nomination for Larry Gelbart, Bernard Dilbert and Laurence Marks.

"The Consultant" features a guest appearance by Alan Alda's father, Robert Alda, as Dr. Borelli. Hawk and Trap meet Borelli at a conference in Tokyo. He takes them up on an offer to visit the 4077 to put new surgery techniques into practice. But Borelli's previous war experience is no help as the OR action is too gruesome. After he fails to perform surgery using his technique, he is found chasing the war with alcohol. Hawk and Borelli debate the merits of alcohol as a coping mechanism. Borelli warns Hawkeye that this is Hawk's first war—he has seen much more.

"Iron Guts Kelly" focuses on how an aide to a visiting General Kelly absurdly attempts to give his general a glorious send-off after he dies in the throes of passion with Margaret. His search for a battle in which the general can die "heroically" ends when the ambulance into which he has put the body gets filled with Korean prostitutes, then has an accident before the body can be delivered to the front.

"Aid Station" finds Hawkeye, Margaret and Klinger on temporary duty at the front. They realize how advanced the working conditions are at the 4077 as they work under fire. The teamwork and dedication they display results in a rare compliment for Margaret by Hawkeye—a first for the two frequent adversaries.

An episode at the end of year two, "Crisis," reflects a period of difficulty for the 4077 that was similar to what the show's audience was experiencing at the time. "Crisis" concerns the unit's coping with a cutoff of supplies from headquarters. Fuel is at a premium; even the legs to Blake's desk are sacrificed for a little heat. The episode aired on February 9, 1974, when Americans were experiencing the effects of the Arab oil embargo that had been imposed on the United States and other supporters of Israel in October 1973 after the brief war between Egypt and Israel.[5] This followed the energy crisis of early 1973 when spot shortages of natural gas, heating oil, and jet fuel reflected the depletion of oil stocks. While the government elected to increase import quotas, a sense of dependency on foreign oil began to make policymakers nervous.[6] When the Arab oil embargo was announced in late 1973, consumers found themselves waiting in long lines for gasoline, and shortages of all forms of energy were common. Moves were made to eliminate unneccesary lighting. Americans were asked to keep their homes at least a few degrees colder and carpooling became more commonplace. Use of fuel for leisure activities was frowned upon. A standby rationing system for gasoline was developed. Many Americans viewed the oil companies as having an interest in driving up prices and were suspicious of the figures put out by the industry.[7] The embargo would be lifted by March 1974, but concerns about depending on foreign sources of energy would continue.[8]

The timing of the "Crisis" episode was uncanny, with a population's sudden worry about the loss of formerly abundant fuel and energy sources giving the show's theme real resonance. While the viewers of 1974 didn't have to cope with a war on top of their energy crisis, the reduction of lighting, the rationing of fuel, and the belt-tightening due to rising fuel prices undoubtedly gave the audience a certain sense of identification with this episode of *M*A*S*H*.

Episodes that offer a critique of United States military behavior and bureaucracy seem to be balanced by episodes like "Radar's Report," aired the week before "For the Good of the Outfit." In this episode, a wounded Chinese prisoner is brought into the OR only to wreak havoc by pulling a knife. A bottle of plasma for Trapper's American patient breaks, and the patient later dies. Trapper, blaming the Chinese prisoner, walks into post op and considers pulling out his IV tube, but Hawkeye stops him. This episode (which was nominated for a Writers Guild Award for Sheldon Keller) and others like it put the doctors squarely in the middle of the conflict, making them the somewhat neutral observers of the horrors of war made possible by both sides. More episodes would evoke criticism of the United States military's insensitivity to civilians and the gung-ho attitude of some officers, all while the surgeons at the 4077 put men from both sides back together. This balancing act—portraying United States wrongdoing while reminding audiences who the real enemy is—probably helped to neutralize or dissipate any criticism of the show for lack of patriotism. Episodes like "For the Good of the Outfit" are rare enough that they become lost in the weekly medical heroics of the 4077. Thus, at least some of the army (the medical corps) is seen to redeem what other aspects of the military destroy.

Indeed, the theme of "*M*A*S*H* doing good" is no better exemplified than in the episode "The Trial of Henry Blake." Blake is charged with giving aid and comfort to the enemy by (who else?) Margaret and Frank. The ensuing court-martial finds Hawkeye, Trapper, and Radar scrambling to vindicate Blake. Just as he is about to be put in the stockade, they march in with Meg Cratty, an American nurse who works with refugees and orphans from the North. These lost and displaced persons are the ones who have been receiving supplies and aid from the 4077. The charges are dismissed, and Henry is able to resume his command. This episode garnered an Emmy nomination for writing (McLean Stevenson) and a film editing award (Fred Berger and Stanford Tischler).

Frank and Margaret's super-patriotism provides both comic relief and the chance to point up the absurd aspects of the military view of the world. Episodes such as "Five O'Clock Charlie," "The Sniper," and "The Choson People" in year two and "Rainbow Bridge" and "Big Mac" in year three find Frank and Margaret trying to enforce military discipline or emphatically expressing their patriotism in the face of foreign threats. In "Charlie," Margaret and Frank take seriously a local renegade pilot who comes by every day to bomb a weapons depot near the 4077 and always misses.

"Big Mac" (for which Laurence Marks received a Writers Guild nomination) finds Margaret and Frank admiring the VIP tent prepared for a visit by General MacArthur (a visit that doesn't turn out as planned). The lusty officers get carried away while sitting on Mac's bed, and Margaret exclaims, "Oh Doug!" as Frank becomes passionate. Before this scene, Frank morally cleanses the camp by burning books he deems unfitting for Mac's visit. While played comedically on *M*A*S*H*, book-burning was a serious issue in the real world. A 1973 report by the American Library Association said more than 100 communities across the country attempted to ban books such as *Catcher in the Rye*, *Soul on Ice*, *Huckleberry Finn*, and *The Grapes of Wrath*. In September 1974, Christian fundamentalists in West Virginia attempted to ban books deemed "anti-religious, Communistic and pornographic" through a boycott of schools. They partially succeeded, winning removal of some textbooks and a promise that a review committee would be formed.[9]

Frank and Margaret's hypocritical moralism and hyperpatriotism approach a state of frenzy when Colonel Flagg (Edward Winter) arrives at the 4077. Flagg, the would be super-spy CIA agent, made his first appearance on the show at the end of year two. Flagg brought to the show an even more absurdly patriotic and paranoid perspective than that of Frank and Margaret.

Edward Winter made six appearances as Flagg over the life of the program—three of them in years two and three—but Winter's first *M*A*S*H* outing was in the role of Captain Halloran of the CID (the Defense Department equivalent of the CIA). The Halloran character arrives at the 4077 in "Deal Me Out," an episode in which army psychiatrist Sidney Freedman (Allan Arbus) clashes with Halloran over a battle-fatigued patient. Halloran is called to the 4077 by Frank, who has received an injured CID man. Frank refuses to operate on the seriously wounded man because military procedure requires that another CID man be present. Hawk and Trapper discover the man may not make it until then and proceed to operate. When Halloran arrives, he threatens to court-martial Hawk and Trap. Later, a patient (played by John Ritter) who doesn't want to return to the front has a gun on Frank, who is in the in the showers. Macho Halloran threatens to take the man out, but Freedman successfully talks the soldier down, and Trapper manages to take his gun away. Freedman would encounter Flagg late in the series to clash over a soldier experiencing "shell shock." "Deal Me Out" received nominations for an Emmy in directing and a Directors Guild Award for Gene Reynolds.

Winter's first appearance as Flagg came in the last episode of year two. "A Smattering of Intelligence" is a comic look at competing United States spy agencies. Flagg arrives on a chopper with minor injuries. He refuses morphine for pain and insists Hawk take him to his CO. Flagg orders Blake not to even mention his presence or the helicopter crash. In the meantime, an old friend of Trapper's, Vinnie Pratt, arrives as a G-2 agent (army counterintelligence) to see why Flagg is there. He contends the accident and injury to Flagg are a set-up so Flagg can investigate the 4077—a theory soon verified when Flagg purposefully breaks his arm so he can't be released from the hospital. Hawk and Trap fuel the "Spy vs. Spy" game by planting two separate files on Frank, one that gives him a fascist identity and a second that "proves" he's a communist. When both spies converge on the Swamp and try to arrest Frank,

Hawk and Trap reveal the ruse, and the two spies leave to have a cup of coffee together.

Two episodes from year three further develop the hyperpatriotic, paranoid Flagg. In "Officer of the Day," Hawk is appointed OD (officer of the day) but refuses to carry a gun. In a sequence that exemplifies the show's clever wordplay, Hawk eloquently voices his pacifism, describing all the things he will happily carry ("carry over, carry forward, Cary Grant...") but insisting that a gun will never be among them. Meanwhile, the OD duty is anything but routine. Flagg arrives, insisting a wounded civilian is a "gook"—a North Korean. Flagg wants the patient released so he can kill him. Hawkeye refuses and looks for a way to get the man out of the hospital without Flagg's knowledge. Frank, who is serving as temporary CO, orders Hawkeye to sign the release forms. Hawk defies the order until Flagg pulls his gun and says he will take the prisoner regardless. But Hawkeye still gets the last laugh: Flagg gets a man to take with him, but he doesn't realize it's Klinger, dressed for a night on the town as the ambulance pulls out.

Flagg's fourth appearance captures the absurdity of the whole spying enterprise. "White Gold" concerns a rash of thefts of the camp's stock of penicillin. A GI from another MASH unit is caught, and Hawkeye and Trapper assume the man is stealing the drug to sell on the black market. Flagg arrives to investigate and lets the GI escape, injuring himself to make it look like there was a struggle. Klinger later hears noise in the supply tent, and Hawk, Trap, and Klinger go in and catch the thief: Flagg. Even Margaret, usually impressed by Flagg's virility, is disappointed and confused at this turn of events. It turns out Flagg is stealing medicine to use to barter information. The original thief is recaptured and confesses he was merely trying to get help for his unit at the front. Hawkeye and Trapper search for a way to take Flagg out of action for awhile. At last they drug him and take out his appendix.

Flagg's function in the series is similar to Frank's. As a caricature, Flagg offers an easy way to point up the absurdity of blind patriotism and machismo masquerading as competency and steadfastness. Even supporters of the Vietnam War or military types could laugh at Frank and Flagg because they acted like overzealous fools. Thus their foolishness likely took the edge off some of the pointed commentary about jingoism and blind patriotism. But Flagg's occasional appearances at the 4077 also parallel events in the mid–1970s that revealed the misbehavior of the FBI and the CIA.

MR. NIXON'S WARS:
FROM VIETNAM TO WATERGATE

The withdrawal of American forces from Indochina continued amid a cease-fire and peace agreement that seemed to unravel almost from the beginning. With an escalation of war in Cambodia, the entire region found itself mired in conflict. Efforts by the Viet Cong to hold more territory in South Vietnam gave them an opening for a provisional government. *Newsweek* reported in July 1973 that there was a virtual "third Vietnam"—the North, the South, and the considerable territory controlled by the Viet Cong in the South.[10] Some predicted eventual victory by the North and the Viet Cong over the South. Meanwhile, United States bombing of Cambodia and support for another shaky government generated controversy in the summer of 1973. Congress negotiated an end to the bombing on August 15 but remained wary of an administration that had lied about its bombing of Cambodia in 1970. In one bombing incident, military sources announced that the damage was minimal, while reporters who went to the site described the incident as the worst bombing error of the war, an error that resulted in 137 civilian dead and 268 wounded. One man whose entire family had been killed implored a newsman to take his picture so Americans could see what had happened.[11]

By early 1975, events were coming to a head in both Cambodia and Vietnam. United States president Gerald Ford was still asking Congress to appropriate money to prop up the governments in both countries. A resistant Congress saw it as throwing good money after bad, since both situations seemed hopeless for the United States–backed regimes. The debate over aid to Cambodia presaged the debates future military endeavors would create in the post–Vietnam era. The Nixon doctrine of supporting those who could fight for themselves was challenged by the notion the United States should not be the policeman of the world. Mail from citizens was persuading Congress to cut off the aid, though many feared a bloodbath should the mysterious Khmer Rouge rebels prevail.[12]

In Vietnam, the South Vietnamese had failed to show themselves capable of fighting their own war. High numbers of South Vietnamese soldiers were deserting—24,000 per month—and many others were being killed or wounded. President Thieu's regime was cracking down on its opposition and silencing press criticism.[13] A "strategic" retreat at the end of March 1975 was supposed to allow the South Vietnamese army to consolidate its forces for the defense of Saigon but instead served to accelerate the end of the war. Provincial capitals were abandoned, including the ancient city of Hue, territory contested throughout the war. The retreat left behind a lot of United States supplied materiel that could be used by the Viet Cong and the North Vietnamese. The chaos of the retreat allowed even more to desert from the armed forces, and many ex-combatants were terrorizing civilians and looting. Some military strategists still insisted there was an army worth saving. Opinion polls in the United States registered large majorities opposing any military aid for either South Vietnam or Cambodia.[14]

The end came quickly as the United States evacuated its remaining personnel and attempted to help the South Vietnamese military and political leadership escape advancing forces. Ford's request for military aid was now partially rechanneled into humanitarian aid to assist in the evacuation.[15] The initial group of refugees were those brought to the U.S. in a "babylift" before the fall of Saigon in 1975. There were an estimated 1.5 million orphans in the war-ravaged country, but concern was especially directed at the 40,000 racially mixed Asian-American babies who would be treated as outcasts in their country. Two thousand were brought to adoptive parents in the United States after paperwork was cleared and transportation was arranged through seven church-related adoption groups.[16] Phone lines were flooded with Americans who wanted to adopt a child, but concerns were voiced that some children might have been separated from parents presumed dead but actually still alive. Others felt that the effort to airlift children to the United States had the seamy undertone of a public relations gesture designed to deflect attention from the inglorious end to United States involvement in Vietnam. The Vatican, in deference to charges by some Vietnamese that these babylifts amounted to kidnapping, ordered its agencies not to participate in such efforts. The babylift became a tragedy when a plane carrying 243 orphans crashed and killed 150 children in April 1975.

While the evacuation was quick and harried, the immediate aftermath in Vietnam once the United States was gone surprised some observers. As Viet Cong and North Vietnamese soldiers moved into Saigon, a French diplomat claimed that one-third of the people of Saigon greeted them enthusiastically, another third were apprehensive, and the rest were indifferent. The first week of rule found a relaxed situation with little violent retribution, although many high-ranking military were being sent to "reeducation" camps.[17]

While the Vietnam War was winding down, skeletons were beginning to fall out of closets back home. The fact that the Watergate scandal was becoming a major problem for the Nixon administration only added to the attacks on an imperial, arrogant presidency known for pulling out all the stops in its attempt to head off or cover up information that implicated the executive branch in a host of scandals: large campaign donations for political favors, hotel break-ins, spying on United States citizens, and overthrowing foreign governments. Though hearings on the Watergate break-in and the spinoff scandals that emerged during this period (the Ellsberg break-in, the use of the FBI and CIA to spy on citizens and thwart investigation of Watergate, and others) were beginning to come to public attention in early 1973, it would take a presidential resignation and hearings lasting into 1975 to get to the bottom of the activities of a publicly unaccountable government.

Before Watergate had begun to plague Nixon, his adminstration had already come under scrutiny in a campaign contribution scandal. Revelations that International Telephone and Telegraph (ITT) had made campaign contributions at a time when it was seeking favors from the White House were reported in early 1972.[18] The Justice Department was investigating ITT for antitrust violations as it grew into the nation's eighth largest industrial concern. About the time the Justice Department decided to pull back from the action, ITT made a contribution to the Republican Party for its San Diego convention. A memo from ITT lobbyist Dita Beard suggesting a connection stoked up the controversy. In August 1973, a memo from White House special counsel Charles Colson indicated that many higher-ups, including the president, could be implicated in the deal between ITT and the Justice Department.[19] By July 1974, investigators determined there was not enough evidence to prove that political favors had been exchanged for cash, but the case did net the first conviction in the scandals that Nixon would bring on himself as former attorney general Richard Kleindienst pleaded guilty to lying about Nixon's exhortation to drop the ITT case.[20]

ITT was also implicated in a foreign scandal when it was alleged the company had offered to put up to $1 million in a government fund that was to be used to destabilize the democratically elected government in Chile. ITT's sizable investment in Chile was being nationalized by the Allende government after most other corporations had accepted compensation from Chile for the nationalizing of key industries. John McCone, a former director of the CIA and an ITT head, had used his connections with "close friends" Henry Kissinger and then head of the CIA Richard Helms to offer to channel the funds to opposition forces in Chile. ITT had vigorously opposed Salvador Allende's election in 1970, and the startlingly cozy relationship between the spy agency and a multinational corporation prompted Senator Clifford Case, a Republican, to ask, "Is the CIA working for the United States, or for ITT and McCone?"[21]

The unraveling of Nixon's presidency began shortly after his inauguration for his second term. February and March 1973 saw growing attention to the Watergate scandal. The men who actually broke into the Democratic Party Headquarters at the Watergate Hotel were convicted in early February, and in the Daniel Ellsberg case, the government was ordered to release a study showing the release of the Pentagon Papers did not harm national security.[22] Nixon's nominee for FBI director (and acting director), L. Patrick Gray, resigned in April 1973 after it was revealed he had destroyed White House records on Watergate given him by John Dean.[23]

April and May 1973 brought startling developments in the trial of Daniel Ellsberg for releasing the Pentagon Papers. The revelation that White House henchmen G. Gordon Liddy and E. Howard Hunt had burglarized the offices of Daniel Ellsberg's psychiatrist prompted the judge to dismiss the charges against Ellsberg and blast the Nixon administration for its interference in judicial proceedings. The CIA admitted it had given technical assistance to Liddy and Hunt in the burglary.[24]

The involvement of the FBI in the Watergate scandal became a matter of concern as L. Patrick Gray's nomination for director and his connections to the White House were examined. Gray's role in turning FBI files on Watergate over to the White House caused many to question whether his nomination should go forward and stimulated discussion as to how routinely the FBI had served the political purposes of the administration. There were startling revelations about the practices of J. Edgar Hoover, the longtime FBI director, in both cooperating with various presidents and gathering damaging information on them.[25]

Through the Watergate hearings, which began in May 1973, the extent of the Nixon administration's machinations in domestic affairs and electoral politics became clear. Over the next few years, hearings regarding Watergate and the FBI and CIA abuses of authority would turn Nixon out of the White House, promote passage of the War Powers Act in November 1973, and reveal the 25 years of CIA wrongdoing throughout the world as well as the subversion of democracy through FBI and CIA wiretapping and spying on domestic political activity. But few predicted at the beginning of the hearings that Nixon would be impeached or forced to resign.[26] Events would quickly take over and make that a real possibility.

The Watergate hearings exploded with the testimony of White House counsel John Dean that the president himself was involved in the cover-up. Dean reported that Nixon was more than willing to pay hush money to the convicted burglars. Testimony also revealed the existence of a White House "enemies" list with the names of many prominent (especially liberal) Americans. Then Alexander Butterfield's testimony revealed the existence of a White House taping system that would ultimately bring the president down and force him to resign. Nixon refused to turn over the tapes, claiming executive privilege. Legal wrangling over the tapes ensued, and Watergate prosecutor Archibald Cox, pressing to get the actual tapes rather than the summaries offered by the administration, was summarily fired in the now infamous "Saturday Night Massacre," which saw not only Cox fired, but also attorney general Elliott Richardson and deputy attorney William Ruckelshaus, who were fired for refusing to fire Cox. All of this led to a Nixon news conference in which he declared, "I am not a crook," adding that the tapes would vindicate him. A poll reported by *Time* in November 1973 showed growing disgust with the behavior of the Nixon White House. Sixty-eight percent felt he was involved in the coverup. Forty-seven percent felt he was acting above the law and that he was trying to cover up the tapes controversy.[27]

In March 1974, Nixon attempted to generate public support with a series of campaign-style events, but polls would continue to indicate a slide. In May, a majority of Americans voiced a preference for him to resign or be impeached, and the nation's press was beginning to grumble that Nixon's antics only reinforced the idea that he was guilty of a coverup and should resign.[28] He continued to resist release of the tapes, fighting court orders. He tried releasing transcripts only and continued to assert executive privilege. The investigation into an eighteen-minute erasure of a June 1972 (just days after the Watergate break-in) conversation between Nixon and Haldeman created more problems for the White House. Experts concluded the tape could not have been easily erased accidentally, and many felt the conversation probably was the first time Nixon heard of White House involvement in the break-in. These developments led to serious consideration of articles of impeachment by the House Judiciary Committee in early summer 1974.[29] The committee also issued subpoenas for the tapes, which were refused by the White House. A Supreme Court ruling on the tapes against Nixon's claim of executive privilege on July 24 more or less sealed his fate. On July 30, the committee approved three articles of impeachment.[30] Nixon resigned on August 8 after finally releasing tapes that incriminated him in the scandal as early as June 23, 1972.

The trial of Nixon's henchmen would begin in the fall, and convictions would be issued in January 1975. Four men—John Mitchell, Nixon's attorney general; close aides John Ehrlichman and H.R. Haldeman; and Robert Mardian, a security chief for the Justice Department—were convicted for their roles in the coverup. More would join them, but Gerald Ford pardoned Nixon shortly after replacing him, which meant that Nixon would never have to defend himself in court.[31]

The investigations of the CIA and FBI began with revelations that each agency had gathered a considerable number of files on American dissidents, especially those involved in the civil rights and antiwar movements. The charges against the CIA were particularly serious as the agency was forbidden to operate domestically.[32] In September 1974, more revelations on CIA activities would emerge and propel a lengthy investigation of the 25 years of CIA covert operations.[33] The most immediate allegation concerned possible CIA involvement in the overthrow of the government of Chile. The three-year experiment with democratic socialism in Chile had ended in September 1973 when the Chilean military overthrew the democratically elected president Salvador Allende. The coup bore similarity to tactics the CIA had used in getting rid of other governments, and it was alleged that Washington was aware the coup was going to occur and did not tell Allende. Allende attempted to rein in military discontent by bringing high-level officers into his cabinet. Nonetheless, one of the reasons given for the coup was that Allende was trying to usurp the authority of the military.[34] The military's pretext for the coup was an alleged plot by leftists to kill several high-ranking military leaders.

The coup was a bloody affair and ushered in a harsh period of human rights abuses in Chile. It was thought that several thousand were killed in the first days of the coup alone. One indicator of a possible United States role was the lack of response from Washington. Though the coup was condemned worldwide, the United States was silent about the fall of this democratic government. Aside from any involvement by the CIA, United States policy had been hostile to Allende from the time he took office, putting pressure on the

World Bank and the Export-Import Bank not to extend loans to Chile. The economic destabilization helped fuel social discontent. And the Pentagon did remain very friendly with the Chilean military and help to keep it well equipped.[35]

Fears about the intentions of the military leaders, especially General Augusto Pinochet, proved well founded in the days and months after the coup. Human rights abuses and the elimination of civil liberties cast a pall on the people of Chile. While the wealthy, along with some elements of the middle class, remained supportive of the coup, those who had benefitted from the Allende policies found themselves targeted for repression and elimination.[36] The communist and socialist parties were outlawed, 7,000 people were put in prison, and universities were put under the direct supervision of the military.

In the ensuing months, torture and repression continued, and the Chilean congress was disbanded. There was no indication the military was interested in elections and democratic rule. A year later, President Ford admitted CIA involvement and confessed that $8 million had been spent to undermine the government of Chile from 1970 to 1973. Henry Kissinger was criticized for his lack of candor when he appeared before Congress to deny a United States role in the coup. Chile would remain a human rights dungeon as the generals would remain in power sixteen years before democratic elections were conducted.[37]

The CIA was very busy trying to keep all sorts of irresponsible behavior from the public. Ex-CIA agents who had become disaffected by the agency's behavior were trying to publish "kiss and tell" books detailing the abuses in which they had participated. Victor Marchetti and John Marks's *The CIA and the Cult of Intelligence* was published in April 1974 after a court ordered 15 deletions instead of the 168 desired by the agency. Philip Agee, a twelve-year agent, would soon publish his book *Inside the Company: A CIA Diary*, which detailed the dirty tricks he had conducted. Agee termed the agency "the secret political police of American capitalism." The revelations included a 1953 coup against Mohammed Mossadegh, the elected Iranian premier whose fatal act was to nationalize a British-owned oil company; the 1954 overthrow of the democratically elected Jacobo Arbenz government of Guatemala for the benefit of United Fruit; a 1967 military coup in Greece; the killing of Cuban revolutionary Che Guevara in Bolivia in 1967; and deep CIA involvement in the wars of Indochina—the secret war in Laos, the Phoenix program in Vietnam, and the bombing in Cambodia. Congress would delve further into these operations in hearings over the next year.

All of this made the attitudes and actions of Frank Burns and Col. Flagg on *M*A*S*H* seem surreal or prescient. *M*A*S*H*'s comedic critique of hyper-patriotism, military machismo, and the commie-under-every-bed world view came at the same time when the far less humorous revelations about the CIA emerged. Because Burns and Flagg were largely caricatures, everyone could laugh at their antics, regardless of what they thought about the United States' role in the world. Thus the humor of *M*A*S*H* served a disarming role as well. A country weary of war, corrupt presidential behavior, and the ugliness associated with being a military and economic superpower could find solace in the ongoing belittling of the fictional warmongers on *M*A*S*H*. Lacking any immediate, direct ability to change the behavior of real political actors, the public could at least feel some satisfaction in the ridicule of similar, if fictional, fools of war and militarism. In this sense at least, *M*A*S*H* was as much cathartic as it was critical of institutions.

AFTER A HARD DAY'S SURGERY...

A consistent feature of the early episodes of *M*A*S*H* is the prevalence of alcohol as a means of diversion from the war. *M*A*S*H* was a situation *comedy*, after all, and the slapstick humor and frequent jokes of the early years serve to offset some of the more serious themes. Drinking and jokes about drinking are prominent in episodes from years one, two, and three. Larry Gelbart has commented that after introducing the still into the Swamp and using it as plot device occasionally, the creative team sought to play down drinking in the later years.[38]

Alcohol use was prolific in both the novel and the film version of *M*A*S*H*. The prevalence of alcohol use in the first year of the television series is evidenced in the battles between Frank and Hawkeye and Trapper over the still. Even Radar, who later would become much more of a neophyte about alcohol, is seen in several early episodes enjoying a drink. The use of alcohol was largely played comedically in years two and three. Henry Blake is often seen drunk at 4077 parties (e.g. "Dear Dad...Three," "For Want of a Boot," "Check Up," and "Abyssinia Henry") and clearly is given a reputation as a souse. Blake's attachment to alcohol is seen in year two in such episodes as "Divided We Stand" as he offers a drink to an army investigator who arrives one morning. In "Crisis" Blake takes a drink even as he talks about a test of leadership and vows no alcohol because of the seriousness of the situation.

The use of alcohol to party or to forget about the horrors of war extends to virtually all of the main cast. For the most part, drinking is shown as a way to blow off steam. It is seen during parties for Frank ("For Want of a Boot") or Trapper ("Check Up"), poker games ("Deal Me Out"), an Easter celebration with a contingent of Greek soldiers ("Private Charles Lamb"), waiting for "Five O'Clock Charlie" to arrive and when the nurses have evacuated the 4077 during an offensive ("There Is Nothing Like a Nurse"). The episode "Officers Only" features the building of the Officers' Club (which Hawkeye quickly turned into an everyone's club), where much drinking takes place.

The still, as a fixture of the Swamp, becomes a plot device when temporary CO Frank decides the camp is going dry ("Alcoholics Unanimous"). This episode, which garnered an Emmy nomination for Hy Averback's directing, shows that just about everyone (including Margaret, but excepting Frank) relies on alcohol to take the sting out of the war. Father Mulcahy, ordered by Frank to give a temperance lecture, takes a few snorts to get his nerve up for the sermon and gives a rocky speech. But even Frank gets his snootful: the alcohol ban is lifted when Frank takes a drink to dull the pain of a kick in the groin.

Sometimes alcohol is integral to the plot as in "Local Indigenous Personnel." In this episode, Hawkeye and Trapper, trying to help a GI get army approval to marry his Korean girlfriend, get a racist investigator drunk so they can blackmail him into approving the marriage. Alcohol also comes into play when anxiety about home sets in. Trapper's longing for his little girl leads him to go on a drinking rampage in "Mail Call." He decides to pack his bags and go AWOL. Hawkeye tries to stop him but is knocked down by Trapper as he leaves the Swamp. In "Hot Lips and Empty Arms," Margaret finds out an old friend has married a now successful doctor she rejected. ("I'd have loved him if I had known!" she says.) She vows to transfer after Hawk and Trapper undermine her authority with the nurses only to have her get drunk with them. When casualties arrive, they sober her up, she thanks them, and eventually she decides to stay. Loretta Swit says this episode was the first to reveal Margaret's dissatisfaction with her relationship with Frank, her second-class status with the doctors, and her efficiency as a nurse.[39]

One episode breaks from the image of drinking as fun to see alcohol as problematic. In "The Consultant," Hawk learns a serious lesson about his own propensity for booze. Critical of Dr. Borelli's bailing out of surgery, he confronts Borelli in the swamp. He tells Hawk he is getting old; this is the third war he's been in. He asks Hawk to look inside himself to see how he is coping with his first war. The episode ends with Hawkeye staring into his martini glass.

Such serious treatments of alcohol were rare in the early years. The frivolous portrayal of alcohol in the first three seasons came at a time when American society was experiencing a more open atmosphere with respect to alcohol and recreational drugs. The lowering of the voting age to 18 in 1969 prompted many states to lower the drinking age as well. Between 1970 and 1975, 29 states lowered their drinking age from 21 to 18 or 19.[40]

In March 1973, the National Commission on Marijuana and Drug Abuse urged treatment for drug users and asked for recognition of alcoholism as a drug problem. A study by the Health, Education and Welfare Department said alcohol was the number one drug problem in America, causing some $15 billion a year in lost work time and playing a role in 28,000 traffic deaths per year.[41]

A well-publicized incident involving a congressman would remind the public that alcohol was problematic for many Americans. Powerful chair of the House Ways and Means Committee Wilbur Mills would see his career slip away as the result of a series of drunken romps with stripper Fanne Foxe. An incident involving Park Police near the Jefferson Memorial made public what had been rumors about Mills's drinking problem. Mills was stripped of his chairmanship and eventually sought treatment for his problem.[42]

Meanwhile, the social debate over the effects of marijuana saw the development of support for its decriminalization. A report from the National Institute of Mental Health in 1971 summarized the existing research on marijuana. The report said that marijuana was not harmful for most people and there was little evidence that smoking it led to use of harder drugs. The report also noted an increase in the use of marijuana by college students.[43] The National Commission on Marijuana and Drug Abuse urged an end to penalties for private possession and use of marijuana and stated that its use at the level of that time (March 1972) did not "constitute a major threat to public health." *Newsweek* reported a poll supporting President Nixon's opposition to this recommendation, with 79 percent considering marijuana harmful. The poll also showed pot smoking had tripled in two and half years, with 11 percent of respondents over eighteen saying they had tried it.

In July 1972, the American Medical Association debated its position on marijuana and reversed its 1969 stance against legalization, suggesting instead that possession of "insignificant" amounts of marijuana not be considered illegal.[44] In 1973, *Time* reported an upswing in attempts to decriminalize or legalize marijuana in localities, and states were moving possession from a felony to a misdemeanor. Oregon completely removed criminal penalties and instituted a $100 fine for amounts up to one ounce.[45] In the meantime, cocaine would begin to surface at the posh night clubs and parties of Manhattan. The high cost of the drug made it a status symbol among the affluent, and it was estimated that 4.8 million Americans had tried it by 1974.[46]

The party atmosphere of *M*A*S*H*, while showing how the unit dealt with the overwhelmingly depressing nature of war, reflected as well the tenor of the early 1970s with respect to drinking and recreational drugs. This sentiment would change as the decade and the show went on. It would not be long before drinking and drugs would be viewed more critically both in society and on *M*A*S*H*.

RACISM AND HOMOPHOBIA
ARE PUT IN THEIR PLACE

Two other ongoing social issues received attention in *M*A*S*H* story-lines. Racism and homophobia became subjects for critique in years two and three. Through Frank's intolerance of Koreans and foreigners, the comments of guest characters, and the righteous indignation of Hawkeye, racism is clearly portrayed as ignorant and unacceptable. Several episodes dealing with racism focus on the attitudes of Americans toward Koreans and army policy toward intermarriage. In "Local Indigenous Personnel" (the army's bureaucratic term for civilians in war zones), Hawkeye and Trapper try to help a GI who wants to take his baby and common-law wife home but needs to be "officially" married. An obstacle arrives in the form of an army investigator, who refers to the mother as a "broad." In the middle of it all, Hawkeye breaks off a date with a nurse who refers to the baby as a "gook." In the end, Hawk and Trap blackmail the investigator into approving the marriage in time for the GI to take his family home with him. An episode in year three, "Love and Marriage," finds Hawkeye and Trapper discovering a GI wants to marry a Korean woman not for love but for money. The GI has been offered $1000 for marrying the woman as a way to get her to the United States, where she will become a prostitute. Meanwhile, Frank is objecting to a Korean orderly's desire that his wife give birth to their child at the 4077. Frank objects based on military policy against nonemergency medical procedures for civilians. Frank's general intolerance for Koreans and other non–Americans is seen several times in the episodes of the first three seasons.

Racism against African Americans within the military is also the subject of two episodes from years two and three. In "Dear Dad...Three," Hawkeye, Trapper, and African American nurse Lt. Ginger Baker teach a lesson to an injured GI who requests "white" blood. They feed his paranoia by applying iodine to his skin while he is sleeping. Ginger comes along and compliments the man for being able to pass as white. Later, Trapper brings him a meal of fried chicken and watermelon. When the man raises his fears with Hawkeye, Hawk tells him about Charles Drew, the African American doctor who developed the technique for preserving blood plasma but was refused treatment at a whites-only hospital in the South after an accident. The show closes with a contrite man who salutes Lt. Baker.

A guest appearance by Harry Morgan as General Bartford Steel in year three's "The General Flipped at Dawn" finds him playing a racist buffoon who comes to inspect the 4077 with a reputation as a stickler. The unit quickly discovers Steele is not only strict but crazy when he decides the unit needs to bug out and relocate. Hawkeye refuses to let him take a chopper that is transporting a patient. The general's threat to court-martial Hawkeye causes concern until Steele proves himself a racist nut by asking an African American soldier to do a musical number: Blacks "have it in their blood," according to Steele. When the MP witnesses this, he concludes the general is crazy and packs up his briefcase. Harry Morgan won an Emmy for Outstanding Single Performance for this role and has said it was one of the most fun roles he had ever played.[47] He would become a regular cast member as Colonel Sherman Potter in year four.

The show critiques military hierarchy and makes a statement about egalitarianism in "Officers Only." When a general builds an officers' club for the 4077, Hawkeye and Trapper get the cold shoulder from the enlisted, who are angry about being shut out of the club. The two doctors' sense of justice leads them into goading the general to make an exception for his injured enlisted son. Hawkeye claims all the other 4077 enlisted as his relatives and lets them in, breaking the caste system between officers and enlisted.

THE STRUGGLE FOR EQUALITY HITS SCHOOLS AND WORKPLACES

Though the tumultuous period of civil disturbances in urban America in the 1960s had receded, race relations were still very much an issue in American life as affirmative action policies and busing to achieve integration in schools were hotly debated.

Attempts to deal with past discrimination against blacks and other minorities were manifested in affirmative action programs—court decisions and federal legislation that attempted to compensate for previous instances of discriminatory hiring and promoting practices in the workplace. United States businesses such as AT&T and Bethlehem Steel were ordered to make back-pay reparations and develop revised seniority systems so that blacks and women could be treated equally with white males. Many in the business community feared "hiring goals" would become "enforced quotas" and were leery of government actions. A court case over admission to the University of Washington Law School heard in 1974 would test the policies of giving women and minorities "special preference" in access to education. Ethnic groups, business groups, and the AFL-CIO filed briefs in support of a white student who felt he been discriminated against because a school had admitted minority students with lower test scores ahead of him. Meanwhile, reports indicated that affirmative action was not effective for those it was supposed to help. Increased college admissions for minorities were incremental and came nowhere close to representing the minority percentage of the general population. This was the beginning of a lengthy social debate and a series of court decisions on the whole idea of affirmative action.[48]

School busing to achieve educational integration was also creating divisions between the races. A court-ordered program in Boston was fiercely resisted by whites who did not want their children bused to inner city schools or blacks attending their neighborhood schools. The hurling of insults and rocks was reminiscent of the South's resistance to integration in the 1960s— yet it happened in the supposedly more tolerant North.[49]

If the legacy of race still divided blacks and whites, Native Americans were also organizing and asserting their claims as part of the legacy of the civil rights movement of the 1960s. Wounded Knee, South Dakota, was the site of a clash between the American Indian Movement (AIM) and the FBI in March 1973. AIM had been formed to struggle for justice and dignity for Native Americans and had earlier taken over Alcatraz Island (1969) and the Bureau of Indian Affairs in Washington (1972). Though the larger issue was the abrogation or ignoring of treaty obligations by the federal government, the immediate trigger at Wounded Knee was the charging of a white man with manslaughter instead of premeditated murder in the death of a 51-year-old Sioux. Internal power disputes between AIM supporters and other Native Americans complicated the dynamics of the protest. The site was surrounded by federal marshals, and senators McGovern, Abourezk, Fulbright, and Kennedy tried to negotiate an end to the stalemate. The standoff resulted in the prosecution of two AIM leaders, Russell Means and Dennis Banks, who were charged with conspiracy, larceny, and assault. Just as in the Ellsberg case, the judge ultimately threw out the charges against the two based on government withholding and doctoring of documents and bribery of witnesses.[50]

With respect to gays, the early years of M*A*S*H are a mixed bag. As we have already discussed, frequent gay bashing and homophobic jokes were a part of year one. Year two began to reflect a different attitude. An episode aired in February 1974 critiques homophobia. "George" involves a GI who confides to Hawkeye that that he was beaten up by other men in his unit because he is gay. Hawkeye effectively deflects Frank's threats to expose the man and accepts the man's desire to "prove" himself by going back to the front. This episode represented a turnaround for the show. Though gay bashing would still occur in other episodes of years two and three, such humor clearly dissipated with this episode. It seems this development was a response to the changing understanding of homosexuality. In December 1973, the American Psychiatric Association reversed its long-held position that homosexuality is a mental illness. Recognizing that sexual orientation was no affliction, NBC apologized for its portrayal of gays and vowed to seek advice from gays in future programming.[51] An article in Time pointed out that gays were beginning to appear in other television series as well. An episode of Marcus Welby in spring 1973 introduced a gay patient (though activists determined the show treated homosexuality as a disease). This followed more sympathetic treatment in episodes of Medical Center, The Bold Ones, Room 222 and an award-winning

TV movie, *That Certain Summer,* in which a divorced father reveals he is gay to his son. Even Archie Bunker discovered that one of his buddies, a former football star, was gay.[52]

Moves by gays to become more visible and to attain protection from discrimination were being reported in the nation's news media. *Newsweek* reported that attempts to get politicians to deal with discrimination against homosexuals were finding some successes in the courts. Lesbian mothers were gaining attention.[53] The treatment of gays and lesbians was also becoming a subject of controversy within the church. Some gays were beginning to form their own churches in the face of discrimination. The United Presbyterian Church, whose official doctrine since 1970 had held that homosexuality was a sin, was rocked by furious debate when a Presbyterian publication asserted that being gay was not a sickness or a sin.[54] These kinds of changes inevitably led to reaction from those who maintained a gay "lifestyle" should not be regarded as normal. The governor of New Hampshire was deluged with protests over the recognition of a gay students' organization at the University of New Hampshire. The protests resulted in a banning of all gay organization activities. Similar threats were made at the University of Maine.[55]

Nonetheless, the evolution of the treatment of gays is a clear example of how media follow the lead of real-world trends and changes. It is difficult to imagine a real-world MASH of the 1950s treating the issue of gays in the military in a sympathetic way. The episode "George" clearly features updated perspective, as well as a 180-degree turn for the series, given the number of gay-bashing jokes early on in the show. As we saw with the character of Flagg on *M*A*S*H* and the real-life ongoing revelations of FBI and CIA abuses of authority, television programming doesn't so much promote social change as it reflects real-world trends, weaving them into storylines that make sense for that particular show. In the case of "George," the creative team picked up on the changing attitude toward homosexuality and made its own statement, perhaps as an oblique apology for its early homophobia.

The episode that in some ways might be considered the most controversial for the early years is not one that challenges United States military policy or geopolitical behavior. Rather, it features the death of a departing character, Henry Blake. The episode represented a first for television: A major character leaving a series dies in a tragic way. McLean Stevenson, who left at the end of year three, was hoping to land his own show by departing *M*A*S*H* and did have a short-lived series. He later acknowledged leaving the show was a bad career move, and he did resent the fact that being killed off at the end of year three left him no opportunity for returning to the show.[56]

The conclusion of "Abyssinia Henry" was kept a secret from most of the cast in order to provoke an honest reaction of shock and disbelief. Most of the episode is lighthearted. Blake finds out he's acquired enough points for discharge.[57] The camp responds with a party in which we see the frequently drunk Blake drunk one last time. Blake boards a chopper after a marathon kiss with Margaret and heartfelt goodbyes to everyone. The show closes with Radar coming into OR with the news that Blake's plane has been shot down in the Sea of Japan with no survivors found. The long camera pan of the operating room to show the unit's reaction is done with only the sound of doctors operating. The last shot focuses on Hawkeye, whose welling tears probably represented the audience's reaction as well. (The episode's sign-off featured shots of Blake from lighter moments of the show.)

Such an expression of the horrors and arbitrariness of war produced both praise and disapproval from the audience. Thousands of letters expressing both reactions were received, but most viewers apparently saw Blake's death as consistent and necessary given the show's mix of comedy and tragedy.[58]

The show would move on. It was now a hit by any definition; indeed, these two years garnered the highest ratings of all the years of the series. It is ironic, given network concerns, that the program's "heaviest" antiwar episodes occurred during the years it received the highest ratings. It suggests the American public was more open to challenging, innovative television than many network executives believed. In many ways, *M*A*S*H*'s success and growth as a sitcom came in spite of close network control. Even today, assumptions about acceptable television programming seem to have more to do with commercial television's conservative and redundant approach to programming than with what the American public will tolerate. The fact is that as *M*A*S*H* became more mainstream in later years, taking fewer and fewer risks, its popularity declined, and it would never again attain the ratings it received in its two most daring seasons.

The critical acclaim began to roll in as well. The show won Emmys for Outstanding Comedy Series, and Alan Alda won awards for Outstanding Lead in a Comedy Series and Actor of the Year for the second season. Gary Burghoff, McLean Stevenson, and Loretta Swit were nominated for supporting role awards, and Stanford Tischler and Fred Berger were nominated for Outstanding Editing. In year three, *M*A*S*H* was nominated for Outstanding Comedy Series, Outstanding Lead Actor (Alda), Supporting Actor (Burghoff and Stevenson) and Supporting Actress (Swit). Alda won a People's Choice Award for Outstanding Male Television Performance (tied with Telly Savalas as "Kojak") and a Golden Globe Award for Best Actor in a Comedy. The episode "O.R." garnered an Emmy for outstanding directing for Gene Reynolds and a Writers Guild Award for Larry Gelbart and Laurence Marks.

The next two years would bring changes to the show both behind and in front of the camera, but *M*A*S*H* would remain a solid audience favorite for years to come.

CHAPTER 5

Hearts and Minds*—
Years 4–5, 1975–77

For each of the first three years, *M*A*S*H* was given a different day and time slot. Year four (1975-76) brought yet another move—this time to Friday night at 8:30—as well as the first significant cast changes. Both McLean Stevenson and Wayne Rogers had departed at the end of the third season, which meant replacement characters would have to be introduced. Additionally, the ensemble cast was expanded as Jamie Farr joined the regular cast in year four and William Christopher joined in year five. Larry Gelbart would depart as executive producer at the end of year four, but not without leaving behind a final moving episode, "The Interview." These changes meant that by year five (1976-77) some new dynamics were present that would gradually change the character of the show. These were years of transition for the nation as well. With Richard Nixon's departure from the White House and the scandal of Watergate receding, there seemed to be a desire to move on from the tumultuous politics of the previous few years.

The creative team took its time introducing the audience to Mike Farrell as B.J. Hunnicutt and Harry Morgan as Colonel Sherman Potter. A one-hour episode opened year four. "Welcome to Korea" created a transition between the departure of Trapper and the arrival of B.J. The episode opens with a gung-ho Frank Burns serving as CO—something he will soon be disappointed to find is a temporary situation. Hawkeye returns from Tokyo on a rickshaw only to discover Trapper has just shipped out for home. Hawkeye tries to head for Seoul to say goodbye to Trapper—in defiance of Frank's orders—with Radar, who is picking up Trapper's replacement. Hawk fails to catch Trapper, but they pick up B.J. and introduce him to army life.

B.J. quickly learns Korea is no picnic. On the way to the 4077, they encounter a farming family using the daughters to check for land mines to protect their cows. A land mine explodes, injuring one daughter. While

The title of this chapter is drawn from the 1974 Academy Award–winning feature documentary Hearts and Minds, directed by Peter Davis. The film includes the use of the phrase by President Lyndon Johnson: "We must be ready to fight in Vietnam, but the ultimate victory will depend on the hearts and minds of the people who actually live over there."

taking her to the hospital, they blow a tire. A group of locals walks by, then suddenly disappears. Hawkeye, B.J., and Radar barely get the tire on as the gunfire starts. Presumably out of danger, they encounter a group of GIs, only to have shells rain down on them. As B.J. tries to help the injured men, the gruesomeness of one soldier's death makes him physically sick. The jeep later stops at Rosie's, where Hawk and B.J. share the first of many drinks together. Margaret and Frank, who have made plans to mold B.J. in their image, greet the three when they finally pull into camp. Hawk introduces a drunken B.J., who tells Frank, "Hey, ferret face!" The episode won Emmys for Outstanding Directing (Gene Reynolds), Film Editing (Fred Berger and Stanford Tischler) and a Writers Guild Award (Everett Greenbaum and Larry Gelbart).

Potter arrived the following week in "Change of Command." In this episode, Frank is disappointed at being turned out of office and goes AWOL. Hawk, B.J., Radar, and Klinger fear that the new CO, a career army man, will bring regimentation to the not-regular-army 4077. Potter quickly discovers what he is up against. He notes Hawkeye's disdain for procedure and authority. He praises Margaret's record, but is befuddled when he calls Frank's name and Margaret responds, "Just friends, sir." Potter asks them all to behave for the next eighteen months until he retires, and then they discover he hasn't operated in two years. The arrival of wounded and a long OR session sorts some things out; afterward Potter declares he could "use a belt" and proceeds to advise Hawkeye on how to improve the hooch from the still. Klinger's attempt to get Potter's attention nets him no more than, "Nice outfit, Klinger." Potter apparently has seen many other men try the same scam. Frank returns with his bruised ego to a mothering Margaret. The more things change, the more they remain the same at the 4077.

Images and stories of war take on a different complexion beginning in years four and five. More and more the war is defined by periods of lull followed by a deluge of casualties. The emphasis in episodes such as "Deluge" and "Post Op" is on the heroic efforts of the medical team to undo the damage done by war, rather than on critiquing the larger issues of war and the geopolitical perspectives that foster it. In "Deluge," the unit faces a shortage of gloves that forces the doctors to wash in alcohol while the shelling comes and a fire starts outside the OR. A bowl of alcohol is mistaken for water and is thrown on the fire, which causes more havoc. The end of the episode finds the unit getting a medal for meritorious conduct. A blood shortage in "Post Op" generates concern and angry calls to HQ by Potter and Hawkeye. The medical staff hears stories from the front, including one soldier's face-to-face encounter with a Chinese soldier he kills solely for survival. Characters occasionally experience the war directly, as Father Mulcahy and Radar do in "Mulcahy's War," and Hawkeye and Potter get caught in shelling while on the road in "Hawkeye Get Your Gun." As we will see, how individual characters cope with war became a primary theme in these years and continued into the years that followed.

Episodes also begin to explore in greater detail the struggles of civilian Koreans in wartime. Going beyond the occasional visits by Nurse Cratty and the orphans in episodes such as "The Kids," plots offer a taste of Korean culture as well as a view of how the nation was affected by the war. For instance, audiences for "Welcome to Korea" saw that the war forced civilians to make desperate choices as they coped with maintaining their livelihood in wartime.

"The Bus" finds Hawkeye, Potter, B.J., Radar, and Frank returning from a medical conference when they get lost and the bus breaks down. While they are stranded, a North Korean soldier surrenders to them. Frank, of course, brings his intolerance of foreigners and his "us vs. them" attitude to the situation, seeing the man as a threat. When the man helps get the bus started, they are gratified, and he then seems content to be taken care of by them. In "Dear Ma," Frank's prejudice and paranoia create a scene when he suspects two South Korean officers being hosted by B.J. are the enemy. He tackles one and is rewarded with the wrath of both B.J. and the officers. Frank also manages to embarrass himself in "Korean Surgeon," in which he gets used by two North Koreans posing as South Koreans to get supplies from the 4077. They flatter Frank to get him to come with them. Once they get past the checkpoint, he is abandoned and forced to walk home. Meanwhile Hawkeye and B.J. try to save a North Korean doctor from languishing in a prioner's camp and allow him to use his skills for the allied side.

But the show goes beyond the occasional cross-cultural encounter to show viewers that the Korean people have a long history and elaborate culture. In "Souvenirs," Hawkeye and B.J. see Frank questioned about an antiquity he has purchased that may be stolen. When Frank is told the vase is over 800 years old, he ignores the MP's warning about looting Korean national treasures and tries to send the vase home to his wife. Hawk and B.J. intercept the package, return the vase, and substitute a bedpan in the package home. "Exorcism" shows viewers a side of Korean spiritual and religious beliefs. Potter orders that a spirit post brought to the camp by some local Koreans be moved off the base. After Radar moves it, a series of glitches befall the 4077—OR lamps burn out, gauges malfunction during surgery, and Potter's new lighter won't work. When a elderly Korean man comes to the MASH after being hit by an ambulance, he insists an exorcist remove the evil spirits before he gets treated. His daughter tells them he got hit trying to scare the spirits away. A priestess performs an elaborate ceremony, and everything gets back to working correctly. Potter tells Radar to put the spirit post back in camp. In "Ping Pong," a Korean orderly named Joe wins the camp Ping-Pong match. When he tells B.J. and Hawkeye he wants to get married, they try to arrange a wedding at the 4077. His fiancée becomes concerned when he fails to return from a trip to Seoul. He arrives wounded—he was "drafted" and put on the front line all in one day. The episode closes with a Korean wedding in which Frank gripes about local customs, Potter gives the bride away, and Father Mulcahy describes the symbolism of the ceremony.

Later years would bring further understanding of Korean culture and the experience of the Koreans in coping with war. These encounters between Americans and Koreans in the show would come at a time when many Vietnamese refugees were arriving on American soil. The refugee issue took many twists and turns and generated some controversy as well. What to do about refugees would be the first question to emerge in the aftermath of the war, and the problem would become a crisis in the years to come. The refugees from South Vietnam first began to leave their country as the United States withdrew in 1975. Many of those who worked for the United States–backed regime during the war felt threatened by a North Vietnamese takeover. *Time* estimated that as many as 200,000 government officials, soldiers, policemen, and other Vietnamese who had worked for United States interests would be fleeing. How to select those who could leave was a controversial issue. It appeared those who were taken out were the more affluent elements of South Vietnamese society. It would eventually be estimated that only about half of the 115,000 the Americans helped evacuate were those the United States identified as having legitimate concerns for their safety.[1]

The refugees who were evacuated during the final United States withdrawal found a less-than-hospitable public in the United States.[2] The country was experiencing a recession, and there were concerns that non–English speaking refugees would place a burden on social services throughout the country. The Ford administration declared it would waive immigration restrictions for up to 130,000 refugees from Vietnam and Cambodia. This was done to assure that "high-risk" Vietnamese could escape expected vengeance from North Vietnam. The Congress, however, initially voted not to fund the administration's request for humanitarian resettlement assistance, primarily sticking on the issue of whether United States troops would help the effort in Vietnam. Eventually Congress appropriated humanitarian resettlement funds for the effort. If congressional representatives were experiencing mixed feelings, they probably had their eyes on opinion polls, which showed that a majority of Americans felt the refugees should be resettled in other countries.[3] The refugees were brought to the United States gradually, with many of them staying for months in resettlement camps in Guam and the Philippines. Resentment grew among the more affluent refugees over the poor conditions in the camps and the menial jobs they were given once they arrived in the United States, and they resented the presence of some of the less affluent Vietnamese among them. By summer 1975, some were requesting to be taken back to Vietnam. Some had been swept up in the evacuation frenzy and had never really desired to leave. Others—many of them men wanting to be reunited with their families—decided their homeland was the best place for them, regardless of the government in charge. Eventually 2,500 would petition to return.[4]

The war in Vietnam would generate other aftereffects. Many people would suffer psychological wounds as a result of their experience. On *M*A*S*H*, years four and five brought episodes that looked at the often hidden injuries suffered by men and women in war.

THE MIND
AS A BATTLEFIELD

M*A*S*H's fourth and fifth seasons introduced new elements for audiences to consider. Viewers still saw war's intrusion into the lives of the 4077 and the men they physically repaired. But more and more, the show began to address the psychological scars of war. Episodes from these years include numerous incidents of battlefield stress and trauma, illustrating that not all the wounds of war are physical.

In "It Happened One Night," the unit battles cold weather. Klinger strips down and tries to get frostbite while the 4077 gets shelled by its own army. The shells come close enough to send one GI in post-op into a panic. The shelling returns several times, and the traumatized man has to be subdued by injections.

In "Smilin' Jack," a soldier arrives with his second injury from the war. Frank admires the soldier's second purple heart, but the recipient reveals his fears of going back to the front to both Radar and B.J. Radar gives him a four-leaf clover for better luck in the field, which seems to help the man face the prospect.

Sidney Freedman returned for four appearances in years four and five. Viewers saw Freedman in year two, when he dealt with disarming a man who didn't want to return to the battlefield, and in year three when he helped a man overcome hysterical paralysis. He also managed to challenge Klinger to admit he's not really crazy. Perhaps the most telling episode dealing with battle fatigue (or, as it would be called in the post–Vietnam era, post-traumatic stress syndrome[5]) is "Quo Vadis, Captain Chandler." "Chandler" concerns a captain who has flown a record number of bombing missions. When he arrives at the 4077, he tells Radar his name is Jesus Christ. He denies his real identity, saying, "That was a long time ago." When Freedman tries to convince him he is a bomber pilot, he responds "Why would I hurt my children? I'm not Chandler, but I hope you can find him." In the meantime, Flagg has arrived at the 4077 to challenge Freedman's diagnosis. He wants to get Chandler back in bombing mode. Freedman deflects Flagg's threats, and Potter takes his advice that Chandler can be helped but it will take a long time.

Year five brought four episodes dealing with the psychological scars of war. In "Hawk's Nightmare," Freedman comes to the 4077 to help Hawkeye deal with a bout of sleepwalking his way through camp while acting like he's back in Crabapple Cove, Maine. He plays jacks with Radar, who he thinks is his childhood friend "Stinky." He has nightmares about boyhood friends, but when he calls them he finds that they are OK. When Freedman arrives, he shows Hawkeye that the dreams that take him home are a way of escaping the war but that Hawkeye's work on young injured men is the real nightmare that he can't avoid.

In "Out of Sight, Out of Mind," Hawkeye is able to empathize with a blinded soldier when he temporarily experiences blindness. Hawkeye and the man bond quickly as the soldier struggles with how to tell his wife.

Another episode finds Freedman coming to the 4077 for, of all things, solace. In "Dear Sigmund," Freedman comes for a poker game and stays two weeks. Viewers hear the letter he writes to Sigmund Freud to explain why he appreciates the people of the 4077. Freedman is trying to understand how they cope with the misery and pain they face daily. Freedman is actually there to overcome a sense of failure he is experiencing after losing a patient to a suicide he felt he should have seen coming. B.J. finds the letter to Freud and asks Freeman if the mind doctor isn't going crazy himself. Freedman tells B.J. the 4077 is a form of therapy for him, and it's actually B.J.'s own coping strategy—practical joking—that helps Freedman get back on the road to helping others. He helps B.J. play a joke on Frank by yelling, "Air raid," after B.J. has filled one of paranoid Frank's foxholes with water.[6]

While Sidney Freedman plays a particular, if occasional, role in helping the 4077 deal with the mental anguish created by war, other characters use their own special skills to help traumatized GIs. Father Mulcahy proves something to himself and in the process gains credibility in the eye of an injured soldier in "Mulcahy's War." In this episode, a man's self-inflicted foot wound draws Frank's curiosity and a threat of a court-martial. Hawkeye deflects Frank's accusation and asks Mulcahy to talk to the man. The man rebuffs Mulcahy when he finds out Mulcahy has never experienced the war at the front—"You're a chaplin, not a solider," the man tells him. A call to the unit from an aid station has Hawkeye telling Radar to go pick up a patient who needs surgery soon. Mulcahy jumps in the jeep with Radar as an opportunity to get the experience of the front. On the way home, he performs a tracheotomy with instruction over the radio from Hawkeye. Mulcahy returns to face the rebuke of Potter for leaving camp without permission and the respect of both Hawkeye and the man who rebuffed him.

Radar has a similar opportunity in "End Run." In this case, the war has ended a promising football career for Billy Tyler, a running back for the University of Iowa, Radar's home state. A leg injury necessitates an amputation, leaving Tyler embittered and suicidal. Radar's frustration at not being able to help Tyler finds him in a rare drinking session with Hawkeye, who has faced Tyler's hostility for taking his leg from him. Radar eventually reminds Tyler that when he was an All-American he always found a way to beat the other team. "You just have to keep trying till you find it," Radar says. Tyler starts his long trip home as he pulls out in an ambulance and waves goodbye to Radar and Hawkeye.

While the trauma of physical and psychological injuries in war would be an ongoing theme throughout the life of the series, the episodes just mentioned reflect a growing realization of the tragedies men were bringing home from Vietnam as the war subsided. Psychological wounds from war certainly were not unique to the Vietnam era. All wars produce men who suffer from these nonphysical injuries, variously called battlefield stress, shell shock, or combat fatigue. Trying to understand the nature of the problems some men brought home was a regular feature of postwar eras.[7] Stories about men who returned from Vietnam with war's nightmares in tow first began to appear in the early 1970s.[8] Early stories noted that many bought drug addictions home with them. A study by the Pentagon found that vets returning home from Vietnam were addicted to heroin in about the same proportion as civilians—about 1.3 percent of those studied could be classified as addicted to narcotics.[9]

Veterans faced many other difficulties in adjusting once they returned, especially with respect to getting jobs. It seemed the 3 million Vietnam veterans were not being given the same kind of help World War II and Korean veterans received when they returned.[10] Funding programs for the new vets were problematic, and policymakers were hesitant about allocating funds for drug treatment, education grants, and medical benefits for families. Other vets faced specific problems adjusting due to injuries that had deprived them of arms and legs; some 25,000 out of an estimated 225,000 physically disabled were residents of VA hospitals and permanently disabled from mines and bullets.

But the psychological problems for some vets represented about one-third of the VA hospital admissions each month. An early investigation by a Senate committee found the reception afforded veterans returning from this unpopular war may have exacerbated the psychological effects of their service, especially for those involved in heavy combat. An article by psychiatrist Robert Jay Lifton in *Saturday Review*[11] explained that those who fought the war from the skies were able to separate the act of killing from the idea of killing. Guilt was more easily avoided or put off. The dehumanizing of the enemy by labeling them "gooks" also served, at least initially, to make killing easier. Returning home to a country that didn't want to hear about it only helped to sublimate the anguish further, according to Lifton.

The case of John Gabron, a vet in Los Angeles who took hostages during a flashback episode, received wide attention in the news in September 1974.[12] Experts began to attribute similar incidents to the uniqueness of Vietnam—a nation's citizenry was projecting the guilt over the war on the men who were sent to fight it. In past wars, men could deal with their combat nightmares and return home to sympathetic families and neighbors. In the case of Vietnam, reports of atrocities created fear of vets among families and acquaintances, as well as the general population. Other news reports attempted to point out that the number of men who suffered these traumas was relatively small and most men coming home were more concerned with getting jobs.

Stories about veterans with psychological problems would continue to surface in the news in the mid–1970s.[13] Not until the late 1970s and early 1980s, however, would the issue become a matter of national focus and concern. The country's relationship with its veterans of a controversial war would finally begin to heal with the dedication of the Vietnam War Memorial in 1982.

The episodes on *M*A*S*H* that dealt with men experiencing similar trauma differed from the real-world cases coming home from Vietnam in that the men on *M*A*S*H* were treated in the field and often sent back to the front. What's more, *M*A*S*H* could solve the problems of these men in a half-hour episode. Families and relatives of Vietnam veterans were discovering that it would take years for some men. Obviously, the format of television speeds up the resolution of problems in a way that leaves out long-term pain or implications. While *M*A*S*H*'s treatment of war's psychological wounds may have helped the country to sympathize with men returning from Vietnam, a "quick fix" from Sidney Freedman or a kind visit from Father Mulcahy was a deceptively simple resolution to what was often a long-term affliction.

SERVING THE COUNTRY OR SERVING TIME?

The attempts of Klinger to get out on psychological discharge or go AWOL are played comedically for the most part. In years four and five he valiantly tries to take advantage of Potter's arrival to gain his discharge. In "Quo Vadis, Captain Chandler," he provides comic relief to the episode's concern with a man who thinks he's Jesus by appearing in the epilogue dressed as Moses. In "It Happened One Night," he accidentally gets shot and uses that to try to get home. Then he wears only underwear and tries to spend the night in the bitter cold to freeze himself sick. "Mail Call Again" provides another attempt to go home when he says two nonexistent brothers have died. But he also makes attempts to get home by trying to bring prisoners into the 4077 when he hears capturing prisoners gets points for discharge in "The Most Unforgettable Characters." Later in the episode he tries to alarm Potter by threatening to pour gas on himself. Potter fools him by having Radar switch the can Klinger has filled with water with one full of gas. Klinger gets a nasty surprise when he actually pours the real gas on himself. In "38 Across" he tries to eat a jeep to get out of the army, and in "Souvenirs" he tries to get out by sitting on a pole in the cold. Potter challenges him to set a fantasy "record," and he does.

The frequent clashes between the militaristic Frank Burns and "resister" Max Klinger metaphorically represent a debate going on in the United States at that time. Burns and Klinger snipe at each other in "Welcome to Korea," "Deluge," "The Interview," "Bug Out," "End Run," and other episodes. Burns never exhibits any sympathy for an antiwar perspective, and Klinger's attempts to get out are as much about not seeing any sense in the war ("The Interview") as saving his neck. Some of their arguments are played for comic relief in episodes that have a serious elements, while others occur in largely comedic episodes.

While Klinger and Frank clashed over the trivial, America's debate over the serious issue of amnesty for Vietnam draft evaders and army deserters was heating up. Clemency, prison, pardon, and amnesty were the vocabulary of the debate. While he was president, Richard Nixon refused to consider anything but punishment for those who expressed their opposition to the war by refusing to serve in it (an odd position for someone raised in a Quaker family). Those who opposed the war had more sympathetic attitudes.[14] When Gerald Ford took office after Nixon's resignation, discussion of a pardon or amnesty for war opponents again took the stage, especially after Ford pardoned Nixon and protected him from prosecution. Ford created a clemency program requiring those who returned to do service and work in public institutions. Most of the more than 100,000 individuals eligible chose not to apply for amnesty; only about 8,500 entered the program.[15]

Ford's program reflected the divisions and ambivalences of the country. It was a controversial program that reopened the debate on amnesty for Vietnam War resisters.[16] By some estimates, 28,000–50,000 men were thought to have evaded the draft or deserted while in the armed forces, and some 500,000 men may have not registered for the draft or were given less than honorable discharges. A Gallup poll showed that the divisions among the American public over Vietnam carried over into how to deal with those who refused to serve in a war they considered immoral. Pluralities favored amnesty for those who evaded the draft but not for military deserters. Larger percentages thought the amnesty should have a price such as public service. War resisters, on the other hand, felt a pardon was inappropriate when no wrong had been done; they felt they had done the morally right thing in opposing the war and had helped to end United States intervention in Vietnam.

As the debate continued, Ford faced a challenge from the conservative wing of his party in the 1976 elections. A cowboy out of the West, Governor Ronald Reagan of California, launched a campaign that was critical of Ford's attempts to mediate the divisions of the country over Vietnam and Watergate. Reagan came into the race too late to overcome the sitting president, but he did force Ford to cover his right flank by responding to Reagan's charges of weakness and lack of ideological clarity. Reagan's 1976 efforts were just a warm-up for what would be a successful run against Jimmy Carter in 1980.[17]

When Jimmy Carter entered office in early 1977, he devised yet another approach. Carter's program was broader; it included men who never registered for the draft and offered reviews of those who were less than honorably discharged. But it did not offer anything to those who deserted the military during the war. Carter's announcement at the very beginning of his term of office was opposed by veterans' groups and those who had supported the war. On the other hand, many of those who were targeted by the program felt they did not need to be pardoned for opposing an immoral war. ABC News reported mail to the White House ran 3–2 against the program. By June, Congress had voted not to fund the program, and in August Carter was not invited to speak to the Veterans of Foreign Wars convention. Such events illustrate how divisive the legacy of the war would continue to be in the United States. Supporters and opponents of the war continued to be unforgiving for what each side thought the other had done to the country.[18] War "hawks" feared that things like amnesty and a defeatist attitude resulting from the war were symptoms of America's weakened resolve and moral decay. Antiwar "doves" were trying to use amnesty programs and opposition to military involvement throughout the world to write a postwar history that would perceptibly alter the role the United States would play in the post–Vietnam world. Neither of these perspectives would totally prevail, nor would either become extinct through the end of the 1970s.

THE "GOOD GUYS" IN BLACK HATS

The larger issues remaining from the Vietnam era were having an impact on the nation as well. The war may have formally ended, but the country was still dealing with the revelations concerning the CIA's secrecy and the FBI's intrusion into citizens' civil liberties. Furthermore, Americans were asking what the legacy of the war would mean for the future of the United States role in the world.

The growing revelations about CIA and FBI activities at home and abroad were beginning to generate a response in Washington. The military coup in Chile had also fueled suspicions of CIA involvement. Former CIA agents were beginning to tell their stories and bringing some of the CIA methods to light. The involvement of the CIA in the coverup of the Watergate and related crimes brought further suspicion that the spy agency was out of control.[19]

Early 1975 brought the appointment of a "blue ribbon" commission by President Ford to investigate the revelations of a CIA domestic operations division that had infiltrated and spied on antiwar activist groups in the 1960s.

Reportedly more than 10,000 citizens had been spied on in the 1950s and 1960s. Longtime spymaster James Angleton resigned as chief of counterintelligence in the wake of the revelations. The commission itself was controversial as many felt the commission members were too sympathetic to the agency and would go easy on the CIA.[20]

The commission focused on the rather narrow issue of CIA involvement in domestic spying on black radical and antiwar groups.[21] The final report from the commission would generate comment and criticism more for what the commission chose not to look into—namely whether the agency had been actively involved in assassinations and overthrowing other governments. These issues would be taken up by the congressional investigations, especially in the Senate.[22] The commission did review whether Cuba's Fidel Castro was involved in the assassination of President Kennedy. It found no evidence for that claim, but it chose not to look into revelations that the CIA had tried to assassinate Castro. The commission's report pointed the finger at both the Johnson and Nixon administrations for pushing the agency into domestic spying. (The CHAOS project had been initiated in 1967 and was designed to determine whether the antiwar movement was getting support or being directed from outside the United States. The commission did report on the tragedy surrounding the agency's sponsorship of research testing LSD on unwitting subjects. That research had resulted in the suicide of army biochemist Frank Olson, who had been working on such a project in 1953.[23])

Beginning in January 1975, the Senate and House investigations of both the FBI and the CIA examined these issues and more. *Time* reported that the scope of the FBI's domestic spying on dissidents extended to members of Congress and other public figures. A counterintelligence program called COINTELPRO had been active for fifteen years before being terminated in 1971. The project mounted a total of 2,730 operations designed to get information on or discredit civil rights and antiwar groups. Especially shocking was the ongoing campaign against Martin Luther King, Jr., including a "poison pen" effort to try to get him to commit suicide. Other reports indicated that J. Edgar Hoover had used the FBI to dig up dirt on prominent politicians as preventative blackmail should some executive or legislator criticize Hoover or his agency. Indeed, the FBI had performed political services and investigations for all presidents since FDR.[24]

The congressional probes of the CIA began to consider whether the clandestine nature of the agency was a contributing factor in why the agency had acted above the law. The resulting reports added a lot of detail to the revelations that had been coming out for the last year. Seventy-five witnesses and 8,000 pages of testimony mined the issues the presidential commission had chosen to ignore. The reports revealed the CIA had been involved in assassination attempts of foreign leaders, including Fidel Castro of Cuba and Patrice Lamumba in the Congo, and implicated in the assassinations of Rafael

Trujillo of the Dominican Republic and President Diem of South Vietnam.[25] It had even gone as far as setting up a permanent means to engage in assassinations called "Executive Action." Other revelations brought into light a series of CIA front businesses that facilitated covert operations. Several airlines had been created and used to transport personnel and cargo needed for CIA operations. One of them, Air America, was implicated in the narcotics business while serving the agency's efforts in Southeast Asia. Unofficial connections to legitimate banks, law firms, and other businesses revealed the agency's coziness with multinational corporations; for example, 200 agents had used corporate titles as identity covers. The reports issued by the investigating committees made 183 recommendations for protecting civil liberties of citizens and putting a leash on covert operations.

Meanwhile, the CIA was officially absolved of direct involvement in the overthrow of Chilean president Salvador Allende in 1973. The CIA did spend $13.4 million, including funding for opposition newspapers and groups, and United States businesses contributed some $700,000, more than half of which came from International Telephone and Telegraph.[26] The legacy of the coup—military dictatorship by the Pinochet regime and severe human rights abuses—was met with benign neglect from the United States government throughout the 1970s and 1980s. Chile's much-touted economic miracle was good for some but hardly miraculous for most.

With the Vietnam War over and revelations about spying and assassinations so much in the news, official Washington was fretting over the meaning of the Vietnam and CIA debacles for the United States role in the world. A report on Vietnam on the one-year anniversary of the United States evacuation found the country at relative peace; the feared bloodbaths of revenge had not materialized. The victorious North, trying to reunite the country, did require former South Vietnamese government and military officials to be "reeducated" under often harsh conditions, and some were given the dangerous tasks of mine clearing.[27] The nation as a whole did suffer from the aftereffects of the war, as bombing and defoliants made agriculture difficult, and the fact that promised reconstruction aid never materialized made recovering from the war an even more arduous task.

But civil wars in Cambodia and Angola now occupied United States policymakers, who were concerned that the withdrawal from Vietnam might signal to the rest of the world a "lack of resolve." The public was in no mood to begin a new military adventure, having just departed from Vietnam, yet conservative policymakers asserted that failure to assist "friendly" forces in Cambodia and Angola would allow the Soviet bloc to run rampant throughout the world. Cambodia's Khmer Rouge had been battling the United States–backed government of Lon Nol, which had received almost $2 billion in aid over five years. The aid proved useless in preventing a Khmer Rouge takeover, and the world would eventually learn about the Khmer Rouge's way of governing as they eliminated a large section of Cambodian society through outright murder and policies that promoted starvation. Shortly after the Khmer Rouge took power, the United States merchant ship *Mayaguez* was seized and charged with spying within Cambodian territorial waters. The United States military retook the ship in a rescue operation that killed 15 soldiers and wounded 50 to save the crew of 39. The operation found support in public opinion polls, though some legislators expressed reservations about the use of force. But the larger point for many was that it showed the United States continued to assert its power. This was especially important to the South Koreans, who were skeptical about United States global commitments in a post–Vietnam foreign policy.[28]

The question of Angola later in 1975 and 1976 would again be put in the context of United States resolve in the face of Soviet "expansionism" in Africa. The oil-rich former Portuguese colony saw three factions locked in civil war, with varying levels of superpower support. The Cuban- and Soviet-supported MPLA gained the upper hand in the fighting. President Ford and his secretary of state, Henry Kissinger, blasted Congress for refusing to make a Cold War response to these developments by backing a "pro–Western" faction. European experts, however, generally regarded the United States–supported FNLA as sure losers and saw South Africa's support of the same group as an albatross for most of Africa. The larger issue was whether the United States should continue its policy of détente with the Soviet Union in light of the Soviet military and political support for the eventual winner of the conflict. A Democrat running for the presidential nomination, Henry Jackson of Washington, was particularly critical of continuing to deal with the Soviets on arms talks and grain purchases while they intervened in Africa. Curiously, such rationale didn't seem to apply to the United States when it was in Vietnam. Ford, who would face a challenge for the Republican nomination from arch-conservative Ronald Reagan, was being criticized for turning détente into a one-way street favoring the Kremlin.[29]

The election of Jimmy Carter brought a proclamation of a United States foreign policy based on human rights. The attempt to shift from longtime support of dictators throughout the developing world to a recognition that support of such dictators fosters resentment among their citizens would bring more complicated issues in the near future. The return of the Panama Canal and the withdrawal of support for the Shah of Iran and Anastazio Somoza in Nicaragua would provide fodder for the debate among factions who saw the proper United States role in the world in vastly different terms. The "Vietnam Syndrome" would come to mean different things to different sides of the debate. For many, the experience of Vietnam demonstrated that United States dominance had a high cost in terms of both American casualties and the destruction rained upon millions of people trying to eke out a living in the developing world. For others, Vietnam was a symbol of what happens when

American forces don't fight to win, and a sure sign that the Soviet Union and other governments would take advantage of "weakness" to wreak havoc in other parts of the world.

THE WAR AND I

The winding down of the Vietnam War brought subtle changes in how war themes were developed for *M*A*S*H*. The relatively few episodes dealing with friendly fire and those that critiqued a boorish, imperial military mindset began to give way to episodes focusing on war's impact on individual characters, or how those characters functioned or survived in war.

Some of those episodes focus on people trying to profit from war or satiate their militaristic urges. In "The Kids," Frank applies for a purple heart based on a minor injury he suffered inside the camp. The episode features another appearance by nurse Meg Cratty, who brings her orphans to the 4077 in refuge from bombing. She mentions how the kids lose legs looking for spent shells—the brass brings good prices. "Kids" garnered an Emmy nomination for directing (Alan Alda). An episode from year five ("Souvenirs") takes another look at this theme as a soldier entices kids to hunt for war trash and then pays them very poorly for it. A lecture by Potter to the entire unit fails to change the man's behavior. Hawkeye and Margaret voice their disgust but threats against the man don't seem to work until Hawkeye decides he looks real sick and talks about grounding him. The man finally promises he will stop the merchandising. Profiting from war recurs in "Post Op," when a soldier who's making money as a middle man selling liquor and Polaroid snapshots is disappointed to learn he's going home.

Hawkeye and B.J. clash with an aggressive colonel in "Some 38th Parallels." The episode opens in the OR with Father Mulcahy reporting that there is no more room in post-op. B.J. mentions that many of the casualties they are working on were wounded while trying to pick up dead soldiers. Later, the colonel who sent these men to collect the dead arrives injured himself. As the colonel tries to leave the 4077, B.J. confronts him on one of his men who has just died. But all that matters is that he kills more of the enemy soldiers than he loses of his own. Hawkeye arranges for a helicopter to "accidentally" dump garbage on the colonel as his jeep pulls out of camp.

"The Novocaine Mutiny" finds Hawkeye facing charges from Frank. Frank is trying to blame Hawkeye for his own failure of command while Potter was gone. Frank's delusional version of events, which focuses on how heroically he behaved while the rest of the unit fell apart, disintegrates rather quickly when Hawkeye, B.J. and Radar testify that Frank was drunk with power when he made the unit bug out and move across the road. The judge throws the charges out and upbraids Frank for his own incompetence.

Dealing with the attitude that "rank has its privileges" is the theme of "The General's Practitioner." A general has decided that because another general has a personal physician, he needs one as well. The general's aide comes to the 4077 because he has heard Hawkeye is the best. Hawkeye resists, saying that he's there to save the lives of the gravely wounded and that war is worse than hell: "Hell doesn't have innocent bystanders. Except for generals, everyone in war is an innocent bystander." Hawk gets a visit from the general and gives him a hard time about his cigars-and-scotch lifestyle. The general is insistent about having Hawkeye as a personal physician but relents when Hawkeye asks him, "Do the men come first or not?"

Hawkeye experiences the worst kind of bureaucratic snafu in "The Late Captain Pierce." He learns he has been declared dead when B.J. takes a phone call from Hawkeye's grieving father in Maine. Attempts to reach his father to tell him he's okay are thwarted. In the meantime, a GI arrives to pick up his body; his paycheck is stopped; and he stops getting mail. He has become a nonperson in the eyes of the army. As the casualties pour in, he boards a bus to return home, telling B.J. he's tired of the endless stream of casualties. Ultimately, however, he returns to his duties.

In "Dear Sigmund," Hawkeye teaches a lesson to a pilot who comes to the 4077 after bailing out of his plane. The man tells Hawkeye the war is easy for him—he just dumps his load and returns home to his wife in Tokyo. When a little girl arrives with injuries from a bombing incident, Hawkeye brings the man to her table. The pilot asks whose bombs hit her village—ours or theirs? Potter responds that it doesn't matter to her. Hawkeye tells him he seems like a decent man—too decent to believe war is easy. The man breaks down, realizing his connection to the little girl's pain.

Larry Gelbart's final episode, "The Interview," which closed year four, stands as one of the more unusual, introspective episodes of the entire series. In this episode, Clete Roberts, a journalist covering the Korean War, arrives to interview the 4077 staff about their experiences in Korea. Filmed in black and white, the episode was written in a unique way. Gene Reynolds had the cast spontaneously answer questions as they felt their characters would. After the footage was edited, the script was "written." Many of the questions focus on how the characters are coping with the war, how they feel about being so far from home, and what they want to do when they returned. Some of the questions deal with their reactions to the war. "Do you see any good coming out of this?" Roberts asks. Frank Burns says it is a shining example of benign United States military intervention. Klinger critiques the words "police action"—"It sounds like you're handing out tickets. War is just killing, that's all," he says.

But the best responses come to the most personal question: Has the war changed you? Frank says certainly not. Father Mulcahy's response is the most heartrending of all: "When the doctors cut into a patient and it's cold, the way it is today, steam rises from the body and the doctor will warm himself over the open wound. Could anyone look at that and not feel changed?"

It is clear that the antiwar nature of the series changed during this period. Early critique and ridicule of things military and political receded and were supplanted with personal anguish and individual suffering over various aspects of the war. In this respect, the show moved from a protest mode to a "feelings" mode. Granted, it had never consistently reflected the anti-imperialist sentiment of many Vietnam War opponents; nor had it been designed to promote critical thinking about war. Nevertheless, beginning in the mid–1970s, the show more than ever encouraged people to feel rather than to think.

LIFE LESSONS FOR THE 4077

Society's transition from the Vietnam era to the "Me" decade finds parallels in the changes in how stories are told on *M*A*S*H*. With actors getting to know their characters better, more and more storylines begin to deal with individual crises and growth. Members of the ensemble cast behave more like a big family, as opposed to the raucous party atmosphere that characterized the first years of the show. The humor begins to change as well, from lots of one-liners and slapstick to a more introspective comedy. This change is exemplified in "Dear Mildred," a "letter" episode in which Potter relates slices of life at the 4077 to his wife. The unit comes together to make him feel welcome and help him celebrate his wedding anniversary. Such family unity was often disrupted by spats, such as the rivalry between Hawkeye and Frank ("The Novocaine Mutiny") and the clashes between Klinger and Frank. On the other hand, these years also find Margaret and Hawkeye moving from hostility to at least a grudging respect for each other. Indeed, as Margaret becomes engaged and distances herself from Frank, she and Hawkeye grow closer. "Hepatitis" finds her confiding in Hawkeye about letters she received from her future in-laws. She feels they are treating her in a condescending way. She gets upset with Hawkeye for his remarks about her when he comes to give a gamma globulin shot to prevent the spread of Father Mulcahy's case of hepatitis. She demands that he respect her as an officer. Hawkeye suggests that the same demand for respect might just work with her future in-laws.

The other characters of the *M*A*S*H* ensemble also experience change or challenge in their lives. It takes an inspection by a tough chaplin ("Dear Peggy") and an experience on the front ("Mulcahy's War") to have Father Mulcahy realize his own value and worth to the unit. Happily married B.J. falls off the fidelity wagon while trying to be a friend to a nurse in "Hanky Panky." War would prove to have lessons for all the members of the 4077.

Hawkeye's past with women and his inability to make a commitment haunt him in "The More I See You." In this episode, Blythe Danner guest stars as Hawk's old flame, Carlye, who's now married and assigned to the 4077. Carlye and Hawk renew their romance at least temporarily until she decides to get a transfer. Hawk proposes to Carlye and asks her to leave her husband. His proposal is more like an internal debate with himself, during which he literally walks himself into a corner. "Hawkeye," a unique episode that is basically a monologue by Alda, finds Hawk suffering head wounds from a jeep accident and spending time with a Korean family as he waits for help. This episode received Emmy nominations for writing (Larry Gelbart and Simon Munter) and cinematography (William Jurgensen). In a later episode, Hawkeye gets temporarily blinded and obtains new insights in "Out of Sight, Out of Mind."

Radar's growth from a naive teenager continues as a theme in the show. "Soldier of the Month" finds him winning a contest whose prize is six days in Tokyo. In "The Interview" he recalls he had fun on the Tokyo trip but says he can't remember much because he was drunk. "The Gun" finds him facing an angry colonel whose gun has been stolen while in Radar's possession. A drunken Radar stumbles into post-op to tell the colonel off; later he gets off the hook when Frank proves to be the culprit. But perhaps the most poignant moment for Radar over these two years takes place in "Some 38th Parallels." When B.J. credits him for noticing an IV disconnected from a patient, Radar is proud that he helped save a man's life. The man develops post-operative complications, but after a second session of surgery, he seems okay, and Radar makes friends with the man. The patient dies suddenly, however, sending Radar into a state of shock while the rest of the unit plods along. Radar would experience war's harshness and more growing pains in his travails as company clerk in future years.

But the most significant changes come to Margaret Houlihan, who becomes closer to her nurses, finds Hawkeye can be an important friend, and discards Frank for a husband. Margaret and Frank begin to part ways soon after Frank's glory days as temporary CO are finished when Potter arrives in year four. Fearing that his wife will find out about his affair, Frank destroys Margaret's tent looking for his old love notes in "It Happened One Night." Margaret begins to react less harshly toward Hawkeye, and she consents to being part of a jeep-stuffing prank in "Dear Peggy." "Soldier of the Month" brings Margaret the indignant realization of just how little Frank thinks of her when he writes a will while under a fever. (He leaves her his clothes.) In this episode, Margaret compliments Hawkeye on his work with a patient.

Frank's troubled marriage back home gets worse when his wife hears about Margaret in "Mail Call Again." She threatens divorce until Frank assures her that Houlihan is "an old war horse, an army mule with bosoms." Having overheard this, Margaret gets revenge by throwing a chair at Frank. In "The

Price of Tomato Juice," B.J. and Hawkeye create further division between the two when they set Frank up by sending a proposal note to Margaret to keep her from a rendezvous with a general in Seoul. She gets angry when she finds the proposal was a joke.

Year five brings big changes in Margaret's life. The first episode of the year, "Bug Out," finds her and Hawkeye staying with a patient whose spinal injury prevents him from being moved during a bug-out. Margaret and Hawkeye grow closer as she shares her anxiety about shelling. In "Margaret's Engagement," which aired the following week, Margaret returns from a conference in Tokyo with an engagement ring. Frank takes the news very poorly, and Margaret rubs it in with talk of fiancé Donald Penobscot's virility. Frank makes a desperate attempt to dissuade her from her marriage plans, but she rebukes him. But Frank gets his own digs in when he makes plans to go out with Hawkeye to pick up nurses. In the later episode "The Colonel's Horse," the separation process continues when Margaret insists that Hawkeye, rather than Frank, perform surgery on her when her appendix needs removing. When Frank objects to Hawkeye's role, she orders Frank out of the OR.

Margaret's relationship with her nurses changes as well. "The Nurses" begins with Nurse Baker (Linda Kelsey) getting a surprise visit from her husband, Tony (Greg Harrison). They were unable to have a honeymoon, and he's come to the 4077 to make up for lost time. Margaret plays straight army with her nurses, objecting to fudgemaking in their tent as well as to their drinking. They give her a hard time in return, and the spat gets Baker put on report. Hawkeye and B.J.'s plan to get the Bakers a night alone together ends up putting Margaret in the nurses' tent for the night. In the morning, Margaret tells Baker she will throw the book at her. As they prepare for an OR session, the nurses confront Margaret. They tell her she's too much by-the-book when it comes to military discipline. She tells them she's tired of their lying. She expresses great frustration at being excluded by the other women in camp, never offering her so much as "a lousy cup of coffee."

Later, a disaffected nurse is brought to tears as she holds a baby they have delivered. In the denouement, Margaret comes into the nurses' tent to find them making fudge again. They offer a taste. "It's awful," she laughs, but she accepts their offer of a cup of coffee. The episode received an Emmy nomination for directing (Joan Darling).

Frank makes another attempt to win Margaret back in "Hanky Panky." Margaret discovers her fiancé is in the hospital, and Frank tries to woo her with a Japanese umbrella. Frank says he just wants to be friends, but he can't seem to keep his hands off her. In "Souvenirs," she tries to get Frank to return a ring she gave him that is a family heirloom. He says he doesn't have it. He later sees someone going through his things and jumps the would-be thief. The thief overpowers him and is revealed to be Margaret, who has found the missing heirloom in his footlocker.

But Frank ends up inadvertently doing Margaret a favor when he taunts her about the lack of a wedding date in the last episode of year five. The taunt leads Margaret to approach Donald about when they will get married. Penobscot arrives at the 4077 to announce they will get married immediately—and that he has Frank to thank for persuading him. Of course, the wedding would be incomplete without a wedding dress from Klinger and Potter giving the bride away. But the best laughs come from Hawkeye and B.J.'s plot to put Penobscot in a body cast when he "breaks his leg" after passing out at the end of his bachelor party. They try to tell Margaret about the cast when she gets ready to leave for a honeymoon. An unsuspecting Margaret never understands what they are trying to say over the noise of the helicopter.

More changes were in store in the next few years of the show for the whole cast. Margaret's marriage to Penobscot would wither. Charles Winchester's arrival would bring new challenges for Hawkeye, and Radar would keep working his way through the transition to manhood. The show would continue to lose its antiwar edge and become a more conventional sitcom focusing on individual crises and challenges and "family" issues within the 4077.

These changes in the show marked the direction many Americans were taking in the mid–1970s. A return to introspection—"getting in touch with one's feelings"—would sweep America in the post–Vietnam era. The focus on the self would take on many forms; religious and spiritual exploration, secular seminars on the self's relationship with others, even the narcissism of disco began to move the country away from social concerns toward the search for individual fulfillment or self-indulgence.

While the ratings for year four declined, putting *M*A*S*H* in fifteenth place (this was the only year besides year one that it was not in the Top Ten), in year five the show came back to fourth place. Rankings aside, *M*A*S*H* received critical acclaim in both these years. Year four brought more Emmy nominations for Alan Alda, Harry Morgan, Gary Burghoff, and Loretta Swit for their roles, and for Larry Gelbart and Gene Reynolds as producers. Alda won a Golden Globe award for Best Actor in a Comedy or Musical, and the program received the prestigious George Foster Peabody Award for Broadcast Excellence. Year five brought more nominations and an Emmy win for Gary Burghoff as Best Supporting Actor.

CHAPTER 6

This War Just Isn't
Working Out for Me—
Years 6–7, 1977–79

Years six and seven brought qualitative changes in the directions *M*A*S*H*
took, the stories it told, and the subjects it took on. They also brought more
changes behind and in front of the camera. Executive producer Gene Reynolds,
like Larry Gelbart before him, left that role after being with the program from
the beginning. He would continue to serve as creative consultant. Burt Metcalfe would lead the creative team, and cast members such as Mike Farrell,
Alan Alda, and Harry Morgan would play greater roles as writers and directors. The most immediate change for viewers in year six was the departure of
Frank Burns, who never got over the trauma of losing Margaret to another
man. Charles Winchester (David Ogden Stiers) arrived as Frank's replacement to take up residence in the Swamp. This shift brought a more formidable rival for Hawkeye and less opportunity to ridicule the militarism and
jingoism that Frank embodied.

In year seven, the show moved from Tuesday to Monday night at 9:00,
where it would stay for the rest of its prime-time run. These years moved the
show still further from the horrors of war and the absurdities of war makers
to an emphasis on how individuals cope with war. *M*A*S*H* became a show
focusing on the individual lives and struggles of the members of the 4077,
moving toward a family sitcom model in which the members of the unit began
to treat each other as family.

The country was changing as well. The election of Jimmy Carter as
president signaled further distancing from the national traumas of Vietnam
and Watergate. People were turning inward, too, focusing on personal issues
after having dealt with the politics of an unpopular war and a disgraced
presidency. The country as a whole was moving toward greater concerns with
self and less concern for others. The post–Vietnam era would seemingly create a shift to the right politically, though the extent of that shift was much
debated.

"HOT LIPS" BECOMES MARGARET

Margaret's big changes occur over years five through seven (1976–79). During this time, she gets engaged, married, and divorced. Her engagement and marriage in year five to Donald Penobscot—a very masculine marine whose muscles and prowess are the subject of much bragging by Margaret—reflect a woman who chooses men based on their virility or military rank. To this point, she is very male-identified and dependent.

However, at the beginning of year six when she returns from her honeymoon in "Fade Out, Fade In," it is clear her marriage has become problematic. The honeymoon has revealed to her that her husband will not cope well with a woman who beguiles high-level officers. She tells Hawkeye and B.J. that Donald lost his desire when he and she spent time with military brass with whom she had been involved in the past. In a later episode called "In Love and War," Margaret hears through the nurses' grapevine that Donald has been making sport of chasing nurses. She discovers he is the one who has wooed a nurse who recently arrived at the 4077 from Tokyo when the nurse tells her he kept licking her fingernails. At the end of the episode, however, Margaret decides to take him back.

"Comrades in Arms," a two-part episode aired one month later, marks a turning point for both Margaret's marriage and her relationship to Hawkeye. Margaret and Hawkeye are assigned temporarily to another unit to demonstrate new techniques. Hawkeye can tell Margaret is upset and tries to get her to talk. When she does, she reveals that Donald is seeing other women—Margaret has a letter from him written to another woman. Encountering jeep trouble, Hawkeye and Margaret spend the night in an abandoned hut. When the shelling begins, they are drawn to each other and become lovers for the night. This affair is short-lived and not without a few bumps in the road as both Margaret and Hawkeye eventually realize their physical attraction won't overcome their basic personality differences and philosophies. Margaret uses the incident to gain retribution against her cheating husband, and it produces another benefit as well: Over time, she and Hawkeye become friends and learn to appreciate the positive qualities in each other. Indeed, "Comrades in Arms" is a watershed episode in the transformation of Margaret and how others in the unit treat her. She learns they are not all out to get her and are even eager to help her when they can. This episode garnered an Emmy for Outstanding Directing and a Directors Guild Award for Burt Metcalfe and Alan Alda.

Margaret's changes are further illustrated in her relationship with Klinger when he accidentally throws away her engagement ring in "Patent 4077." Margaret jumps all over Klinger when he reveals he threw away a wrapping of tissue that had the ring inside. A sympathetic Hawkeye teams up with Klinger to get a new, seemingly identical ring from a local Korean merchant. But their good intentions go awry when the merchant mangles the special inscription inside the ring. Margaret is furious at first, thinking Klinger and Hawkeye did it to make fun of her but she learns to appreciate the gesture for what it was—two friends trying to ease the pain of another.

Margaret's marital trouble would continue in subsequent episodes. Donald's financial management becomes objectionable and she makes her own changes in "The Merchant of Korea." She then ambivalently faces a possible pregnancy in "What's Up Doc." Not only is she dealing with the uncertainties of a troubled marriage, but pregnancy would mean an automatic discharge for someone who thinks of herself as career army. It turns out she's not pregnant, and she is relieved yet wistful.

Margaret's character growth occurs in other ways as well. In "Images" she has a clash with a new nurse, Nurse Cooper, who is having a hard time adjusting to the gruesomeness of the operating room. Margaret takes a hard line with the nurse at first, demanding that she shape up or ship out. Potter makes her give Cooper a second chance. Later in the episode, Margaret breaks down when she hears a little dog to whom she had been sneaking food scraps has been run over by a jeep. Hawkeye tries to comfort her by telling her he saw her feeding the dog and she has every right to be upset. Margaret's next encounter with Cooper finds her more sympathetic.

Later in year six, Margaret gets a visit from a fellow army brat and nurse in "Temporary Duty." At first she is thrilled to see an old friend, and Margaret and Lorraine Anderson have good laughs remembering old times. But as Anderson falls for the teasing and charm of Charles Winchester, Margaret gets upset and becomes "military" with Anderson. After Anderson decides to bunk with the other nurses, Margaret urges her to stay and reveals that she is jealous of Anderson's openness and freedom. Margaret comments that she has no friends at the 4077. Anderson tells her to not let "Major Houlihan" run her life. Margaret tries the tactic the next morning after Anderson has returned to her unit when she asks B.J. and Charles to join her for a cup of coffee.

In year seven, Margaret shows compassion for her nurses after one gets injured when the camp's water tower collapses during high winds in "They Call the Wind Korea." Margaret brings her some toiletries to assuage her feelings of responsibility for the nurse but maintains her tough exterior as she performs the gesture. Margaret's relationship with the wounded also takes a new course as she frequently is seen comforting recovering soldiers. An especially poignant scene occurs during "Point of View" when she sponge-bathes a soldier who cannot talk due to a throat injury.

In year seven, her tumultuous marriage reaches a resolution: She files for divorce, and by the middle of the season she gets it. In the meantime, she becomes more focused on living life on her terms. In "Major Ego," the complications of her divorce and her lack of access to money lead her to have a one-nighter to experience her newfound freedom (she also turns down the man who wants more than one night). However, even when her divorce becomes finalized and she comes up with a plan for nurses to become more involved in triage, she is forced to confront the sexism of superior officers in "Hot Lips Is Back in Town." After she invites a general to inspect her new triage operation, he offers her a post in Tokyo. She takes this to mean she will have an opportunity to take her program to other units, but his intention is for her to serve as his mistress. Dejected, she angrily turns him down, and the euphoria of liberation she felt from the divorce withers away.

The penultimate episode of the year finds her in complete charge of her life. In "A Night at Rosie's," she meets Sgt. Scully, a soldier she finds attractive, but she is somewhat appalled when he tells her he's AWOL. However, she chooses an unlikely course in helping him escape from the MPs who come into Rosie's looking for him. This is something her straight by-the-book military mindset would not have permitted her to do in the early years of the show. Scully promises he will see her again, and indeed she would develop a brief relationship with him in year eight.

Meanwhile, Hawkeye's romantic encounters begin to take on a different tone as well. He now shows interest in women as human beings and not merely desirable playthings. In the episode "In Love and War," Hawk learns that appearances are deceiving when he discovers that a seemingly wealthy Korean woman is actually enduring all kinds of hardship to keep her family together. His relationship with her is tender yet brief as the woman has to relocate her family away from the 4077.

In other episodes, Hawkeye and the other men of the 4077 are forced to confront their own male chauvinism. A visit by a Swedish female doctor (Mariette Hartley) in "Inga" reveals Hawkeye's and Charles's sexism. At first, both anticipate romance with this attractive doctor. She shows interest in Hawkeye, but he is put off when she tries to show him a new technique in surgery. He also can't handle her assertiveness in romantic situations. Charles is also "shown up" by Inga and comes to loathe her for besting him in the operating room. Margaret calls both of them on their sexist attitudes. "Inga," written and directed by Alan Alda, garnered its creator an Emmy nomination for directing and an Emmy award for outstanding writing.

In "Ain't Love Grand," both Klinger and Charles learn you can't always get what you want when each is romantically rejected. Charles falls for a Korean prostitute whom he tries to reform, and Klinger falls for a nurse who is amused by his penchant for dresses. Charles's attempts to turn the young woman from a life of prostitution are rebuffed, and while Klinger wants to believe his relationship is serious, the nurse makes it clear she's just in it for the kicks.

THE BATTLE FOR WOMEN'S RIGHTS

The women's movement was in full swing in the mid–1970s, and much energy was devoted to the struggle to get the Equal Rights Amendment ratified by at least 38 states. By the end of 1974, the amendment had been ratified by 34 states, and it was generally thought that ratification would come in 1975. But that year brought setbacks as Oklahoma, Arizona, Georgia, Utah, and Nevada voted the amendment down, Indiana tabled it indefinitely, and Illinois, where it was expected to pass, postponed any action. Two states that had approved the amendment, Nebraska and Tennessee, rescinded their approval. Attempts to pass ERAs at the state level also foundered, with ballot initiatives in New York and New Jersey going down to defeat. Anti-ERA groups were campaigning that such amendments would undermine the family and promote unisex bathrooms and homosexual marriages.[1] As the constitutional time clock on ratification ran down, advocates of the ERA went to Congress to get an extension for the deadline. In October 1978, both houses of Congress approved an extension until June 1982. As anti–ERA forces gathered steam to oppose first the amendment and then the extension, it became clear that the extension was no guarantee the amendment would finally get four more states' ratification.[2]

Opposition from religious groups—conservative Catholics, fundamentalist Protestants, and Mormons—was making the last four states' approval a tough hurdle. In an attempt to give the Catholic Church's position on abortion some teeth, the Bishop of San Diego announced anyone who was a member of a group "promoting" abortion would not be able to receive communion.[3] There was fallout from the legalizing of abortion as well. A Supreme Court decision in July 1977 found that though states could not make abortion illegal, they were not compelled to pay for abortions for poor women.[4] Many states were expected to take this ruling as a reason to remove abortions from the list of procedures funded by Medicaid programs. Congress had passed a law banning federal funding of abortions, which then was challenged in the courts as well. The future of federally funded abortions would continue to be debated.

On other fronts, feminists were finding it necessary to defend some hard-won gains. The issue of reverse discrimination—a belief that affirmative action merely legalized discrimination against whites and males—was also being challenged in the courts as the Supreme Court agreed to hear the Bakke case in March 1977. By June 1978, the court had decided that the University of California had discriminated against Allan Bakke, a white man twice turned down for admission to medical school. Cover stories on the case in *Newsweek* and *Time* described a fragmented decision that involved six separate opinions. The swing vote came from Justice Lewis Powell, who sided with a plurality holding that the University of California's affirmative action plan was a quota system that could only be employed where past discrimination had been proved. On the other hand, he also agreed with an opinion maintaining that race could be a factor in considering admission to educational institutions. School administrators maintained that almost no minorities would be admitted without such programs. The landmark Bakke decision, which would remain the focus of debate for years to come, affected the status of women as well as racial minorities.[5]

On other fronts, however, women were gaining more equality with men. A law that banned discrimination in the granting of bank loans and the issuing of credit cards was passed around the same time women began to organize their own financial institutions like the First Women's Bank in New York and the Feminist Federal Credit Union in Detroit. Regulations passed forbade the consideration of sex or marital status in judging worthiness for credit and mandated that banks give reasons for refusing credit upon request from the applicant.[6]

Women were beginning to have a global voice as well. Six thousand women attended a United Nations–sponsored conference during the International Women's Year in 1975. The delegates met for two weeks in Mexico. But even the Mexican president's wife learned about male dominance when her husband passed her over to appoint his attorney general as president of the women's assembly.[7]

Collegiate sports were beginning to respond to the times—and to the requirements of the 1972 Title IX Educational Amendments Act—as women's sports programs and scholarships were beginning to be increased. It was estimated that 10,000 scholarships would be granted at 464 schools in the 1977-78 school year. This was a considerable increase from the 60 schools that were granting sports scholarships to women in 1974. Increases in athletic participation by high school girls also went up dramatically in the 1970s, from about 300,000 in 1970 to 1.6 million in the 1976-77 school year.[8] Educators and psychologists praised this development for the positive effects it would have on young women's self-esteem. In women's professional sports, women were far from parity with men in terms of pay, but golfers such as Carol Mann and jockeys such as Mary Bacon were beginning to have an impact as well. The notion of sports as a male bastion was clearly being challenged as more women gained access to college scholarships and stars in various sports began to emerge.

Something that would have made Margaret Houlihan proud was the fact that the first women to enter the military academies had just completed their first year as "plebes." A report on their adjustment showed that they dropped out at rates lower than men in the air force and army academies. There were incidents of resentment and harassment by male cadets, but such incidents were expected to fade as women became regular fixtures at the academies.

Women were also enlisting in the armed forces and were now required to train with M-16 rifles. By 1979, the recruiting goal for women would reach 50,000, and women would increasingly take on responsibilities the army had once reserved for men.[9]

The world of the media also saw some breakthroughs for women. Phyllis George's hiring by CBS Sports to report on football was greeted with skepticism by feminists and dismissive men alike. Both believed the primary reason she was hired was that she was the 1971 Miss America. George sought to divert people's attention from that achievement and direct it toward her football knowledge and interview skills. *Newsweek's* report the week before she would work the Super Bowl seemed designed to help her accomplish just that.[10] A breakthrough also occurred at one of the nation's most prestigious newspapers, the *New York Times*. Lee Anne Schreiber, at the age of 33, became the paper's first female sports editor after a stint as a reporter at *Time* and as editor at *Womansports* magazine. The paper shouldn't be given too much credit, though, since this move was likely prompted by an out-of-court settlement of a discrimination lawsuit just one month before. The agreement by the *Times* committed the paper to filling at least 25 percent of its senior news positions with women.[11]

In May 1976, ABC News announced the signing of Barbara Walters to co-anchor the evening newscast with Harry Reasoner. The longtime queen of NBC's early morning news program *Today*, Walters was no doubt helped in her rise to anchor by the Emmys she won and by being named Woman of the Year by *Ladies Home Journal*. When she jumped to ABC, she was signed for the then unheard-of sum of $1 million per year, a figure that raised questions about the news business as show business. But the signing of Walters liberated her and other women from their previous relegation to the network's morning news shows. The promotion of one woman to join an evening news program was a visible breakthrough for women and a reminder that the presence of women in previously male domains was not a passing fad.[12]

In contrast to Walters's success, women in the film business still lacked the respect and the kinds of roles that would give them dignity. Actresses claimed the roles for women largely consisted of neurotic housewives, prostitutes, and cooks. Women were caught between their need to work and their reluctance to settle for roles they found demeaning and unrealistic. Many actresses of the day maintained the situation resulted from a preponderance of men occupying creative and decision-making roles as scriptwriters, directors, and producers.[13]

In the area of religion, a major breakthrough came in the fall of 1976, when the Episcopal Church's General Convention voted to allow the ordination of women priests. Previous votes by the convention in 1970 and 1973 had rejected the idea of ordaining women to roles beyond deacon. The

Philadelphia Diocese had violated these votes by ordaining eleven women in 1974. While some traditionalists were expected to resist this vote, the first woman was ordained January 1, 1977.[14] By early 1978, a schism developed within the church over the ordination of women. A dissident group of bishops were ordained for the "Anglican Church of North America," a body of traditionalists formed in opposition to official Anglican approval of women clerics. [15]

The efforts of women to make their case in the political arena were on the rise as well. The National Women's Conference in Houston in November 1977, an attempt to formulate a series of national policy initiatives for women, had been given impetus by the 1975 International Women's Year. Given the growth of women's groups on both the pro– and anti–ERA sides of the fence, the conference had its own controversies—so much so that 15,000 women with a conservative outlook met separately across town to plan strategies that would oppose much of what the official conference would advocate. Women at the official conference used the event to make an accounting of the progress of the women's movement—how far it had come and just how much it had yet to accomplish. Resolutions were passed advocating ratification of the ERA, greater representation of women in the arts and in business, stronger enforcement of recently passed credit legislation, and adoption of measures to prevent wife-beating and domestic violence. Women from both political parties were present for the conference, which featured a show of unity by then first lady Rosalyn Carter and former first ladies Betty Ford and Lady Bird Johnson.[16]

While legislation and court rulings were creating more opportunities for women, the women's movement was also beginning to raise awareness of rape as one of the fastest growing violent crimes. The publication of Susan Brownmiller's *Against Our Will* brought discussion of this formerly taboo subject front and center in the national consciousness.[17]

Interpersonal issues and struggles between women and men were also being played out in the homes and bedrooms of the country. The release of two books by Marabel Morgan, *The Total Woman* and *Total Joy*, ignited a debate over just how women should treat the men in their lives and vice versa.[18] Feminists raged at Morgan for her advocacy of inequality in marital relationships and her belief that women who made their husband's daily routines easier and their sex lives spicier would have happier marriages. For her part, Morgan maintained her techniques for revitalizing stale marriages would help women develop poise and self-confidence and help them discover who they really were. Most analysts saw the books as part of the self-help craze that was sweeping bookstores in the mid- to late 1970s and advocated positive thinking as a key to self-fulfillment. The books touched a chord in some sectors of American society. *The Total Woman* sold over 3 million copies, and Morgan received over 100 letters per day in which she was asked to deal with various aspects of "housewife blues." Furthermore, her "Total Woman" seminars brought her message of self-fulfillment through self-submission to thousands of largely white, middle-class women in more than 60 cities.

A *Newsweek* cover story broadened the debate over the effects of the women's movement on society by looking at how men were (or weren't) changing as women rose toward a more equal footing.[19] Psychologists assessed how men were responding to women's demands for such changes as more independence, meaningful work outside the home, and more involvement by men in child-rearing. According to the article, men's acceptance of these changes was related to their age, with younger men seemingly more accepting of women working outside the home and men becoming more involved with child care.

A sidebar story in this issue focused on the choice of ABC newsman Ted Koppel to take an eight-month leave (actually a significantly reduced workload) to care for the kids while his wife, Grace Anne, completed a law degree at Georgetown University. Koppel described how he came to appreciate the demands of housekeeping and child-rearing, including his frustration at having cooked a dinner for which his wife was an hour late in getting home. The article concluded that men were having conflicting feelings about women working outside the home and their greater involvement with children and family was resulting in a greater reluctance to do a lot of business traveling or moving for the sake of career advancement.

Relations between the sexes would continue to evolve as more and more women asserted themselves in their jobs and in their relationships. On *M*A*S*H*, just as Margaret would continue to make sense of her life and career, so would the men of the 4077 learn a few lessons about respecting women and treating them as equals. More generally, it was a time of personal introspection for many in American society and for the characters in *M*A*S*H*. The move in the program from themes critiquing politics and militarism to themes addressing individual crises and growth followed from the changes occurring in the nation. People in the mid- to late 1970s began to search for meaning and self-fulfillment in their lives, looking for psychological, spiritual, and material comfort in a world of upheaval and uncertainty. While the 1970s evolved into the "Me Decade," the evolution of *M*A*S*H*'s characters in a 1950s time frame offered viewers new ways of relating program themes to events in their own lives and the world around them.

*M*A*S*H* AND THE ME DECADE

While Margaret's changes certainly reflect the larger struggle of women for respect and dignity, Charles Winchester's arrival at the 4077 signals a change in the show's storytelling. Character studies become a feature of the show as it begins to explore the relationships among the main cast.

"Fade Out, Fade In" tells the story of how Frank leaves the 4077 and Charles arrives to take his place. In this hour-long episode, we learn that Frank is late returning from R and R. A telephone call from Tokyo eventually clears up the mystery. It seems Frank has taken Margaret's marriage very hard. His antics in Tokyo add up to a "lost" weekend experience in which he accosts a couple whom he mistakes for Margaret and Donald. The couple turns out to be a general and his wife. Frank gets arrested and held for psychiatric observation. Ultimately, Frank not only gets to return to the States but also gets a promotion and a cushy job in an army hospital. Even as they celebrate this development, Potter, Hawkeye, and B.J. express their frustration at Frank's amazing luck.

In the meantime, Potter obtains what he at first thinks is a temporary replacement for Frank. Potter's call to Tokyo arrives at an inopportune moment for Charles Winchester, who is safely ensconced there and has just been playing—and winning—cribbage with a colonel. The colonel takes the call from Potter just as Winchester is counting up what the colonel owes him. The colonel decides that Charles is expendable and proceeds to assign him to the 4077.

Charles arrives at the camp on an oxcart, something he clearly regards as an indignity to someone of his lineage. Coming from a wealthy family in Boston, Charles is always eager to remind people of his Harvard background. His first stint in the operating room shows he is an excellent if deliberate surgeon, but his arrogance immediately begins to turn Hawkeye, B.J., and Potter off. After Potter learns Frank is not returning, he contacts Tokyo and asks them to make Charles's assignment permanent. A bit later, a difficult case that Potter assigns to Charles instead of Hawkeye touches off the battle of egos between Hawkeye and Charles. "Fade Out, Fade In" won an Emmy for Outstanding Film Editing and an ACE "Eddie" for film editors Stanford Tischler and Larry L. Mills. Jim Fritzell and Everett Greenbaum won a Writers Guild Award for their script.

As a new personality at the 4077, Charles opens up new plots for the show. A series of episodes defines his basic arrogance, egotism, and selfishness. Later in year six, Charles is faced with his own imperfection when a patient nearly dies after Charles gives him the wrong medicine in "The Light That Failed." "The Winchester Tapes" introduces the audience to the Winchester family as Charles tape-records a letter home. This occurs as Charles's encounters with other members of the unit fully expose his greed and arrogance. B.J. plays a series of jokes on Charles, the last one (a rubber chicken in Charles's teapot) prompting him to reiterate his pleas to his family to "get me the hell out of here."

Charles's selfishness is the subject of several episodes. He and B.J. clash over a jacket given by an appreciative patient in "The Grim Reaper." In the same episode, he tries to woo Margaret by sharing a package of delicacies from home. A canned pheasant makes them both ill and Margaret becomes less impressed with him. In "Change Day," Charles tries to use a change in army scrip (the currency soldiers are paid in) to benefit himself. He shows that his greed knows no bounds as he hatches a plot to exploit local Koreans who have scrip from their dealings with GIs. He makes a deal to give them a fraction of the new scrip's worth while he pockets the rest. Hawkeye and B.J. get wind of his plan and hatch a counterplot that leaves Charles literally holding the bag—a sack of worthless currency that he is prevented from exchanging. Charles later uses his affluence to gain advantage over B.J. and Hawkeye when they ask for a loan in "The Merchant of Korea." After he loans them the money, he begins to ask for "favors" that result in them waiting on him hand and foot. Seething at his arrogance, they decide to invite him to play poker. He wins for awhile until they realize that he is unintentionally sending signals about his hand. In the end, Margaret, Potter, Mulcahy, Radar, Hawkeye, and B.J. take him to the cleaners.

In year seven's "Baby, It's Cold Outside," Charles has a much more comfortable time with the Korean winter than the rest of the unit. He decides to trade Margaret his gloves while staying comfortable in his goose-down jacket, a concession he regrets as he later tries to cajole her into giving them back. Another episode, "The Billfold Syndrome," finds Charles extremely upset at being turned down for chief of thoracic surgery at Massachusetts General Hospital. He takes the news so badly that he stops talking to everyone else in camp. Hawkeye and B.J., after initially showing some empathy for Charles, take his vow of silence as a challenge and fake a telegram telling Charles that he is still in the running for the post. Once Charles learns the source of the telegram, he retaliates by using a jeep to collapse the Swamp tent with Hawkeye and B.J. in it.

Charles's inability to deal with a woman doctor in "Inga" is followed two weeks later by his resentment in "The Young and the Restless" when he and the other surgeons are shown up by a young doctor who teaches them a new technique in heart surgery. Charles takes this development poorly, going out on a drinking binge.

Charles's character proves not to be as much a caricature as his predecessor, Frank Burns. He is revealed to be fallible and vulnerable in "Dr. Winchester and Mr. Hyde" when he becomes dependent on amphetamines in an attempt to keep up with his work and stave off exhaustion. In "Major Ego," Charles saves a man's life through heart massage only to see another patient have complications due to his surgical oversight. During this time, Charles is pursued by a reporter who feeds his ego. In the end, however, a chastened Charles rips up the reporter's story because he realizes his arrogance almost cost a man his life. In the 1978 Christmas episode ("Dear Sis"), Charles learns a lesson about giving. Charles is genuinely touched when Radar and Father Mulcahy arrange to have his mother send his childhood tobogganing cap. He awkwardly thanks Mulcahy for the gesture and has a happy moment recalling the fond memories associated with the cap.

The changes in Margaret's character and life and the arrival of the egotistical Charles are indicative of an inward turn for the program, and other characters are likewise presented with situations that cause them to engage in self-examination. Perhaps the best example of this is Father Mulcahy. Several episodes offer viewers insight into the camp chaplain's character. As an extra for the first few years, Mulcahy's character doesn't get much treatment. The shift in themes toward self-exploration and individual crises brings Mulcahy more fully into the program. For the most part, Mulcahy's self-examination revolves around his feelings of inadequacy and sometimes purposelessness in his duties at the 4077. Year six's "Tea and Empathy" finds Mulcahy learning through a soldier's confession that the man was trafficking in stolen medical supplies. He learns this as the unit is being victimized by a theft of penicillin. In the course of the confession, the man reveals to Mulcahy where the stolen goods are. After considering the ethical difficulties in telling Potter about the location of the goods, Mulcahy gets Klinger and they take off to retrieve the goods to save the day for the doctors and their patients. In year seven, Mulcahy's resourcefulness helps the unit obtain sodium pentothal despite Charles's interference in "Out of Gas."

Later in year seven, Mulcahy confronts the indignity of being passed over for promotion after learning a chopper pilot has been promoted twice in six months in "An Eye for a Tooth." Potter presses the case for him but to no avail. Late in the episode, Mulcahy assists the chopper pilot. The pilot is called to get a wounded soldier but lacks his balancing dummy, a counterweight he needs when he has only one wounded man to transport. Mulcahy volunteers to go on the mission to serve the function of the dummy. Upon returning, Potter greets Mulcahy, honors his courage, and tells him he will put in for a commendation.

A letter from Mulcahy to his sister ("Dear Sis") describes the unit as it approaches the holidays. His letter describes his frustration at not feeling more useful—he's asked by Radar to lend a prayer as a cow back home gives birth, he solicits contributions for the orphans' Christmas, and he prays for the dead. Then, during triage, he punches a soldier who knocks Margaret over and generally presents a difficult time. His use of violence disturbs the priest, and he resents Hawkeye's teasing. The episode closes with a Christmas party in which Hawkeye toasts Mulcahy as someone gives them strength "just by his decency."

Radar and Hawkeye are also subjects of self-exploration and discovery. Early in year six, their relationship takes a new turn in "Fallen Idol." This episode, which garnered writer and director Alan Alda an Emmy nomination for writing, concerns Radar's frustration at still feeling like a kid instead of a man. He approaches Hawkeye and tells him he has yet to "become a man." Hawkeye tells him to go to Seoul and take care of it. B.J. expresses some objection to this advice, but Radar heads for Seoul to fulfill his desire. Later, Radar arrives wounded and is placed on Hawkeye's table. Hawkeye catches the wrath of Potter and blames himself for encouraging Radar to go to Seoul.

Hawkeye drinks himself into a stupor over Radar's injury, and a hangover forces him to have another doctor cover for him in surgery when he gets sick. Potter confronts him and tells him to clean up his act and visit Radar. When he finally does visit, Radar calls him "sir" and brings up Hawkeye's sickness during surgery. Radar expresses his disappointment in Hawkeye walking out on the patient. Hawk responds with anger, telling Radar he's not there to be admired.

Having further inflamed the situation, Hawkeye takes heat from Mulcahy, Margaret, and Potter for his treatment of an injured friend. When Hawkeye comes in to apologize for his behavior, Radar tells him off. They meet at Rosie's sometime after that and slowly begin to converse. The scene ends with Hawkeye trading his beer for Radar's grape Ne-Hi. The episode closes with a rare salute from Hawkeye.

An episode from later that year finds Radar still dealing with the manhood issue. In "Images," he decides he wants to get a tattoo. B.J. and Hawkeye try to talk him out of it by getting a tattooed soldier to tell him about his bout with hepatitis and how the tattoo turns women off. Radar discovers the setup and decides to get a tattoo just to spite the doctors. When Radar returns, Potter orders him to show them the tattoo.

Year seven's "Hot Lips Is Back in Town" finds Radar falling in love. Following the advice of Hawkeye, he tries to play it cool, but he can't pull it off and has to tell the nurse his true feelings. She and Radar are the talk of the camp the next night as they dance at the officers' club.

Hawkeye's character takes some new twists and turns beyond the changes in his relationships with women. In the first episode of year seven, he is left in charge of the unit when Potter is called away for meetings in "Commander Pierce." Hawkeye starts his stint as CO rather lightheartedly but soon finds himself inundated with bureaucratic snafus and a dispute among the nurses. He really loses his cool, though, when his pal B.J. leaves the camp to get a wounded man without telling Hawkeye, who has just learned that a lot more wounded are about to arrive. When Potter returns, he tries to get the two friends to stop feuding by sharing some good whiskey he brought back from his trip.

In "C*A*V*E," Hawkeye is seen dealing with claustrophobia. The unit has bugged out to avoid a shift of the war toward their camp, and Potter decides the best spot is a cave. This decision causes Hawkeye problems as he tries to treat a patient inside the cave. His patient worsens and they decide he needs to be reopened. He and Margaret return to the camp for the operation, and he learns of her fear of loud noises as they operate amidst shelling.

Others in the cast struggle with personal issues as well. In "Potter's Retirement," Col. Potter faces anonymous charges of running a less-than-military unit from someone at the 4077 when he is called to Seoul to meet with superiors. When he returns to camp, he cracks down on the unit and gets the camp in shape for inspection, then announces his retirement. When the snitch turns out to be an informant placed in the unit by army command, Hawkeye, B.J., and Radar convince him to postpone his retirement. In "Lil," Potter finds himself attracted to the visiting Col. Lillian Rayburn, who is inspecting the nurses. Their common age leads to a couple of days of fun. Lil wants more, however, and as attracted as Potter is, he tells her he must remain true to his wife, Mildred. In "The Young and the Restless," phlebitis puts Potter off his feet and out of the OR. A visiting young doctor who substitutes for him gets rave reviews and makes Potter feel unneeded by the unit.

B.J.'s concerns about home put him into a funk in "Mail Call Three." He frets about wife Peg's problems with the household and whether she might be attracted to the man who comes to fix things. In year seven's "B.J. Papa San," he develops a relationship with a Korean family—treating a sick father, repairing their hut, and otherwise trying to right the wrongs the war has imposed on the family. He returns one day to find the family has abandoned their home, and he realizes his good works just can't make things right for the Koreans. Finally, in "The Party," B.J.'s family orientation inspires him to get the others to help organize a party for their relatives to get to know each other in New York. The others are skeptical about their families' participation, but B.J.'s insistence makes the party happen.

These kinds of episodes reveal the heart of the show's concerns for the rest of its duration. The sight of *M*A*S*H* characters coping with the world around them was something the audience could probably relate to, since the entire country seemed in one way or another to be looking inward. People's distrust of institutions like the government and big business—a large component of the years of protest—was devolving into an obsession with their own well-being, whether psychological, spiritual, or material. This shift in American society explains why the 1970s became known as the "Me Decade," a title popularized by the guru of "new" journalism, Tom Wolfe.[20] Wolfe's chronicling of the self-help movement and the religious revival sweeping the country provided the link between the secular and spiritual forms of introspection. These two developments, linked with the narcissism of the disco scene, summarize how people dealt with the shifting sands of the era. The Vietnam debacle and the corruptions of power evident through Watergate and related scandals gave people little to hope for outside their daily lives.

LOOKING OUT FOR NUMBER ONE

News stories on these trends began appearing in early 1975. California was seen as the point of origin of the self-help phenomenon. Werner Erhard's "est" movement gathered its steam there, according to a March 1975 article in *Newsweek*.[21] "Est" seminars would soon spread beyond the West Coast so that by mid–1976 more than 83,000 people in twelve cities had taken the $250 two-weekend experience.[22] Erhard and his seminars would attract a lot of attention from the psychology community, not all of whose members were enthralled with est, since many became convinced that its biggest accomplishment was the enrichment of Erhard. The est method drew upon many strains of classic and modern introspective techniques including Zen Buddhism, meditation, Gestalt psychology and transactional analysis, to name a few.

Erhard himself was a controversial personality. Almost a cult figure among his adherents, and especially those who worked for him, he rose out of nowhere. He decided to take his new name, discarding his former (Jack Rosenberg) along with his wife and four children when he moved to the West from Philadelphia in 1960. He was a trainer for Mind Dynamics, a firm that trained businessmen in "humane managerial techniques" until pursued by the state of California for making fraudulent claims.[23] His success with est had certainly left him with a comfortable lifestyle at age 40—a $100,000 house, a corporate plane, and a Mercedes.

As word of the seminars and Erhard spread, a number of writers took the est seminar and reported on it. Their reports varied, some saw value in the experience, while others decided it was absurd to pay money to be verbally abused and humiliated.[24] The seminars involved physical deprivation—food and bathroom privileges were scarce, verbal haranguing and a series of "processes" were designed to help students to "get it." Those who didn't feel they got it were told there was nothing to get. Participants who found the experience a positive one told of their willingness to let go of things they could not control. Yet at the same time, the oft-repeated phrase "I am the cause of my world" seemed to endow them with a desire to act on the world. Platitudes such as "What you do has no effect on anything else" and "Choose to let the world be and it won't bother you anymore" apparently served as guideposts for seminar graduates. Eventually, Erhard would create a spinoff project, the Hunger Project, based on the idea that as people take responsibility for themselves, they will eventually take responsibility for the world. About $700,000 in donations to the project was collected by August 1978, but none of it went toward feeding hungry people.[25]

Some saw these seminars as helpful for people who were unsure of themselves. Others maintained that if seminar graduates said they had been transformed, then the seminars must be doing some good. A *Newsweek* article noted that a recent psychiatric study had documented psychological harm to at least five graduates who were mentally stable before the experience. One graduate went home and tried to breathe underwater; another became so paranoid that he carried a bow and arrow and a handgun with him. Many analysts gave scorching reviews to what was variously called the "self-help" or "human potential" movement.[26] A lengthy analysis by Peter Marin in the October 1975 issue of *Harper's* castigated est and related experiences and called the whole self-help movement the "new narcissism."[27] Calling these developments a form of spiritual tyranny (others used the term "spiritual fascism"), Marin said the self-help movement was a "deification of the isolated self." It was a way of rationalizing selfishness and moral blindness that encouraged a survivalist mentality. Marin ridiculed the efforts to reduce the dynamics of the social world to individual pursuit. Such efforts, she said, deny the complexities that people face and encourage the denial of history and the larger social world's influence on behavior and values.

Est was just one of a series of self-help techniques that garnered attention in the mid- to late 1970s. A cover story in *Newsweek* detailed many of these developments,[28] which collectively the magazine termed the "consciousness revolution." The article described most of these techniques as amalgams of Western psychotherapy and Eastern spirituality. Some efforts were seen as earnest and in many cases helpful, while others were viewed as a fast way for their leaders to make money—snake oil for the mind. The development of such techniques as psychosynthesis, biofeedback, Arica, and Silva Mind Control was rooted in post–World War II psychology through such theorists and practitioners as Carl Rogers, Gestalt therapist Fritz Perls, and Abraham Maslow. A new entity, the Association for Humanistic Psychology, was created to facilitate the exchange of ideas in this area.

The new narcissism could also be seen in the rise of "assertiveness training," whose goal was to teach people how to achieve what they wanted to in work and life situations.[29] Two books by Robert J. Ringer encouraged people to realize that looking out for themselves was the way to happiness. Ringer's *Winning Through Intimidation* had sold 1.7 million copies since its 1973 release. In 1977, he followed that up with *Looking Out for #1*, which sold 200,000 copies in one month. Ringer's books were a paean to Machiavellianism, which held not only that you should buy friends, but that doing so was really the only way to make friends.[30]

The self-help craze, like the spiritual "revival" and the disco scene described below, was primarily a white, middle-class phenomenon. After all, self-help seminars were expensive, and many people just couldn't afford enlightenment. But by and large, these developments took place when middle America, shaken by a military loss in Vietnam and a political system bound up in its own corruption, was suddenly absent the certainties that life had appeared to offer in the 1950s and early 1960s. Given the widespread frustration with crumbling institutions and the inadequacy of social protest at creating social change, it was inevitable that many Americans would conclude that they were forced to make sense of the world on their own. While many turned to psychology and self-help, others searched for spiritual satisfaction.

The revival of religion in the mid–1970s was seen by some as part of a larger swing toward a more conservative orientation for many Americans. The involvement of clergy in the civil rights and antiwar struggles of the 1960s had brought a more activist orientation to spiritual faith. The societal trend toward introspection shifted this activism inward, emphasizing a fundamentalist orientation to the Bible and individual transformation and morality. While this shift originated largely in the evangelical Protestant churches, other Protestants as well as the Catholic and Jewish faiths experienced the phenomenon.[31] Some of the faithful were called "Jesus people" or "Jesus freaks," and many were taking a cue from the rock festivals of the Woodstock era to recreate traveling revivals of earlier days. Young people were targeted for conversion, while prominent celebrities, from Watergate convict Charles Colson to former Black Panther Eldridge Cleaver to Senator Mark Hatfield of Oregon, were declaring their allegiance to Christ. Seen as a "back to basics" approach, the revivalist movement was less institutional than some of the mainstream religions and more aggressive at trying to win converts. The success of the revivalist approach was reflected by which denominations were experiencing growth in attendance. Large mainstream bodies such as the Episcopalians and United Methodists showed little growth, while more conservative large churches such as the Catholics and Southern Baptists had modest gains. The churches with the greatest rise in membership—Seventh Day Adventists, Assemblies of God and the Mormons—were the most conservative and tended to emphasize individual piety and salvation. Also emerging during this period was a new church headed by the Rev. Sun Myung Moon, whose followers functioned more as a cult, with a belief in the divinity of their leader. Moon arranged marriages among his faithful and demanded total submission to his will and world view.

In a Gallup poll in the fall of 1976, one-third of Americans said they had had a "born again" experience. Forty percent of those responding indicated they believed the Bible was to be taken literally. The results, combined with then candidate Jimmy Carter's own professed beliefs, prompted Gallup to declare 1976 the "Year of the Evangelical."[32]

These developments began to take on increasingly political overtones and implications. Carter's campaign victory prompted many to wonder if his professed religious beliefs were a factor in his election. *Newsweek* speculated that even if Carter benefited from the support of devout Christian voters, the Democratic party could not draw comfort from the fact, given evangelicals' largely conservative orientation.[33] "Evangelical" was what most born-again Christians called themselves, yet such an umbrella term tended to conceal differences among various groups over such issues as the infallibility of the Bible and the prescription for a truly Christian life.

Religious-based political activism began to rise in 1977 with Anita Bryant's crusade in South Florida to repeal a Dade County ordinance forbidding discrimination based on sexual preference. The effort gained nationwide attention and support for both sides of the issue.[34] Bryant would eventually prevail, and this religious movement would find a home in right-wing political circles. A *Time* cover story portended this development in December 1977.[35] The story detailed some of the trends giving prominence to the movement—ambitious plans by the Campus Crusade for Christ, the emergence of 2,000 broadcast preachers reaching an estimated 114 million radio listeners, the rise of televangelism as Oral Roberts and Pat Robertson (the 700 Club) and Jim Bakker (the PTL Club) put money into broadcast facilities and programming. Some of the mainstream religious groups were disturbed at a blend of "show biz and salvation."

Network news programs began to take note of these trends as well. NBC reported on an increase of faith healing, particularly within the "charismatic" movement in the Catholic Church.[36] ABC ran a story on the upsurge in evangelism, pointing out that Rex Hubbard was operating an $18 million budget for his church.[37] In October 1977, NBC ran a three-part series exploring the Catholic charismatic movement, Charles Colson's conversion experience, the publishing of Christian Yellow Pages (which advertised things like "Glory to God Pest Control"), and Pat Robertson as the "Christian Johnny Carson."[38] A *CBS Evening News* report addressed the growth of religious television, citing the popularity of such preachers as Robert Schuller, Pat Robertson, and Jerry Falwell.[39] By the time the 1980 election rolled around, these developments would play a significant role in the election of Ronald Reagan and in the composition of the Senate. No longer would born-again Christians be dismissed. The drive to create a more "moral" America would become a force to be reckoned with politically.

This is not to say, however, that the entire country went searching for spiritual satisfaction in the mid- to late 1970s. There were other, more self-indulgent paths to personal satisfaction or gratification. The obsession with self would create a sea of change in how Americans amused and entertained themselves. A major indicator of this change was the emergence of a new musical form. Rock and roll's rebelliousness had typified the protest era of the 1960s, but disco music came along to challenge rock's preeminence during the "Me Decade" 1970s.

Disco first received due notice in 1975 and 1976 when *Newsweek* and *Time* begin to track the rise of nightclubs featuring disc jockeys playing music instead of live bands and the careful orchestration of music with a light show that bathed dancers in a dizzying array of lighted floors, mirror balls, and strobe lights.[40] At first, such clubs played primarily rock music, but eventually they would generate music with its own beat and pacing. A cover story in *Newsweek* celebrated the return of "good grooming and touch dancing."[41] The article estimated there were 10,000 clubs in 1976 compared to about 1,500 two years previously. New dances such as the hustle were developed, drawing upon such Latin rhythms as the mambo. The article cites the origin of the discos in the gay community, which sought places where people could let go and be themselves. Disco became popular with young adults who were searching for something beyond their daily routines. Disco was an escape from the boredom of the nine-to-five work world. The urban sound quickly moved into the suburbs, and discos became the new place for women and men to meet.

By 1977, disco was so popular that many clubs offered restricted memberships so that the serious dancers could have a regular place to go and avoid waiting in long lines to get into clubs. In larger cities, some of these clubs catered to an exclusive, affluent crowd, with some charging from $300 to $1,000 in yearly membership fees.[42] As hot as it was, the trend only grew hotter with the release of *Saturday Night Fever*, a film depicting urban youth's use of disco to escape a dreary, dead-end job world.[43] The film elevated John Travolta to superstar status, and the soundtrack was the Bee Gees' best-selling album to date.

Disco was now big business.[44] The number of discos climbed to 15,000 in 1978 and 20,000 in 1979, and the clubs were generating an estimated $4 billion in business per year. *Saturday Night Fever* expanded the popularity of the music beyond the young adult crowd the clubs had been catering to. There were disco proms, disco cruises, and disco roller rinks. Some clubs were beginning to open their doors during the day to accommodate teens and children who wanted to experience the lights and sounds. An estimated 200 radio stations had adopted a disco format. Disco had clearly made its mark on the Me Decade.

The narcissism typified by self-help psychology, religious movements focused on personal salvation, and the self-indulgent, sexually tinged disco scene marks a clear departure from the values of the 1960s protest and social change movements. After years of social turmoil, America was retreating inward as there seemed to be no reason to put one's body on the line for a cause. As the Vietnam era receded from national consciousness, the politics of the country would take some twists and turns as well, with the hawks of the war days finding new external threats with which the United States would have to contend.

THIS WAR IS ABOUT ME

M*A*S*H's drift into individualism and character studies had an influence in how the war would be treated in years six and seven. Instead of directly addressing the philosophical and political aspects of war as they had in the early years of the show, plots now focused on how individual members of the unit coped with being put in the danger of war. Critiques of a brutish, insensitive government would give way to identifying the occasional officer who pushed his men too far or put personal ambition ahead of the safety of the troops. The focus on individual militarism pushed institutional militarism well out of the picture. *M*A*S*H* would continue to remind its viewers that war is hell, but less and less would it convey the idea that war is the product of a set of forces encouraged by Machiavellian governments seeking greater and greater global power.

Nowhere is this trend so evident as in the hour-long "Fade Out, Fade In" when Father Mulcahy deals with an injured soldier who doesn't want to return to the front. It's not because he fears for his own life, but because he has killed three people and doesn't want to be forced to kill anymore. Later in the season ("The Smell of Music"), a soldier whose rifle misfired has to deal with the fact that he will have a disfigured face for the rest of his life. When Potter tries to comfort him, the man tells him he doesn't want to return home and face his girlfriend. After the man makes one suicide attempt, a nurse is told not to let him out of her sight. When a distraction in the camp diverts the nurse's attention, the man goes into the OR and tries to gas himself to death. Potter comes in and challenges the man to go through with it. The man resists Potter and looks at him like he's crazy. Potter relents, telling him, "That's more like it—now you're fighting to stay alive."

Another soldier's frustration with the war creates tension at the 4077 when the soldier takes Charles hostage in "What's Up Doc?" The man's sergeant has been killed and he is now the one supposed to lead his men into combat. He tells B.J. that he is an art history major who took ROTC—not a combat leader. Charles's attempt to mollify the man with Harvard-Yale talk only results in his being taken hostage. Klinger, seeing another chance to get out, eventually takes Charles's place. The man, however, is too weak to endure the wait and passes out as Klinger tries to take him to the chopper that is supposed to begin the trek home.

A psychological crisis for a medic brings Sidney Freedman to the 4077 in year seven's "The Billfold Syndrome." Hawkeye gets on a bus full of wounded to do triage and discovers that the usually competent medic Jerry Nielsen is disoriented—he doesn't recognize the familiar faces of the 4077. Freedman examines Jerry and determines that something has happened that Jerry has repressed. With B.J. and Hawkeye's help, Freedman hypnotizes Jerry and simulates a battle scene. The effort reveals that Jerry's kid brother has been killed and Jerry, whose mother told him to look out for his brother, is filled with guilt. When Jerry comes out of hypnosis, he breaks down—a first step in his recovery.

Year seven's second episode, "Peace on Us," finds Hawkeye frustrated at being told the number of points needed for rotation has been increased. He decides to take the peace talks into his own hands and travels to Panmunjon after learning that the talks have failed. He gets into the negotiating room by pretending to be the general's physician. He gives a speech to both sides, who sit there stunned at his audacity. When he gets back to the 4077, the unit throws a party for him. At the end of the episode, a hungover unit scrambles when the PA announces the arrival of more wounded. It's a depressing reminder that the war will go on.

In a later episode called "Dear Comrade," Hawkeye wins a jeep in a poker game. Looking forward to a big date, he procures the jeep, only to discover an artillery weapon is hitched to it. When Potter orders the gun out of camp, Hawkeye decides to disarm it by filling the barrel with cement.

Hawkeye's antiwar sentiments create a rift with B.J. when he decides to keep a too-eager officer out of action for a little longer in "Preventative Medicine." Hawkeye discovers by talking to some of the wounded that their commander, Colonel Lacy, has little regard for his men when it comes to taking a hill from the North Koreans. Even Margaret, initially impressed by Lacy's machismo, is appalled when the colonel tells her the offensive will result in a 20 to 30 percent casualty rate. When Lacy announces that he will trick his commanders into thinking the North Koreans have initiated the battle, Hawkeye spikes his drink to give him a severe stomachache. He then diagnoses Lacy's "bad" appendix. As Hawkeye preps Lacy for surgery, B.J. confronts him on the ethics of operating on a healthy man. Hawkeye does the deed and is comforted to think that the man won't be sending them casualties for a while. When he returns to the Swamp, B.J. tells him Radar has just announced more wounded are arriving. A chastened Hawkeye reluctantly heads for the OR.

These episodes typify how the show's orientation to war changes in the post–Vietnam 1970s. Reducing the war's impact to the role it plays in disrupting individuals' lives dampens the spirit of antimilitarism found in the early episodes. And while Hawkeye spent his early years challenging the military and political institutions that were prosecuting the war, now he is making one-man statements about war. Such one-man protests make him an admirable character, but his moves are shown to have no lasting impact. He is no longer taking on militarism as a whole; instead, he deals with the individual militarists who cross his path. Keeping a colonel from the front for a little while, temporarily disrupting the peace talks, and trying to keep a young Korean from being drafted ("The Price") are not actions that challenge the political ideology underlying the American presence in Korea. This "Me Decade" approach to antiwar statements would become the show's primary method for addressing war in general. Even the OR sessions so frequent in the early years would decline in number now that Americans who had once watched bloody battles on their nightly news no longer had a war on their minds. Making strong antiwar statements had given way to pulling at the heartstrings of viewers.

Two episodes in year seven epitomize *M*A*S*H*'s revised approach. Reprising the format of Larry Gelbart's final year four episode, "The Interview," Korean War–era journalist Clete Roberts returns in the hour-long "Our Finest Hour." Most of this episode, which combines interview segments with footage from previous episodes, focuses on how individual members of the 4077 cope with the war and misery around them. The mix of the serious elements with some of the memorable physical comedy of the show also includes newsreel footage from the early 1950s. The personality profiles of each character in the ensemble bring back scenes from the era of Henry Blake and Frank Burns. Mostly, the interview captures how the characters are surviving the war. The antiwar highlight of the episode is a brief soliloquy by Hawkeye that was not aired in any previous episode (although it may have been edited from a previous episode). The speech reflects Hawkeye's view of the American intervention in Korea and is perhaps his strongest statement against the superpowers' imperialist attitude which rationalized war: "I just don't know why they are shooting at us. All we want is to bring them democracy and white bread. Transplant the American Dream—freedom, achievement, hyperacidity, flatulence, technology, tension. The inalienable right to an early coronary sitting at your desk while plotting to stab your boss in the back. That's entertainment!"

"Point of View" is a critically acclaimed episode filmed from the perspective of a soldier from the time he arrives at the 4077 on a chopper until he leaves it to return home. Private Rich meets everyone in the ensemble—Klinger in his nurse's uniform, the efficient Radar, a comforting Margaret, a joking Hawkeye, and a troubled Potter. The episode won a Writers Guild Award and an Emmy for writing (Ken Levine and David Isaacs) and a Directors Guild Award and an Emmy for directing (Charles S. Dubin).

The show would continue to branch out creatively in later years but would never revisit the satirical, antiwar attitude of the early seasons. By their own admission, program leaders like Burt Metcalfe and Alan Alda took the show more and more into poignant storytelling that stressed personal relationships. In year seven, they made a conscious attempt to do more episodes outside the camp and make the show more visually interesting—for example, using a bugout to relocate in a cave, or doing a whole episode in Rosie's bar. Radar's departure was planned for the end of year seven but was postponed so it could be a two-part episode in year eight. Many in the cast continued to get involved in writing and producing; Mike Farrell and Harry Morgan would join Alan Alda in those tasks. The show would continue to garner yearly nominations— Burt Metcalfe for producing, Alda for outstanding lead actor, Harry Morgan and Gary Burghoff for supporting actor, and Loretta Swit for supporting actress. Alda received a People's Choice Award for favorite male television performer, and the program won the People's Choice for favorite comedy. Clearly the show had developed a loyal audience as it remained in the Top Ten for both years.

A SHIFT TO THE RIGHT?

All this occurred throughout years of change in the political world. Politics were taking a distinct turn away from the trends of the late 1960s and early 1970s. In the post–Watergate, Jimmy Carter years, America's world role would continue to be debated. The further the war years ebbed from memory, the more the spirit of those years gave way to media and political perspectives trumpeting a return to conservative policies. Such proclamations would begin with the emergence of Ronald Reagan to challenge President Gerald Ford for the 1976 Republican nomination.[45] Conservatives upset with the rather moderate Ford were pushing for a challenge. Other conservatives were talking about a third-party effort.[46] While Ford staved off Reagan's challenge in the 1976 primaries, the election of Jimmy Carter ignited greater passion among conservatives in the late 1970s for electing Reagan in 1980. Conservatives objected to much of Carter's foreign policy, from the Panama Canal treaties in 1977 and 1978 to his human rights focus in foreign policy matters.[47] Conservatives claimed that Carter had diminished the role and power of the United States in the world. The events of the Carter presidency, especially the taking of United States hostages in Iran, would make a repackaged Reagan, once defined as too conservative, ready to challenge Carter in 1980.

Attempts to discern the ideological direction of the country persisted until Reagan's election to the presidency in 1980. The precise meaning of such labels as "liberal" and "conservative" was widely debated in the late 1970s.[48] The tax revolt of 1978, beginning with the passage of Proposition 78 in California, was cited by columnists and pundits as a sign of the country's move from the liberal antiwar years toward a model of government that had less and did less.[49] As the popularity of citizen initiatives to cut taxes spread from California to states like Ohio and New Jersey, the notion that the country as a whole was turning to a conservative outlook was debated in the nation's media. A cover story in *Newsweek* pointed to a series of developments that seemed to indicate a growing conservative mood. Restoration of the death penalty, mandatory recitation of the pledge of allegiance in schools, and opposition to the ERA were seen as markers of a growing trend.[50]

Yet public opinion showed the situation was more complex than many opportunistic conservatives claimed. While more people were describing themselves as conservative,[51] some observers saw not so much a conservative mood as a public that was less interested in helping others, given their own uncertain status. Polls showed that economic worries were the motivation behind much of the tax-cutting mood. Inflation, the high cost of living, and unemployment were genuine worries of the mid- to late 1970s. The same polls showed that people were supportive of federal spending on education, health, public housing, law enforcement, and aid to the poor, with far less support for defense and foreign aid—hardly the kind of policies being advocated by the "new" right.[52] Public sentiment seemed to indicate that many people wanted to shift the costs of government toward the rich, with a corresponding emphasis on government spending for the benefit of the working and middle classes. Even conservative pundits such as James J. Kilpatrick noted that the public was more contradictory in its political mood than the alleged "rising conservative tide" suggested.[53] What was evident was that conservatives were becoming more effective at fundraising and making their perspective prominent in the media.[54] The primary obstacle some conservative politicians encountered was reconciling traditional economic conservatism (favoring lower taxes and government efficiency) with the social conservatism (opposing abortion and the ERA, favoring moralistic groups such as the Moral Majority) of the emerging new right. Bringing together these divergent blocks of interest would prove perplexing as the prodigious fundraising and extensive media coverage did not really translate into success at the polls.[55] The ideological rigidity of many new-righters turned off more moderate voters, and insurgent conservatives found incumbents hard to defeat. An emphasis on open seats in the 1978 midterm elections brought greater success for the new right and set the stage for the election of Ronald Reagan, complete with long coattails, in 1980.[56]

Probably the greatest impact the higher profile conservatives were achieving was in the area of foreign policy. The Carter presidency was attacked for many of its foreign policy initiatives. The Panama Canal treaties negotiated by Carter faced a lot of opposition before finally being approved. Carter's declared emphasis on human rights considerations in the formulation of foreign policy also ran into domestic opposition; moreover, it presented practical difficulties as longtime United States allies who abused their citizens' human rights were challenged at home by rising discontent and insurgencies.[57]

One such ally was Shah Reza Pahlavi of Iran, who faced challenges from Islamic fundamentalists for his brutal rule and repression. From the United States perspective, the shah was a front-line defender against whatever designs the Soviets might have on the oil-rich Persian Gulf and Middle East. The shah's family had been restored to the throne in 1953 through a CIA coup of the democratically elected Mossadegh government, which had made the mistake of trying to nationalize its oil industry, then in the hand of British and United States petroleum interests. A visit by the shah to the United States in 1977 provoked protests by Iranian students at the White House. The protests had to be quelled with tear gas, which drifted onto the White House lawn where the shah was being ceremonially welcomed. The students were especially interested in pointing out the shah's use of the SAVAK, the secret police in Iran, who were torturing and holding 25,000 to 100,000 political prisoners.

The Carter administration faced another problem in Nicaragua, where the Somoza family owed its long reign primarily to United States backing for nearly 50 years. The latest Somoza to rule Nicaragua, Anastasio, ruled harshly as he used his United States trained and funded National Guard to repress his opposition. A civil war that had been brewing since 1972, when citizens saw Somoza pocketing the disaster relief provided to the country after a disastrous earthquake, was now moving into high gear. A daring takeover of the legislature by the Sandinista Front for National Liberation in August 1978 was the boldest effort the rebels had yet launched to challenge the regime, and such efforts would continue into 1979.

These developments fueled foreign policy conservatives' claims that Carter was weak in dealing with the world and was diminishing United States power and influence. This alleged weakness would eventually become known as the Vietnam Syndrome, which might be generally described as a reluctance to project United States power in the wake of a defeat at the hands of a small country. Writing in *Harper's,* conservative Norman Podhoretz decried what he called the culture of appeasement, which he said was a product of the Vietnam era's demonizing of the United States role in the world. Podhoretz maintained that the cynicism emerging from the Indochina experience had created attitudes of pacifism and anti–Americanism (among Americans themselves) that were undermining the need to spend more to meet the "Soviet threat." He maintained the USSR was increasing its military prowess to the point where it was a threat to United States domination. Podhoretz opposed Carter's human rights policy for failing to make distinctions between allies and enemies. He said the Soviets could take comfort in the fact that their human rights situation had now become part of a policy that was creating unease for repressive United States allies.[58]

Podhoretz was hardly alone in this outlook. Indeed, the claim of United States weakness in comparison to Soviet military prowess had become a conservative mantra shortly after the United States left Vietnam in 1975.[59] Jimmy Carter's term in office brought on a rising tide of prominent voices who criticized what they saw as a diminishing of United States power in the face of

greater Soviet military and nuclear abilities. A series of reports in news week-
lies began to compare United States and Soviet military capacities. A special
section in *U.S. News and World Report* presented a graph showing the United
States military was lagging behind the Soviets in such areas as ballistic missiles, naval ships, tanks, and artillery weapons. The same graph, however,
showed the United States ahead by a three-to-one margin in warheads those
nuclear missiles could carry and advantages in combat aircraft and helicopters,
to say nothing of the qualitative differences between United States and Soviet
military technology. The Soviets were clearly defined as the aggressors with
their assistance in Africa to Ethiopia and Somalia, although the mainstream
media did not seem to regard United States intervention in Central America
as particularly aggressive.[60]

A cover story in *Newsweek* sang a similar chorus in June 1978.[61] Focusing on alleged Soviet and Cuban backing of rebels in Zaire, the article highlighted the rise of Zbigniew Brzezinski within the Carter White House as
someone who would bring a renewed militancy in opposing the Soviet "threat"
to the United States, whether through Third World proxy wars or in the
nuclear theater. The drumbeat would continue as hardline anti-communist
politicians and media would continue to paint pictures of a Soviet menace
going unchallenged by a globally timid United States.[62] While the Carter
administration grappled with popular revolts in Nicaragua and Iran, it also
was forced to respond to the chorus of conservative voices clamoring for a
defense buildup. However, events would overtake Carter, and Ronald Reagan's
run for the presidency in 1980 would outflank him on the right by making it
clear who would be tougher with the Soviets.

By early 1979, it would become evident that any reluctance the foreign
policy and defense establishment might have experienced in the wake of Vietnam was quickly dissipating. America the superpower would begin to flex its
muscles and learn to wage war in ways that did not cost so many American
lives. While the legacy of Vietnam would continue to mean different things
at different ends of the political spectrum, for the political and military leadership, it was eventually reduced to a public relations problem. For these people, the problem was not the heavy-handed use of American military power
or the support of regimes that abused their people. The problem was how to
foster public support—a problem they would overcome through propaganda
campaigns and scare tactics coupled with the use of proxy armies, instead of
American soldiers, to help them restore the United States to its pre–Vietnam
glory days.

CHAPTER 7

The Party's Over, and Radar Goes Home— Years 8–9, 1979–81

The end of the 1970s would bring more changes to the 4077 and to the country as a whole. Gary Burghoff, the only *M*A*S*H* actor who played in both the movie and the television series, would leave the program in the beginning of year eight. As the show continued to focus on the trials and tribulations of the cast, it would become more serious. The once partying and rebellious 4077 would gradually downplay drinking and become a straighter military outfit. Year eight would be the last year in which a full season of 25 episodes would air. The show's popularity continued as it garnered a 25 rating and fifth place overall for 1979-80 and a 25 rating, fourth-place finish for 1980-81.

America's brief Jimmy Carter era would come to a close with the election of Ronald Reagan in November 1980. This development would take the country in new directions both domestically and in the rest of the world. By now, the culture and politics of the country were a far cry from those of the early 1970s in which the show had premiered. The pendulum had unquestionably swung to the right as Reagan ushered in an era that celebrated military power, reasserted superpower authority, and continued to encourage self-interest over social responsibility.

FROM "HANGOVERS R US" TO "JUST SAY NO"

In all its iterations—novel, feature film and television series—*M*A*S*H* had always involved a lot of drinking and partying. In the early episodes of the television show, alcohol is a primary subject of humor as various characters from Henry Blake to Hawkeye Pierce are portrayed as happy drunks and party animals. Alcohol is also seen as a means to escape, if only for a little while, the cruel realities of war. In contrast, episodes from the middle years of the show begin to evince change in how alcohol and those who consume it are portrayed. In "Fallen Idol" (year six), alcohol and drugs are seen as problematic when Hawkeye blames himself for encouraging Radar to go to Seoul to "become a man." Radar's injuries in a vehicle accident on the way send Hawkeye into a tailspin of guilt and anger, provoking a drinking binge that leaves him too hungover to operate. "Fallen Idol" closes with Hawkeye trading his bottle of beer for Radar's grape Ne-Hi. In a later episode from the same year ("Tea and Empathy"), B.J. has to deal with a soldier he's treated before who has returned with another wound. B.J. learns the second injury is just an excuse to get more of the morphine to which the soldier became addicted after his first injury. "Dr. Winchester and Mr. Hyde," which aired at the end of year six, shows Charles dealing with a dependency on amphetamines to help him stave off exhaustion and get through his workday.

The use of alcohol as a plot device leading to serious themes continues in the late 1970s and early 1980s episodes. For example, in "Period of Adjustment," B.J.'s desperate longing for his family back home leads to a drinking binge when Radar visits B.J.'s wife and little girl, Erin, in San Francisco on his way back to Iowa. B.J.'s binge begins when Peg writes about meeting Radar and tells him that Erin called Radar "Daddy" because he was wearing a uniform like B.J. does. The despairing surgeon teams up with Klinger, who is tired of people complaining about missing Radar and criticizing the way Klinger has handled his new job as company clerk. They manage to close Rosie's together and then break into Potter's liquor cabinet. Potter and Hawkeye find them and talk them back to a more sober view of things. The epilogue finds Hawkeye thanking Klinger for getting crucial parts to rebuild the still.

Two episodes that confront problem drinking more directly are "Bottle Fatigue" (year eight) and "Bottoms Up" (year nine). In "Bottle Fatigue," Hawkeye decides to give up drinking for a week after Igor hands him his bar tab for the previous month. Margaret and B.J. joke about it, and Charles tells him that drinking is a reaction to the war which will change once he leaves Korea, but Hawkeye issues himself a challenge to give booze up for a week. The results are mixed. Hawkeye relishes his new sober life but he drives his compatriots crazy with his self-righteousness as he criticizes their drinking. An intense episode in the OR with a wounded Chinese prisoner who has a grenade brings Hawkeye into the officers' club to join the others saying he needs a drink. Then he hears what he just said, puts the drink down, and declares he will have a drink when he wants it, not when he needs it.

"Bottoms Up" finds Margaret elated at the visit of an old childhood friend who's now a nurse about to return home. When the nurse makes several serious medical errors and is caught hiding and drinking in the supply tent, Margaret at first defends the woman. Later, the woman has delusions—seeing things on her mess tray that aren't there. The episode closes with a letter to

Margaret from the woman, who is now back in the States and receiving treatment.

Two other episodes involve alcohol in a significant if less critical way. "Old Soldiers" finds the unit worried about Potter as he takes off for Tokyo after a late-night call. When a mysterious package arrives for Potter and is followed by handwritten invitations to the 4077's main characters, Potter brings them together for a drink of brandy dating from World War I. It turns out Potter is the last surviving member of a group of four friends from that war, and he has his friends at the 4077 join him in the tontine—a bottle of brandy that the four young men pledged would be consumed by the last one alive.

In "Taking the Fifth," Hawkeye is chastened for his sexist attitudes when he literally advertises a rare bottle of wine as a premium to be given away in a date with one of the nurses. Hawkeye figures it's the surefire seducer and proceeds to promote himself as a great date with a great bottle of wine. The nurses retaliate by setting him up, then piling into the supply tent when the would-be date whistles them in as Hawkeye pours the wine.

The last two years would bring another episode involving alcohol in the plot. In "Blood and Guts" (year ten), famous journalist Clayton Kibbee visits the 4077 and makes Hawkeye jealous with his wooing of women. Kibbee's reporting proves to be embellished by his drinking, and he turns B.J. off when he takes a motorcycle B.J. has lovingly restored for a joyride while drunk. Hawk and B.J. find him injured on the side of a road and the motorcycle ruined. A chastened Kibbee reworks his stories into a more honest account after Hawkeye and B.J. put him back together.

These episodes are a far cry from the "everything goes" attitude toward alcohol seen during the early years of the show. American attitudes toward alcohol and drugs were changing, and the lowered drinking ages and more permissive attitudes of the late 1960s and early 1970s were giving way to the raising of drinking ages and to Nancy Reagan's "Just Say No" antidrug crusade.

Evidence that the lowering of drinking ages had lowered the threshold age at which teens began to use alcohol was presented in the January 1975 issue of *Parents Magazine*.[1] In a 1974 study by the National Institute on Alcohol Abuse (NIAA), said *Parents*, 14 percent of male high school seniors reported getting drunk at least once a week, and 23 percent of all students reported they got drunk at least four times a year. Researchers accounted for this rise by noting the decline in use of other drugs. Teenagers said that police and parents had a lax attitude about alcohol compared to other drug usage. On the other hand, doctors pointed out that of all addictive agents, the two most physically damaging and life threatening are alcohol and tobacco. A report in *U.S. News and World Report* noted that the increase in teenage drinking explained why young people accounted for 60 percent of traffic fatalities and why treatment programs were seeing a rise in teenage clients. The lowering of drinking ages in 1971, which followed the drafting of eighteen-year-olds for service in Vietnam and the subsequent lowering of the voting age, was identified as the primary reason for the increase, since many younger than eighteen now had access to alcohol through legal-age friends.[2]

A 1976 report estimated that nearly a quarter of all teenagers were potential addicts and problem drinkers. The report warned that the mixing of alcohol with medications could be life threatening.[3] The *NBC Nightly News* cited research projecting nearly one half million teenage alcoholics, as well as data showing that most seventh graders had tried alcohol.[4]

In related events, a debate emerged when some treatment research showed some alcoholics could successfully resume drinking in moderation. Research funded by the NIAA on 1,340 alcoholics found that 70 percent were "under control" and that a majority of them were drinking moderately eighteen months after treatment. The findings sparked controversy, and groups such as the National Council on Alcoholism and Alcoholics Anonymous criticized data that relied on the self-reports of drinkers.[5]

The media, especially television, came under fire for glorifying drinking as well. A report on the *CBS Evening News* quoted former Los Angeles Dodger Don Newcombe as saying alcohol destroyed his career. He also said television reinforces the notion that alcohol will help people and that it is a necessary and important part of life. The report also quoted a vice-president of CBS Television, who stated that he wasn't aware of any alcoholics who began to drink in response to television commercials and portrayals of alcohol consumption.[6]

Since the mid–1970s, news stories had reported that lowered drinking ages were resulting in greater numbers of teens and young adults dying in alcohol-related car accidents. Such reports continued to appear in 1977 and 1978.[7] What's more, new statistics found still heavier usage of alcohol by teenagers—the NIAA now said one-half of all high school seniors were drinking at least once a week and one-half of all teens had tried it at least once. Related figures correlated drinking with greater criminal activity and violence by young people. Minnesota was the first state to reverse the trend toward lower drinking ages, raising its minimum from eighteen to nineteen in 1976. Maine raised its drinking age from eighteen to twenty in 1977.

Network news covered Senate hearings on the NIAA report on teenage drinking in March 1977, and in December, CBS cited another NIAA study relating traffic accidents to drinking among eighteen- to twenty-year-olds.[8] By 1978, there was a solid trend in states returning to higher drinking ages.[9] From 1976 on, nine states raised their drinking ages from eighteen to nineteen, six states raised them to twenty, and seven others raised them to twenty-one. By 1983, twenty-two states had raised their drinking ages and joined twelve who already had twenty-one-year minimums.

These developments dovetail with the kinds of changes *M*A*S*H* exhibits in its portrayal of alcohol. Once a mere source of jokes and physical comedy, alcohol and drugs began to be viewed more seriously as real-world America wrestled with the negative consequences of alcohol consumption among the nation's youth. Such shifts are probably evident in most programming of that time; television storytelling has often served to raise the consciousness of the citizenry when it is generally agreed that attitudes need to be changed. The most notable thing about this aspect of *M*A*S*H* is that it reveals again how the media do not tend to lead such changes but instead reflect and work off trends occurring in larger society. It should also be noted that *M*A*S*H* is not preachy about its treatment of alcohol in the later episodes and certainly does not totally disdain its use. *M*A*S*H* successfully presents a nuanced perspective, neither underplaying nor exaggerating the fact that alcohol and drugs in general have problematic aspects. Thus *M*A*S*H* reflected the contradictions about alcohol and drugs that were manifest in American society.

RADAR AND THE 4077 FAMILY

Throughout years eight and nine, changes in *M*A*S*H* continue to reflect the "Me Decade" phenomena of the mid- to late 1970s. The show also continues its move toward a family sitcom model, with plots about members of the unit helping each other or having (familial) spats. The big event in the *M*A*S*H* family in these years is the departure of Radar O'Reilly. Originally planned for the last episode of year seven, the departure was moved to year eight so it could be given it a two-part treatment. Gary Burghoff chose to leave for fear of being typecast in "Radar" roles for the rest of his career. Radar's character didn't grow the way Margaret's or Hawkeye's did. If anything, Radar became more of a caricature over time—he actually was less of a stereotype in the early years, when he was often a part of Hawkeye's scheming and regularly pulled the wool over Henry Blake's eyes. It is implied he loses his virginity in year one's "Cease Fire"—yet this is contradicted by year six's "Fallen Idol," a perfect example of how Radar was reduced to a naive momma's boy in later seasons. Nonetheless, Radar's importance in the show was acknowledged in the use of two episodes to chronicle his departure and the kinds of changes it would cause at the 4077.

"Goodbye Radar" aired in October 1979. The episode begins with Radar on R and R and the unit coping with a generator breakdown during an OR session. Klinger and Zale try to make the generator work but to no avail, leaving the rest of the unit craving Radar's return, which is delayed. Meanwhile, as Radar waits for a flight back to Seoul, he meets a nurse who is headed home to Missouri. They discover they aren't that far from each other back in the States. Their brief encounter leads to pledges to look each other up when Radar gets home.

When he finally gets back to the 4077, he is besieged with problems. The generator still won't work, and his office has been left a shambles by his substitute, Klinger. The generator proves problematic even for Radar, who can't find a trade for a new one. Part 1 abruptly ends with Potter telling Radar his Uncle Ed has died and he must return home to his mother.

Part 2 finds Radar reminiscing about his stay at the 4077 while trying to pass on basic knowledge about clerking to Klinger. Radar's resourcefulness doesn't secure a generator, but he manages to improvise lighting when he rounds up vehicles and uses the headlights to shine into an open-air OR. This event convinces him he's indispensable to the unit and really can't leave. When Klinger finally makes a deal for a generator, he gets cheers from the rest of the unit, and Radar realizes his mother needs him more. A goodbye party for him is cut short by a deluge of wounded. A touching goodbye from Potter and a salute from Hawkeye send him on his way. The episode closes with Hawkeye finding Radar's teddy bear on his bed, which prompts him to say, "Goodbye, Radar." The script for "Goodbye Radar" won a Writers Guild Award for Ken Levine and David Isaacs.

Radar's departure creates an ongoing storyline concerning Klinger's promotion to company clerk. In "Period of Adjustment," Klinger's organizational skills come under fire as the rest of the unit places demands on the inexperienced and overwhelmed company clerk. He gets tired of hearing about how he doesn't measure up to Radar. Potter is especially upset with how Klinger is handling the paper work. It takes Father Mulcahy to point out that Radar wasn't always the model of efficiency that Potter found when he arrived at the 4077. Potter then apologizes to Klinger and tells him to make the job Max Klinger's. "Period of Adjustment" garnered a Directors Guild Award and Emmy nomination for Charles S. Dubin and a Writers Guild Award for John Rappaport and Jim Mulligan.

A later episode ("The Yalu Brick Road") finds Klinger trying to do the right thing but seeing it turn out wrong when he makes trades for turkeys. The turkeys only make the rest of the unit sick, forcing Margaret, Charles, and Father Mulcahy to care for the others. This episode won film editors Stanford Tischler and Larry Mills an ACE "Eddie" and an Emmy nomination for editing.

In year nine, Klinger's travails are further chronicled. In "Your Retention Please," Klinger gets word from Toledo that his ex-wife is marrying his best friend. This sends him into an emotional tailspin and leaves him vulnerable to a reenlistment officer (Barry Corbin) who is anxious to fill his quota. Klinger quickly comes to regret his reenlistment, and when Hawkeye fears Klinger has gone AWOL, Potter confides that he had Klinger recite the wrong oath. Klinger's fortunes take a turn for the better when he saves Charles's life in "Operation Friendship." Klinger then begins to milk Charles's appreciation for all it's worth—this after Charles had abused him during Charles's stint as temporary CO in "Tell It to the Marines." In "The Red/White Blues," Klinger is criticized for being lazy. It turns out Klinger is having an adverse reaction to the malaria preventative the unit is taking. The drug's side effects are particularly pronounced in people of African and Mediterranean heritage.

Charles's troubles are also the subject of several episodes in years eight and nine. In an early year eight episode, "Mr. and Mrs. Who," Charles returns from R and R with a severe hangover only to begin receiving mysterious telegraphs from a "Mrs. Winchester." Pictures from his trip show he had a wild time at what looks like a wedding. When his mystery wife finally visits, Charles is relieved to learn that it was all a joke. Later, in "Stars and Stripe," Charles and B.J. clash over who gets the credit for a paper they are requested to write for the American College of Surgeons. A jealous Hawkeye gets his digs into both of them until Potter reminds them the whole unit had role in the operation. They decide the byline should credit the whole 4077.

Charles's prejudices surface when he tries to prevent his sister's marriage to an Italian in "Bottle Fatigue." He is forced to retract a nasty letter to his sister after an incident in OR (a wounded Chinese prisoner wields a hand grenade) reminds him of the preciousness of life. A similar situation in year nine's "The Life You Save" finds Charles obsessed with dying after a sniper's bullet puts a hole through his stocking cap. Eventually, he goes to the front and holds the hand of a dying soldier. As he asks the man to describe what he is going through, the man gasps and dies. Charles closes the scene in tears and leaves his hat at the aid station. Finally, Charles's loyalty to others in the unit emerges when he defends Margaret from an unscrupulous colonel in "No Laughing Matter."

Other characters' trials and tribulations are examined as well. Father Mulcahy again faces the indignity of not being promoted in "Captains Outrageous." This time, his files get lost in Pentagon bureaucracy, and it takes a persistent Potter to track down the paper snafu and secure the promotion for Mulcahy. In "Blood Brothers" (year nine), Mulcahy gets a visit from a cardinal. His all-out efforts to impress the cardinal leave him embarrassed at the rest of the unit's behavior. Mulcahy learns a lesson when he hears Hawkeye tell about a patient who has leukemia. He relates the lesson in a Sunday sermon, which the cardinal attends. Mulcahy compares his concern about impressing the cardinal with the concerns of the man (Patrick Swayze) who has been told he must soon confront death but is more worried about his buddy. He breaks down as he says he's not there for a pat on the back but rather to serve God's children.

Hawkeye learns about putting egos aside to achieve common goals when Alan Alda's real-life father, Robert Alda, reprises his role as Dr. Borelli in "Lend a Hand." Hawkeye and Borelli clash but then are forced to work as a team when they injure their hands while providing help at a battalion aid station. In "Bless You, Hawkeye" (year nine), Hawkeye is bothered by sneezing fits while treating wet wounded soldiers. Sidney Freedman is brought in when he continues to get worse. Freedman determines Hawk is reacting to a repressed childhood memory that was revived by the unique smell of the wet soldier's uniform. It was the same odor he smelled when he was saved from drowning by an older cousin he looked up to. Questioning by Freedman brings out the fact that the cousin had actually pushed him into the water—a cruel joke that scarred Hawkeye emotionally.

The episodes of years eight and nine bring challenges to B.J., first when he encounters a female journalist who captures his attention in "War Co-Respondent." This episode brings journalist Aggie O'Shea (Susan St. James) to the 4077. Hawkeye fawns over the journalist, but she seems to have only eyes for B.J. However, B.J. resists her flirtations and tells her he must remain true to his wife.

B.J.'s longing for home is the subject of several episodes, such as "Period of Adjustment," in which he goes on a drinking binge after learning from wife Peg that their little girl, Erin, called Radar "Daddy" during his visit to San Francisco. Year eight's "Dreams" finds B.J. dreaming about home, where he dances with Peg before being taken away to Korea. B.J.'s domestic concerns are also examined in "No Sweat" when he worries about Peg hiring men to do jobs around the house. In "Oh, How We Danced," the unit honors his family dedication when they throw an anniversary party for him using home movies and his own words on a tape recorder to make his anniversary away from Peg a little easier. Finally, when B.J. notices a mortally wounded man has a young child, he valiantly tries to make sure the man doesn't die on Christmas in "Death Takes a Holiday." While the rest of the camp celebrates Christmas, B.J., Margaret, Hawkeye, and Father Mulcahy stay with the man and move the clock forward a half-hour when he dies at 11:30 p.m. on December 25.

The program continues to evoke feminist themes, not only through Margaret Houlihan, but through other characters as well. Margaret's brief affair with Scully is developed in year eight. Scully returns to the 4077 in "Guerrilla My Dreams" as an injured soldier to woo and charm her. A later visit in "Stars and Stripe" finds Margaret upset with Scully for being demoted from sergeant to private after he hit a superior officer. She's also offended that he has turned down promotions in the past. He dismisses her as an officer. This infuriates her, and he gets mad and walks out. Later, she tries to patch things up by putting on a fancy dress. He takes this as a concession and proceeds to talk about making her into a new woman, making it clear that he's at the front of their "chain of command." She tells him she will miss him but that being just a wife is not good enough for her. Scully leaves, to return no more.

In year nine, Charles comes to Margaret's aid after he unwittingly sets her up with the lecherous colonel who sent him to the 4077. In "No Laughing Matter," Charles desperately tries to get Col. Baldwin to take him back to Tokyo. Charles serves the boor's every whim, even to the point of getting the man a companion for the evening from Rosie's bar. When Margaret comes into the colonel's tent, he mistakes her for his "date" and tries to force himself on her. Looking to Charles to lie for him, the man accuses Margaret of improper advances and behavior. Charles, in a fit of decency, decides not to go along and defends Margaret's honor.

Other critiques of sexism in the military occur. In "Nurse Doctor," Father Mulcahy tries to help a young nurse study for medical exams. Mulcahy is horrified when the nurse mistakes his help for amorous intentions, giving him a generous hug. Margaret tries to help the woman with some of her tough love—defending the prospective doctor from jealous fellow nurses and not letting her transfer or back down from taking the exams when the nurse is upset after the incident with Mulcahy. In "Your Retention Please" (year nine), a male nurse is frustrated by the lack of respect he gets for his work and by not being promoted like other nurses. Even Charles comes around as he praises the man for his work and compliments him on his knowledge. The unit honors the man by making him an honorary first lieutenant.

PROGRESS AND SETBACKS FOR FEMINISTS

These developments in the program reflect the real world concerns of several cast members—most notably Alan Alda and Mike Farrell—as the drive to ratify the Equal Rights Amendment continued. Alda became a very visible and outspoken advocate of women's issues, appearing at ERA rallies and otherwise using his celebrity status to promote equal opportunities for women.[10]

The political climate for women, however, was decidedly mixed, and the ERA extension ultimately failed to produce the necessary ratification. Feminists also faced the challenge of the ascendancy of the religious right as a force in the country's politics. Meanwhile, women continued to break through barriers in what were considered male domains. By the late 1970s women were serving as mayors of some of the largest cities in the country.[11] Jane Byrne was elected mayor of Chicago in April 1975, joining women like San Francisco's Dianne Feinstein (who was appointed to serve out the remainder of the term of George Moscone after he was assassinated) and Phoenix's Margaret Hance (first elected in 1975 and reelected in 1977). Raleigh, North Carolina; Oklahoma City; and San Jose also had female mayors.

President Jimmy Carter went beyond opening the doors to women when he proposed requiring women as well as men to register for the military draft in February 1980.[12] The decision was debated throughout the country and fueled the ongoing argument over whether there should be a draft at all. Polls showed the return to the draft was opposed by a majority of 18- to 24-year-olds. Most men that age felt that if there was a draft, women should be included, while most women that age were opposed. A further question concerned whether women should serve in combat. Many said that if a woman volunteered to do so, she should be allowed. The issue was a vexing one for feminists, who on the one hand understood the significance of women's draft registration as a sign of growing equality, while on the other hand they questioned the need to restore the draft. Leaders in the women's rights movement also worried about the proposal's effect on ratification of the ERA as leading ERA opponent Phyllis Schlafly described the proposal as a stab in the back of American women. Meanwhile, with women entering the military as volunteers and through enrollment at the military academies, the service branches' experience of women in the armed forces was judged quite positively on the whole. The first female graduates made up 8 percent of the graduates of West Point, Annapolis, the Air Force Academy in Colorado and the Coast Guard Academy in Connecticut. Women, however, still faced hazing problems, and they had a slightly higher dropout rate in the academies.

For all the doors the women's movement was opening, there were other, more vexing issues that were slower to change. Michelle Triola Marvin's "palimony" suit against actor Lee Marvin generated a lot of publicity in 1979. The issue under litigation was whether a woman who lives with a man without marrying him should receive alimony when the relationship ends. The judge determined that Triola Marvin was not eligible for half of Marvin's earnings during their life together, but he did grant her over $100,000 for her adjustment to living alone. Other issues being debated in courtrooms and living rooms were the notion that only men should pay alimony when marriages break up, the growing trend of "prenuptial agreements," and custody battles over the children of divorcing parents.[13]

These issues were being decided incrementally, case by case, across the country while the ERA ratification effort continued to flag. In theory, the amendment would have obviated many of the issue-by-issue fights over women's rights by providing a general mandate for equal treatment. Feminists looking to the 1980 elections were only disappointed as Ronald Reagan rode a crest of conservatism into office, a victory that ultimately sealed the amendment's fate.

With Reagan's election, the religious right became a force in American politics. Jerry Falwell's Moral Majority, founded in 1979, developed into a politically formidable organization with a reported 72,000 ministers and 4 million lay members. Falwell's use of television helped spread his message that the country was in moral decline and needed to be rescued through political action. Falwell claimed he had registered 3 million new voters from among his followers to fight the "evils" of abortion, pornography and homosexuality. Later, the Moral Majority would coalesce with other groups to endorse a broader agenda of school prayer, tax cuts, and opposition to the ERA.[14]

Throughout the 1980 campaign, the media reported a significant rise in activism on the right. A "Washington for Jesus" rally in April 1980 brought

200,000 for a "non-political" rally to purify the nation. The fall campaign brought a spate of reports to network television on the influence of religious conservatives in the presidential and congressional campaigns.[15] In September, Jerry Falwell endorsed Reagan, saying President Carter had betrayed Christianity. Fundamentalist groups were credited with helping turn out liberal senators, especially by supporting Charles Grassley in Iowa as he defeated incumbent John Culver. After the election, a group of liberals led by *All in the Family* producer Norman Lear organized People for the American Way as an antidote to the Moral Majority.

The religious right would continue to influence the nation's politics on such issues as abortion.[16] Passions on both sides of the abortion issue heated up as religious conservatives organized to try to overturn the 1973 *Roe vs. Wade* decision which had legalized a woman's right to choose abortion. The National Right to Life Committee, after six years of existence, claimed 11 million members and 1,800 chapters across the country. The Hyde amendment, named after anti-abortion congressman Henry Hyde of Illinois, continued to bar federal funds to pay for abortions except in cases of pregnancy resulting from rape or cases that placed a woman's life and health in danger.

Conservative religious groups also began to take on the media. *NBC Nightly News* reported on increasing attempts to censor materials in libraries. In April 1981, Jerry Falwell and Donald Wildmon formed the Coalition for Better Television, which sought to put pressure on advertisers sponsoring "immoral" programs. The campaign had an effect on large advertiser Procter and Gamble, which announced it would drop its sponsorship of 50 programs.[17]

These events indicate the clearest change in direction from the concerns and attitudes of the antiwar days of the early 1970s. However, the country's conservative swing was evident not just in the domestic arena. Ronald Reagan's election as president also brought changes in military and foreign policy, which would swing back to a pro-interventionist, military-oriented attitude toward the rest of the world.

REFUGEES—PRESENT AND PAST

Though fully five years had passed since the withdrawal of the American presence in Vietnam, the war's legacy continued to present the country with challenges—this time in the form of the "boat people," Vietnamese refugees who were fleeing postwar Vietnam for a better life.

As mentioned in Chapter 5, the victory by the North produced a wave of refugees in 1975. A second wave of refugees, called "boat people," began leaving Vietnam in 1977 and 1978. Leaving in small, shaky boats for dangerous open seas, they headed for such countries as the Philippines, Malaysia, and Thailand. These people hoped to escape a number of problems plaguing

Vietnam, including political repression, economic hardships, and a country-side devastated by war and no longer productive. Some estimates claimed that over one-half of those who left perished at sea.[18] Countries in Asia, saddled with their own economic difficulties, at first reluctantly created refugee camps for Vietnamese and Cambodians flocking from their homelands, but soon the stress on their own resources was too much to bear. They implored the United States, Canada, and Western Europe to resettle some refugees in their countries and began to turn back boat people who continued to land on their shores. Many of the Vietnamese refugees were ethnic Chinese who faced particularly harsh treatment in Malaysia, where hatred toward ethnic Chinese was well known. Refugees in Malaysia numbered 12,000 in July 1978. By November the number had swelled to 45,000, with a total of 80,000 refugees throughout the region. One poignant incident involved 2,500 refugees, half of them children, aboard a rusting ship named the *Hai Hong*. Malaysia refused the boat entry into its port, and no other nation in the region would permit it to land either. Many of the refugees had paid large amounts of money to board the ship (which had been scheduled to be sold for scrap), but none of those who took their money could be found. The Malays threatened to tow the ship out to sea and leave the refugees stranded there. France and the United States eventually pledged to take them into their countries.

Incidents like this one brought the problem to a head in 1979.[19] There were 250,000 in temporary camps throughout the region by May 1979, out of a total of 900,000 refugees from Indochina since 1975. About 200,000 had settled in the United States. Malaysia declared in June it would begin to forcibly remove the refugees by towing 76,000 out to sea and shooting any who tried to return. While condemning Vietnam for using the situation to rid itself of its 1.1 million ethnic Chinese, western countries continued to drag their feet in coming to the refugees' aid. The United States was taking in about 7,000 refugees per month and was considering increasing that number to 9,000. China had accepted another 230,000, and 100,000 had gone to France, Australia, West Germany, and Canada since 1975. There were about 300,000 remaining in the region, and many other countries were beginning to adopt the harsh treatment meted out by the Malaysians.

A two-day conference on Indochinese refugees sponsored by the United Nations in July 1979 brought representatives from 50 nations to Geneva, Switzerland.[20] United States vice-president Walter Mondale brought an American commitment to use naval and air operations to pick up people at sea and pledged almost $1 billion in funds for refugee relief. Other participating nations promised to take in 250,000 refugees. This conference marked the beginning of the end of at least one legacy of the war.

The treatment of Koreans in *M*A*S*H* often reflects the real-world refugees' dire situations, particularly in episodes from years eight and nine. For example, Klinger's attempt to preserve a young Korean woman's honor is misinterpreted by her mother in "Private Finance." While sitting in Rosie's one day, Klinger notices a very young woman trying to pick up some of the GIs. He tries to stop her—she's just a kid, he figures. Unfortunately for Klinger, her mother comes along during this exchange and assumes Klinger is trying to pick up her daughter. She then strikes out at Klinger with a vengeance. When Margaret and Potter approach the woman to try and convince her otherwise, they learn of her losses due to the war. When the daughter speaks up for Klinger, the woman relents. The unit decides to use the money left by a dead soldier who gained it through all kinds of illegal activities to help the woman and her family move away from the front to a safer place.

The 4077 later deals with the child of a Korean woman and an American GI in "Yessir, That's Our Baby." A baby is abandoned by its mother at the camp with a note indicating the father is American and the mother cannot adequately care for the child. Father Mulcahy remarks that the child will face much hardship because she is a mixed-race baby. Such children are treated as outcasts, sometimes killed or forced to become virtual slaves. Horrified at such a prospect for this child, Hawkeye and B.J. set out to deal with the bureaucratic red tape involved in sending the child to the States. As they proceed, they learn the United States is the only government that does not accept the children of its men. The 4077 is left with no alternative but to leave the child at a local monastery where she can be raised. As he leaves her for the monks, Hawkeye says, "You brought a little light into a dark and dismal place."

Child refugees resurface in "Old Soldiers." This time, a Red Cross representative walks the children to the camp after their village is shelled. Roughed up by war, the children are inoculated for tetanus and treated for their wounds. They also experience the warmth of the unit, who see the children's presence as a respite from the drudgery of war.

In the last episode of year nine, "The Foresight Saga," the unit gets a letter from Radar back home. The letter paints a rosy picture of his life in Iowa but is soon contradicted when they try to call Radar and talk to his mother instead. She tells them things aren't so rosy. In the meantime, the unit has been treated to some fresh vegetables supplied by a Korean boy whose mother was cared for by the 4077. It turns out he has lost track of his grandparents and lost his land. The members of the 4077 decide to send the boy and his farming skills to help Radar's family and to gain a new life in the United States.

Dealing with refugees is one way the show weaves war-related plot lines into episodes. Other war-related episodes continue to focus more on how individual members of the unit deal with the war. The most innovative episode of this type during these years is "Dreams," which was written and directed by Alan Alda and garnered an Emmy nomination for directing. The episode follows each member of the ensemble as he or she takes a break from a deluge of wounded.

During the brief respite, each has a dream. Margaret's dream finds her dressed as a bride soon overwhelmed by injured men. B.J. dreams about dancing with wife Peg. They waltz into an OR, where Potter taps him on the shoulder, and B.J. begins to operate. Col. Potter dreams about playing polo as a young boy.

Charles's dream finds him playing the role of magician and doing quite well. When Potter appears and shows him a gurney with an injured soldier, he has difficulty—he can't do his magic on the man.

Mulcahy takes a break from the action to dream about being the pope. When he opens his Bible, he finds blood dripping on it. When he looks up to see where it's coming from, he sees a GI hanging on a cross.

Klinger lies down and finds himself dreaming of Toledo, only to see Col. Potter operating on him in Tony Packo's cafe.

Hawkeye is the last to get a break. His dream finds him in a classroom where the teacher asks him how to reattach a limb. When Hawkeye says he doesn't know, the teacher asks for his arm, pulls it off, then asks for his other arm. Hawkeye then finds himself floating in a boat surrounded by all kinds of detached limbs and is awakened by the sound of choppers.

The episode closes when the staff, sitting around a mess table, decide to avoid going to sleep as they recall their nightmares.

This episode, while artistically creative, is a perfect example of how the program deals with war in the later years. Most episodes focus on individuals' stories of coping with the horrors of war. Other episodes see the unit as a family doing good or getting through tough times together. Hawkeye is often the lead character in these episodes. For example, "Letters" finds him with the toughest letter to answer when the unit gets a bunch of letters from the fourth grade class in Crabapple Cove, Maine, his hometown. Hawkeye's letter comes from a bitter boy whose brother was injured in Korea, treated by the doctors, and sent back to the battlefield, where he was killed. Hawkeye responds that he often hates what he does, but tells the boy to "look for good wherever you can find it."

When the unit receives a shipment of a half-million tongue depressors, Hawkeye uses them to build a monument to the stupidity of war and all the injured men who have come through the 4077 in "Depressing News." An army information officer arrives to photograph and do a story on the monument, saying it would help recruitment back home. Hawkeye decides no such thing will happen and rigs the monument to be blown up as the reporter photographs it. The confused man asks Hawkeye why he blew it up. Hawkeye responds: "Senseless destruction."

Other episodes show encounters with North Koreans. The first episode of year nine ("The Best of Enemies") finds Hawkeye returning from R and R when he gets shot at and captured by a North Korean soldier. The soldier takes him to another man who is severely wounded. Hawkeye, thinking his own life is at stake, tries desperately to save the man to no avail. Hawkeye and the Korean then dig a grave for the man using their helmets. In "The Yalu Brick Road," B.J. and Hawkeye have a soldier surrender to them when they have a jeep accident on the way back to the 4077. They try to lose the man until they encounter another group of North Koreans. The first soldier then acts as if they are his prisoners. They decide the man wants to be with them, and they take him to camp.

"Guerrilla My Dreams" is a serious episode in which B.J. and Hawkeye try to keep an injured North Korean woman from a South Korean lieutenant who is known to torture and kill prisoners. She escapes from her bed to try to kill another patient, only to pass out on the floor. The 4077 staff believes she is trying to avoid the South Korean, and they try to sneak her out of camp. The woman says she would just as soon kill them for saving the lives of her enemy. A chastened staff looks on in shock as the man takes her away in a jeep.

A visiting surgeon reacts to the horrors of war in "Heal Thyself." Edward Herrman guest-stars as Captain Newsome, a replacement surgeon for Winchester and Potter, who are sick with the mumps. At first impressed with the way the man works, B.J. and Hawk hear some of his stories from working closer to the action. But Newsome becomes unhinged when the wounded begin to overwhelm him. He walks out of the OR and is found later in Potter's tent. Potter suggests they call Sidney Freedman to help the man. Freedman also comes by in "Goodbye Cruel World" to help a Chinese-American GI who is suicidal with suppressed guilt. Freedman determines he is experiencing an identity conflict—to be a good American, he has to kill Chinese; to be a good Chinese, he has to kill himself. Freedman uses hypnosis to help the man.

Other "helping" episodes build the legacy of the 4077's compassion and care for wounded. "Life Time," co-written by Alan Alda and Walter Dishell (the medical adviser for the show), involves a patient whose aorta is lacerated. Temporarily cutting off the blood supply to the spine, the staff must work quickly to prevent paralysis. The episode proceeds in real time with a clock superimposed in the corner of the screen for viewers. Waiting for the graft donor to die takes up precious time, and B.J. incurs the wrath of a man whose dying friend will ultimately provide the graft.

Charles comes to realize he can't save a soldier's most precious skill in "Morale Victory." Charles is pleased that his work saved a man's legs, until he learns from the bitter man that he'd rather have lost his legs to save his hand— he's a budding virtuoso pianist. Charles encourages the man to look for other ways to use his skill—writing, teaching, and conducting.

Potter's statement about the Korean war being different from other wars he's been in prompts Mulcahy to compose a song in "Dear Uncle Abdul." During an OR session, Potter says the reasons for the war aren't clear, and Mulcahy agrees there's no unity of purpose, no slogans to rally around.

Mulcahy makes several attempts before settling on a song that concludes "Perhaps at last we've asked ourselves what we should have asked before, with the pain and death this madness brings what were we singing for." To which Hawkeye replies, "Amen."

The lack of movement toward peace is touched on in "A War for All Seasons," which follows the 4077 over a year's time. Two consecutive New Year's Eve parties find Potter toasting the hope that they might go home in the next year.

Finally, the 4077 staff comes to Margaret's rescue in "Are You Now, Margaret." This episode finds Margaret being investigated by a congressman's aide. The McCarthy witch-hunt for communists has reached the 4077, and the investigator wants Margaret to admit she dated a "known communist." Hawkeye and B.J. set the aide up by getting him to try to seduce Margaret. They find a way to blackmail him and he backs off his investigation.

The treatment of war in these years clearly lacks the spirit of antimilitarism that characterizes the early episodes of the show. By emphasizing how various members of the main cast and guest characters cope with being stuck in an ugly war, the show continues to focus on individuals during a time when the "Me Decade" was in full swing. Supervising producer John Rappaport acknowledges that the method used to develop storylines was to begin with the personalities of the characters, then imagine how they might react to various situations.[21]

An actors' strike after year eight pushed scripts for year nine into a tenth year. Would *M*A*S*H* go on forever following the changes and personal crises confronting cast members? About this time, a decision was developing to bring the show to a close, but given the high ratings and the accolades from the television industry, it was not time to kill the goose that had laid so many golden eggs.

The show's creative team continued to turn out artistically compelling stories that helped maintain the show's popularity. *M*A*S*H* continued to receive awards for those in front of and behind the camera. Among a host of nominations, Alan Alda, Harry Morgan, and Loretta Swit garnered Emmys for year eight, while Alda won the People's Choice Award for Favorite Television Performer and for All Around Male Entertainer. The show also won the People's Choice Award for Favorite Television Comedy Program. In year nine, Alda would win an Emmy for Outstanding Lead Actor in a Comedy and the People's Choice Award for Favorite Male Television Performer and Loretta Swit would win an Emmy for Best Supporting Actress for a second year. The show would garner a People's Choice Award for Best Television Comedy Series and a Golden Globe Award for Best Television Comedy/Musical Program.

REAGAN RAISES THE FLAG

All of this occurred as the country was shifting into a much more militaristic mode. The siege mentality that swept the country during the 1979 hostage crisis in Iran, coupled with the election of Ronald Reagan, who pledged to take on the Soviets and rehabilitate the United States military, produced an effort to roll back the clock to the glory days of the post–World War II era, when the United States asserted its authority on a global scale.

The Iranian crisis was the culmination of a series of events that began with the fall of the shah of Iran, a longtime United States ally, in February 1979.[22] The arrival of the Ayatollah Khomeini as Iran's new leader ushered in a fundamentalist Islamic government. The Carter administration's decision to admit the deposed shah to the United States for cancer treatment was the last straw for Khomeini's followers, though anti–United States sentiment had long existed among Iranians because of America's support of the shah and his harsh rule. A group of students seized the United States embassy and held its occupants hostage. This situation became the backdrop for the 1980 presidential campaign. Though America's allies were sympathetic to the hostages, generating a united economic response to Iran was problematic. The Europeans were alienated by Carter's previous foreign policy decisions and their greater dependence on Iranian oil. April saw a rescue attempt that only resulted in further embarrassment for the United States and Carter.[23] The rescue attempt was aborted when the aircraft involved broke down in a staging area in the Iranian desert. The midair collision of a plane and helicopter as the mission began to retreat resulted in the deaths of eight servicemen. The Iranians ridiculed Carter over the failure, and though he received a brief boost in the polls after the debacle, as the election approached it became clear the Carter campaign was doomed as a result of events in Iran. The Carter administration suffered a final humiliation when the release of the hostages, though negotiated by Carter's team, occurred seconds after Ronald Reagan took office.[24]

The Pentagon budget was another subject of complaint for the growing conservative voice, which claimed that the United States military machine had been weakened in the aftermath of Vietnam. Carter's declared human rights emphasis and negotiation of a Panama Canal Treaty had already made him vulnerable to criticism for allegedly reducing the image of the United States in the eyes of the world. He had responded to such charges with his support of a neutron bomb, only to be criticized by European members of NATO. Though many of the European military supported the production of the bomb, the Dutch and Germans were far more reluctant. Popular opposition throughout Europe was based on the bomb's ability to destroy human life while leaving buildings intact, as well as the fact that it would tend to close the gap between conventional battlefield weapons and nuclear war. Carter eventually pledged to delay production of the bomb on the condition that the Soviet military behavior did not violate any agreed-upon limits. This vacillation only fueled the fire and rhetoric of Carter's Cold War critics.[25]

More general criticism was directed at the military's preparedness and fueled calls for a military buildup to "catch up" with the Soviets. Critics said the all-volunteer army had failed to meet its quotas and budget austerity had brought the defense establishment to its worst situation since before World War II.[26] The Carter administration had already begun to increase military spending when the president "discovered" a Soviet brigade in Cuba in October 1979, and the Soviet invasion of Afghanistan occurred in January of 1980.[27] Carter's embargo on grain sales and boycotting of the Olympics in Moscow wouldn't win him many points for assertiveness, and the effect of the grain embargo on the nation's farmers undoubtedly lost him some votes in the farm belt of the Midwest.

As the 1980 campaign heated up, Reagan made strong pledges that he would respond to such threats and proposed massive increases in defense spending to put the United States substantially further ahead in the arms race. Once in office, Reagan would demonstrate his intentions early in his administration with the bombing of Libya,[28] a strong indication of the active militarism Reagan would pursue. Several years earlier, Libyan leader Muammar Kaddafi had made a declaration extending Libya's territorial waters in the Mediterranean beyond internationally recognized boundaries. Upon gaining office, Reagan used Libya to demonstrate his determination not to let lesser powers challenge international conventions or United States superiority. No immediate issue prompted the maneuvers in the waters off Libya, and Libyan jets had many times approached the naval flotilla only to be turned around by American aircraft. But the choice to confront eventually resulted in the downing of two Soviet-made Libyan aircraft. The action was irritating to some of the United States allies, with only Britain's Margaret Thatcher coming out in clear support of Reagan. Other European leaders and the public saw the event as indicative of Reagan's wild cowboy approach to foreign policy. His plans to upgrade the nuclear forces were similarly met with protest and skepticism in Europe.[29] It was clear Reagan's "go it alone" tendencies had put the allies on edge.

But Reagan's foreign adventures would not stop with Libya, as he followed up on campaign pledges to try to roll back the Sandinista Revolution in Nicaragua and bolster support for the right-wing regime in El Salvador. These attempts would involve shoring up and rehabilitating the Central Intelligence Agency. Roundly criticized in the mid–1970s, the CIA would be revived under a long-time advocate of covert operations, William Casey.[30] Reagan would issue guidelines fostering covert operations and allowing the CIA to become more involved in domestic situations. Though such actions met with protest from civil liberties groups and those opposed to United States intervention in Central America, Casey would lead the agency back into a Cold War mode and would revive the sponsoring of proxy armies via the formation and training of the contras in Nicaragua.

With Reagan's election, the legacy of Vietnam was fading. Reagan himself offered a revision of the Vietnam experience, calling it a "noble cause" in a speech to the Veterans of Foreign Wars during the 1980 campaign.[31] In contrast, the evocation of El Salvador as "another Vietnam" by those opposing United States intervention in Central America showed that the Americans were still fighting among themselves over the meaning of the war that had created such divisions in the country a decade earlier. The subject would continue to be hotly contested. In the meantime, *M*A*S*H*'s evolution would prompt a discussion among television and culture critics regarding the impact of *M*A*S*H* on American television.

CHAPTER 8

Goodbye, Farewell and Amen— Years 10–11, 1981–83

M*A*S*H's final two years presented viewers with further explorations of character and intrafamily relationships as it wound down toward a grand finale in February 1983. Year ten brought a slip in the ratings to a 22 share and a drop to ninth place overall for 1981-1982. The following year brought it back to third place, probably due to the large audience for the final episode. The actor's strike before year nine pushed some episodes into year ten. According to story editor Dennis Koenig, six scripts left over from year ten were to be used in year eleven as a half-year's worth of shows culminating in a two-hour movie. The network surprised the crew with an order for nine more episodes. As Koenig puts it, "When the network said they wanted nine more scripts, they could have just as well ordered nine hundred."[1]

The creative team used the extra episodes to set up and lead to events in the final movie. Burt Metcalfe returned to Korea between years nine and ten to get ideas specifically oriented toward the end of the Korean War as a way to bring authenticity to the final years. The show's approach to war by now distinctly differed from the antiwar spirit of the early years. According to Thad Mumford and Dan Wilcox, the "war is hell" themes in the show now focused on "showing people in an insane situation acting crazy to try to maintain their sanity. ... We ended up doing different stories in a sense because they weren't as strident about how awful war was although it was always the omnipresent villain."[2]

ALL FOR ONE, ONE FOR ALL

The 37 episodes that make up the final two years continue to focus on issues and crises involving individuals and the unit as a whole. In many ways, the show becomes more a soap opera than a situation comedy as the laugh track is now barely discernible in the show and in some episodes is absent altogether.

This development is nowhere more obvious than in stories dealing with Max Klinger. Just as one-time extra Father Mulcahy gradually gets more attention in the later years, so too does Radar's departure open up more possibilities for Klinger as he takes over Radar's role as company clerk. A two-part episode in year ten, "Snap Judgment/Snappier Judgment," finds Klinger in what is now a common situation for him—trying to do good and getting into trouble instead. "Judgment" begins with Hawkeye and B.J. arguing over who really deserves a Polaroid camera sent in gratitude by a father for the unit's work on his son. During a rash of thefts in camp, the camera disappears. Potter's orders to file a stolen goods report result in Klinger doing the report but inadvertently failing to send it in. Klinger goes to Rosie to recover the camera for Hawkeye and B.J. He gets a camera, only to be stopped by MPs looking for stolen goods who suspect he is the thief. An investigator arrives but feels that he's being set up because everyone in the camp is going out of the way to make Klinger look good. Just as he is seemingly convinced, Rosie comes by and reignites the investigator's suspicion.

The cunning Hawkeye and B.J. work to get Klinger cleared of charges. Meanwhile, Charles tries to serve as Klinger's lawyer, but fails miserably by making a fool of himself in the courtroom. Hawkeye and B.J. uncover an MP as the real culprit when they catch him in the act of stealing.

Klinger also plays a major role when the unit takes on a British holiday tradition in "'Twas the Day After Christmas." In this episode, the unit learns about the British tradition of switching roles on Boxing Day. When Klinger challenges Potter to switch roles with a GI for the day, Potter decides it might be a good idea for officers to learn more about the work the enlisted do and vice versa. Hawkeye becomes an orderly while Margaret and B.J. have KP duty and Charles is serving as the cook's aide. Klinger and Potter switch their roles of clerk and commander. Potter proves to be a less-than-competent clerk and Klinger is confronted with an important decision when a patient needs to be transferred. Klinger turns to Potter to come up with a solution. The episode ends with each member of the unit more appreciative of what others do.

Klinger and Margaret, who have always had a rather chilly relationship, become closer in "The Birthday Girls." This episode finds Margaret trying to get to Tokyo for her birthday. When she recruits Klinger to take her to Kimpo air base, she gets on his case when he delays. A "shortcut" turns out to be a bad decision, resulting in jeep trouble. A very upset Margaret blames Klinger for the breakdown and shuns him as they settle down for the night. Klinger tries to soften her frustration when he offers her a muffin with a candle and tells her he knows deep down there's a good person beneath her tough exterior.

A more serious episode concerns Klinger's delusions when he has a high fever from a kidney infection in "Follies of the Living/Concerns of the Dead."

As wounded are brought in, Klinger passes out near the spot where a dead soldier named Westin is placed. While Father Mulcahy gives Westin last rites, the delirious Klinger sees the man get up and try to talk to Father Mulcahy. Westin turns to Klinger and tells him he doesn't feel dead and doesn't want to die. Much of the episode follows Westin as he gradually convinces himself he is dead. All of this is taken in by Klinger during his high fever. The episode closes with Westin walking down a road that many other men are walking in the same direction. As the soldier becomes convinced he is dead, Klinger comes out of his fever and asks everyone about Westin.

Later in year eleven, Klinger's penchant for coming up with get-rich schemes has him seeking Charles as an investor in "Who Knew?" He tries to convince Charles a toy he has invented will pay off, but Charles scoffs at both his inventions: a hula hoop and a Frisbee.

The most interesting twist in Klinger's army days occurs in "Promotion Commotion." This episode finds B.J., Hawkeye, and Charles appointed to the camp promotion board. Rizzo, Igor, and others try to bribe the trio as a way to get promoted. Meanwhile, Klinger impresses the officers with his answers during the exam, which the others fail miserably. Klinger gets the promotion and the others don't—an odd turn of events, given that he has spent most of his days in the army trying to get out.

Klinger's promotion on the show came at a time when the Reagan White House was busy boosting the funding of the Pentagon. While Reagan urged a thrifty approach to the rest of the federal budget, promoting cuts in social spending and income tax cuts that would benefit people in higher income brackets, he boosted defense spending beyond increases proposed by Jimmy Carter's projected budgets. His five-year plan was to spend $1.7 trillion, investing in new military hardware that some said would be of questionable value.[3] All of this was part of Reagan's plan to rehabilitate the image of the military.

Thus Klinger's 180-degree turnaround, from would-be Section 8 trying to get out of the army in any way he could imagine to a straight, competent, crisply uniformed soldier provides an interesting parallel to events in the real world. Max Klinger represents a microcosmic example of how the 4077 changes over the years as well—from a group of nonconformists stuck in the army to an efficient and militarily competent medical unit which saves the lives of brave soldiers.

Episodes of the last two years also provide insight into the characters of B.J. Hunnicutt and Father Mulcahy. Throughout the series, B.J.'s role as family man gets quite a bit of attention—the soldier stuck in Korea who is missing his daughter's formative years and his happy marriage. Year ten's "Wheelers and Dealers" finds B.J. fretting about Peg taking a job to pay off a second mortgage. A poker game brings out the worst in him when he decides he will bet on just about anything in order to send enough money to have Peg quit the job. When B.J. sends the bidding way up, the others object at the transformation of what was a friendly game. This leads B.J. to a confrontation with Hawkeye and Margaret. Things come to a head when B.J. tells Margaret she doesn't know what it's like to have a child. Margaret responds that it could be a lot worse, adding, "Maybe you've got the most to lose because you've got the most."

B.J.'s concerns over his daughter also leads to a temporary spat between him and Hawkeye in "Picture This." When Hawkeye moves out of the tent to get away from B.J. and Charles, the two remaining Swampmen quickly discover their differences. Charles tires of B.J.'s baby stories, and B.J. gets saturated with Charles's classical music. In the end, the Swampmates make up by deciding to put up with each other's idiosyncrasies. Another episode that finds B.J. and Hawkeye at odds is "The Joker Is Wild." In this episode, B.J. bests Hawkeye when Hawk challenges him to try to play a practical joke on everyone in the ensemble. The episode proceeds with Charles, Potter, Father Mulcahy, Margaret, and Klinger all seemingly victimized by B.J. The next morning, Hawkeye thinks he has won the bet and strolls into the mess to collect, only to learn that B.J. has set him up for the ultimate practical joke—Hawkeye was victimized by his own paranoia as all the others were in on B.J.'s prank.

Two more serious episodes focus on B.J.'s conscientiousness as a doctor. In "Bombshells," B.J. struggles with being given a bronze star for an act he considers a failure. When he goes out fishing with a chopper pilot, they try to pick up several wounded trapped by enemy gunfire. B.J. tries to get a man to grasp a rope from the chopper, but the pilot orders B.J. to cut the rope when the chopper comes under fire. When a general presents B.J. with a medal for heroism, he rejects it, feeling no pride over abandoning the man. In the epilogue, B.J. gives his medal to a recovering soldier.

B.J. confronts the fact that doctors can't work miracles when he is forced to amputate a soldier's leg in "UN, the Night and the Music." He makes the mistake of telling a man who arrives with a wounded leg he will be OK. As the man's case grows worse, he is taken back into the OR, where his leg is amputated. This time B.J. learns a lesson in bravery and unflappability when the man reacts to losing his leg by telling B.J. not to tell his wife and makes a joke about how his wife will have no trouble keeping him at home.

In similar ways, Father Mulcahy both teaches and learns life's lessons as he closes out his days in Korea. In "Identity Crisis," he counsels a man who he discovers has taken another man's identity. The man confesses to taking a dead soldier's dog tags in the hope of getting home. Mulcahy tells the man to think of all those who will be victimized by this deception—the dead man's family, his family, and most of all himself. He brings the man the mail from the dead man's family, which convinces the man he must come clean on the dog tag switch.

In "A Holy Mess," Mulcahy peacefully ends a distraught soldier's attempts to use his Sunday service as a sanctuary from a lieutenant who wants to arrest him. Disturbed by the fact that his wife has had a baby when he's been gone over a year, the soldier asks for Mulcahy's help. Mulcahy valiantly tries to support the man's request for sanctuary but talks him into giving up his gun when the man gets desperate.

"Heroes" finds Father Mulcahy reverting to his childhood days when a boxer visits the 4077. Gentlemen Joe Cavanaugh's tour of Korea brings him to the camp, where Mulcahy fawns over his boyhood hero. The boxer dutifully humors the men in post-op while indicating he is tired of army cots and the whole tour in general. During a dinner in his honor, the boxer collapses from a stroke. Mulcahy is taken aback at the once strong athlete's misfortune and can't believe someone he thought invincible now lies near death. In a quiet moment at the unconscious boxer's bedside, Mulcahy tells the man how he inspired him in his childhood.

In "Trick or Treatment," Father Mulcahy's attempt to administer last rites to a man declared dead actually helps to save the man's life. What seems a miracle is explained by a mistaken death declaration due to a very low heartbeat.

Mulcahy also does good when he becomes the camp's representative in a footrace with the 8063 in "Run for the Money." He successfully guilt-trips a superior opponent into throwing the race to him with talk about the plight of the orphans and how the money bet on the race should go to them. To top it off, just as he gets to the finish line, he makes the rest of the 4077 donate their winnings to the orphans.

Col. Potter faces a variety of issues in the last two years, mostly concerning his surgical skills, his health, and his wife back home. A visit by a USO troupe in year ten's "That's Show Biz" brings him face to face with Brandy Doyle, an aging stripper who captured his fancy as a young man. She makes some moves on him, but he falls asleep when she gets him drunk. In "Setting Debts" (year eleven), Potter becomes convinced his wife has bought a houseboat when Hawkeye gets a letter from her and won't reveal the contents to him. He really gets himself worked up, only to learn she has paid off the mortgage. The staff helps him celebrate by burning the mortgage. In "Strange Bedfellows," the colonel worries about his daughter back home when he deals with the sexual indiscretion of his son-in-law during a visit. He inadvertently learns his son-in-law has been with another woman and is determined to tell his daughter, but a talk with Father Mulcahy convinces him otherwise. Instead, Potter shares a story of his own youthful infidelity with his son-in-law, who pledges his love for Potter's daughter.

A few episodes of the final years address issues of sexism and racism. One episode that tackles racism within the military is "The Tooth Shall Set You Free," in which the unit confronts a racist officer. Laurence Fishburne guest-stars as a black soldier who reveals his bitterness toward an officer who wants to send his black soldiers home. Hawkeye notices the officer seeks to send a lightly wounded black man home while telling a more seriously wounded white soldier he will soon be back with the unit.

When it is revealed that although the officer's unit is 11 percent black, blacks make up 46 percent of the wounded, Potter sets the officer up by portraying himself as racially intolerant only to spring another black soldier posing as a major on him. When the white officer is given a choice of facing a court-martial or resigning his commission, he realizes his time is up.

The second episode ("Give 'em Hell, Hawkeye") dealing with racism concerns a local Korean boy who comes to the 4077 speaking American slang. He identifies heavily with things American to the point that he asks the doctors to give him "American eyes" because Korean women will like him more that way. Margaret convinces him that his own good looks will do him just fine.

Sexism again rears its head when Margaret is reminded for the umpteenth time that she is truly in a "man's army" in year ten's "Follies of the Living/Concerns of the Dead" and "Sons and Bowlers." In "Follies," she learns that nurses get no respect when she suggests a solution to Klinger's sickness. While Potter, Charles, and Hawkeye debate why he is sick, she tries to suggest they work on getting his fever down first. They ignore her until Potter comes up with the same solution. Similarly, "Bowlers" finds Margaret excluded from consideration as Potter recruits bowlers for a tournament against the marines. He does come to her, however, to ask her to distract and divert the star "pro" bowler for the marines using her "seductive" powers. When Hawkeye is called away from the bowling match, Potter reluctantly lets Margaret take his place. She helps the unit win.

Hawkeye and Charles learn further lessons about dealing with women in year eleven. In "Hey, Look Me Over," Hawkeye is up to his usual antics when the nurses return after being evacuated for a few days. The men create a mess in OR. During the clean-up, Hawkeye strikes out with one nurse, but nurse Kelly makes it clear she would like to be wooed. Her hurt is all too evident when Hawkeye doesn't respond. At the officers' club later, Kelly gets the nerve to ask Hawkeye to dance, and he obliges until the music turns slower. While he buys her a drink, he ignores her when he is distracted by another, more attractive nurse. Kelly later confronts Hawkeye in the hospital during an inspection, which only upsets Margaret as their argument is heard by the inspecting nurse. Later, Hawkeye inadvertently hears Kelly as she quietly consoles a gravely wounded soldier. He remedies his earlier behavior by showing up at the nurses' tent in a tuxedo, flowers in hand, only to find Kelly has another suitor for the evening.

Charles's perspective on women undergoes a challenge when he falls for a visiting French nurse in "Foreign Affairs." Charles woos her with fine wine and talk of Paris until she tells him about living with a man several years ago.

When the woman speaks about meeting his family, Charles hesitates and avoids her. Later, he tells the woman that his family wouldn't approve of her given her past affairs and that he can't accept her "bohemian" ways.

M*A*S*H's feminist and egalitarian tendencies were indeed a reflection of the kinds of contradictions and changes women were facing in American society in the 1980s. But by the time the show went off the air, the political climate for feminism had changed. Even as the show became more feminist over the years, women's rights advocates were taking it on the chin. The ratification extension for the ERA expired in June 1982 without gaining the three remaining states necessary for ratification. While Phyllis Schlafly and her supporters celebrated the death of the amendment, the feminists tried to regroup and develop a post–ERA agenda, looking to the electoral arena to get rid of state legislators who opposed ratification in their states.[4] The National Organization for Women pledged to take on the national Republican Party directly in the 1982 congressional elections, partly by encouraging more women to run for office.

Feminist leaders were pleasantly surprised when Reagan nominated a woman to the nation's highest court in July 1981.[5] Sandra O'Connor's Supreme Court nomination proved controversial among the women's groups who had opposed the ERA. The "new right" felt betrayed by Reagan's choice as they felt he did not live up to his anti-abortion rhetoric. Conservative fundraiser Richard Viguerie and Moral Majority leader Jerry Falwell were incensed at what they saw as O'Connor's support for abortion rights measures and the ERA during her service in the Arizona state senate. When she was confirmed by the United States Senate in September 1981, Republican stalwart Barry Goldwater criticized O'Connor's conservative critics and defended his fellow Arizonan.

It was clear that the factions debating the role of women in American society would continue to press their cases. A cover story in the July 12, 1982, issue of *Time* summarized the ups and downs for women to that point.[6] The article noted a striking increase in the number of women holding office nationwide, from 5,765 in 1975 to 14,225 in 1979. On the other hand, women numbered just 19 of the 435 members of Congress, and only 2 women occupied seats in the Senate. Women were still getting paid less than men for the same work and were relegated to "pink collar" positions on the whole. Furthermore, the primary reason women were entering the workplace continued to be economic need rather than self-fulfillment. Over half of married women were now in the labor force, and mothers who worked outside the home now outnumbered those who did not. And although more women were becoming lawyers and doctors, those who had made it to middle-level management were discovering a "glass ceiling" that prevented movement into the upper echelons of the business world.

The plight of single mothers was also beginning to attract attention as sociologists came to identify the feminization of poverty, citing statistics that showed one-half of all families headed by women fell below the poverty level in 1980 and 70 percent of absent fathers were failing to provide child support. These issues would continue to confront policymakers as the 1980s marched on. Women would continue to make progress in some areas while falling back in others, providing the fuel for both sides of the gender equality debate.

BANGING THE DRUMS OF WAR

M*A*S*H's evolution in the last years of the show brings more soap opera–like themes into the way war issues are addressed in the program. Most of the episodes which deal with war-related issues continued to focus on individual cast members or others coping with the harsh realities of war.

Generally, such episodes show a member of the 4077 in a situation that causes him or her to reflect on the absurdity, danger, and futility of war. These individual experiences really don't provide any questioning of the powers that be, although in a couple of episodes the notion of trying to gain propaganda advantages is brought out, and the media are shown playing a role in banging the drums of war. "Blood and Guts" is an excellent example. This episode finds journalist Clayton Kibbee coming to the 4077 to write a series of stories on how some donated blood he brings from the United States is used to help the wounded. As it turns out, the blood is used in cases that are not even battle-related, much less examples of glory and valor. In each case, Kibbee produces a story that distorts the reality. Kibbee is brought back to reality when he is injured and has been given some of the blood intended for wounded GIs.

In "Foreign Affairs," army propagandists claim that a downed North Korean pilot has actually defected to the United States side. A public information officer arrives at the 4077 after hearing about the man and tries to give him an award for bringing Soviet jets into South Korean territory. There's just one hitch: the North Korean doesn't want to defect and insists on being treated as a prisoner of war. The information officer becomes desperate for a worthy defector and Hawkeye and B.J. find a way to satisfy him. It turns out the South Korean who translated for him is all too anxious to get to the United States and is willing to pose as the "defecting" pilot.

These episodes provide some insight into the role of propaganda in convincing citizens of a war's worthiness or success. They expose the sometimes shallow motives and the necessity to project certain appearances so that the politicians and the public "back home" can be proud of the war effort and continue to support it. Like earlier episodes involving the media, "Blood and Guts" and "Foreign Affairs" show journalists are all too willing to distort reality for their own purposes, glorifying war to increase public support, or furthering their careers with dramatic stories.

Other episodes critique field officers who are using their men to get their own glorious moment. In "Friends and Enemies," Potter finds himself in conflict over the arrival of an old friend, "Woody," who is injured in battle. B.J. and Hawkeye learn from the wounded under his command that Woody took foolish risks in leading the men. Potter, at first defensive about his friend, eventually confronts him with what he finds out about the battle and files a report to insure that he isn't allowed to the front again.

"Say No More" brings the war home in a personal way to a general. An act of heroism by a young lieutenant saves two of his mens' lives and brings his father to the 4077. As Hawkeye cares for the lieutenant, he comes to resent his father and warns the general that while his son may seem okay, there is a threat of an embolism that could take his life abruptly. The son suddenly dies, and the general shares a poignant story about his son as a little boy. Hawkeye thinks he's seeing another side of the man, but that is cut short when the general gets back on the phone with his demands for the next battle.

"Give and Take" is a perfect example of how the show deals with war in the later years. This episode puts an American GI in a hospital bed next to the North Korean he shot in battle. The GI at first takes pride in his action— he shot the man after being injured and feeling the man tug at his boots. When the Korean develops an infection from the frostbite, the man reluctantly offers his blanket. Later, the North Korean declines a candy bar from Klinger and gestures to give it to the GI who gave him the blanket. The North Korean's condition later deteriorates, and he dies. When Potter visits the GI later, the man is remorseful. Potter responds that it should be a rule of war to know who you are shooting. The man breaks down, saying he will think about it each time he puts on shoes.

Episodes dealing with individual lessons from war occur throughout the final two years. B.J. has to deal with getting a medal after leaving a man in the field in "Bombshells." Hawkeye gets upset at the slow pace of the peace talks in "Give 'em Hell, Hawkeye" and writes an angry letter to President Truman. Two Korean brothers on opposite sides of the war end up at the 4077 in "Communication Breakdown." The South Korean guard tells Hawkeye that the sick man is his brother. Hawkeye learns the family consciously split the boys into the opposing armies to insure that the one on the victorious side could help the family after the war.

The ever-present threat of death provides Hawkeye with a reason to reflect in "Where There's a Will, There's a War." In this episode, Hawkeye is sent to a battalion aid station that is without a doctor. The continuous shelling at the station and Hawkeye's discovery that the doctor he is replacing was killed inspire Hawkeye to write his will. Meanwhile the unit worries about him, and they really become concerned when they hear a doctor has died. As Hawkeye writes the will, clips of the characters he has worked with and come to love are shown. When Hawkeye is finally given permission to return to the 4077, an aide at the station asks if he finished writing his will. The man says he's seen a lot of wills written there.

The regular episodes of *M*A*S*H* conclude with a "mini" final episode ("As Time Goes By") in which the unit organizes a time capsule to leave behind. Hawkeye and Margaret tee off over the time capsule—she wants to take a serious approach, while he sees potential for humor in the effort. Eventually, they come together. Hawkeye contributes a broken fan belt from a helicopter, and then they present items for those who have passed through— Radar's teddy bear is left to symbolize all those boys who came to Korea and returned home as men, and one of Henry Blake's fishing lures represents all the men who didn't make it home. Father Mulcahy gives some boxing gloves as a way to settle all future wars. Hawkeye suggests he and Margaret should bury the hatchet.

This softening of the military's image and the reduction of war to individual experiences and tragedies were accompanied in the real world by the Reagan administration's increasing assertion of American power abroad. Reagan's revival of militarism took on many forms—boosting the defense budget, developing new weapons of mass destruction, and promoting his strident anti-communism wherever he saw interests opposed to the United States.

A November 1982 report in *Newsweek*[7] revealed covert CIA organizing and funding of a guerrilla army (which came to be known as the "contras") to take on the Sandinista government in Nicaragua. Reagan had made Nicaragua a target of his blustering throughout the 1980 presidential campaign. Now in office, Reagan wanted to make an example of Nicaragua as a country that had defied United States hegemony in Central America and now was going to pay for it. It really didn't matter that for 50 years, the United States government had backed one of the most ruthless dictators in Latin America, Anastasio Somoza. Reagan sought to "restore" democracy to a country that he said was subverting other governments in Central America. It also didn't matter that the Sandinista government was bringing land reform, literacy crusades, and health care to Nicaraguans who were treated as beasts of burden by the Somoza family. In Reagan's world of absolutes, Nicaragua was a communist threat. Furthermore, many analysts in the foreign policy apparatus worried about the example a Nicaragua independent from United States control might set for other countries in the region.

In El Salvador, the 1980 murder of four United States churchwomen and the Bishop of San Salvador at the hands of United States–backed and –trained forces did not prevent a continuation of aid to the country in its civil war with leftist rebels. Such aid ($116 million) was premised on the accusation that the Sandinistas in Nicaragua were trying to spread their revolution to neighboring countries in Central America. Such evidence proved to be spotty at best, and the 22,000–strong Salvadoran army was continually embarrassed by guerrilla forces numbering between 4,000 and 6,000.[8] Central America became a political battleground in Congress as well as a military battlefield in which thousands would die. Debates over aid to the contras and the Salvadoran government would rage throughout the early 1980s, bringing protesters to Washington to prevent what they felt might be "another Vietnam." By the mid-1980s, the Iran Contra scandal would expose the secret funding of the contra army after the cessation of overt aid by Congress. While the scandal would not bring down the Reagan presidency, his image and place in history would surely be affected by it.

Reagan's anticommunism would also focus on Europe and the Soviet Union. The Polish government's imposition of martial law and attempts to disband the independent trade union Solidarity gave Reagan the opportunity to demonstrate his resolve in taking on the Soviets, who it was feared might intervene directly. In December 1981 and January 1982, the crackdown in Poland was met with fierce United States rhetoric and an attempt to get European allies to isolate Poland and the Soviet bloc.[9] A symbolic lighting of candles during the Christmas holiday and ample coverage of the defection of the Polish ambassador to the United States typified the symbolic gestures Reagan used to defy the communist machinations in Eastern Europe. More concrete measures such as the imposition of sanctions against Poland or the Soviet Union were more difficult to pull off without significant participation by European allies, who were anxious to maintain the appearance of détente between the East and the West. There was a general refusal to cut off food aid to Poland as that would only hurt the people the West was supposedly supporting. Similarly, European interests with a contract to build a petroleum pipeline from Siberia to Western Europe prevailed over the Reagan administration, which wanted the project postponed or canceled.[10]

Reagan's buildup of the military, especially the development of new nuclear weaponry, provoked massive protests on both sides of the Atlantic and stirred passions that would revive a movement to ban all nuclear weapons.[11] Major demonstrations in Europe and the United States sought to head off a new, expensive arms race. Protesters pointed out that both superpowers already had enough nuclear weapons to destroy the world several times. Reagan's "peace through strength" ideology would negate any hopes for ratification of the SALT (Strategic Arms Limitation Talks) agreement that had been negotiated during the Carter presidency, and his drastic increases in military spending would swell the deficit he had pledged during the campaign to reduce.[12]

But perhaps the biggest event in the early years of the Reagan administration was the decision to commit troops to Lebanon in September 1982. Ostensibly undertaken to escort Palestine Liberation Organization fighters from Beirut after Israel's invasion and occupation of Lebanon, the commitment of 800 marines along with some Italian and French forces was the first major intervention of United States forces on foreign soil since the Vietnam era. Their mission was to help evacuate the PLO from Beirut and to get Israel to withdraw. (There was a somewhat familiar feel to this use of United States troops; they had also been committed in 1956 by President Eisenhower to support a then allied Lebanese government.) Subsequent to the arrival of the Marines, a Christian militia allied with the Israelis conducted a massacre of hundreds of Palestinian civilians in the Sabra and Shatila refugee camps.[13] The American public cast a wary eye on Lebanon as several of the United States troops lost their lives over the next months.

GOODBYE, FAREWELL AND AMEN

February 1983 bought the final two-and-a-half-hour episode of *M*A*S*H* to the American public. "Goodbye, Farewell and Amen" was originally scheduled as a two-hour movie, but the creative team had so much material to include that the final product was a half-hour longer. Burt Metcalfe's trip to Korea provided much of the substance. He found that many Americans stayed on after the war, so the team came up with a subplot involving one member of the 4077 who stays. The subplot about captured Chinese musicians was provided by a doctor who served in Korea. And the primary plot involving the accidental smothering of a baby was a story he heard early on in his trip, a story he was reminded of again and again as others described similar situations. The actual broadcast of the armistice announcement was recreated using the voice of the actual journalist, Robert Pierpoint. Static was added to lend authenticity.

Advertising for the final episode garnered $450,000 per 30 seconds, a higher rate than what was charged for the Super Bowl at the time. CBS grossed $13.6 million for the show and attracted an estimated audience of 125 million viewers—a 60 rating and a 77 share, which exceeded the audiences for that year's Super Bowl as well as the *Roots* miniseries.[14]

The movie begins with a long pan of an unfamiliar hospital and dialogue between Hawkeye and Sidney Freedman. Viewers soon learn that Hawkeye is under observation at a psychiatric ward on a base in Korea. Freedman is having Hawkeye repeat a story that Hawkeye has apparently told him many times. Meanwhile, there is a buzz around Korea that peace is imminent; negotiators are trying to finalize a truce.

Back at the 4077, they are beginning to anticipate the end of the war. Margaret is planning for her army career after Korea. Soon Lee, a young Korean woman who was falsely accused of being a guerrilla in "As Time Goes By," is still trying to find the parents from whom she was separated. Klinger has fallen for her and is trying to help her in her quest. Charles, returning from a trip to the "ravine latrine," encounters a group of four Chinese men carrying musical instruments. They surrender to him and follow him home.

Charles discovers his musician prisoners have a classical music repertoire, and he decides to teach them how to play Mozart.

The film bounces back and forth between the 4077 and Hawkeye and Freedman, who continue to discuss a beach party and the bus ride home. Each time, Freedman digs a little bit more out of Hawkeye. Trying to keep everyone quiet, Hawkeye gets upset with a woman and her noisy chicken.

B.J. visits Hawkeye and tries to tell him he's on his way home, but Hawkeye never lets him get that far. When B.J. mentions his daughter, Hawkeye seems to get upset and protests to B.J. about being locked up. Hawkeye resists telling the story about a noisy chicken. Eventually it is revealed that the chicken is no chicken at all—in his mind, Hawkeye has substituted the chicken for a baby in the woman's arms. Freedman presses and presses until Hawkeye remembers that the woman smothered the baby in her attempt to quiet its cries during the passing of an enemy patrol. Hawkeye breaks down when he discovers what he has been suppressing inside of himself.

Father Mulcahy suffers hearing loss when he tries to free the prisoners trapped by the shelling of the camp. Klinger travels much of Korea with Soon Lee trying to find her parents. As they search, they declare their love for each other and decide to get married. When Klinger says he wants to take her home, Soon Lee says yes, but only after she finds her parents.

The armistice is announced. Unfortunately, no one has told the field commanders that the war is over, and suddenly more wounded arrive at the 4077. Charles is taken aback when he discovers the Chinese musicians among the wounded and dead. He walks back to the Swamp, puts on a Mozart record, and as soon as he hears the first bars, he picks the record up and breaks it.

In the OR, Hawkeye faces the ultimate test as a wounded little girl is placed on his operating table. He takes a deep breath and thanks Sidney before he begins.

The final party for the 4077 consists of humorous and poignant moments as each member of the unit tells about his or her future plans. This segment really serves as a microcosm of the show—illustrating the different backgrounds of each person, expressing the affection the members of the 4077 have had for each other, hinting about where their lives will take them after the war and revealing how some of them have been changed by their experiences. Charles says that music was a refuge from the misery of war for him, but now it will serve as a reminder. Margaret tearfully thanks her nurses. Father Mulcahy says he has decided to work with the deaf. Klinger provides the biggest surprise of all—that he is staying with Soon Lee and they will be married the next day.

The wedding ceremony precedes the goodbyes among Hawkeye, B.J., Margaret, Charles, Klinger, Mulcahy, and Potter. Some are humorous, some are poignant, all are loving. Hawkeye gives a 30-second goodbye kiss to Margaret. B.J. and Hawkeye give Potter a salute as he rides out of camp on his horse, Sophie. B.J. and Hawkeye are the last, with Hawkeye telling B.J., "I'll never shake you." B.J.'s difficulty telling Hawk goodbye is solved when Hawkeye rises in a chopper to see GOODBYE spelled out with painted white rocks. And so the story ends.

The final episode was a major cultural event for the nation. Special parties and events such as *M*A*S*H* lookalike contests provided the hoopla surrounding the broadcast of the movie, and extensive press coverage reflected the kind of attention the end of this long-running show generated.[15] The large audience for the movie undoubtedly was a reflection that at some point throughout its lifetime, the show had attracted the interest of millions of Americans of all kinds of backgrounds and every political stripe.[16]

Media perspectives on the show's closing episode gave it high praise for its innovative approach and decried the fact that television had become driven by market research. Gene Reynolds is quoted in *Newsweek* as saying, "A lot of good programming is defeated that way. Audience research usually says eliminate the pain. But you have to put viewers through the pain, conflict and obstacles."[17] Lawrence O'Toole, writing in *Macleans*, compared the show to an Irish wake: "rollicking, raucous and recuperative."[18] Harry Waters's final take on the show for *Newsweek* described it as "the most original, courageous and successful enterprise in the annals of series television" and tracked the history of the show and its relevance for contemporary American society.[19] These analyses find the strength of the show in its ability to mix comedy and tragedy. It may have started cautiously as a sitcom but from the second season onward it grew into a show deserving of its reputation as unique in the history of television and, especially, situation comedy.[20]

Some commentators credited the program with altering the American psyche and raising antiwar consciousness[21] while another review applauded *M*A*S*H* for keeping up with the news and becoming bolder over time— bringing in Col. Flagg during the years of the investigations of the CIA, for example, and experimenting with new ways to tell stories.[22]

Whether these appraisals of the program reflect the audience's perspective or not, it is clear that *M*A*S*H* constitutes a cultural phenomenon. *M*A*S*H*'s relevance for the real world of the 1970s and 1980s should be viewed as a bonus achievement for a show set in the 1950s. And while "Goodbye, Farewell and Amen" truly focuses on the end of the Korean conflict for those who fought in it, this final episode also perhaps provides some insight into the America of the 1980s. The episode emphasizes how ordinary people placed in a state of war are changed by that experience. So, too, many Americans had thought that the Vietnam experience would forever change the way the United States dealt with the rest of the world. The primary plot in "Goodbye, Farewell and Amen" focuses on Hawkeye's recognition of and recovery from the trauma he suffered when he held himself responsible for the woman suffocating her crying baby. Hawkeye's denial in the early stages of the episode may be seen as a metaphor for the denial of America's role in Vietnam. In the wake of Reagan's renewed emphasis on military prowess and the "inherent goodness" of American intentions in the world, the final episode of *M*A*S*H* at least implicitly tries to remind the country there is no real glory in war. Reagan's revisionism of Vietnam as a "noble cause" can be seen as a symbol for how the country had either forgotten or chosen to deny the human destruction wrought on a people and culture in the name of anticommunism. If there were any lessons for the millions of American who watched the final episode, the warning about the consequences of denying the past was perhaps the most important.

The opening and dedication of the Vietnam Veterans Memorial in November 1982 would reopen the controversies over Vietnam.[23] The stark, low-key structure containing the names of all United States citizens who died there was criticized by some for being too morose. Opponents wanted a more traditional monument like the Iwo Jima Memorial in Arlington Cemetery. But most Americans who visited the memorial in the first year found it a fitting and proper remembrance for those Americans who perished.

But other events that occurred a little less than six months after the airing of "Goodbye, Farewell and Amen" would prove the prophetic metaphor presented in the movie. By October 1983, the United States would again involve itself in the affairs of other countries and lose American lives in the process. Though not the first casualties suffered in Beirut, the bombing of the marine barracks in Lebanon in October 1983 would leave more than 200 Americans dead and reignite the debate over why they were sent there in the first place.[24]

A few days later, the United States would invade the Caribbean island country of Grenada, which had experienced a coup. The pretense for the invasion was a "threat" to the lives of American medical students on the island.[25] Though the invasion was short-lived and for all practical purposes the 6,000 United States troops faced little opposition, the friendly fire casualties that accounted for most of the American deaths raised concerns about where Reagan was taking the country. Larger concerns were voiced by European allies and the American press corps.[26] The French called it a violation of international law, while the Germans, Italians, and others expressed opposition and concern about the precedent it would set.

The American press corps objected to being put on the sidelines, unable to get a firsthand view of the invasion. Many saw this as the implementation of a lesson the Pentagon learned in Vietnam. The notion that the press coverage in Vietnam had undermined the United States effort there was popular in military circles. The effective barring of the press in Grenada during the invasion eliminated the possibility of the media witnessing any embarrassing actions by the United States forces. Indeed, the White House had denied the invasion was going to occur at all when the White House press corps inquired in the days before the invasion was launched.

Others speculated whether the invasion of Grenada was a foretelling of United States designs on Nicaragua or was perhaps meant to have an intimidating effect on the Sandinistas. These considerations contributed to a debate over the use of force in other countries and arguments about whether Reagan had followed the letter and spirit of the post–Vietnam War Powers Act.[27] A report in the Canadian news magazine *Macleans* revealed some of the less-than-admirable actions of the United States forces in Grenada. The bombing of a hospital housing mental patients on the first day killed an estimated 47 patients. Documents purporting to identify Soviet and North Korean support for Grenada were criticized as overblown: Grenadian arms were well outdated and hardly constituted a threat to the island's neighbors.

Reagan's invasion of Grenada and use of troops in Lebanon accompanied his efforts to use the CIA to accomplish foreign policy goals. Though some reports identified the use of the Green Berets as a change from their days of CIA operations,[28] William Casey had different plans at the CIA. Many congressmen looked skeptically at Casey's work with the agency, whose budget had seen a growth rate of 17 percent annually for the three previous years.[29] When the battle over contra aid was seemingly won by its opponents, Casey used the CIA to create a separate funding source for the contras fighting the Nicaraguan government. Congress would learn that the number of covert operations conducted by the CIA would rise from two or three per year in the Carter era to twelve to fourteen with Casey at the helm for Reagan. Besides the contras, the CIA was actively supporting Islamic rebels fighting the Soviet-backed Afghanistan government. The CIA would come under scrutiny again when the Iran Contra scandal would break in 1986. These events present strong evidence that the "Vietnam Syndrome" ended around the same time *M*A*S*H* left network television for a long run in syndication that lasts to this day.

With a review of the show complete, it is now appropriate to consider the legacy of *M*A*S*H* in terms of its role in changing American television and shaping the American psyche. The next chapter considers the social change reflected in the show, and the final chapter will explore the show in the context of the values television projects.

CHAPTER 9

The Legacy
of M*A*S*H

*M*A*S*H*'s long run on American network television, its innovative mix of comic and tragic elements, and its occasional foray into politically charged issues make it a unique phenomenon of television and American history. This chapter takes a look at the legacy of *M*A*S*H*—what is the meaning of this program beyond its prime-time life? What does the program's history say about the relationship between commercial television and the politics of culture? Does television lead social trends or lag behind them? This chapter reviews the political and cultural trends in the show and in American society with the aim of assessing the relationship between media trends and the larger sociopolitical culture in which programming emerges.

SOCIAL TRENDS IN *M*A*S*H*,
SOCIAL CHANGE IN AMERICA

Over its eleven-year run, *M*A*S*H* took on many issues and went through many changes. This section reviews some of those changes and the corresponding trends in American society. Four elements are identified: the presence of sex and sexism, the use and portrayal of alcohol or drugs, the portrayal of war and militarism, and critiques of institutions and individuals.

Sex and Sexism

The early years showed the military setting to be a male-dominated world. The presence of nurses in the camp, however, made it different from typical military units of the day. Through the lead character of Hawkeye Pierce, the *M*A*S*H* audience got a world view that judged nurses almost exclusively in male terms. The preponderance of sexist humor in the early years was the primary indicator of how the world of *M*A*S*H* was defined by male sexual desire. This orientation changed throughout the life of the show as characters and situations evolved. Two characters were particularly

143

exemplary in this respect. Margaret's transformation from a sex-hungry, male-dependent vamp into a woman who had had her share of hard knocks in a male-dominated institution provided much script material. Beginning in year five, Margaret became a model of feminist evolution as she married, became alienated in that marriage and divorced, and then proceeded to define her life and relationships on her terms.

Hawkeye's changes similarly reflected an evolving male consciousness that moved toward multi-dimensional evaluations of women rather than those based on physical beauty alone. His early skirt-chasing, sexually driven character gave way to someone who was at least occasionally put in his place by intelligent, strong women. Such changes in Hawkeye were as important for men to see as Margaret's evolution was for women. Other characters also reflected an evolving feminist consciousness in *M*A*S*H*. Charles Winchester, B.J. Hunnicutt, and Sherman Potter all learned lessons about the women in their lives. Female guest stars provided challenges to men's behavior and assumptions about what women could do and how they could act in their relationships with men. In all, the trend in *M*A*S*H* was rather clear. By the time it went off the air, it had made almost a 180-degree turn in how women were considered and portrayed. Sexist humor of the early years nearly disappeared in the later years. Nurses moved from being decorative background or the object of sexist comments to asserting themselves and sometimes putting Hawkeye, Frank, and later Charles in their places.

The relationship between this trend and the events in the real world over this time is obvious. Hawkeye's changes were literally authored by Alan Alda, whose involvement in the drive for ratification of the ERA paralleled his character's changes. But interestingly, the show's rather consistent trend toward greater respect and treatment of women was not reflected in the real world. Indeed, the defeat of the ERA and the rise of conservative women's groups to reassert traditional roles for women were a part of the wave of social conservatism that Ronald Reagan rode into office. But the defeat of the ERA did not mean women would not make strides in the workplace and professional worlds. Women accomplished many "firsts"—in media, religion, academia, sports, and the military—over the lifetime of *M*A*S*H*. Many of these domains were the exclusive province of men before the women's movement.

Women's progress despite the defeat of the ERA reflects a degree of dissension in American society throughout the 1970s over the evolving roles of women. Whatever setbacks the ERA's defeat may have handed the women's movement, progress was made socially and at the individual level as women and men began to negotiate their roles in intimate and familial relationships. In this sense at least, there was no looking back, either on *M*A*S*H* or in American society.

Alcohol and Drugs

The use of alcohol on *M*A*S*H* also reflected the changing attitudes in American society in the 1970s. The first few years of the show clearly projected an "anything goes" attitude toward alcohol. Parties were a frequent occurrence in the early years, and those who did not imbibe were largely ridiculed or made to appear as spoilsports. By the middle years, drinking became more neutralized. Alcohol was still consumed, but it was more of a background activity than a constant feature of life at the 4077. In the later years of the show, several episodes critiqued the abuse of alcohol and other drugs as the regular cast and guest stars coped with their own dependencies. The later years took on not so much a puritan attitude toward alcohol as a more nuanced position. So, while the unit did not become a group of teetotalers, alcohol was not always a source of merriment in those years, and its power to take the edge off the war was questioned or treated ambivalently. Alcohol and drug addiction were shown as problematic for some characters, who were dealt with sympathetically.

This change clearly followed the pendulum of society as America moved from lowering drinking ages in the late 1960s and early 1970s to raising them just a few years later. In 1972, presidential commissions on drugs and alcohol were suggesting that another "recreational" drug, marijuana, be decriminalized because its effects were judged to be on a par with or perhaps less harmful than alcohol. By the mid–1970s, the trend started reversing. A rise in drunk-driving arrests and fatalities caused a reassessment of the drinking age. Public sentiment related to the lowering of the voting age to eighteen and the fact that eighteen-year-olds were serving in war gave way to concerns about those less than eighteen having greater access to alcohol through their older friends. By the late 1970s many states had raised minimum ages to at least nineteen and many times back to twenty-one.

The parallels in the societal trends and the trends in *M*A*S*H* provide an illustration of the iterative function of television and mass media. That is, while the media may not be the source of trends and social changes, they appropriate such trends and feed them back to society. *M*A*S*H*'s glamorization of alcohol in the first two years was a way of projecting youth and "hipness." Along with sex, alcohol and partying served a commercial function of attracting an audience. Once it secured a loyal following, the show was able to venture off into some of the more unique elements for which it became famous. The references to sex and alcohol reflected a perceived need to attract the youthful audience that advertisers were demanding.

War and Militarism

Emerging toward the end of the Vietnam War, *M*A*S*H* provided a look at how television could treat issues that went beyond the concerns of

everyday suburban America—the concerns that drove most situation comedies of the time. After a first year that was primarily comedic in focus, the
show began to effectively integrate serious themes, sometimes offering criticism of war planners and makers and the societal delusions that lead countries to war. Years two and three of *M*A*S*H* offered the most serious elements of antiwar sentiment over the life of the show. In those years, *M*A*S*H*
took on military authority in a more direct manner—friendly fire incidents,
overzealous generals and officers, and a general betrayal of humanistic principles were all exposed and critiqued in plot lines from 1972 to 1975. The role
of Hawkeye as a primary source of this critique dovetailed nicely with his
antiauthoritarian perspective. He challenged the army when it abused the very
people it was supposedly helping to liberate. The interplay between himself
and the militaristic caricature present in the character of Frank Burns provided much grist for comments about militaristic thinking as short-sighted,
bigoted, and irrational. Generals were routinely portrayed as self-serving hyp-
ocrites or fundamentally clueless bureaucrats. The military bureaucracy came
up for the harshest criticism; shortages, miscommunication, and obsession
with paperwork enabled the show to critique the irrationality and incompetence of the Pentagon and military planners in general.

Later years of the show moved from these themes to a more diffuse "war
is hell" orientation focusing on how the *M*A*S*H* staff and others coped with
the often brutal realities of war. In these years, the focus was less on the institutional shortcomings of the American military and more on how individuals put in war survive. Bureaucratic corruption and incompetence were reduced
in later episodes to individual greed, selfishness, and glory-seeking. But the
largest element serving to defuse *M*A*S*H*'s antiwar sentiment was the basic
premise of doctors and medical units being put in the middle of a no-win
proposition. In the business of putting bodies, and sometimes lives, back
together, the doctors were a direct contradiction to the function of war, which
is for one side to debilitate and defeat another side. The doctors really were
no match for the destruction, and the audience came to ally with the doctors
in this despairing situation.

The history of this period parallels the evolution in how *M*A*S*H* dealt
with war. The show clearly followed on the sentiment surrounding the Vietnam War in the early 1970s. American society had reached a consensus that
United States involvement was at best a mistake; many saw it as a fundamental wrong for a society that espoused democratic values. Thus, while the
early antiwar themes perhaps represented risk-taking for network television,
for larger society they were a reflection of what the Vietnam War had revealed
to America about itself. These provocative themes first dissipated then almost
disappeared as society moved further and further from the Vietnam War era.
The cease-fire in 1973 and final evacuation from Vietnam in April 1975 took
scenes of war off the nightly newscasts, and American consciousness about the

war faded over time. That the show garnered its highest ratings from 1973 to 1975 is an indication of how people were attracted to a program offering commentary on a society that had been deeply torn by a distant war.

The movement from a political critique of American foreign policy to a "war is hell" perspective illustrates how *M*A*S*H* retreated into safe territory in the wake of the Vietnam War's resolution. The show's more critical edge would not reemerge with the onset of the Reagan era and its reassertion of militarism in United States foreign policy. This fact further indicates that *M*A*S*H* was not as politically provocative as many have maintained.

The marked increase in military decorum over the life of the 4077 is another indicator of how the show was led by the events of the late 1970s toward a reversal of its military criticism in the context of Reagan's celebration and reassertion of military prowess. From the party-oriented, sexually active unit of the early years, the 4077 evolved into a competent and effective part of the war effort. This transformation is nowhere clearer than in the evolution of Max Klinger from a cross-dressing would-be deserter to a competent company clerk. Klinger's dress as a ploy to get out of the army gave way to other tactics he used to get himself declared crazy. But by the time Reagan came into office and more United States resources were dedicated toward military prowess, Klinger had taken on Radar's role as paper shuffler, and he even got promoted for his efforts.

Two other elements of the show deserve mention as we look at war themes. The portrayal of Koreans and the psychological trauma suffered by many soldiers on the show brought to audiences other aspects of the Vietnam experience that became social concerns throughout the 1970s. Episodes about the plight of the Koreans aired as the postwar refugee problem in Vietnam occupied the news. The army's uneasy and contradictory attitude toward Koreans was treated in many episodes in a critical way, especially when children were involved. The difficulty faced by many American GIs who married Korean women or fathered Korean-American children was dealt with sympathetically in the program. The issue of mixed-race children presented in the show was also part of the legacy of the Vietnam War. Traditional societies like Vietnam and Korea looked askance at mixed-race children. The persecution they might face became a concern both on *M*A*S*H* and in the debate over Vietnamese refugees. On *M*A*S*H*, red tape and bureaucratic indifference over mixed-race children and Korean-American marriages represented the military's unwillingness to acknowledge and deal with the effects war has on individuals and relationships.

*M*A*S*H* and, ultimately, the American public looked at these situations with sympathy. However, public opinion about other Vietnamese refugees was slow to evolve. Fears of economic burdens on the government and refugees taking jobs from Americans provoked many Americans' rejection of refugees. But the plight of the boat people in the late 1970s brought heartrending images to television screens in the United States, and though some Americans remained unsympathetic, more recognized the moral imperative involved in helping refugees.

Another product of warmaking—the effect of war on soldiers' psyches— was a fairly frequent theme in *M*A*S*H* episodes. The character of Sidney Freedman provided the intervention needed to get men back to mental health. Such themes began in the first few years and resurfaced with some regularity. Sometimes the show even dealt with the bureaucratic politics of declaring men unfit to serve, making it clear that gung-ho military authorities feared one soldier's reaction to war might lead others to plead battlefield fatigue and psychological trauma to avoid further fighting at the front.

While *M*A*S*H* dealt with men traumatized in battle, too often they were cured in a half-hour television format, while such trauma in the real world required months or years of recovery. Moreover, Vietnam veterans faced particular difficulty in readjusting to American life after their service. Coming back to a country that had grown hostile to the war itself, those men who felt their actions in Vietnam had dehumanized them found the problem compounded by a society that dehumanized, if not demonized, them as well. But the episodes of *M*A*S*H* again paralleled news reports, this time concerning the difficulties faced by many combat veterans returning from Vietnam. In the case of Vietnam veterans, drug addictions were often part of the psychological burden they acquired in the war. While plentiful heroin in Vietnam became a way to escape the pain of war, heroin was not generally a part of the Korean experience. *M*A*S*H* did offer an occasional theme on drugs involving addiction to painkillers. *M*A*S*H* probably served some function in helping Americans understand what many American soldiers had experienced in Vietnam by bringing episodes such as these to audiences.

Beyond the horrors of war, *M*A*S*H* plots addressed the role of espionage and intelligence-gathering during a time that abuses of power and authority by intelligence agencies became a concern in the real world of the 1970s. Mostly through the character of Col. Flagg, *M*A*S*H*'s pointed critique of the espionage mentality evolved around the same time the abuses of power of the FBI and the CIA in dealing with domestic dissent and geopolitical machinations were being exposed to the American people. The caricature of Flagg as a gung-ho, tough and not very intelligent intelligence officer provided a sketch of the military and Machiavellian mindset of those who enter the cloak-and-dagger world. Flagg's absurd and paranoid world view served as an updating of the McCarthy era. As 25 years' worth of CIA wrongdoing was exposed from 1974 through 1976, viewers of *M*A*S*H* saw Flagg proved wrong, ridiculed, and defied whenever he tried to intimidate various characters on the show. Flagg's over-the-top persona served as the butt of all kinds of jokes directed at the kind of hyperpatriotic, paranoid consciousness that led to abuses of authority at the FBI and CIA. The death of FBI director J. Edgar Hoover gradually opened the doors to reveal just how effectively Hoover had used his position to prevent challenges from the many administrations under which he served as FBI director. And while Flagg never tried to overthrow another government on *M*A*S*H*, his Cold War mentality certainly exemplified the above-the-law arrogance that had led the FBI to spy on American citizens involved in the civil rights and antiwar movements. So, while the American public learned about exploding cigars meant for Fidel Castro, *M*A*S*H* posited that the most gung-ho are the ones whose behavior should be monitored.

From Institutional Critique to Individual Concerns

There were also some larger, overarching trends during those years, in *M*A*S*H* and in American society. *M*A*S*H*'s evolution from its early critiques of institutional and bureaucratic behavior to its later focus on individual characters' trials and triumphs reflects a shift in the American consciousness from concern about war, nuclear brinkmanship, and human rights atrocities to an inward focus, a search for individual fulfillment or redemption.

The politically charged years of the early 1970s produced a public that was more skeptical and cynical about institutional authority and politics. As the Vietnam War wound down, Americans turned away from political and collective critique and activism against bureaucratic institutions toward a search for self-definition and a focus on relationships, families, and spirituality. Some felt their protests had been successful and thus were no longer necessary; others felt their efforts had proved futile in effecting social change. In either case, many felt a need to turn inward for answers to life's questions. This need gave rise to the self-help movement, a move toward inwardly focused religious experience, and the indulgence of the disco world, which together represented a clear break from the more collectively oriented protests of the late 1960s and early 1970s.

Similarly, while *M*A*S*H*'s first few years provided a lot of criticism of institutional heavy-handedness and gung-ho militarism, the move to the "Me Decade" both in America and on *M*A*S*H* signaled a change from outer- to inner-directed concerns. Each of the ensemble cast on *M*A*S*H* took turns learning life's lessons and experiencing individual growth. This move toward inward-looking character development and a focus on the individual reflects how the show shifted with the perceived and real changes of society.

Television and Society: The Chicken-Egg Question

The cultural debate over the meaning and effect of television programming seems to recur with each new generation. It is often assumed that television introduces negative trends and images to the social world, causing negative effects among the population. The eleven-year run of *M*A*S*H* reveals something different about the relationship between television programming and society. This analysis shows that television doesn't so much lead society into new trends or encourage negative behaviors as it reflects the tensions and contradictions existing in society at particular moments in time. That is, television tends to follow changes occurring in society and to offer a repackaged, idealized set of images that interpret those changes in some way.

M*A*S*H certainly did not foment antiwar sentiment. Rather, its emergence on television followed several years of social discord over United States intervention in Vietnam. Had a show like *M*A*S*H* premiered five years earlier, when protests over the Vietnam War were just beginning to challenge the Johnson administration's perspective, we might conclude that it helped turn public opinion against the war. Instead, *M*A*S*H* premiered on network television after the nation had reached consensus on the need to get out of Vietnam.

War and militarism were treated more sharply in the early years of the show while the Vietnam War was occupying time on the nation's nightly newscasts. By the 1980s, war themes in the show were reduced to examinations of how individuals coped with war, and the 4077 became a much more conventional military unit that got high marks for its work. Reagan's revival of military prowess as a national source of pride paralleled these developments in the show. Absent the antiwar spirit of the Vietnam era, Reagan's interventionist and nuclear philosophies were not subjected to critique through program themes in the same way the program had commented on the United States experience in Vietnam.

The fact that sexism was so prevalent in the early years of the show—at a time when the women's movement was coming into its own—demonstrates that *M*A*S*H* actually lagged behind the times in its treatment of women. The early celebration of alcohol in the program was a reflection of relaxed attitudes and the lowering of drinking ages in the late 1960s and early 1970s; a more critical treatment of alcohol and drugs came in the late 1970s, when society began viewing drinking and recreational drug usage as more of a problem. The cultural trend from the collective protests of the 1960s and 1970s to the "Me Decade" of the mid–1970s was followed in the show as its tendencies to ridicule political and military leaders gave way to a focus on individual lives and crises, ranging from marriage and divorce to missing one's family and coping with the psychological pressures of war.

These trends reveal that television programs tend to follow social trends rather than create them. Innovation in television programming is generally driven by a desire to reach a particular audience. Most television programming hews closely to a lowest-common-denominator formula, discouraging provocative efforts that may offend some audience segments. CBS's transformation from a schedule built around rural comedy to more "hip" programs with an urban appeal was an acknowledgment of the changes occurring in American society in the late 1960s.

The themes of *M*A*S*H*, and the changes in those themes over the years, seem remarkable when one considers *M*A*S*H* was set in the 1950s. Furthermore, considering the research done by the creative team on the Korean War and the United States in the 1950s, one might have expected the show to reflect the politics and values of that era. Instead, the creative team used its research to lend authenticity to the program while making the stories relevant to the lives of viewers. This kind of bridge between two historical eras makes the consistency of the trends identified here more apparent. Writers and producers exist in the same social milieu as their audience. Thus, the key in the creation and success of *M*A*S*H* lay in the contemporary experiences and world views of the creative team as they took the events of the 1950s and gave them a post–Vietnam interpretation.

Except for the emergence and flourishing of feminism in the show, the themes in *M*A*S*H* drifted toward the conservatism that the nation's news media increasingly portrayed from the mid–1970s to the Reagan era. *M*A*S*H*'s tendency to roll with the political punches of society demonstrates commercial network television's need to stay within some rather well-defined, if implicit, boundaries of politics and culture. The nature of these boundaries, in the context of the "values" debate surrounding television and mass culture in general, is the subject of the following chapter.

How network television anticipates and reflects real-life trends plays a major role in determining the kinds of values television projects. The pluralism of American society provides many dilemmas for network programmers, and as American society demonstrates contradiction, tension and dissension, so will television recast such tensions and contradictions in ways that idealize them. Television's projected "solutions" to the social problems and issues of the day never take on the political and economic structures that may have fostered them. Instead, television provides audiences with ways of coping with social change that may have negative individual consequences. The "values" of television, we will see, do not so much create the problems extant in society as they provide audiences with a means of interpreting and coping with the world around them.

CHAPTER 10

Television, Values, and Social Change

The debate over the values projected by television and the sociocultural meaning of television in American society has been an ongoing contest since the medium was born. A long-running series like *M*A*S*H* allows for a "big picture" look at the role of television in a nation's culture and politics. As we will see, there is no consistent set of values projected by *M*A*S*H* over its lifetime, something that can probably be said of most programming. Instead, television can project different kinds of values and even reflect contradictory values and tendencies existing in society. This chapter identifies four types of values that offer different orientations to the world—values that emphasize different political, economic, and cultural priorities. These four value orientations are (1) commercial or economic values that drive the television industry; (2) universal values reflecting the human condition and experience; (3) religious or moral prescriptions and prohibitions that focus on often mythical standards of the past; and (4) countercultural or oppositional values that challenge the status quo. Following a definition of each of these value orientations, this chapter will consider how this typology of values is reflected in *M*A*S*H*. Finally, this chapter will examine how these values conflict and compete with each other as a result of the economic, political, and cultural trends and conflicts existing in society at any given time.

THE VALUES OF TELEVISION: IMPERATIVES AND CONTRADICTIONS

Commercial Values

The function of television today is no different from the function of the other mass media that evolved and predominated before it. There has always been social turmoil over the introduction of new media and what they bring to their audiences. The telegraph, motion pictures, and radio all were criticized for purported negative effects on individuals and society as a whole. With its rapid expansion in the post–World War II era, television brought a new technology into homes and immediately began to play a role in postwar prosperity. Television's development drew upon radio's evolution as a mass medium earlier in the twentieth century. While the economic and political struggle over the development of radio stations created a debate on the meaning of public ownership of the airwaves, there was no such debate over television. From the outset, the medium would be organized and rationalized as part of the capitalist system. Private ownership of television meant that from the beginning it would function at least in part to produce profits for owners and stockholders of stations and networks. Television's reliance on advertising as a primary source of income required that audience size be determined, so television borrowed the notion of the ratings services from radio. The "bottom line" for television was achieving large audiences that could be exposed to sponsors' messages.

Such definitions of success in television came to conflict with notions of aesthetics and creativity. The drive to create mass audiences produced programs intended to appeal to mass tastes, while quality programming that failed to achieve large audience appeal was often summarily dumped. The commercial or economic values of television can be seen as fomenting some of the trends that some groups in society have judged to be negative. Sexual titillation and pandering gradually brought to television a tendency to appeal to people's baser instincts. And it is no surprise that this tendency should be present in advertising as well. Sex sells; that's why it surfaces in both programs and advertisements. Encouraging the growth of consumer society means creating and exploiting social fears and anxieties. Successful advertising convinces consumers that they can make themselves attractive and sexually desirable by buying things to compensate for their perceived shortcomings. Television's rather consistent projection of an upper middle-class lifestyle in its programs is also an indirect way of perpetuating the materialist values of consumer society. Encouraging consumers to define themselves by the cars they drive, the clothes they buy, and the goods they acquire is part of television's function. The imperative of television to provide audiences for its advertisers and profits for its owners influenced the development of programming, which moved away from educational and enlightening fare and toward the use of the medium to serve seemingly more frivolous, yet implicitly corporate priorities and values.

Universal Values

Commercialism does not completely comprise television's goals and value orientations. At its best, television projects a set of universal values, just as any phenomenon central to a culture must provide a vision of human dignity and social solidarity as a means of socialization. Universal values are the most fundamental human values required for the basic functioning of society; they represent the nearly unassailable truths that are supposed to govern everyday behavior and contribute to a more humane and socially tranquil society. Just as oral and written traditions passed on to new members of society contain certain expectations of how one should treat other humans, so does television bring stories that emphasize doing good in life—helping others, being honest and sincere, showing faithfulness and loyalty towards others, and generally internalizing the basic social rules needed for society to survive. Universal values hold across time and culture. They are the "morals of the story" found in so many of the family sitcoms of the late 1950s and early 1960s such as *Leave It to Beaver, Donna Reed,* and *Ozzie and Harriet.* Programs in all genres rely on universal values as morals of the story—punishing antisocial behaviors such as greed and dishonesty while advocating truth, sincerity, and strong character. Critics citing particular shows as "television at its best" are typically pointing out programs that consistently project universal values in a way that is relevant to contemporary society.

Moral Prescriptions and Prohibitions

The last two values orientations in this discussion are not so much inherent in television as they are reflections of social tendencies that competing elements of society want television to project. Both of these orientations can be seen at least implicitly as challenges to commercial or market-driven values that bring programming deemed in some way objectionable, undesirable, and socially harmful. Both of these reflect a belief in "the way things should be" in life and the social world.

Moral prescriptions and prohibitions can be seen as providing codes that define a world of absolute rights and wrongs. These kinds of codes differ from universal values in that they are derived from a fundamentalist orientation to religious texts and beliefs. Groups built on such traditions strive to get networks to provide more "wholesome" entertainment, which usually means shows that present a highly idealized version of contemporary life in which real-world problems are glossed over or easily solved by individual transformations of character.

Groups of this nature have described their value orientation as traditional "family" values. They place great stock in the belief that television leads society to change. They decry deviation from an institutionally defined "proper" life with respect to sex, drugs, alcohol, marriage, forms of dress, and so forth. They see television as a morally corrupting and disrupting force in society. Attempting to roll back cultural trends to a mythical past, many pressure groups seek to prescribe an exclusive set of values for TV to project; they tend to discount or ignore real-world conditions beyond television that may be fostering undesirable behavior.

Such value orientations are especially directed at programming aimed at children and youth. The drive to develop technology that allows parents to control access to certain programs and networks is a manifestation of efforts to influence what young people learn from television. Because such efforts sometimes place economic pressure on networks and program sponsors, the groups initiating the efforts are often able to influence policy and the direction programming takes. This value orientation, though it conflicts with notions of pluralism and diversity basic to America's ideals of democracy, often prevails because its perceived economic and political clout brings corporate media compliance or compromise.

The question then arises: If television often reinforces "traditional" values, why are those who cast themselves as defenders of those values so critical of television programming? Their objections seem to focus more on television's willingness to portray the problems of modern society, rather than on how those problems are resolved. Programs that take on teenage pregnancy or drug use rarely, if ever, wind up glorifying the problem. Instead, the resolution usually proceeds along lines that should be welcomed by those who espouse "traditional" values and morality. Such defenders of tradition apparently would prefer that television turn back the clock to a time when such problems were less prevalent or less visible. Television's need to remain at least somewhat contemporary and relevant to the times is what seems to draw criticism from religious and moral traditionalists.

Countercultural or Oppositional Values

The final value orientation is the one that falls the most outside the economic, political, and cultural boundaries of "mainstream" society. Countercultural and oppositional values on television are rare and tend to occur during periods of social upheaval and tension. Such values challenge society's notions of itself, identify the contradictions between ideology and reality and suggest that social structures and institutions privilege some social groups over others.

The opposition that grew around the Vietnam War offered a challenge to America's self-perception as a world leader and force for democracy and peace. *The Smothers Brothers Show* and *All in the Family* are two of the few programs that confronted America with its contradictions: values of freedom and tolerance versus tendencies toward control and closemindedness; ideals of diversity versus the reality of racism; the supposed practice of peaceful leadership versus the actual promotion of nuclear arms and the use of war as an instrument of foreign policy.

The modest introduction of some countercultural or oppositional values in network television lagged behind the rise of oppositional values in society when the civil rights, antiwar and women's movements began to challenge America's vision of itself. The playing out of the Vietnam War brought a drawdown of the domestic tensions it had fueled. Whatever cues the counterculture of the 1960s provided in influencing television content, they were no match for the more central commercial values that steer content away from controversy, less popular ideas, and values that challenge basic assumptions about power and authority. Given the medium's own institutional linkages to corporate power, television is predisposed toward ignoring or downplaying these values.

Television's value system, then, is inherently conservative in two senses. First, it is conservative in taking risks and attempting innovation. Change in television lags behind society's changes. Trends in the real world must find a wide following before television will appropriate them and re-present them to society in a more commercialized (and therefore acceptable) form. Second, television is politically conservative, by virtue of the commercial imperatives and effective pressure by adherents to moral prescriptions and prohibitions. When television programs portray individual and social problems, they pose solutions that do not question basic assumptions about the economic and political order. Rather, most solutions in fictional television dilemmas focus on the individual level. Such solutions are the foundation of conservative ideology.

It is clear that universal values are safe territory for television to tread. These values represent the bulk of television's storytelling. Such values promote social solidarity, reflect some larger sense of the human condition, and stress the importance of empathy and compassion for others. While there is sometimes conflict between commercial and universal values, such as the use of violence to attract audiences, for the most part television's appropriation of universal values tends not to interfere with its commercial interests.

The value orientations outlined above provide a structure for examining periods of social change and upheaval, which in turn represent good opportunities to consider how television reflects and reshapes the values disputes of the day. The next section explains how the four value orientations help us understand *M*A*S*H*'s changes over its eleven-year run.

THE VALUES OF *M*A*S*H*

*M*A*S*H* emerged on television during a historical period of change and upheaval. The show represents a unique conjunction of cultural and historical circumstance—it took the stage at a time when television was searching for ways to reflect the issues of the day. With its unusual status as a sitcom that dealt with war and other unfunny issues, *M*A*S*H* also provides a means to test just how pliable the boundaries of television culture are. As an antiwar comedy, it would try to capture the antiwar and antiestablishment spirit of the late 1960s and early 1970s. Thus, a close look at how *M*A*S*H* reflected changes in values throughout its prime-time run will help tease out the role of values in fictional television and contribute further to an understanding of television's political predilections.

Undoubtedly, commercial concerns were part of what brought *M*A*S*H* to network television. The show was conceived to help CBS bring in younger, hipper audiences, and the heavy reliance on sexual titillation and partying in first-year episodes demonstrates how primarily commercial values drive a new show. In fact, the prevalence of drinking and sex in the novel and film versions of *M*A*S*H* probably provided the commercial incentive for trying this new kind of situation comedy.

The security of renewal for a second season allowed the program's creators to venture into more serious antiwar themes and take more risks creatively and politically. Sexual frivolity and the party atmosphere of *M*A*S*H* dissipated as the show got its own legs and acquired a loyal and commercially desirable audience.

Universal values really are the primary values in *M*A*S*H*. Being true to self, caring for others, rewarding honesty, and punishing behavior that is dishonest or violates social solidarity are recurrent themes. The show's sympathetic portrayal of Koreans as their culture is disrupted is at once a critique of war and an understanding of the universality of the human condition and human ability to empathize.

Universal values are *M*A*S*H*'s strong point and probably help account for the show's broad appeal and enduring popularity, even today in syndication. Many of *M*A*S*H*'s award-winning episodes reflect such universal values, though the specific emphasis on these values did change over the life of the show as it moved from critiquing the horrors of war early on to watching the main cast of characters gain self-insight and personal growth in the later years. Individual striving and integrity are strong themes and serve as a reflection of the prototypical American value system. The development of *M*A*S*H* "family" themes that put value on looking after and caring for others in the 4077 family also became a staple in the later years of the show.

Because its run bridged the antiwar era and the Ronald Reagan presidency, *M*A*S*H* provides a window into how television responds to real and perceived changes in the contemporary world. *M*A*S*H* retreated from the uninhibited drinking and sex of its first season into a more traditional outlook on alcohol, drugs, and sexuality. The implied infidelity and partying atmosphere of the early years were almost nonexistent in the later years, and indeed, several episodes in the later years offered critiques of infidelity and overindulgence, instead celebrating virginity and steadfastness. Themes of the horrors of war and the desirability of peace were depoliticized in the later years, and there was far more respect for authority figures and less ridicule of hyperpatriotism. As America "stood tall" with Ronald Reagan in office, *M*A*S*H* came to reflect a more conservative moral orientation.

Oppositional values surfaced occasionally in the early years of the show, as military authority figures were criticized for being too gung-ho, hypocritical, and insensitive to the human casualties of war. Friendly fire incidents, witch-hunts by Colonel Flagg, and the idea that the United States was in Korea to do good were all held up to some degree of critical scrutiny. Such episodes represent occasional attempts by the program's creative team to stretch the boundaries of network television. Though some of these efforts were resisted or censored outright by network powers, *M*A*S*H*'s more provocative years were also the years it garnered its highest ratings. It might reasonably be concluded that American audiences are more accepting of provocative programming that challenges the conventional wisdom than are the networks or advertisers, who are more concerned with not offending some desirable segment of the audience. Countercultural or oppositional values are rare on network television, and *M*A*S*H* stands as one of the few shows in television history that occasionally brought such values to the American public.

That television tends to adapt to the mood of society is evidenced in *M*A*S*H*'s lack of antimilitarism and anti-imperialism themes as a response to Reagan's military buildup and interventionist policies in Central America. Having largely shifted to "proxy wars," which meant fewer U.S. troops fighting, even Reagan's position on Vietnam as a "noble cause" failed to trigger widespread opposition to his policies and also failed to reignite provocative, challenging themes on *M*A*S*H*. Without the antiwar spirit that characterized the early years of the show, there would be little inclination to make statements about potential "new Vietnams" through critical episodes.

In this context, *M*A*S*H*'s early and only occasional forays into these areas actually serve as evidence *against* the conventional wisdom about the politics of television and the values it projects. As oppositional moments of the show, these themes illustrate not that television programming is provocative and responsible for social trends but instead that it can only occasionally challenge the limitations of the network masters. These relatively minor critiques, occurring at the end of the antiwar period, illustrate that television's basic orientation is inherently conservative. As one of the few shows to occasionally challenge institutional authority and the ideology of America's role in the world, *M*A*S*H* might well be characterized as a relatively provocative program. But at the same time, it offers evidence that television as a whole is far from being the liberal provocateur its many conservative critics describe. Rather, the fact that it is a rare example of politically provocative storytelling shows just how cautious and politically conservative television tends to be.

THE "BOTTOM LINE" ON VALUES

The commercial imperatives of television tend to keep it in "safe" territory. Institutionally, network television is an integral part of American capitalism and as such can hardly be expected to challenge that system. Television's function of encouraging a materialistic, consumer society necessitates projecting a value system of individual striving for material happiness. Television's predominantly upper middle-class world is rarely touched by real-world problems, and when it is, those problems are by and large solved in ways compatible with "mainstream" American values.

M*A*S*H, for all its antiwar reputation, clearly retreated from occasional and modest critiques of warmaking and came to focus on how individuals cope with being put in war. In this context, *M*A*S*H* indeed stands as an example of a slightly more provocative approach to television storytelling. In today's even more bottom-line-oriented media environment, a program like *M*A*S*H* would have difficulty getting a pilot episode shot for network consideration. Cable systems with 50-plus channels mean commercial values pervade even more as network television increases sexual titillation and violence to compete with premium cable channels offering uncut R-rated films. Such developments do not indicate a more "liberal" political philosophy on television so much as they demonstrate the role commercial values play in shaping media content.

Such commercial values are beginning to conflict with the universal values that have shaped the storytelling role of television since its inception. Family life, as modeled in a program like *Married with Children*, is far removed from the usual family sitcom; at the same time, it represents a further devolution of television in serving commercial interests almost exclusively. Countercultural or oppositional values are virtually nonexistent in network television. At best, some police or courtroom programs may suggest the justice system fails to serve the interests of justice. Alternative visions of community, society, and the world are absent at a time when new organizing and governing principles for the world are needed. As long as mass culture primarily exists to serve corporate bottom lines, it will rarely provide social enlightenment or empowerment. If television's ability to criticize and inspire falls into permanent disuse, the medium will never contribute to problem-solving and positive social change. The obvious task for media reformers is to wean television from its obsession with the commercial imperatives of its corporate masters. Until then, any movement to reorient the role of television in American society is bound to be frustrated.

There may never be a show quite like *M*A*S*H*, just as America may never experience a time quite like the post–Vietnam era. Television's increasing emphasis on commercial values in determining the kind of programs presented to United States audiences clearly would preclude a show like *M*A*S*H* from making it to network television today. As United States society takes its twists and turns, programming may occasionally criticize powerful institutions like the government and military in a manner reminiscent of *M*A*S*H*. But it will take more significant change within the world of television itself before more provocative programs are allowed to proliferate.

Episode Guide

Cast and crew credits at the beginning of each year represent those individuals who served in various capacities for all or part of the season. Other credits are drawn from show credits at the beginning and end of each episode. The episode descriptions are drawn from airings of the show in syndication. In general, episodes got shorter over the years as networks inserted more advertising time in each time block. It is apparent that some episodes were edited from the original versions, probably because uniform episode lengths were needed for syndication.

YEAR 1, 1972-1973

Cast and Crew

Regular Cast: Alan Alda as Hawkeye Pierce, Gary Burghoff as Radar O'Reilly, Larry Linville as Frank Burns, Wayne Rogers as Trapper John McIntire, McLean Stevenson as Henry Blake, and Loretta Swit as Margaret Houlihan. *Produced by* Gene Reynolds. *Executive Script Consultant* Larry Gelbart. *Developed for Television by* Larry Gelbart. *Associate Producer* Burt Metcalfe. *Production Supervisor* Jack Sonntag. *Unit Production Managers* Mark Evans, Wes McAfee. *Assistant Directors* James Engle, Robert Doudell. *Directors of Photography* William Jurgensen, Richard A. Kelley.

Film Editors Fred W. Berger and Stanford Tischler. *Music by* Johnny Mandel, Duane Tatro. *Music Supervision* Lionel Newman. *Art Directors* James Sullivan, Jack Senter. *Set Decorators* Jerry Wunderlich, Stuart Reiss, Ralph Sylos. *Medical Advisor* Walter D. Dishell, M.D. *Executive Consultant* Ingo Preminger. *Based on a Novel by* Richard Hooker. *Post Production Supervisor* James Blakely. *Theme* Johnny Mandel.

*M*A*S*H Pilot (9/17/72)*

Written by Larry Gelbart. *Directed by* Gene Reynolds. *Nominated for* Emmy, Outstanding Directorial Achievement (Gene Reynolds); Emmy, Outstanding Writing Achievement (Larry Gelbart); ACE Eddie Award, Editing (Stanford Tischler). *Winner:* Directors Guild Award (Gene Reynolds). *Guest*

Stars: Karen Philipp, Patrick Adiarte, G. Wood, Timothy Brown, Linda Meiklejohn, Laura Miller, George Morgan, B. Kirby, Jr., John Orchard, Odessa Cleveland.

The Swamp's houseboy, Ho-Jon, is accepted into Hawkeye's alma mater. They decide to raise money for tuition. Hawkeye and Trapper plan a party and raffle off a weekend in Tokyo with a nurse. Frank is in charge while Henry Blake is away, and Hawk and Trap clash with him over the party. Frank gets put out of action by Hawkeye and Trapper, and an onslaught of casualties brings out their surgical skills. Father Mulcahy wins the raffle.

To Market, to Market (9/24/72)

Written by Burt Styler. *Directed by* Michael O'Herlihy. *Guest Stars:* G.Wood, Robert Ito, Jack Soo, John C. Johnson, Odessa Cleveland, Sorrell Booke.

The hijacking of a hydrocortisone delivery forces Hawkeye and Trapper to use the black market. They get one businessman interested in Henry Blake's antique oak desk and trade it to get some of the drug. Margaret and Frank become suspicious about their plotting, and about the Koreans who come to check out the desk. Henry, very fond of his desk, watches it get hoisted away on a helicopter.

Requiem for a Lightweight (10/1/72)

Written by Bob Klane. *Directed by* Hy Averback. *Guest Stars:* Marcia Strassman, Sorrell Booke, John Orchard, William Christopher. *Note:* This is the first appearance by William Christopher as Father Mulcahy. Mulcahy was played by George Morgan in the pilot.

Hawkeye and Trapper seek to keep a nurse from being transferred by Hot Lips, and they vie for her affection. Henry Blake, challenged by another commander to a boxing tournament, makes Trapper box a big, intimidating soldier in exchange for keeping the nurse at the 4077. Hawkeye and Ugly John use a glove soaked with ether to insure Trapper's victory, which impresses the nurse. Margaret and Frank's attempts to unfix the match fails, and they get crushed by the falling boxer.

Chief Surgeon Who? (10/8/72)

Written by Larry Gelbart. *Directed by* E.W. Swackhamer. *Winner:* Writers Guild Award, Teleplay (Larry Gelbart). *Guest Stars:* Linda Meiklejohn, Jack Riley, Sorrell Booke, Timothy Brown, Odessa Cleveland, Jamie Farr, Bob Gooden, John Orchard. *Note:* This is Klinger's first appearance in the show.

Frank Burns complains about Hawkeye's disrespect. Henry responds by appointing Hawkeye chief surgeon. The rest of the camp "coronates" Hawkeye while Margaret and Frank complain to General Barker. Barker's visit provides him a view of life at the 4077. Camp hijinks, a poker game, and a surgery session during his visit show MASH has fun but gets the job done.

The Moose (10/15/72)

Written by Laurence Marks. *Directed by* Hy Averback. *Guest Stars:* Paul Jenkins, Virginia Lee, Craig Jue, Barbara Brownell, Patrick Adiarte, Timothy Brown, John Orchard, Linda Meiklejohn. *Note:* In this episode, Radar is much more "street smart" than he is for most years of the show.

A GI arrives in camp with a "moose"—a Korean female slave—who was bought from her family for $500. Hawkeye, Trapper, and Radar conspire to cheat at poker to win her back from the GI. They try to return her but learn that her family, in the person of her wisecracking brother, will resell her. They try a "Pygmalion" effort to give her self-respect.

Yankee Doodle Doctor (10/15/72)

Written by Laurence Marks. *Directed by* Lee Phillips. *Guest Stars:* Ed Flanders, Bert Kramer, Herb Voland, Marcia Strassman, Tom Sparks.

The 4077 is designated as the setting for the making of an army film on MASH units. Hawkeye is chosen as the star while Margaret and Frank write a script. Hawkeye objects to the piece of propaganda that filmmaker Lt. Bricker is producing and creates his own film, making fun of glorifying doctors while closing with a serious speech about the hell of war: "Guns have more power to take life than surgeons have to preserve it."

Bananas, Crackers and Nuts (11/5/72)

Written by Burt Styler. *Directed by* Bruce Bilson. *Winner:* ACE Eddie Award, Editing (Fred W. Berger). *Guest Stars:* Stuart Margolin, Marcia Strassman, Odessa Cleveland.

Heavy casualties leave Hawk exhausted and desiring R and R. His attempts to get Frank to sign a pass by acting crazy only result in Frank and Margaret ordering a psychiatric examination. Hawkeye continues his act by telling Capt. Sherman, the psychiatrist, he is in love with Frank. Sherman is ready to commit him until Hawkeye and Trapper set him up to make a pass at Margaret and discredit him.

Cowboy (11/12/72)

Written by Bob Klane. *Directed by* Don Weis. *Guest Stars:* Billy Green Bush, Joseph Corey, William Christopher, Mike Kobelo, Jean Powell, John Orchard, Patrick Adiarte.

Chopper pilot Cowboy is expecting a letter—he's worried his girlfriend at home is leaving him for another man. He wants to go home, but Henry refuses. A series of misfortunes befall Henry: He gets shot at while golfing, his tent gets run over by a runaway jeep, and the latrine blows up while he's in it. Cowboy offers to fly him to Seoul and then threatens to push him out. The letter arrives assuring Cowboy he is loved. Hawkeye uses the radio to get the Cowboy to come down, thus sparing Henry.

Henry, Please Come Home (11/19/72)

Written by Laurence Marks. *Directed by* William Wiard. *Guest Stars:* G.Wood, John Orchard, William Christopher, Patrick Adiarte, Timothy Brown, Odessa Cleveland, Linda Meiklejohn, Bill Svanoe, Jeane Pleet, Noel Joy, Kasuko Sakuro.

M*A*S*H gets a high efficiency rating and, as a reward, Blake is transferred. This leaves Frank in charge, and he proceeds to make life miserable for everyone at the 4077. After Frank takes away their still, Hawkeye and Trapper plot to get Henry back. They go to Tokyo to convince Henry that Radar is sick and needs him. Radar gives himself away, but Henry decides to stay anyway.

I Hate a Mystery (11/26/72)

Written by Hal Dresner. *Directed by* Hy Averback. *Guest Stars:* Bonnie Jones, Linda Meiklejohn, Timothy Brown, Odessa Cleveland, Patrick Adiarte, William Christopher.

A rash of thefts in camp is victimizing everyone. During a search, the goods are found in Hawkeye's footlocker, and he lacks an alibi. Hawkeye identifies the real thief by playing Sherlock Holmes. It turns out to be Ho-Jon, who has been stealing stuff to bring his family together. The camp pitches in to reunite his family.

Germ Warfare (12/10/72)

Written by Larry Gelbart. *Directed by* Terry Becker. *Guest Stars:* Robert Gooden, Karen Phillip, Byron Chung, Timothy Brown, Patrick Adiarte, Odessa Cleveland.

Hawkeye and Trapper fight the transfer of a wounded North Korean prisoner—they try to hide him in the Swamp. Frank objects to the prisoner, who needs blood only Frank can provide. Hawkeye and Trapper tap into Frank for a pint while he's sleeping. The patient gets ill after receiving blood, prompting concern that Frank has hepatitis. After further hijinks, Frank turns out to be all right.

Dear Dad (12/17/72)

Written by Larry Gelbart. *Directed by* Gene Reynolds. *Guest Stars:* Bonnie Jones, Lizabeth Deen, Gary Van Orman, Buck Young, Bill Katt, William Christopher, Jamie Farr, Odessa Cleveland.

Hawkeye's letter home tells about the Christmas season at the 4077. Father Mulcahy and Trapper do good for Korean orphans. Klinger and Frank clash over Klinger's clothes while Radar sends a jeep home piece by piece. Margaret and Frank fear peace talks may break them up. Hawkeye is called on to treat an injured man on the battlefield while wearing a Santa suit he was using to give gifts to the children.

Edwina (12/24/72)

Written by Hal Dresner. *Directed by* James Sheldon. *Guest Stars:* Arlene Golonka, Linda Meiklejohn, Marcia Strassman.

Klutzy nurse Edwina tells nurses she hasn't had a date. The nurses boycott men until someone dates her. The men draw straws and Hawkeye is the chosen one. Hawkeye tries to woo her, but Edwina is a walking disaster and the date is a catastrophe. Hawkeye tries to convince her to relax and be herself.

Love Story (1/7/73)

Written by Laurence Marks. *Directed by* Earl Bellamy. *Guest Stars:* Kelly Jean Peters, Indira Danks, Barbara Brownell, Marcia Strassman, Jerry Harper.

Radar's been jilted by his girlfriend back home, but he quickly falls in love with a new nurse officer who's well read and cultured. Hawkeye tries to help Radar fake his way through classical literature and music as he tries to impress her. When Frank and Margaret object to the relationship between an officer and an enlisted man, Hawk and Trap keep them from their own trysts until they get off Radar's back.

Tuttle (1/14/73)

Written by Bruce Shelly and David Ketchum. *Directed by* William Wiard. *Nominated for* Writers Guild Award Teleplay (Bruce Shelly and David Ketchum). *Guest Stars:* Herb Voland, Mary-Robin Redd, James Sikking, William Christopher, Dennis Simple.

Hawkeye creates a fictional soldier, Capt. Tuttle, to cover his own attempts to help a local orphanage by getting supplies and back pay and giving them to the orphans. Hawkeye embellishes the phantom captain's reputation as Henry, Frank, and Margaret try to figure out who Tuttle is. The episode closes with a humorously ironic eulogy of Tuttle given by Hawkeye.

The Ringbanger (1/21/73)

Written by Jerry Mayer. *Directed by* Jackie Cooper. *Guest Stars:* Linda Meiklejohn, Leslie Nielsen.

Hawkeye and Trapper discover an injured colonel has a high casualty rate for his outfit. They try to keep him at 4077 for a while by faking concern about an undefined illness they make up. He tries to get a second opinion from the other doctors, but they convince him Henry's a lush and Frank's gay, so the colonel is afraid to let either one examine him. Then they tell Margaret he needs comforting. Eventually, they persuade him to admit he has battle fatigue and send him back to the States.

Sometimes You Hear the Bullet (1/28/73)

Written by Carl Kleinschmitt. *Directed by* William Wiard. *Nominated for* Writers Guild Award Teleplay (Carl Kleinschmitt). *Guest Stars:* James Callahan, Ron Howard, Lynnette Mettey, Chuck Hicks, Fred Lerner, William Christopher.

Hawkeye is reunited with an old friend who's writing a book about the war from a GI's point of view. Hawkeye and Trapper discover an underage soldier—a broken-hearted 15-year-old trying to prove his manhood. Hawkeye first tells the boy he won't send him home, but he changes his mind after his friend returns gravely wounded and dies on his operating table. Other events include Frank injuring his back in camp and applying for a purple heart, and Hawk's romantic date being continually interrupted by Radar.

Dear Dad...Again (2/4/73)

Written by Sheldon Keller and Larry Gelbart. *Directed by* Jackie Cooper. *Guest Stars:* Alex Henteloff, Gail Bowman, Odessa Cleveland, William Christopher, Jamie Farr. *Note:* Hawkeye tells his father to give his mother and sister a kiss. In later episodes, Hawkeye is an only child and his mother is dead.

A man impersonating a surgeon performs well at 4077 until he's discovered. Hawkeye loses a bet with Trapper that he can walk into mess naked and not be noticed. Frank and Margaret are on the rocks and Hawkeye and Trapper try to get them back together. Meanwhile, Radar tries to get his diploma, and with Henry's help, he does.

The Long John Flap (2/18/73)

Written by Alan Alda. *Directed by* William Wiard. *Guest Stars:* Kathleen King, Joseph Perry, Jamie Farr, William Christopher.

A lack of winter supplies has the camp shivering. Hawkeye feels guilty about having long johns when Trapper gets sick. He "loans" them to Trapper, who loses them to Radar in a card game. Through a series of trades, tricks, and maneuverings, the long johns work their way through most of the camp before Hawkeye gets them back.

The Army-Navy Game (2/25/73)

Written by Sid Dorfman. *Story by* McLean Stevenson. *Directed by* Gene Reynolds. *Guest Stars:* Alan Manson, William Christopher, John A. Zee, John Orchard, Jamie Farr, Sheila Lauritsen, Bobbie Mitchell.

The unit has fun anticipating the Army-Navy game until the war interrupts—an unexploded shell lands in camp. Calls to HQ for help only demonstrate that HQ is more interested in the big game. Margaret and Frank prepare to die together, while Radar takes advantage of the impending doom to get intimate with a nurse. They eventually learn the bomb was dropped by the CIA. Hawkeye and Trapper try to defuse it, and it turns out to be a propaganda bomb that showers the camp with leaflets.

Sticky Wicket (3/4/73)

Written by Laurence Marks and Larry Gelbart. *Story by* Richard Baer. *Directed by* Don Weis. *Guest Stars:* Wayne Bryan, Lynnette Mettey, John Orchard.

The 4077 gets lots of casualties and the OR becomes a verbal battlefield between Hawkeye and Frank. Frank demands a public apology. Hawkeye's patient won't get better, and he can't figure out what's wrong. Frank harasses him about the case and his competence. Hawkeye becomes absorbed with the case to the point that he even declines a date with a nurse. He rebuffs Margaret's suggestions until he opens the patient up and discovers a hard-to-find fragment.

Major Fred C. Dobbs (3/11/73)

Written by Sid Dorfman. *Directed by* Don Weis. *Guest Stars:* Harvey J. Goldenberg, Odessa Cleveland. *Notes:* Larry Gelbart and many others regard this episode as one of the worst. The episode emerged from the fact that South Korea was the fifth largest producer of gold in the world.

Hawkeye and Trapper alienate Margaret and Frank—they put Frank in cast as a joke and tape-record one of their liaisons. Their practical jokes push Margaret and Frank to demand Henry Blake give them a transfer. Meanwhile, Radar is convinced there is gold nearby and begins to hunt for it. Fearing replacements will be worse than Margaret and Frank, Hawk and Trap set Frank up to believe there's gold near camp to keep him at 4077.

Cease Fire (3/18/73)

Written by Laurence Marks and Larry Gelbart. *Story by* Larry Gelbart. *Directed by* Earl Bellamy. *Guest Stars:* Herb Voland, Jamie Farr, William Christopher, Marcia Strassman, Bonnie Jones, Patrick Adiarte, Odessa Cleveland, Bruce Kimmel.

A rumor from top that a cease-fire is imminent gets the camp celebrating. A skeptical Trapper is less than excited. The camp says goodbye to each other—Margaret graciously tells Frank to go back to his wife, while Hawkeye tells three nurses he's married so they won't expect to continue a relationship with him back home. Photos at a cease-fire party reveal Margaret's liaisons with General Clayton. When the cease-fire and armistice turn out to be false, the Swamp has been stripped of just about everything.

Showtime (3/25/73)

Written by Robert Klane and Larry Gelbart. *Story by* Larry Gelbart. *Directed by* Jackie Cooper. *Guest Stars:* Joey Forman, Harvey J. Goldenberg,

John Orchard, William Christopher, Stanley Clay, Sheila Lauritsen, Oksun Kim. The singing "Miller Sisters" are Marilyn King, Jean Turrell, and Joan Lucksinger.

A USO show is interrupted by casualties, and Trapper has an especially hard case. Father Mulcahy, worried about his effectiveness, helps save a soldier's life. Henry is worried about his wife back home who's about to give birth. In the meantime, Frank plays series of practical jokes on Hawkeye, while a dentist about to return home is afraid of getting injured.

YEAR 2, 1973-1974

Cast and Crew

Regular Cast: Alan Alda as Hawkeye Pierce, Gary Burghoff as Radar O'Reilly, Larry Linville as Frank Burns, Wayne Rogers as Trapper John McIntire, McLean Stevenson as Henry Blake and Loretta Swit as Margaret Houlihan. *Produced by* Gene Reynolds and Larry Gelbart. *Script Consultant* Laurence Marks. *Developed for Television by* Larry Gelbart. *Associate Producer* Burt Metcalfe. *Production Supervisor* Mark Evans. *Unit Production Manager* Ted Butcher. *Assistant Directors* J. Russell Llewellyn, Leonard S. Smith, Jr. *Director of Photography* William Jurgensen. *Film Editors* Fred W. Berger and Stanford Tischler. *Music Supervision* Lionel Newman. *Music by* Duane Tatro, Earle Hagen, Benny Golson. *Music Editors* Ken Wannberg, John Harris. *Supervising Music Editor* Len Engel. *Art Directors* Rodger Maus, Walter McKeegan. *Set Decorators* Ralph Sylos, Don Webb. *Medical Advisor* Walter D. Dishell, M.D. *Post Production Supervisor* Joseph Silver. *Theme* Johnny Mandel.

Divided We Stand (9/15/73)

Written by Larry Gelbart. *Directed by* Jackie Cooper. *Guest Stars:* Herb Voland, Anthony Holland, Jamie Farr, Linda Meiklejohn, Odessa Cleveland, Bobbie Mitchell, Lesley Evans.

Gen. Clayton sends a psychiatrist to investigate the 4077 to see if it should be disbanded. Frank and Margaret have been sending him negative reports. The psychiatrist experiences Klinger and watches the hijinks of Hawkeye and Trapper and the trysts of Frank and Margaret. While the man confronts the unit on its behavior, choppers begin to arrive and everyone heads for the OR. The onslaught of casualties shows 4077's true side, and the psychiatrist tells Clayton it would be crazy to break the unit up—they are doing an impossible job in an impossible place.

Five O'Clock Charlie (9/22/73)

Written by Larry Gelbart and Laurence Marks. *Story by* Keith Walker. *Directed by* Norman Tokar. *Guest Stars:* Herb Voland, Corey Fisher, William Christopher, Odessa Cleveland, Lloyd King, Sarah Fankboner, Gail Bowman, Deborah Newman.

The unit has to deal with an incompetent mad bomber who strikes at 5 P.M. every day. Five O'Clock Charlie provides amusement for Hawkeye, Trapper, and the rest of the unit as they place bets on by how much he will miss the target. Meanwhile, Frank and Margaret take the threat seriously and get General Clayton to place a gun in camp to take him out. When Frank fires the gun at Charlie, it lands on the ammunition dump Charlie is trying to take out.

Radar's Report (9/29/73)

Written by Laurence Marks. *Story by* Sheldon Keller. *Directed by* Jackie Cooper. *Nominated for* Writers Guild Award, story (Sheldon Keller), Teleplay (Lawrence Marks). *Guest Stars:* Joan Van Ark, Allan Arbus, Jamie Farr, William Christopher, Derick Shimatsu. *Note:* Allan Arbus's first appearance is as Milton Freedman; in his later appearances he is Sidney Freedman.

Radar's weekly report to HQ tells about the unit's experiences with a wounded Chinese prisoner. Meanwhile, Margaret and Frank try to get rid of Klinger. A psychiatrist offers to get Klinger out if he will admit he is a homosexual and a transvestite. Klinger takes offense and refuses. Hawkeye is interested in a new nurse but when he talks of marriage she decides to transfer.

For the Good of the Outfit (10/6/73)

Written by Jerry Mayer. *Directed by* Jackie Cooper. *Guest Stars:* Frank Aletter, Herb Voland, Odessa Cleveland, Lesley Evans, Gwen Farrell. *Note:* This episode reportedly brought heavy network criticism for its pointed critique of United States military behavior.

The 4077 gets a lot of casualties, all Korean civilians. Hawkeye and Trapper determine the wounds are from "friendly fire." Major Stoner arrives after Hawk and Trap submit a report and tells them there will be a full investigation. They then read about the shelling in *Stars and Stripes* which fails to mention the shells came from the United States. When Hawkeye writes his father to have him tell his senator, General Clayton arrives and suggests the army may move Hawk and Trap to the front. Frank and Margaret bring forth more fragments and evidence and reopen the investigation. Hawkeye learns from his father that the senator can't help him—he's been indicted for influence-peddling.

Dr. Pierce and Mr. Hyde (10/13/73)

Written by Alan Alda and Robert Klane. *Directed by* Jackie Cooper. *Guest Stars:* Buck Young, Herb Voland.

Hawkeye spends 24 hours in OR only to hear more choppers as he gets into bed. It happens a second time and Hawkeye is nearly asleep on his feet. The rest of the unit tries to get him to go to bed, but he decides to try to stop the war. He telegraphs Harry Truman and asks him, "Who's responsible?" Later, inspired by Frank's declaration that the enemy is jealous of American hygiene, he decides to deliver a latrine to North Korea.

Kim (10/20/73)

Written by Marc Mandel, Larry Gelbart, and Laurence Marks. Directed by William Wiard. Guest Stars: Leslie Evans, Edgar Miller, Maggie Roswell, Momo Yashima, Jamie Farr, William Christopher.

A young Korean boy with a minor injury charms the camp. When it appears he has no family, it prompts Trapper to ask his wife about adopting the boy. While he waits for an answer, each member of the unit entertains the boy in his or her own way. While with Margaret and Frank, the boy drifts into a minefield. After a comedy of errors trying to read the minefield maps, Trapper and a helicopter rescue him. A truck pulls up with a nun from the orphanage and the boy's mother. A dejected Trapper walks back to the camp slowly.

L.I.P. (Local Indigenous Personnel) (10/27/73)

Written by Carl Kleinschmitt. Directed by William Wiard. Guest Stars: Corinne Camacho, Burt Young, Jerry Zaks, Odessa Cleveland, Jamie Farr, William Christopher.

A GI with a Korean woman and baby wants to get married and take his family to the United States. He asks Hawkeye to help him. After a mountain of paperwork, a CID officer arrives to investigate. He treats the situation with disdain and refers to the woman as a "broad." Using staged photos of the officer in a compromising situation, Hawkeye blackmails him into approving the marriage. Meanwhile, Hawk's romantic encounter with a nurse ends abruptly when Hawkeye discovers the woman has racist attitudes.

The Trial of Henry Blake (11/3/73)

Written by McLean Stevenson, Larry Gelbart, and Laurence Marks. Directed by Don Weis. Nominated for Emmy, Outstanding Writing in Comedy (McLean Stevenson). Winner: ACE Eddie Award, Editing (Fred W. Berger and Stanford Tischler). Guest Stars: Hope Summers, Robert F. Simon, Jack Aaron, Bobbie Mitchell, Roy Goldman, Jamie Farr.

Henry and Radar go to HQ where they learn that Henry is charged with giving aid and comfort to the enemy. Faced with the prospect of having Frank permanently in charge, Hawkeye and Trapper decide to counter with their own evidence. Frank puts them under house arrest, but they manage to get to HQ. They testify that Blake's "aid and comfort" has been going to Meg Cratty, a nurse who runs an orphanage. Frank at first insists on pressing the charges, but a note from Hawkeye that threatens to tells his wife about Margaret helps Frank decide otherwise.

Dear Dad... Three (11/10/73)

Written by Larry Gelbart and Laurence Marks. *Directed by* Don Weis. *Guest Stars:* Mills Watson, Sivi Aberg, Arthur Abelson, Jamie Farr, Odessa Cleveland, Bobbie Mitchell, Kathleen Nughes, Louise Vienna, William Christopher.

Hawkeye's letter to his father provides a slice of life at the 4077. A "booby-trapped" soldier with a grenade wired to his back requires delicate surgery. Meanwhile, a wounded soldier wants a promise that he will get only "white" blood. To teach him a lesson, Hawkeye and Trapper dye his skin with iodine while he's asleep. Later they explain to the soldier that all blood is the same. They tell the story of Charles Drew, the African American doctor who developed the technique for preserving blood plasma, only to die after an auto accident because the hospital wouldn't accept black patients. Comic relief is provided when Blake, Trapper, Hawkeye, and Radar screen some home movies from Blake's wife.

The Sniper (11/17/73)

Written by Richard M. Powell. *Directed by* Jackie Cooper. *Guest Stars:* Teri Garr, Marcia Gelman, Dennis Troy.

The 4077 is under siege from a sniper. They call HQ for help, but HQ says they can't help until the next day. Wounded arrive, and the staff is forced to work by candlelight after the sniper takes out the generator. Margaret goads Frank into taking matters into his own hands, but he chickens out. The chopper arrives the next day and a wounded sniper raises a white flag—he thought he was firing at MacArthur's headquarters.

Carry On, Hawkeye (11/24/73)

Written by Bernard Dilbert, Larry Gelbart, and Laurence Marks. *Story by* Bernard Dilbert. *Directed by* Jackie Cooper. *Nominated for* Writers Guild Award (Bernard Dilbert, Larry Gelbart, and Laurence Marks). *Winner:* Emmy, Outstanding Directing in a Comedy (Jackie Cooper). *Guest Stars:* Lynnette Mettey, Gwen Farrell, Marcia Gelman, William Christopher. *Note:* The public address system announces that the French anticipate an end to the Vietnamese war.

When a flu epidemic hits the 4077, Hawkeye and Margaret struggle to keep things together while the others are sick. They clash as Margaret asserts her authority but Hawkeye maintains he is in charge in the OR. A drove of casualties arrives as well as some flu vaccine. But shortly after getting injected, Hawkeye becomes sick. The epilogue finds Hawkeye in bed and Radar "checking" on the patient while the others look on.

The Incubator (12/1/73)

Written by Larry Gelbart and Laurence Marks. *Directed by* Jackie Cooper. *Nominated for* Writers Guild Award (Larry Gelbart and Laurence Marks). *Guest Stars:* Robert F. Simon, Logan Ramsey, Ted Gehring, Eldon Quick, Sarah Fankboner, Helen Funai, Jerry Harper, John Alvin.

Hawk and Trap seek to obtain an incubator to help speed their testing. The army won't provide one, so they try an enterprising supplier who's getting rich off war. They make their way to the general in charge and start asking him questions at a press conference, which incites the curiosity of the press. Blake gets a bad report on them and struggles with their punishment. Meanwhile, it turns out Radar has cunningly traded for an incubator.

Deal Me Out (12/8/73)

Written by Larry Gelbart and Laurence Marks. *Directed by* Gene Reynolds. *Nominated for* Directors Guild Award (Gene Reynolds); Emmy, Outstanding Directing in Comedy (Gene Reynolds). *Guest Stars:* Pat Morita, Allan Arbus, Edward Winter, John Ritter, Jamie Farr, Jerry Fujikawa, Tom Dever, Gwen Farrell. *Note:* Edward Winter's first appearance is as Captain Halloran; in later episodes he becomes Colonel Flagg.

Sidney Freedman comes for the weekly poker game. Hawkeye and Trapper operate on a seriously injured counterintelligence officer, defying the rule that another counterintelligence officer be present. In the meantime, Radar is shaken after apparently hitting an old Korean man with his jeep, though the man has no visible injury. When intelligence officer Capt. Halloran arrives, he threatens Hawk and Trap for operating on the counterintelligence officer, but Blake convinces him to join the poker game. Suddenly, shots ring out: A patient who refuses to return to the front has trapped Frank in the showers. Freedman talks him down, and Trapper manages to disarm the man. Radar's accident victim returns for a second time and is recognized as a "professional" accident victim.

Hot Lips and Empty Arms (12/15/73)

Written by Linda Bloodworth and Mary Kay Place. *Directed by* Jackie Cooper. *Guest Stars:* Odessa Cleveland, Sheila Lauritsen, Kellye Nakahara. *Nominated for* Emmy, Outstanding Writing (Linda Bloodworth and Mary Kay Place). *Notes:* Margaret makes reference to her "dead" father. Later in the series, her father visits her at the 4077. Loretta Swit has identified this episode as a first sign of Margaret's dissatisfaction with her life.

The mail finds Henry using a microscope to preview the porno films he ordered from Havana. Margaret is upset over a letter from home saying a friend has married a successful man Margaret turned down. Margaret takes it out on her nurses. When Frank comes to her tent afterward and attempts to console her, she decides she deserves better than him and requests a transfer.

Margaret gets drunk with Hawkeye and Trapper, but then wounded arrive. The doctors sober her up with a shower and coffee. She decides to stay.

Officers Only (12/22/73)

Written by Ed Jurist. *Directed by* Jackie Cooper. *Guest Stars:* Robert F. Simon, Robert Weaver, Clyde Kusatsu, Jamie Farr, Odessa Cleveland, Sheila Lauritsen, Ralph Grosh.

Hawkeye and Trapper operate on a general's badly wounded son. The general arrives to see his son and offers a reward to Hawk and Trap. They request three days in Tokyo. Henry gets periodic updates on their antics. They return to find the general has also built an officers' club. The club's restrictions (only officers are admitted) create a rebellion among the enlisted. At the general's ribbon-cutting ceremony, Hawkeye gets the general to make an exception allowing his own son to be admitted; then Hawk proceeds to let all the other enlisted in as his "relatives."

Henry in Love (1/5/74)

Written by Larry Gelbart and Laurence Marks. *Directed by* Don Weis. *Guest Stars:* Kathrine Baumann, Odessa Cleveland, Sheila Lauritsen, Clyde Kusatsu, Gwen Farrell.

The 4077 suffers the temporary command of Frank while Henry takes R and R in Tokyo. Hawkeye and Trapper get so disgusted they nail Frank inside a large crate. When Henry returns, he isn't interested in hearing about all this from Frank and Margaret. Hawkeye and Trapper can tell something is up. He tells them he's in love, and the object of his affection, Nancy Sue, arrives shortly thereafter. While Henry is called away to surgery, Nancy Sue makes a move on Hawkeye, and he struggles with what he should tell Henry. Radar makes a timely call to Henry's wife, and when Henry talks to her, he remembers who he is in love with.

For Want of a Boot (1/12/74)

Written by Sheldon Keller. *Directed by* Don Weis. *Guest Stars:* Michael Lerner, Suzanne Zenor, Johnny Haymer, Patricia Stevens, Sheila Lauritsen, Jamie Farr.

Cold weather makes Hawk desperate for new boots. He makes a series of deals trying to get them. At last the entire series hinges on one piece of paper: Hawkeye must get Frank and Margaret to sign a psychological discharge for Klinger. Hawkeye fails to get the signatures, the chain of deals falls apart, and Hawkeye closes the show wearing a golf bag over his leg.

Operation Noselift (1/19/74)

Written by Erik Tarloff. *Story by* Paul Richards and Erik Tarloff. *Directed by* Hy Averback. *Guest Stars:* Stuart Margolin, Todd Susman, William Christopher, Patricia Stevens, Lou Elias, Bobbie Mitchell.

A soldier feels that his large nose is ruining his life. He goes to Hawkeye and Trapper to seek a nose job. Although it's against regulations, Hawk calls a plastic surgeon he knows in Tokyo. When the surgeon arrives in camp, he takes a liking to Margaret. Meanwhile, Frank and Margaret are suspicious of the surgeon's presence, so Radar fakes a nose injury playing catch, and Hawkeye and Trap then switch him for the soldier. When the surgeon is diverted by Margaret, he virtually attacks her and creates a scene. Frank and Margaret declare their intention to get to the bottom of who is getting operated on, but they soon find everyone in camp wearing a nose bandage.

The Choson People (1/26/74)

Written by Laurence Marks, Sheldon Keller, and Larry Gelbart. *Story by* Gerry Renert and Jeff Willhelm. *Directed by* Jackie Cooper. *Guest Stars:* Pat Morita, Clare Nono, Dennis Robertson, Jay Jay Jue, Jerry Fujikawa, William Christopher, Bobbie Mitchell.

When locals arrive to reclaim their land, Henry tries to deal with them while Frank again demonstrates his intolerance. Then a Korean woman arrives with a baby and claims Radar is the father. Radar at first denies it, then says the baby is his. A judge advocate officer arrives, and a blood test determines Radar cannot be the father. The woman admits it was a soldier who has left Korea. Radar ends up disappointed—he liked the "respect" he got from being a potential father. The army helps relocate the family further south, and things get back to normal at the 4077.

As You Were (2/2/74)

Written by Larry Gelbart and Laurence Marks. *Story by* Gene Reynolds. *Directed by* Hy Averback. *Guest Stars:* Patricia Stevens, Jamie Farr, William Christopher, Bobbie Mitchell, Kellye Nakahara.

A lull in the war has the camp bored. Hawkeye and Trapper get gorilla suits and try to liven things up. In the meantime, Margaret tells Frank he has to do something about his hernia, and they approach Hawk and Trap to operate. The gorillas discuss it and consent. A rush of casualties amidst a "friendly" shelling of the camp postpones Frank's surgery. Frank's attempts to operate only worsen his condition. The shelling puts out the generator, and they operate with lamps. While Henry delivers a Korean baby, Frank gets his hernia repaired.

Crisis (2/9/74)

Written by Larry Gelbart and Laurence Marks. *Directed by* Don Weis. *Guest Stars:* Jamie Farr, William Christopher.

Henry calls the staff together to announce that supply lines have been cut and there are going to be shortages. Desperation descends as book pages become toilet paper and furniture becomes firewood. They crowd into one tent to conserve heat, and general craziness ensues as they try to get to sleep. Hawkeye and Trapper discover Frank is comfy because of battery-heated socks. Supplies arrive, but Blake needs a new desk—his has been used for firewood.

George (2/16/74)

Written by John Regier and Gary Markowitz. *Directed by* Gene Reynolds. *Guest Stars:* Richard Ely, George Simmons, William Christopher, Patricia Stevens, Bobbie Mitchell.

Hawkeye notices bruises on a GI who comes in wounded. Later, the man tells Hawkeye that he wants to return to the front; he says the reason he has bruises is that he got beat up by others in his unit when they learned he was a homosexual. Hawkeye tells Trapper and then learns Frank knows about the GI's secret and is threatening to get him discharged. They then trick Frank into admitting he cheated on his medical exams and use that as blackmail to stop his report about the GI.

Mail Call (2/23/74)

Written by Larry Gelbart and Laurence Marks. *Directed by* Alan Alda. *Guest Stars:* William Christopher, Jamie Farr. *Note:* Hawkeye gets a sweater from his sister. In later episodes he is an only child.

Mail call brings something for everyone in camp. Frank is bragging about his stock trading in defense interests. In the meantime, Klinger is trying to get out of the army with a series of letters about deaths and pregnancies in his family back home. Hawkeye and Trapper set Frank up for a fall when Hawkeye makes him think he's got a hot stock tip. A drunk Trapper decides to go home to see his girls and knocks Hawkeye down when he tries to stop him. Hawkeye tells Frank about the stock ruse.

A Smattering of Intelligence (3/2/74)

Written by Larry Gelbart and Laurence Marks. *Directed by* Larry Gelbart. *Guest Stars:* Edward Winter, Bill Fletcher. *Note:* Edward Winter becomes Colonel Flagg of the CIA after previously playing Captain Halloran.

An injured Colonel Flagg refuses morphine and asks to speak to Blake. He tells Blake he is a CIA agent and produces a bunch of alias identities. Blake promises to keep his identity secret, but Radar tells everyone who he is. Then Vinnie, an old friend of Trapper's, arrives—a G-2 intelligence man. Vinnie is there to see what Flagg is up to. When Flagg realizes Vinnie's in camp, he rebreaks his arm so he can find out what Vinnie is up to. Hawkeye and Trapper set them up by using Frank's files as a foil. To one agent, Frank is a communist. To the other, he's a fascist. Hawk and Trap admit they set the two spies up. Vinnie and Flagg decide to go off for a cup of coffee.

YEAR 3, 1974-1975

Cast and Crew

Regular Cast: Alan Alda as Hawkeye Pierce, Gary Burghoff as Radar O'Reilly, Larry Linville as Frank Burns, Wayne Rogers as Trapper John McIntire, McLean Stevenson as Henry Blake, and Loretta Swit as Margaret Houlihan. *Produced by* Gene Reynolds and Larry Gelbart. *Developed for Television by* Larry Gelbart. *Associate Producer* Burt Metcalfe. *Production Supervisor* Mark Evans. *Unit Production Manager* Ted Butcher. *Assistant Director* Leonard S. Smith, Jr. *Directors of Photography* William Jurgensen, Joe Jackman. *Film Editors* Fred W. Berger and Stanford Tischler. *Music by* Benny Golson. *Music Supervision* Lionel Newman. *Art Director* Rodger Maus. *Set Decorator* Norman Rockett. *Medical Advisor* Walter D. Dishell, M.D. *Post Production Supervisor* Joseph Silver. *Theme* Johnny Mandel. *Original Songs Sung and Composed by* Loudon Wainwright III.

The General Flipped at Dawn (9/10/74)

Written by Jim Fritzell and Everett Greenbaum. *Directed by* Larry Gelbart. *Nominated for* Emmy, Outstanding Single Performance by Supporting Actor (Harry Morgan); Emmy, Outstanding Film Editing (Stanford Tischler and Fred W. Berger). *Guest Stars:* Harry Morgan, Jamie Farr, Bill Christopher, Lynnette Mettey, Theodore Wilson, Brad Trumbull, Dennis Erdman.

An inspection by a general puts the camp on edge. When the general arrives, the unit's behavior leaves much to be desired, but so does the general's. After talking to a chopper pilot, he decides too much fuel is being wasted and orders a bug-out to move the camp closer to the front. At this point, everyone except Frank has decided the general is nuts. When Hawkeye sends a chopper off with a patient on it instead of letting the general use it for himself, the general calls for a court-martial. When the military hearing is assembled, the general asks the African American pilot for "a musical number" because he has it in his blood. Thus the general exposes his own mental instability, and the MP cancels the hearing.

Rainbow Bridge (9/17/74)

Written by Larry Gelbart and Laurence Marks. *Directed by* Hy Averback. *Guest Stars:* Jamie Farr, William Christopher, Mako, Loudon Wainwright III.

Hawkeye and Trapper get ready for R and R in Tokyo only to have casualties interrupt their plans. The unit gets a call from the Chinese to pickup some American wounded. The pick up point is fifty miles inside North Korea, and they are to bring no guns. Frank and Margaret think its a setup. Trapper, Hawkeye, and Radar go, and Margaret goads Frank into going because there could be a medal in it for him. She also gives him a little pistol—Hawkeye and Trapper don't find out about this until they arrive at the site. Things go well until Frank panics and goes for the pistol, but it's so tiny the Chinese doctor laughs. When they return, Radar packs for their trip to Tokyo, then finds the doctors passed out on their cots.

Officer of the Day (9/24/74)

Written by Laurence Marks. *Directed by* Hy Averback. *Guest Stars:* Jamie Farr, Edward Winter, Dennis Troy, Jeff Maxwell, Jerry Fujikawa, Tad Horino, Richard Lee Sung. *Note:* This episode features Hawkeye's antigun ("carry a gun") soliloquy.

Blake is gone and Frank is in charge, doing his military-regimen bit. Hawkeye is appointed officer of the day, and the job dogs him. Local Koreans, all named Kim Luc, seek medical attention. Flagg arrives with a North Korean prisoner and asks that the prisoner be treated so he can be killed. Klinger tries to escape in a nun's habit and later as a "business girl." Alarmed at Flagg's plan to kill the prisoner, Hawk and Trap devise a plan to stall him. Frank and Margaret take Flagg's side, and he forces them to sign the release. Hawkeye and Trapper get the last laugh as they load Klinger on the ambulance instead of the prisoner.

Iron Guts Kelly (10/1/74)

Written by Larry Gelbart and Sid Dorfman. *Directed by* Don Weis. *Guest Stars:* James Gregory, Keene Curtis, Bobbie Mitchell, Byron Chung, Alberta Jay, Jeff Maxwell, Dennis Troy.

The 4077 prepares for a visit by General Kelly. Both Margaret and Frank fawn over the general, but the general has eyes for Margaret. Soon after the general's arrival, he dies in Margaret's bed. Hawkeye and Trapper help a frightened Margaret drag the body back to the VIP tent. His aide objects to the way he died and plans to have him "die" gloriously in battle instead. Radar has a hard time finding any fighting, so the aide decides to put the body in an ambulance and drive to the front. Margaret manages to conceal the incident from Frank with a tall tale. Before the ambulance leaves camp, some GIs sneak some "business girls" in it; then it pulls out. A phone call brings word that the ambulance has had an accident—the girls are OK, but the general is dead. The newspaper reports the general died in battle.

O.R. (10/8/74)

Written by Larry Gelbart and Laurence Marks. *Directed by* Gene Reynolds. *Winner:* Emmy, Outstanding Directing in Comedy Series (Gene Reynolds); Writers Guild Award (Larry Gelbart and Laurence Marks). *Guest Stars:* Jamie Farr, William Christopher, Allan Arbus, Odessa Cleveland, Bobbie Mitchell, Bobby Herbeck, Orlando Dole, Jeanne Schulherr. *Note:* The laugh track is not used in this episode.

A heavy onslaught of casualties keeps the unit in the OR. An Ethiopian soldier expresses gratitude to Hawkeye, while Frank nearly takes a healthy kidney out of a patient who has only one. Then Hawkeye performs an open-heart massage to revive a patient. Sidney Freedman arrives for the weekly poker game and is told to scrub up and operate. The camp and OR get shelled. Hawkeye learns the heart massage patient has died. A fire starts in OR, causing further panic. When it's over, Hawkeye and Trapper pass out on OR tables.

Springtime (10/15/74)

Written by Linda Bloodworth and Mary Kay Place. *Directed by* Don Weis. *Guest Stars:* Alex Karras, Jamie Farr, William Christopher, Mary Kay Place, Greg Mabrey, Roy Goldman, Jeff Maxwell.

Hawkeye operates on a very large soldier, Lyle, who becomes eternally grateful to him. Radar has his eye on a nurse but is shy about approaching her. Margaret and Frank trade sweet nothings on a picnic. Klinger's girlfriend in Toledo accepts his marriage proposal, and he decides they can get married by telephone. Radar makes a date to read poetry with the nurse, only to have her throw herself at him when he begins to read a poem. Lyle's protection of Hawkeye gets Frank in trouble for harassing Hawkeye. Klinger's wedding ceremony (by radio) gets done just as Radar stumbles in rather disheveled.

Check-Up (10/22/74)

Written by Laurence Marks. *Directed by* Don Weis. *Guest Star:* Jamie Farr.

Blake orders the annual physicals for the unit but Trapper avoids his. Hawkeye confronts Trapper on the exam and Trapper reveals he has an ulcer. Hawkeye tells him that's his ticket home. While the rest of the unit prepares for a farewell party, Radar comes and tells Trapper the army won't be sending him home—he can be treated in Tokyo or at the 4077. They go to the party, where a drunk Margaret tells Trapper she's always admired him. Trapper tells the unit about staying and tells Margaret he will see her later.

Life with Father (10/29/74)

Written by Everett Greenbaum and Jim Fritzell. *Directed by* Hy Averback. *Guest Stars:* William Christopher, Sachiko Penny Lee, Patricia Stevens.

The mail brings some diversion for Hawkeye—a puzzle with the prize of a pony. A Korean woman is looking for a rabbi to perform a bris on her baby, whose father is at the front. Meanwhile, Blake is worried that his wife might be unfaithful. Margaret and Frank object to the bris, since the surgery is against regulations. Radar gets a rabbi on a navy ship, and Mulcahy (who has his own worries after a disturbing letter from his sister) stands in for him for the bris. The bris is completed, and Trapper finds a way to keep Frank from reporting the ceremony. In the meantime, a call from Blake's wife has eased the colonel's mind.

Alcoholics Unanimous (11/12/74)

Written by Everett Greenbaum and Jim Fritzell. *Directed by* Hy Averback. *Nominated for* Emmy, Outstanding Directing in a Comedy Series (Hy Averback); Directors Guild Award (Hy Averback). *Guest Stars:* Jamie Farr, Bobbie Mitchell, William Christopher.

Blake is in Seoul, and Frank is in charge. He bans alcohol and dismantles the infamous still. Hawkeye, Trapper and Margaret later get drunk and then are caught by Frank, who is appalled. He orders Father Mulcahy to give a temperance lecture. Klinger has Mulcahy gear up for the sermon by taking a nip from a bottle. Mulcahy delivers a rather wobbly sermon. Hawkeye and Trapper, on each other's nerves, begin to clash. Frank accidentally gets kicked in the groin, Margaret gives him some booze to ease the pain, and Hawkeye declares the Eighteenth Amendment has been repealed.

There Is Nothing Like a Nurse (11/19/74)

Written by Larry Gelbart. *Directed by* Hy Averback. *Guest Stars:* Jamie Farr, Loudon Wainwright III, William Christopher, Bobbie Mitchell, Jeanne Schulherr, Leland Sun.

A threatened offensive means the nurses have to evacuate and the men are left on their own. Frank has the men digging foxholes and Klinger tries to leave with the nurses. A session in OR without the nurses is chaotic and leaves the OR a shambles. Hawkeye and Trapper listen in on a conversation between Frank and Margaret. Angry, he chases them until he falls into one of the foxholes. They cover it by parking a jeep over it. They watch a home movie belonging to Frank—a hilarious film of his wedding. All rejoice when the nurses return.

Adam's Ribs (11/26/74)

Written by Laurence Marks. *Directed by* Gene Reynolds. *Guest Stars:* Jamie Farr, Basil Hoffman, Joseph Stern, Jeff Maxwell.

A bored Hawkeye has had it with army food and starts a rebellion in the mess tent. Blake, upset with the antics, orders him to come up with diversion for the camp. He dreams up a scheme to get some carryout barbecued ribs from Chicago. Just when the ribs make it to the 4077, casualties arrive, and Hawkeye has to pull himself away from his long-awaited feast.

A Full Rich Day (12/3/74)

Written by John D. Hess. *Directed by* Gene Reynolds. *Winner:* ACE Eddie Award, Editing (Fred W. Berger and Stanford Tischler). *Guest Stars:* Jamie Farr, William Watson, Sirri Murad, Curt Lowens, Michael Keller, Kellye Nakahara.

Hawkeye's letter home to his father describes a full, rich day. An injured soldier from Luxembourg is presumed dead but can't be found when his superior officer arrives. Then, a gun-wielding lieutenant insists his injured sergeant be operated on first. A Turkish soldier panics in the OR, wields a syringe, and stabs it in Henry's hand, causing him to pass out. Later, a drink with a sedative meant for the Turk is drunk by Radar. Radar and the Turk take off in the jeep only to return a short time later with Radar passed out. The Luxembourg officer becomes offended when his soldier can't be found, so they put on a memorial ceremony for the man. As it turns out, however, the man is alive.

Mad Dogs and Servicemen (12/10/74)

Written by Linda Bloodworth and Mary Kay Place. *Directed by* Hy Averback. *Guest Stars:* Michael O'Keefe, Shizuko Hoshi, Arthur Song, Jeff Maxwell, Bobbie Mitchell.

A scratch on Radar's hand is from a local dog, and Hawkeye is concerned about rabies. Radar and Blake search for the dog but come up empty-handed, so Radar begins rabies shots. Meanwhile, Frank is giving a hard time to a patient with hysterical paralysis—he wants to send him to Tokyo. Hawkeye and Trapper consult Sidney Freedman. Blake sees the dog in camp and tries to catch it but causes panic throughout the camp as he does so. It turns out the dog is okay. Trapper gets the paralyzed soldier to talk, and eventually he gets up and walks.

Private Charles Lamb (12/31/74)

Written by Larry Gelbart and Sid Dorfman. *Directed by* Hy Averback. *Nominated for* Writers Guild Award (Sid Dorfman). *Guest Stars:* Ted Eccles, Titos Vandis.

Several wounded Greek soldiers come to the 4077 for treatment. A Greek colonel brings an Easter feast to the 4077 in gratitude. Radar is alarmed that a lamb will be used for the feast. Meanwhile, a soldier with a foot wound suspected to be self-inflicted visits Father Mulcahy's tent and mistakes Frank for the padre. He confesses his wound is self-inflicted, and Frank tells him he will report him. When Hawkeye and Trapper remind him he was impersonating a priest, Frank backs off. The lamb disappears—Radar had Blake sign the lamb's discharge. The episode closes with the Easter feast, complete with spam lamb.

Bombed (1/7/75)

Written by Jim Fritzell and Everett Greenbaum. *Directed by* Hy Averback. *Nominated for* Emmy, Outstanding Achievement in Cinematography (William Jurgensen); Directors Guild Award (Hy Averback). *Guest Stars:* Jamie Farr, William Christopher, Louisa Mortiz, Edward Marshall. *Notes:* Margaret implies her father is dead. Later in the series her parents are divorced, and her father visits her at the 4077 in year nine's "Father's Day."

Heavy shelling of the 4077 during an onslaught of casualties creates chaos. A booby-trapped soldier arrives; Hawk and Trap disarm him. Radar's calls to HQ elicit the information that the shelling is "friendly." Margaret and Trapper get stuck in the supply tent overnight when a shell causes the door to jam. When they are freed the next morning, Frank becomes obsessed with what might have transpired between them. Jealous, he proposes to Margaret to prove his love, but he recants when the bombs stop flying.

Bulletin Board (1/14/75)

Written by Larry Gelbart and Simon Munter. *Directed by* Alan Alda. *Nominated for* Emmy, Outstanding Directing in a Comedy (Alan Alda). *Guest Stars:* Jamie Farr, William Christopher, Johnny Haymer, Patricia Stevens, Kellye Nakahara.

This episode is a slice of life at the 4077. Hawkeye and Trapper seek new ways to pass the time. Margaret comes to ask Frank for a loan, and he balks. Trapper's letter to his little girl tries to explain what he does—like operating in cold weather. A frozen soldier comes into camp, and Frank declares him dead, but Trapper checks him and finds a pulse. Hawkeye convinces Henry the unit needs diversion and they reschedule a cancelled picnic. At the picnic, Frank runs into the finish of a nurses' race. The episode closes with a tug of war in which everyone gets muddy. Then, Radar announces more choppers are on the way.

The Consultant (1/21/75)

Written by Larry Gelbart and Robert Klane. *Directed by* Gene Reynolds. *Guest Stars:* William Christopher, Robert Alda, Joseph Maher, Tad Horino. *Note:* Alan Alda's father, Robert Alda, guest stars as Borelli.

While in Tokyo for a surgical clinic, Hawkeye and Trapper meet Dr. Borelli, a civilian medical consultant with service in both world wars. A chopper arrives at the 4077 shortly thereafter with Borelli aboard. When the wounded arrive, Borelli suits up and tells them they can save a soldier's legs with artery grafting. But when the graft is delivered, Borelli is found in the Swamp holding a glass of booze. A resentful Hawkeye completes the procedure and later confronts Borelli in the Swamp. Borelli challenges Hawk to think where he might be after two wars.

House Arrest (2/4/75)

Written by Jim Fritzell and Everett Greenbaum. *Directed by* Hy Averback. *Guest Stars:* Jamie Farr, William Christopher, Mary Wickes, Bobbie Mitchell, Jeff Maxwell, Dennis Troy, Kellye Nakahara.

A visit by a fussy colonel coming to inspect Margaret and the nursing staff has Margaret nervous. An edgy Frank irritates Hawkeye, and their quarrel ends with Frank getting punched. Frank presses charges against Hawkeye.

Witnesses Trapper and Margaret have different stories. In the meantime, the inspecting colonel has her eyes on Frank and tries to seduce him. He resists, but she manages to frame him with cries of rape. Margaret decides Hawkeye didn't hit Frank after all.

Aid Station (2/11/75)

Written by Larry Gelbart and Simon Munter. *Directed by* William Jurgensen. *Guest Stars:* Jamie Farr, William Christopher.

The unit gets a call for a medical team to go to an aid station at the front after their surgeon is killed. Hawkeye, Margaret and Klinger will go. (A panicky Klinger starts giving his dresses away.) The trio performs admirably in open-air, live-shelling conditions. Back at the 4077, Frank complains about the primitive conditions while the others worry about the three at the front. The three return triumphantly; while away, each has learned to appreciate something about his or her comrades.

Love and Marriage (2/18/75)

Written by Arthur Julian. *Directed by* Lee Phillips. *Guest Stars:* Soon-Teck Oh, Johnny Haymer, Dennis Dugan, Jerry Fujikawa, Pat Li, Robert Gruber, Jeanne Joe, William Christopher, Roy Goldman. *Note:* Dennis Dugan reappears as Potter's son-in-law in year ten's "Strange Bedfellows."

Frank is complaining about everything during an OR session. Hawkeye and Trapper learn a Korean orderly was a student who was "drafted" so suddenly that he was unable to tell his expectant wife goodbye. Radar tricks Henry into signing a pass for the man. Then a GI comes in and says he wants to marry one of the girls from Rosie's bar. Later, Hawkeye and Trapper learn that American men are being paid to marry women who then become prostitutes in the United States. X-rays reveal the bar girl has tuberculosis, canceling the "marriage." When the Korean orderly is captured and brought back to the 4077, Hawkeye and Radar go get his wife, and she has the baby on the way back to the camp.

Big Mac (2/25/75)

Written by Laurence Marks. *Directed by* Don Weis. *Nominated for* Writers Guild Award (Laurence Marks). *Guest Stars:* Jamie Farr, Graham Jarvis, Loudon Wainwright III.

Radar gets a phone call and scrambles to the OR to get Henry. Blake learns that MacArthur is coming to visit the 4077 in honor of its record. A visit by a colonel details a second-by-second itinerary. The camp spruces up for the visit, and Henry does his best to keep Klinger out of sight. Margaret and Frank visit "Mac's" VIP tent and decide to give the bed a workout. A comical rehearsal is interrupted by the actual visit. "Big Mac" gives a salute from his jeep and keeps moving. He sees Klinger dressed as the Statue of Liberty and gives another salute before rolling on.

Payday (3/4//75)

Written by John Regier and Gary Markowitz. *Directed by* Hy Averback. *Guest Stars:* Jamie Farr, William Christopher, Jack Soo, Eldon Quick, Johnny Haymer, Bobbie Mitchell, Jeff Maxwell, Pat Marshall.

It's Hawkeye's turn as pay officer, and when he has $10 left, Radar panics—he has to file reports. This inspires Hawkeye to jokingly tell Radar to bill the army for all the lost income he could have made back home. When $3,000 from the army arrives, an amused Hawkeye tells Radar he really didn't mean it, and he decides to give the money to Father Mulcahy for the orphanage. Then a captain arrives to investigate regarding the $3,000, which he wants back. When Trapper wins big at the poker game after tricking Hawkeye into a loan, Hawk takes the winnings to pay the captain.

White Gold (3/11/75)

Written by Larry Gelbart and Simon Munter. *Directed by* Hy Averback. *Guest Stars:* Jamie Farr, William Christopher, Edward Winter, Hilly Hicks, Stafford Repp, Michael A. Salcido, Daniel Thorpe.

With Klinger on guard duty, thieves arrive looking for penicillin. One (an American) is caught but refuses to talk. Hawkeye and Trapper suspect the thieves are selling the penicillin on the black market. When Col. Flagg arrives to investigate, his behavior is very suspicious, and the doctors eventually discover that the CIA uses penicillin to barter for information. A resentful Hawkeye reminds him the 4077 uses it to save lives. The MPs bring in the original thieves. They are medics who haven't been getting enough and were buying and stealing to augment their supply. Hawkeye and Trapper subdue Flagg and keep him out of action with an appendectomy.

Abyssinia, Henry (3/18/75)

Written by Everett Greenbaum and Jim Fritzell. *Directed by* Larry Gelbart. *Guest Stars:* Jamie Farr, William Christopher. *Notes:* Blake's departure based on getting enough points is inaccurate for the Korean War. The point system had been abandoned after World War II. The final scene of this episode was kept secret from the cast until just before shooting it. The episode generated a great deal of mail, both positive and negative.

Radar comes in during an OR session to tell Henry that he has enough points to go home. Frank and Margaret plan their takeover while Henry prepares to leave. Radar and Henry have a poignant exchange about feeling like father and son. Trapper, Hawkeye, Blake, and Radar get drunk at Rosie's and demilitarize Henry. When Henry comes out to depart in the morning, he says his goodbyes. Radar salutes him. Radar comes into the OR later to tell the unit that Blake's plane was shot down over the Sea of Japan. There were no survivors.

YEAR 4, 1975-1976

Cast and Crew

Regular Cast: Alan Alda as Hawkeye Pierce, Gary Burghoff as Radar O'Reilly, Mike Farrell as B.J. Hunnicutt, Larry Linville as Frank Burns, Harry Morgan as Sherman Potter, Loretta Swit as Margaret Houlihan, and Jamie Farr as Max Klinger. *Produced by* Gene Reynolds and Larry Gelbart. *Developed for Television by* Larry Gelbart. *Associate Producer* Burt Metcalfe. *Executive Production Manager* Mark Evans. *Unit Production Manager* Ted Butcher. *Assistant Director* Leonard S. Smith, Jr. *Directors of Photography* William Jurgensen, Meredith Nicholson, Andrew Jackson. *Film Editors* Fred W. Berger and Stanford Tischler. *Music by* Pete Rugolo. *Music Supervision* Lionel Newman. *Art Director* Rodger Maus. *Set Decorator* Norman Rockett. *Medical Advisor* Walter D. Dishell, M.D. *Post Production Supervisor* Joseph Silver. *Theme* Johnny Mandel.

Welcome to Korea (9/12/75. One-hour episode)

Written by Everett Greenbaum, Jim Fritzell, and Larry Gelbart. *Directed by* Gene Reynolds. *Winner:* Emmy, Outstanding Directing in a Comedy (Gene Reynolds); Emmy, Outstanding Film Editing for a Series (Fred W. Berger and Stanford Tischler); Writers Guild Award (Everett Greenbaum, Jim Fritzell and Larry Gelbart); ACE Eddie Award, Editing (Fred W. Berger and Stanford Tischler). *Guest Stars:* William Christopher, Robert A. Karnes, Tom Dever, Ted Zeigler, Reid Cruickshanks, Nat Jones.

Frank is in charge and applying his military mindset to the 4077. Hawkeye returns from Tokyo to find Trapper has returned home. Hawkeye wants to go to Seoul to say goodbye, but Frank refuses. When Radar gets in a jeep to get Trapper's replacement, Hawkeye goes along. Margaret and Frank, looking over the new man's record, envision shaping him in their image. In Seoul, Hawkeye learns he just missed Trapper, while Radar has tracked down B.J. Hunnicutt, the newest surgeon for the 4077. They find their jeep stolen when they get ready to return. Before they steal a general's jeep to get home, Hawkeye and B.J. get to know each other. On the way back to camp, B.J. gets his first taste of the realities of war, including mine injuries to civilians, sniper fire, and shelling. Almost home, they stop at Rosie's, and Hawkeye and B.J. get riproaring drunk. Back at camp, B.J. quickly demonstrates he will not fulfill Margaret and Frank's hopes. Frank gets picked up for stealing the general's jeep when he shows lousy timing in using it. The episode closes with a "preview" of the arrival of Colonel Potter.

Change of Command (9/19/75)

Written by Jim Fritzell and Everett Greenbaum. *Directed by* Gene Reynolds. *Guest Star:* William Christopher.

Hawkeye and B.J. finish building the "Henry Blake Memorial Bar" just as Radar comes in with news that a new commander is coming. Margaret is outraged to hear that Frank is being replaced, and Frank weeps in her tent. Potter arrives and quickly meets Klinger, who is anxious to start working him for a Section Eight. An officers' meeting finds Frank has apparently left the 4077. Margaret informs Hawkeye and B.J. he has gone AWOL. Choppers arrive, and after a long OR session, Potter declares he could use a belt. Hawkeye and B.J. are happy to be of service in this matter. Frank finally returns, and when Klinger comes in wearing a sailor's dress to see Potter, Frank is stunned to hear Potter say, "Nice outfit, Klinger!"

It Happened One Night (9/26/75)

Written by Larry Gelbart and Simon Munter. *Story by* Gene Reynolds. *Directed by* Gene Reynolds. *Guest Stars:* Christopher Allport, Darren O'Connor.

It's a cold but active night at the 4077, even though the camp is under blackout conditions due to shelling. A patient who is particularly edgy reacts violently when the shelling comes close. They finally find out it's friendly fire—again. Frank gets upset when Margaret tells him she keeps all his love notes. He goes to her tent while she is on duty and tears the place apart looking for the notes. A new guard accidentally shoots Klinger in the foot, and though it's not much, Klinger acts like he's on his deathbed. Later he comes in from the cold wearing only underwear—he's hoping pneumonia will get him home. After Margaret helps Hawkeye subdue the edgy patient with a sedative, she returns to her tent to find Frank asleep and her tent in shambles.

The Late Captain Pierce (10/3/75)

Written by Glen Charles and Les Charles. *Directed by* Alan Alda. *Guest Stars:* Richard Masur, Eldon Quick, Sherry Stevens, Kellye Nakahara.

Hawkeye is horrified to learn he's been reported dead. He tries to telephone his father immediately, but phones are cut off due to a visit by Eisenhower. Klinger tries to send a telegram but can't do that either. After Hawkeye's mail gets stopped, he gets a visitor from HQ who explains how he became "dead" and describes the mountains of red tape it will take to get him living again in the army's eyes. Frustrated, he gets on a bus hoping to get himself home but returns as the choppers bring wounded. Eventually, he talks to his father.

Hey Doc (10/10/75)

Written by Rich Mittleman. *Directed by* William Jurgensen. *Guest Stars:* Frank Marth, Bruce Kirby, Ted Hamilton, William Christopher.

In another of his elaborately crafted series of deals, Hawkeye (aided by B.J.) succeeds in getting a medical excuse for a sergeant who wants to return home by boat instead of plane. The doctors also manage to acquire some bottles of scotch (subsequently destroyed by sniper fire) and a microscope. Frank gets a chance to drive a tank and nearly runs over the whole camp.

The Bus (10/17/75)

Written by John D. Hess. *Directed by* Gene Reynolds. *Guest Star:* Soon-Teck Oh.

Hawkeye, Radar, B.J., Potter, and Frank are on the bus coming back from a medical conference but get lost. After they stop to try to determine where they are, the bus fails to start when they try to leave. Frank has candy bars but doesn't share. Radar, blaming himself for getting lost, goes out to look for help and doesn't come back. They go out looking for him but come up empty-handed. A North Korean surrenders to them. Radar returns and wakes Frank up and sees the chocolate. The prisoner works on the bus and gets it going. Frank "discovers" his chocolate bars on the way home and shares them.

Dear Mildred (10/24/75)

Written by Everett Greenbaum and Jim Fritzell. *Directed by* Alan Alda. *Guest Stars:* William Christopher, Richard Lee Sung, Buck Young, Patricia Stevens, Barbara Christopher.

Potter writes a letter to his wife and tells her about the 4077. Both he and Radar are having a tough time getting used to each other. Radar learns Potter's anniversary is coming up. Frank and Margaret arrange for a local craftsman to carve a bust of Potter. When a chopper pilot mentions an injured horse near the front, Radar insists they save it. He coaxes the horse to go with them. Hawkeye and B.J. tell him he will have to get rid of it until he decides to give it to Potter.

The Kids (10/31/75)

Written by Jim Fritzell and Everett Greenbaum. *Directed by* Alan Alda. *Guest Stars:* Ann Doran, Mitchell Sakamoto, Haunani Minn, William Christopher, Kellye Nakahara, Chrisleen Sun, Darrin Lee. *Nominated for* Emmy, Outstanding Directing in a Comedy (Alan Alda).

The 4077 hosts Nurse Cratty and the orphans during heavy fighting. While they prepare, Frank shows Margaret a purple heart he received—for being wounded when a piece of eggshell hit him in the eye. Hawkeye and B.J. object to the purple heart and give Frank a hard time. A pregnant woman who's been shot comes into camp. They deliver a baby nicked in the rear by a bullet. While Frank rants and raves about the children, he finds his purple heart being pinned on the new baby.

Quo Vadis, Captain Chandler (11/7/75)

Written by Burt Prelutsky. *Directed by* Larry Gelbart. *Guest Stars:* Allan Arbus, Edward Winter, Alan Fudge, William Christopher. *Note:* The laugh track is not used in this episode.

Among the wounded who arrive on a bus is a man who says he is Jesus Christ. Hawkeye, B.J., and Father Mulcahy all talk to him. Frank and Margaret, convinced the man is feigning mental illness to get out of war, call Col. Flagg. Flagg arrives and says the man is a bomber pilot and wants to send him back to work. Sydney Freedman comes in for a consultation. Flagg implies that Freedman is a communist sympathizer. Flagg wants the man returned to the front; otherwise he's afraid a lot of others would feign battle fatigue too. Sidney recommends Tokyo. When the man leaves, Radar approaches him to bless his teddy bear, and he blesses everyone. In the epilogue, Klinger appears dressed as Moses.

Dear Peggy (11/14/75)

Written by Jim Fritzell and Everett Greenbaum. *Directed by* Burt Metcalfe. *Guest Stars:* Ned Beatty, William Christopher.

B.J.'s letter to his wife, Peggy, tells her about life at the 4077. He does a heart massage to revive a patient Frank had declared dead, and Frank resents him for doing so. Meanwhile, Father Mulcahy is worried about the imminent arrival of Col. Hollister, who is coming to inspect him. Hawkeye organizes a jeep-stuffing prank after he reads about one back home. Hollister arrives concerned about the hijinks and finds Mulcahy at the bottom of the stuffed jeep. Hollister confronts Mulcahy on his style with his own fire and brimstone. As usual, Klinger tries a number of ruses to get out.

Of Moose and Men (11/21/75)

Written by Jay Folb. *Directed by* John Erman. *Guest Stars:* Johnny Haymer, Tim O'Connor.

Hawkeye clashes with a military police colonel on the way home from working on civilians. Meanwhile, at the 4077, Sgt. Zale gets a letter from his wife admitting her infidelity. B.J. tries to help him only to find out later Zale has a "moose" (a Korean female slave) in Korea. Hawkeye and Frank pull in with civilian wounded and the colonel he confronted on the road—a mine went off at the checkpoint. Frank suspects the Koreans of sabotage and becomes paranoid about everything. Hawkeye puts the colonel back together, yet when Potter visits with the man he learns the colonel wants Hawkeye disciplined. Potter defends Hawkeye and tells the man he is living because of him. The man calls Hawkeye to his bed and tells him he will go easy by not court-martialing him. B.J. decides to confront Zale about his infidelity and hypocrisy.

Soldier of the Month (11/28/75)

Written by Linda Bloodworth. *Directed by* Gene Reynolds. *Guest Stars:* Johnny Haymer, William Christopher.

At the staff meeting, Potter tells the staff he is concerned about a fever that has striken many soldiers. He also announces a "Soldier of the Month" contest with a prize of six days in Tokyo. Things get much more military as a result—even Klinger gets dressed in full uniform. Meanwhile, Father Mulcahy tracks down information on treatment for the fever victims. Frank, trying to catch the rats whose lice are thought the source of the fever, gets sick himself. A delirious Frank dictates a will to Mulcahy. Hawkeye and B.J. administer the quiz and expose Klinger for cheating. Radar wins the contest.

The Gun (12/2/75)

Written by Larry Gelbart and Gene Reynolds. *Directed by* Burt Metcalfe. *Guest Stars:* Warren Stevens, William Christopher.

A late-night accident between two American vehicles brings wounded to the 4077. Radar takes a rare pistol from a colonel. Frank admires it while Radar locks it away. Later Frank steals it, leaving Radar in terrible trouble with the gun's owner. Hawkeye and B.J. corner Frank. Meanwhile, Radar drinks his troubles away and goes to the hospital to tell the colonel off. Frank shoots himself as he tries to return the gun.

Mail Call Again (12/9/75)

Written by Jim Fritzell and Everett Greenbaum. *Directed by* George Tyne. *Guest Star:* William Christopher.

This episode follows Radar as he distributes the mail. Potter gets a letter from his son telling him he will be a grandfather. Radar suggests a pool for date, weight and sex of the child. Frank's mail brings bad news—his wife has heard about Margaret and wants a divorce. Upset, he heads for the office to call his wife. He tells her that Margaret is an army mule with bosoms. He gets his wife to call off the divorce and then encounters Margaret throwing things at him. After the staff watches Radar's home movies, the phone rings with news of Potter's granddaughter. Father Mulcahy wins the pool.

The Price of Tomato Juice (12/16/75)

Written by Larry Gelbart and Gene Reynolds. *Directed by* Gene Reynolds. *Guest Stars:* James Jeter, William Christopher.

Radar initiates a series of deals to get a shipment of tomato juice as a surprise for Colonel Potter. The deals begin with a pair of nylons (to be donated by Klinger in return for a pass) and end with Radar procuring the juice, only to discover that Potter is allergic. In between lies everything from a general's interest in Margaret to a fake marriage proposal to Margaret from Frank; and when the general's car arrives to pick up Margaret for a rendezvous, Klinger is smuggled out of camp in her place.

Dear Ma (12/23/75)

Written by Everett Greenbaum and Jim Fritzell. *Directed by* Alan Alda. *Guest Stars:* Redmond Gleeson, Byron Chung, John Fujioka, William Christopher, Rollin Moriyama, Lynn Marie Stewart, Gwen Farrell.

Radar's letter home follows him as he assists Hawkeye in the annual foot inspection. Radar encounters a North Korean soldier in the mess tent, and Frank becomes anxious about enemy invaders. Then Radar takes a call from Mrs. Potter while the colonel is away—she had a premonition Colonel Potter has been injured. Frank overhears two South Koreans with B.J. and tackles one, thinking he is a North Korean. When Margaret and Potter return, he has been shot in the rear by snipers. Frank, who has been avoiding his foot inspection, is tackled by B.J. and Hawkeye, who discover his toenails are painted with Margaret's nail polish.

Der Tag (1/6/76)

Written by Everett Greenbaum and Jim Fritzell. *Directed by* Gene Reynolds. *Guest Stars:* Joe Morton, William Christopher.

Frank gets jealous when he hears that Margaret, on leave in Tokyo, is having fun without him. Col. Potter asks Hawkeye and B.J. to be nice to Frank as he is especially difficult without Margaret. They invite him to play poker. When he gets obnoxiously drunk, they put him to bed and put a body tag on him as a joke. When Frank goes to the latrine, he stumbles into an ambulance, which takes him to the front. When B.J. and Hawkeye go to get him, they run into heavy action. When they return with Frank they discover he has been sleeping the whole time.

Hawkeye (1/13/76)

Written by Larry Gelbart and Simon Munter. *Directed by* Larry Gelbart. *Nominated for* Emmy, Outstanding Writing in Comedy (Larry Gelbart and Simon Munter); Emmy, Outstanding Achievement in Cinematography (William Jurgensen). *Guest Stars:* Philip Ahn, Shizuko Hoshi, Susan Sakimoto, June Kim, Jeff Osaka, Jayleen Sun. *Notes:* Episode is a soliloquy by Hawkeye. In this episode he says he is an only child, though earlier episodes made reference to his sister.

Hawkeye is driving a jeep when he swerves to miss some kids and tips the jeep. A family brings him into their home, and he writes a note to take to the 4077. He realizes he has a concussion, so he tries to stay awake. He talks endlessly in a stream of consciousness. A jeep's horn sounds and he says good-bye. In the epilogue, he returns to the family with gifts.

Some 38th Parallels (1/20/76)

Written by John Regier and Gary Markowitz. *Directed by* Burt Metcalfe. *Guest Stars:* George O'Hanlon, Jr., Lynnette Mettey, Kevin Hagen, William Christopher.

The staff is working on lots of casualties, many from a colonel who loses many men while recovering the dead. Radar notices an IV disconnected from a patient, and B.J. tells him he may have saved the man's life. Radar becomes friendly with the patient. Frank comes up with a scheme to auction garbage to local Koreans. Hawkeye, on a date, "can't" and is worried. More wounded arrive, among them the colonel responsible for so many wounded. Hawkeye and B.J. give him a hard time. The patient Radar is friendly with dies and he is shocked. Hawkeye, who has purchased much of Frank's garbage, uses the garbage to make an effective statement of his feelings toward the gung-ho colonel. Feeling his vigor restored, Hawkeye approaches Nurse Abel.

The Novocaine Mutiny (1/27/76)

Written by Burt Prelutsky. *Directed by* Harry Morgan. *Guest Stars:* Ned Wilson, Johnny Haymer, William Christopher. *Note:* Hawkeye talks about his mother sending him civilian underwear. In later episodes, only his father is said to be alive.

Frank, Potter, B.J., and Hawkeye are at a preliminary hearing. Hawkeye is charged with mutiny for usurping Frank's authority. There are several versions of what happened. According to Frank, he was trying to hold the 4077 together during heavy casualties when everyone else was falling apart. Hawkeye, B.J., and Radar testify that it was Frank who was out of control. The judge drops all charges and puts Frank in his place.

Smilin' Jack (2/3/76)

Written by Larry Gelbart and Simon Munter. *Directed by* Charles S. Dubin. *Guest Stars:* Robert Hogan, Dennis Kort.

Helicopter pilot Jack Mitchell is competing to get the highest number of patients transferred for the year. When Potter notices a sore on Mitchell's hand that hasn't healed, he asks Mitchell about it, but the pilot shrugs him off. Later he admits he's diabetic, a fact he's been hiding to keep from getting grounded. He manages to take off with the chopper to get enough wounded to set the record. Potter radios him, but he brings back four wounded, only to be beaten by another pilot once he is grounded. Meanwhile, Radar encourages a twice-wounded soldier by giving him his four-leaf clover.

The More I See You (2/10/76)

Written by Larry Gelbart and Gene Reynolds. *Directed by* Gene Reynolds. *Guest Stars:* Blythe Danner, Mary Jo Catlett, William Christopher.

Carlye, a new nurse at the 4077, is Hawkeye's former lover. Now Carlye is married, and though she and Hawkeye agree they can just work together, their love for each other becomes reignited. Carlye decides to get a transfer. When Hawkeye finds out, he very awkwardly proposes to her—he convinces himself marriage would be fine. She tells him he is married to his career and says goodbye.

Deluge (2/17/76)
Written by Larry Gelbart and Simon Munter. *Directed by* William Jurgensen. *Guest Stars:* William Christopher, Kario Salem, Anthony Palmer, Lois Foraker, Albert Hall, Tom Ruben, Lynn Marie Stewart. *Note:* Episode is interspersed with newsreel footage, some of it about the French in Vietnam.

Potter is on the phone, asking for more warning when heavy casualties are expected. When those casualties come, Hawkeye and Frank clash. Mulcahy works with a patient who promised God he'd become a priest if he lived. In the OR, all is confusion. A soldier throws a cigarette in a laundry hamper and starts a fire. Klinger, attempting to put it out, throws a bowl of alcohol on it. Then a shell explodes right outside the OR and causes chaos. The epilogue finds Hawkeye and B.J. exhausted while the PA announces the unit has received a medal for meritorious conduct.

The Interview (2/24/76)
Written by Larry Gelbart. *Directed by* Larry Gelbart (his final episode). *Guest Stars:* Clete Roberts, William Christopher. *Notes:* The entire episode is filmed in black and white and there is no laugh track. The episode was scripted in reverse—the interviews were done spontaneously and segments were edited for use in the final product. Clete Roberts was a journalist during the Korean War.

Clete Roberts introduces this episode as his show. He's come to Korea to interview the 4077 because of its 97 percent efficiency rating. He asks a series of questions of Hawkeye, B.J., Frank, Radar, Klinger, and Potter. They talk about how they cope with their situation, what they miss about home, how they feel about the people they work with, and whether they see any good coming from the war.

YEAR 5, 1976-1977

Cast and Crew

Regular Cast: Alan Alda as Hawkeye Pierce, Gary Burghoff as Radar O'Reilly, Mike Farrell as B.J. Hunnicutt, Larry Linville as Frank Burns, Harry Morgan as Sherman Potter, Loretta Swit as Margaret Houlihan, Jamie Farr as Max Klinger, and William Christopher as Father Mulcahy. *Executive Producer* Gene Reynolds. *Produced by* Allan Katz, Don Reo, and Burt Metcalfe. *Story Consultant* Jay Folb. *Developed for Television by* Larry Gelbart. *Executive Production Manager* Mark Evans. *Unit Production Manager* Ted Butcher. *Assistant Director* David Hawks. *Directors of Photography* William Jurgensen, Meredith Nicholson, Sherman Kunkle. *Film Editors* Fred W. Berger, Stanford Tischler, Larry L. Mills, Samuel E. Beetley. *Music by* John Parker.

Music Supervision Lionel Newman. *Art Director* Rodger Maus. *Set Decorator* Bert Allen. *Medical Advisor* Walter D. Dishell, M.D. *Post Production Supervisor* Joseph Silver. *Theme* Johnny Mandel.

Bug Out (9/21/76, One-hour show)

Written by Jim Fritzell and Everett Greenbaum. *Directed* by Gene Reynolds. *Guest Stars:* Richard Lee Sung, Frances Fong, Don Eitner, Barry Cahill, James Lough, Eileen Saki.

A rumor that there's going to be a practice bug-out causes anxiety. When Potter assembles the unit to squelch the rumor, the call comes in to bug out. Meanwhile, Hawkeye begins surgery on a patient with a spinal injury. The bug-out proceeds without him, Margaret, and Radar, and they learn shortly after the unit leaves that they are in the middle of the front. When Potter reaches the buildings he had scouted by helicopter, he finds the house full of "business girls," and Potter gives them Klinger's dresses to persuade them to leave the house. A helicopter comes to evacuate the spinal injury patient, and just as the three get ready to go to the new location, they find the 4077 is already returning.

Margaret's Engagement (9/28/76)

Written by Gary Markowitz. *Directed by* Alan Alda.

When Margaret calls Potter from Tokyo giddy and promising good news when she returns, the whole camp gets curious. When she returns, she shows them an engagement ring. Frank takes it hard and rips the doors off the mess tent. She brags about her beau, Lt. Col. Donald Penobscot. Frank makes one last stab at winning her back, and when she rebukes him, he puts on camouflage and goes looking for enemies. He returns with a Korean family and its cow. Radar places a timely call to Frank's mother, and he cries himself to sleep on the phone.

Out of Sight, Out of Mind (10/5/76)

Written by Ken Levine and David Isaacs. *Directed by* Gene Reynolds. *Guest Stars:* Tom Sullivan, Judy Farrell, Enid Kent, Dudley Knight, Kellye Nakahara, Bobbie Mitchell.

Hawkeye suffers an eye injury that leaves him temporarily blind. Radar impersonates a general to insure a visit by the best eye specialist, who promises nothing. For several days, Hawkeye worries about his future, but he also discovers a new way to experience life. He shares his experience with a patient who has lost his eyesight and is having a hard time writing his wife. When the specialist returns, he is able to see.

Lt. Radar O'Reilly (10/12/76)

Written by Everett Greenbaum and Jim Fritzell. *Directed by* Alan Rafkin. *Nominated for* Emmy, Outstanding Directing in a Comedy (Alan Rafkin).

Guest Stars: Sandy Kenyon, Johnny Haymer, Raymond Chao, Lynne Marie Stewart, Jeff Maxwell.

When a master sergeant fails to pay his gambling debts, Hawkeye and B.J. make a deal with him to promote Radar to lieutenant. Before Radar finds out, he finds himself the object of a nurse's desires. When Potter reads the promotion announcement, he's stunned that Radar has jumped a rank. He gets put down by his buddies and has a hard time giving them orders. To top it off, the nurse no longer wants him because she's attracted to underdogs. Radar goes to Hawkeye and B.J. and asks to have them demote him. They do, and he finds his nurse friend is interested again.

The Nurses (10/19/76)

Written by Linda Bloodworth. *Directed by* Joan Darling. *Nominated for* Emmy, Outstanding Directing in a Comedy (Joan Darling). *Guest Stars:* Greg Harrison, Linda Kelsey, Mary Jo Catlett, Carol Lawson Locatell, Patricia Sturges. *Note:* For Loretta Swit, this episode marks the first major change in her character.

Margaret is uptight in OR and hard on the nurses. When she comes into their tent she gets angry about their unmilitary conduct and general disrespect of her. She clashes with Nurse Baker and confines her to her tent. Things get complicated when Baker's husband, Tony, arrives with a 24-hour pass. They have not seen each other since they married, and Hawkeye and B.J. try to help her find a place where she can be with her husband for the night. The next morning, Margaret is angry with Baker for sneaking out of the nurses' tent. The nurses confront Margaret on her straight military ways, and she tells them she's jealous of their camaraderie—they never once have asked her to join them in a "lousy cup of coffee." In the epilogue, she visits the nurse's tent for coffee.

The Abduction of Margaret Houlihan (10/26/76)

Written by Alan Katz and Don Reo. *Story by* Gene Reynolds. *Directed by* Gene Reynolds. *Guest Stars:* Edward Winter, June Kim, Le Quynh, Susan Bredhoff, Lynne Marie Stewart, Susan Sakimoto, Jon Yune, Jay Fenichel.

Klinger warns Margaret there are North Koreans around the area when she goes with a Korean girl to help a woman give birth. When she is not in camp the next day, Radar begins to panic. Frank decides he will take things into his own hands, mishandles his pistol, and shoots B.J. in the leg. Things get crazier when Col. Flagg arrives to investigate and decides Margaret has been taken by the Chinese. When she strolls into camp with baby and mother, the search is called off. When Flagg tries to leave, he suffers an ignominious injury and has to stay.

Dear Sigmund (11/9/76)

Written by Alan Alda. *Directed by* Alan Alda. *Nominated for* Emmy, Outstanding Writing in a Comedy (Alan Alda); Emmy, Outstanding Cinematography (William Jurgensen); Emmy, Outstanding Film Editing in a Comedy Series (Samuel E. Beetley and Stanford Tischler); ACE Eddie Award, Editing (Stanford Tischler and Samuel E. Beetley). *Winner:* Emmy, Outstanding Directing in a Comedy (Alan Alda) Writers Guild, Teleplay (Alan Alda); Directors Guild (Alan Alda). *Guest Stars:* Allan Arbus, Charles Frank, Bart Breverman, Sal Viscuso, J. Andrew Kenny, Jennifer Davis.

Sidney Freedman is at the 4077 for the weekly poker game, but he stays to do some therapy on himself. He writes a letter to Sigmund Freud about the 4077 and notes how, faced with oppressive conditions, they can respond with lunatic laughter. A series of practical jokes has him wondering who the comic genius is. He talks about how Hawkeye shows the reality of the war to a pilot who hasn't seen what happens when his bombs land. Freedman admires Father Mulcahy, whom he describes as a natural at therapy. When Hawkeye and B.J. ask Sidney why he has stayed so long, and he explains that his business was getting "too good" and he lost a soldier to suicide whom he felt he should have saved. He has a strange conversation with Frank, who is digging foxholes. Discovering the practical joker is B.J., Freedman helps him pull one on Frank. After B.J. fills a foxhole with water, Freedman shouts, "Air raid!" Frank jolts out of the Swamp and jumps into the foxhole.

Mulcahy's War (11/16/76)

Written by Richard Cogan. *Directed by* George Tyne. *Guest Stars:* Brian Byers, Ric Mancini, Richard Foronjy.

Hawkeye and B.J. try to protect a soldier with a self-inflicted wound from Frank's gung-ho machismo. They suggest Father Mulcahy talk to him. When Mulcahy tries to tell the 18-year-old that going back to the front won't be so bad, the soldier gets Mulcahy to admit he has not been to the front himself. The soldier tells him they have little to talk about. When the aid station calls to have a badly wounded soldier picked up, Mulcahy decides to go with Radar against Potter's orders. On the way back to the 4077, the injured man has difficulty breathing. Mulcahy performs a tracheotomy by following Hawkeye's radioed instructions. When he returns, he approaches the self-wounded soldier and asks, "Now can we talk?"

The Korean Surgeon (11/23/76)

Written by Bill Idelson. *Directed by* Gene Reynolds. *Guest Stars:* Soon-Teck Oh, Robert Ito, Larry Hama.

A busload of wounded arrive with some North Koreans among them. One of them is an English-speaking doctor. Frank and Margaret are hostile to the doctor and accuse him of trying to harm a patient, but Potter rebukes them. The doctor mentions he would like to work with them instead of languishing in a POW camp. Radar arranges the paperwork, and they manage to trick Frank and Potter into thinking the man went off to a camp. Later, Frank is fooled into giving medical supplies to two North Koreans, who invite him to go back with them. They take Frank far enough to get past the checkpoints. When Potter figures out who the doctor is, he says the man will have to become a POW. As the man leaves camp, he passes Frank, who is walking home.

Hawkeye Get Your Gun (11/30/76)

Written by Jay Folb. *Story by* Gene Reynolds and Jay Folb. *Directed by* William Jurgensen. *Nominated for* Writers Guild Award, Teleplay (Jay Folb); Writers Guild Award, Story (Gene Reynolds and Jay Folb). *Guest Stars:* Mako, Richard Doyle, Jae Woo Lee, Thomas Botosan, Phyllis Katz, Carmine Scelza, Jeff Maxwell.

Potter gets irritated by Frank's comments about his old age. When a local hospital calls for help, Hawkeye and Potter draw the short straws. As they prepare to head into unsafe territory, Potter insists Hawkeye carry his side arm. They work under even more difficult conditions than the 4077. Exhausted, they get drunk on the way home, only to encounter shelling and snipers. Luckily a platoon of United States soldiers comes by to get them home. When he returns, Potter challenges Frank to do 50 push-ups.

The Colonel's Horse (12/7/76)

Written by Jim Fritzell and Everett Greenbaum. *Directed by* Burt Metcalfe.

Potter is going to Tokyo. Margaret fears she has appendicitis, and she asks Potter to make sure Hawkeye does the operation instead of Frank. Meanwhile, Potter leaves the care of his horse in Radar's hands, and the horse goes down with colic. B.J. talks to his father-in-law in Oklahoma, who tells them the horse needs to be irrigated. Using warm water, they get the horse regular again. Margaret's appendix is removed after she tells Frank to get out of the OR.

Exorcism (12/14/76)

Written by Jay Folb. *Story by* Gene Reynolds and Jay Folb. *Directed by* Alan Alda. *Guest Stars:* Virginia Ann Lee, James Canning, Philip Ahn.

When some local Koreans place a spirit post on the camp's grounds, Potter objects and has Radar move it. Immediately everything in camp starts breaking down; even Potter's lighter quits working. B.J. works on Cpl. Marsh, who has lost his St. Christopher's medal, and Marsh then returns to the 4077 with new injuries. An old Korean gets hit by an army ambulance, and his daughter tells the doctors he insists the camp be exorcised before he gets operated on. They bring in a priestess, who chases the spirits away. Things return to normal, and Potter's lighter lights. Potter tells Radar to put the spirit post back in camp.

Hawk's Nightmare (12/21/76)

Written by Burt Prelutsky. *Directed by* Burt Metcalfe. *Guest Stars:* Allan Arbus, Patricia Stevens, Sean Roche.

In the OR, Hawkeye talks about how the youth of the injured men bothers him. That night he walks in his sleep and acts like a kid. Everyone is spooked. The next night, Hawkeye goes for another walk and later wakes up from a nightmare about a childhood friend getting harmed. A phone call home finds the friend okay. When it happens yet another night, Potter calls Sidney Freedman. Freedman tells Hawkeye he is returning to his youth in his sleep to escape the war. But the harm to his friends in his dreams is the war intruding into his life, a reminder he can't escape it. In the epilogue, Klinger approaches Hawkeye and expresses admiration for his tactics.

The Most Unforgettable Characters (1/4/77)

Written by Ken Levine and David Isaacs. *Directed by* Burt Metcalfe.

Radar is taking a correspondence course in writing and uses the daily reports to practice. Potter asks him to do it the army way. Meanwhile, it's Frank's birthday, so B.J. and Hawkeye decide to stage a fight between themselves for Frank's benefit. He takes the bait and begins to buddy up with B.J. Klinger tries several new tactics to get out of the army, including threatening to set himself on fire. Potter outfoxes him and gets the last laugh. When Radar takes Hawkeye and B.J.'s fighting too seriously, they reveal the ruse, and Frank gets angry with Radar.

38 Across (1/11/77)

Written by Jim Fritzell and Everett Greenbaum. *Directed by* Burt Metcalfe. *Guest Stars:* Dick O'Neill, Oliver Clark, Ron Kolman, Momo Yashima, Bill Shimkai, Gwen Farrell, Rex Knowles.

Boredom has set in, and Hawkeye and B.J. start work on a crossword puzzle. The entire staff pitches in while they work in OR. They get down to one word and get stuck. Hawkeye calls a navy buddy, Tippy, who is a crossword expert. The message he leaves prompts Tippy to come to the 4077 with an admiral who thinks there is some kind of emergency. Meanwhile, Klinger tries to eat a whole jeep to prove he is crazy. When the admiral arrives and Potter discovers why he's there, Potter gets angry with Hawkeye. A deluge of casualties shows the admiral the 4077 has a tough task. Potter makes Hawkeye tell the admiral about the crossword "emergency." Tippy doesn't know the word, but the outraged admiral does.

Ping Pong (1/18/77)

Written by Sid Dorfman. *Directed by* William Jurgensen. *Guest Stars:* Richards Narita, Frank Maxwell, Sachiko Penny Lee, Robert Phalen, Enid Kent. *Note:* Potter says he is retiring in 16 months.

An inter-camp Ping-Pong tournament brings a victory for the 4077 thanks to Joe, a Korean orderly. Later, Joe brings his fiancée by and tells B.J. and Hawkeye they want to get married. Potter meets an old friend, Lt. Col. Becket, when he comes to the unit wounded. He arrives with lots of other casualities. Eventually Potter learns that Becket is a reckless and unqualified commander whose main concern is getting a promotion to increase his retirement pay. Potter tells Becket he will take him out of action—he cannot endanger more troops. Joe fails to return from his trip to Seoul, and his fiancée worries. He comes to the 4077 wounded—he was "drafted" and put into action the same day. Hawkeye informs Potter of the marriage request, and he's hesitant until Hawk tells him he's giving the bride away. The Korean wedding ceremony is performed over Frank's objections.

End Run (1/25/77)

Written by John D. Hess. *Directed by* Harry Morgan. *Guest Stars:* Henry Brown, Johnny Haymer, Tim Tarpey, Peter D. Greene, Greg Mabrey, James Lough.

When a fight takes place in Rosie's, Zale gives Klinger a hard time for not fighting. Meanwhile, a soldier with a badly injured leg comes to the 4077. Radar recognizes him as Billy Tyler, an All-American football player. Tyler learns that he might lose his leg and says he doesn't want to live without it. When Klinger and Zale fight in the mess, Frank organizes a boxing match to settle the matter. When Tyler does lose the leg, he is depressed and so is Radar. Hawkeye tells Radar to talk to Tyler and try to raise his spirits. Meanwhile, Hawkeye gets Klinger and Zale to conspire against Frank, and Frank gets punched by both. Radar's talk gets Tyler back on track.

Hanky Panky (2/1/77)

Written by Gene Reynolds. *Directed by* Gene Reynolds. *Guest Star:* Ann Sweeney.

In OR, Margaret tells Potter she is upset over not having received a letter from Donald in four days. Hawkeye notices a nurse seems interested in B.J., but B.J. says her marriage is going through rough times and she wants a friend, not a date. The mail brings a letter from Donald—he's in the hospital and Margaret panics. The nurse gets a "Dear Jane" letter, and when B.J. gets her to open up, they become intimate. Later, Hawkeye finds B.J. writing a letter to his wife telling her he has been unfaithful. Hawkeye tells him not to send it—what happened was out of kindness, not lust. Meanwhile, Frank tries to woo Margaret, but she beats him out of her tent. B.J. talks to the nurse and they are able to agree to be friends.

Hepatitis (2/8/77)

Written by Alan Alda. *Directed by* Alan Alda. *Note:* This episode was inspired by William Christopher's actual bout with hepatitis, which caused him to miss several episodes.

Hawkeye gets upset when Radar brings mail and news from his hometown paper about the successes of a mediocre doctor. About this time, Hawkeye develops back trouble. But there's another health problem in the unit: Father Mulcahy has hepatitis. The unit mobilizes to prevent further cases, with Hawkeye giving blood tests and gamma globulin. When he visits Margaret, she resists the injection, but he gets her to talk about letters she's getting from her future in-laws. When he horses around over the injection, she demands respect. He then suggests that's what she should demand from her in-laws. B.J. performs a tough surgery and celebrates afterward; when he passes out from drinking, Hawkeye gives him his gamma globulin shot. When Potter gives Hawkeye his shot, he suggests Hawkeye's jealousy of the mediocre doctor back home is the source of his back problem.

The General's Practitioner (2/15/77)

Written by Burt Prelutsky. *Directed by* Alan Rafkin. *Guest Stars:* Edward Binns, Leonard Stone, Suesie Elene, Larry Wilcox.

A colonel arrives looking for a personal physician for a general. He believes Hawkeye might be a good choice, but Hawkeye makes it clear he is not interested in the general's offer. In the meantime, a friend of Radar asks him to care for his Korean girlfriend when he returns to the States. Radar reluctantly agrees and then discovers she also has a baby. Radar gradually feels more comfortable, and is disappointed when his friend returns for his family. The general comes to check Hawkeye out, and though he finds out what Hawkeye is like, he still wants him. Hawkeye tells the general that his skills are best used at the 4077. The general agrees and leaves camp.

Movie Tonight (2/22/77)

Written by Gene Reynolds, Don Reo, Alan Katz, and Jay Folb. *Directed by* Burt Metcalfe. *Guest Stars:* Enid Kent, Judy Farrell, Jeffrey Kramer, Carmine Scelza.

Cleaning detail has everyone cranky. Things get better when Father Mulcahy comes in with mail and a movie. The movie, a Western, is brittle and keeps breaking, so the unit passes the time singing and doing imitations. A driver comes by to pick up nurses to go to Seoul. They decide to stay, and he joins them. Yet another break brings Margaret up for a song, which she continues to sing once the film is repaired. En masse they imitate the final scene of the movie—a shootout where they all play dead. An ambulance comes in, and shouts of "Wounded" get the 4077 scrambling again.

Souvenirs (3/1/77)

Written by Burt Prelutsky. *Story by* Burt Prelutsky and Reinhold Weege. *Directed by* Joshua Shelley. *Guest Stars:* Michael Bell, Brian Dennehy, Scott Mulhern, June Kim, Crandal Jue, Alvin Kim.

Margaret wants Frank to return a ring she gave him, but he denies having such a ring. A GI selling "souvenirs"—jewelry and knickknacks made from weapons casings—has Korean children hunting scrap metal in minefields. In the meantime, Frank finds out a vase he bought on the black market is 800 years old. He tries to send it home, but Hawkeye and B.J. intercept it and put a bedpan in the box instead. Klinger starts a new scam—sitting on a pole in the cold to get sick enough to be sent home. Potter eventually encourages him to break an alleged "record." When Frank sees an intruder going through his things, he jumps and wrestles with the person, only to be defeated—by Margaret, who has recovered her ring from his footlocker. Angry when the souvenir salesman continues his dealings with the children, Hawkeye and B.J. threaten to ground him for medical reasons. He backs off and says he will go out of business. Klinger breaks the "record" and gets a three-day pass.

Post Op (3/8/77)

Written by Ken Levine and David Isaacs. *Story by* Gene Reynolds and Jay Folb. *Directed by* Gene Reynolds. *Guest Stars:* Hilly Hicks, Sal Viscuso, Andy Romano, Daniel Zippe, Richard Beauchamp, Alan McRae, Gary Springer, Andrew Bloch, John-Anthony Bailey, Zitto Kazann.

A shortage has Potter pleading with HQ for more blood. Additional wounded arrive and make the situation more difficult. A lot of stories circulate in post-op: one man describes a face-to-face encounter with a Chinese soldier, another tells how he thought clearing mines was a safe job. Yet another tries to get Margaret to date him. Klinger helps a Puerto Rican soldier who had his mustache shaved for surgery by making a replacement with his own hair. The blood shortage gets dire, and the doctors chase Frank down for a pint. Then a group of Turkish soldiers arrive to give blood.

Margaret's Marriage (3/15/77)

Written by Everett Greenbaum and Jim Fritzell. *Directed by* Gene Reynolds. *Guest Stars:* Beeson Carroll, Judy Farrell, Lynne Marie Stewart, Kellye Nakahara, Patricia Stevens.

Embarrassed by comments from Frank, Margaret urges Donald to set a wedding date. Donald comes to the 4077, and he and Margaret decide to get married the next day. The nurses throw a shower, and Klinger donates a wedding dress to Margaret. The men get very drunk at a stag party. When Donald passes out, B.J. comes up with a prank: They put him in a full body cast. The wedding ceremony gets rushed when choppers start arriving, and scenes in the OR intervene. When Margaret and Donald get ready to leave, she throws her bouquet, and Frank catches it. B.J. and Hawkeye try to tell her Donald doesn't need the body cast, but she fails to understand them. Frank wistfully watches the chopper fly away.

YEAR 6, 1977-1978

Cast and Crew

Regular Cast: Alan Alda as Hawkeye Pierce, Gary Burghoff as Radar O'Reilly, Mike Farrell as B.J. Hunnicutt, Harry Morgan as Sherman Potter, Loretta Swit as Margaret Houlihan, David Ogden Stiers as Charles Winchester, Jamie Farr as Max Klinger, and William Christopher as Father Mulcahy. *Produced by* Burt Metcalfe. *Executive Story Consultant* Jay Folb. *Story Editors* Ken Levine and David Isaacs. *Program Consultant* Ronny Graham. *Creative Consultants* Gene Reynolds and Alan Alda. *Developed for Television by* Larry Gelbart. *Associate Producer* Stanford Tischler. *Executive Production Manager* Mark Evans. *Unit Production Manager/Assistant Director* David Hawks, Michele Futrell. *Directors of Photography* William Cline, Meredith Nicholson. *Film Editors* Stanford Tischler, Larry L. Mills. *Music Supervision* Lionel Newman. *Art Director* Rodger Maus. *Set Decorator* Bert Allen. *Medical Advisor* Walter D. Dishell, M.D. *Post Production Supervisor* Joseph Silver. *Theme* Johnny Mandel. *Casting* Sam Christensen, Joyce Robinson.

Fade Out, Fade In (9/20/77)

Written by Jim Fritzell and Everett Greenbaum. *Directed by* Hy Averback. *Nominated for* Emmy, Outstanding Film Editing (Stanford Tischler and Larry L. Mills); Writers Guild Award, Teleplay (Jim Fritzell and Everett Greenbaum). *Winner:* ACE Eddie Award, Editing (Stanford Tischler and Larry L. Mills). *Guest Stars:* James Lough, Raymond Singer, Tom Stovall, Rick Hurst, Robert Symonds, William Flatley, Joseph Burns, Kimiko Hiroshige.

As they deal with the physical and psychological wounds in a heavy load of casualties, members of the 4077 wonder why Frank is late returning from R and R, and why Margaret returned from her honeymoon in a bad mood. Soon they learn that Frank has been arrested for antics in Seoul; later, Hawkeye and B.J. will learn that Margaret has already encountered marital problems. Radar gets a temporary replacement for Frank, a Major Charles Winchester. Major Winchester arrives and soon finds that he's the permanent replacement when Frank is sent back to the States (with a promotion). Hawkeye and B.J. struggle with Charles's arrogance and professionalism, but they discover that he can give as good as he gets when it comes to practical joking.

Fallen Idol (9/27/77)

Written by Alan Alda. *Directed by* Alan Alda. *Nominated for* Emmy, Outstanding Writing in Comedy (Alan Alda). *Guest Stars:* Frances Fong, Robin Riker, Larry Gilman, Patricia Stevens, Michael Talbott.

Radar is embarrassed by his sexual naivete, and at Hawkeye's suggestion he travels to Seoul to seek some experience. Hawkeye gets a shock when wounded arrive and Radar is among them. His guilt drives him to drink, and the next day he's too hungover to operate. Radar tells Hawkeye his behavior is a disappointment to those who look up to him. Hawkeye, resenting the hero role, blows up at Radar. Some soul-searching by each is required before they begin to rebuild their friendship.

Last Laugh (10/4/77)

Written by Everett Greenbaum and Jim Fritzell. *Directed by* Don Weis. *Guest Stars:* James Comwell, Robert Karnes, John Ashton.

B.J. is suffering a case of mistaken identity that turns out to be a trick by his friend Leo Bardinaro, who is a lifelong practical joker. Bardinaro comes to say goodbye to B.J. before he returns to the States and pulls all the classic jokes—exploding cigars, hand buzzers, etc. B.J. retaliates by grabbing his orders to go home. In the meantime, Margaret is eager to see Donald and begs for a pass. B.J. gets the last laugh on Bardinaro by sending him on his way in a jeep without much gas. Margaret gets her pass and returns in a much better mood after a couple days with Donald.

War of Nerves (10/11/77)

Written by Alan Alda. *Directed by* Alan Alda. *Guest Stars:* Allan Arbus, Michael O'Keefe, Peter Reigert, Johnny Haymer.

Casualties arrive, and Sidney Freedman is among them. Potter notices everyone in camp is on edge and asks Freedman to talk to some of them. Margaret and Charles visit him to complain about each other, and even Klinger comes to see him, convinced that he really is going crazy. In the meantime, a patient Freedman was treating is very bitter at Freedman for sending him back to front. Later, Freedman enthusiastically participates in a "therapeutic" bonfire by shedding his uniform and tossing it on the flames.

The Winchester Tapes (10/18/77)

Written by Everett Greenbaum and Jim Fritzell. *Directed by* Burt Metcalfe. *Guest Stars:* Thomas Carter, Kimiko Hiroshige.

Charles is taping a letter home, telling his family about the 4077 and begging them to get him out of Korea. When Klinger hears of Charles's relative who got out of the army due to fainting spells, he starts passing out. Hawkeye gets an invitation from a nurse to spend a weekend in Seoul and goads Charles into taking his officer-of-the-day duty. But wounded arrive and force

Hawkeye to delay his weekend. B.J. plays with Charles's head by switching his pants to make him think he has gained, and then lost, too much weight. After surgery, Hawkeye's jeep arrives to take him to Seoul, but he is asleep in the Swamp.

The Light That Failed (10/25/77)

Written by Burt Prelutsky. *Directed by* Charles S. Dubin. *Guest Stars:* Enid Kent, Gary Erwin, Philip Baker Hall.

The supply truck is late and the 4077 is running low on light bulbs. When supplies do arrive, they are nonessential summer supplies (delivered in the middle of winter). Mail brings B.J. a mystery novel, which gets the whole camp reading. He gets to the end of the book only to discover the last page is missing. In the meantime, Charles gives the wrong injection to a patient and worries more about himself than the patient. Hawkeye and B.J. revive the patient but get no thanks from Charles. A feebleminded author is no help when B.J. calls her for the ending to the novel. The truck with winter supplies finally arrives.

In Love and War (11/1/77)

Written by Alan Alda. *Directed by* Alan Alda. *Guest Stars:* Kieu Chinh, Susan Krebs, Enid Kent.

Hawkeye meets a Korean woman who is secretly taking care of victims displaced by the war. In the meantime, Margaret hears a new nurse complain about a "Donald" who made a pass at her. Certain details convince Margaret that it was her husband. Hawkeye falls in love with the Korean woman, and rushes to treat her mother after an OR session only to discover she has died and the family is moving away from the front. Later, Margaret and Hawkeye commiserate together. She will take Donald back; Hawkeye must let his love go.

Change Day (11/8/77)

Written by Laurence Marks. *Directed by* Don Weis. *Guest Stars:* Phillip Ahn, Glenn Ash, Richard Lee Sung, Thomas Dever, Peter Riegert, Johnny Haymer.

When Potter announces a scrip exchange. Charles hatches a plot to profit from exchanging scrip held by local Koreans. Hawkeye counterplots against Charles. In the meantime, a wounded MP entrusts Hawkeye to exchange his scrip, and Klinger decides on a new tactic to get out of the army by applying for West Point. The money Hawkeye is supposed to exchange gets stolen during a fight. Hawkeye manages to arrange things so that Charles's money repays the MP. Klinger's attempt to get into West Point fails. Mulcahy gets the stolen money returned to him, and Hawkeye tells him to use it for the orphanage.

Images (11/15/77)

Written by Burt Perlutsky. *Directed by* Burt Metcalfe. *Guest Stars:* Susan Blanchard, Larry Block, John Durren, Judy Farrell, Enid Kent, Rebecca Taylor, Carmine Scelza, Joseph Hardin.

A new nurse is having a tough time adjusting to the gruesomeness of the OR. Margaret shows no sympathy until Potter orders her to give the nurse a second chance. In the meantime, Radar decides he wants to get a tattoo when he sees a patient who is covered with them. Hawkeye and B.J. get a tattooed soldier to discourage him. Margaret breaks down when she hears a little dog she's been feeding scraps to has been run over by a jeep. Hawkeye confronts her and tells her to stop being so tough on the outside. Margaret later apologizes to the new nurse for giving her a hard time. Radar gets wise to the tattoo ruse and he goes off to get a tattoo anyway—but it's not a permanent one.

The MASH Olympics (11/22/77)

Written by Ken Levine and David Isaacs. *Directed by* Don Weis. *Guest Stars:* Mike Henry, Michael McManus.

Hawkeye and B.J. help a GI who is going to be kicked out of the army if he doesn't lose weight. When Klinger learns about this, he decides to try to eat his way out of the army. An accident in the compound convinces Potter the unit needs to get in shape. He organizes a series of Olympic games with three days' R and R for the winning team. When Donald arrives to see Margaret, he goads Hawkeye into letting him represent her team against Hawkeye's. Donald is chosen to run the obstacle race against the overweight GI. He loses the race and receives the wrath of Margaret as they leave for a shorter R and R.

The Grim Reaper (11/29/77)

Written by Burt Prelutsky. *Directed by* George Tyne. *Guest Stars:* Charles Aidman, Jerry Hauser.

When Colonel Bloodworth tells the 4077 to expect a lot of casualties in next 24 hours, Hawkeye and B.J. give him a hard time about body counts. Charles shares a canned pheasant with Margaret which makes them sick. When Hawkeye taunts the colonel for not reaching his casualty quota, he and Hawkeye almost come to blows, and the colonel threatens a court-martial. In the meantime, Klinger meets an injured GI from Toledo and they reminisce about their favorite haunts. B.J. and Charles fight over a jacket given them by a patient. More wounded arrive, this time the colonel among them. Chastened by his injury, he calls Hawkeye over to tell him he won't bring charges against him.

Comrades in Arms, Pt. 1 (12/6/77)

Written by Alan Alda. *Directed by* Burt Metcalfe. *Nominated for* Emmy, Outstanding Directing in Comedy (Burt Metcalfe and Alan Alda); Directors Guild Award (Alan Alda and Burt Metcalfe).

Potter recruits Hawkeye and Margaret to go to the 8063 to demonstrate arterial transplant surgery. The unit becomes concerned when they learn Margaret and Hawk are headed into danger. On the road, Hawkeye learns that Margaret is upset over a letter from Donald. When their jeep breaks down, Margaret gets upset with what she sees as his lack of manhood. They find an abandoned hut, and Hawkeye gets Margaret to read her letter. It turns out that Donald sent her a letter meant for another woman. They settle in for the night, but shells bring them together in an embrace as the episode ends.

Comrades in Arms, Pt. 2 (12/13/77)

Written by Alan Alda. *Directed by* Alan Alda. *Nominated for* Directors Guild Award (Alan Alda and Burt Metcalfe). *Guest Stars:* Jon Yune, James Saito, Doug Rowe, Leland Sun.

The 4077 is upset—Hawkeye and Margaret cannot be found. When Margaret and Hawkeye wake up, Margaret cuddles with Hawkeye and acts like they are longtime lovers. Hawkeye is more reluctant. B.J.'s worry leads him to recruit a chopper pilot to go look for the pair. Margaret sees the chopper but is unable to attract the pilot's attention. Margaret and Hawkeye hide out in a rainstorm. When they get to the 8063, they fight during their demonstration. They vow a professional relationship. When they return to the 4077, she at first denies anything happened. Later, she reads a letter to "Hank" based on their night together, which she will send to Donald.

The Merchant of Korea (12/20/77)

Written by Ken Levine and David Isaacs. *Directed by* William Jurgensen. *Guest Star:* Johnny Haymer.

When Peg telegraphs B.J. to get $200 for a down payment on their dream house property, B.J. is forced to ask Charles for a loan. Charles then uses the loan to ask B.J. for all kinds of little services. When payday is delayed, Hawkeye also becomes indebted to Charles. Hawkeye and B.J. dream up a card game to get back at Charles. He cleans up at the game, until they realize he gives his hand away by his whistling. They win back their money, forcing him to ask for a loan.

The Smell of Music (1/3/78)

Written by Jim Fritzell and Everett Greenbaum. *Directed by* Stuart Miller. *Guest Stars:* Jordan Clarke, Nancy Steen, Lois Foraker, Richard Lee Sung.

Charles is taking up the French horn and driving B.J. and Hawkeye crazy. They are headed for the showers, but when Charles tells them they stink, they decide not to shower until Charles gives up his horn. He refuses, and the competition begins. In the meantime, Potter has a soldier whose severe facial disfigurement has him contemplating suicide. Potter uses a surprising technique that convinces him to give up the plan. The rest of the unit decides

Hawkeye and B.J. are too pungent for the mess tent. Margaret and the rest of the unit call a halt to the bad smells and sounds. They wash down Hawkeye and B.J. and destroy Charles's horn.

Patent 4077 (1/10/78)

Written by Ken Levine and David Isaacs. *Directed by* Harry Morgan. *Guest Stars:* Keye Luke, Brenda Thomson, Harry Gold, Patricia Stevens, Johnny Haymer.

A difficult time with a leg injury has Hawkeye wishing for a new kind of clamp. Zale volunteers to try to build one, but his attempt fails. In the meantime, Klinger accidentally throws Margaret's wedding ring away. When a local merchant offers to try to make the clamp, they discover he is selling wedding rings like Margaret's. They buy one for her, but the merchant gets the inscription wrong. She thinks it's a cruel joke but eventually realizes they meant well. The merchant's clamp works so well that he begins a new line of surgical supplies.

Tea and Empathy (1/17/78)

Written by Bill Idelson. *Directed by* Don Weis. *Guest Stars:* Bernard Fox, Neil Thompson, Sal Viscuso, Chris Winfield, Chris Mulkey, Neil Hunt, Jay Pirelli.

Wounded men from a British regiment arrive at the 4077. Hawkeye is upset when one with a belly wound is put at risk of infection by the tradition of giving the men tea. To make things worse, the 4077's penicillin has been stolen. When the British commander arrives, he talks harshly to his men. In the meantime, a wounded man B.J. works on keeps asking for more morphine. B.J. decides the man is addicted and starts to get him off the drug. When a confession reveals the location of penicillin, Mulcahy and Klinger retrieve the cache. When the British major returns, Hawkeye confronts him on his treatment of the soldiers. He tells Hawkeye he was merely using reverse psychology and wins Hawk's grudging respect.

Your Hit Parade (1/24/78)

Written by Ronny Graham. *Directed by* George Tyne. *Guest Stars:* Ronny Graham, William Kux, Ken Michelman, Johnny Haymer, Patricia Stevens.

A shipment of records has Radar playing D.J. after some lessons from Klinger. A deluge of wounded makes for a long OR session, prompting Potter to tell Radar to keep it up. Potter's frequent request of "Sentimental Journey" prompts Hawkeye and B.J. to ask why. Potter tells them about his infatuation with Doris Day. Hawkeye has a tough case with a rare blood type, and they bring in a drunk bomb defuser to give blood.

What's Up Doc? (1/30/78)

Written by Larry Balmagia. *Directed by* George Tyne. *Guest Stars:* Charles Frank, Lois Foraker, Kurt Andon, Phyllis Katz.

Margaret is uptight and cranky in OR and reveals to Hawkeye that she may be pregnant and will have to leave the army. In the meantime, B.J. has a patient who's worried about his injured sergeant. He learns the man came to Korea from an ROTC program and feels overwhelmed. Charles tries to smooth-talk him but he pulls a gun and takes Charles hostage. He demands a chopper to get him on his way home to Ohio. When Klinger learns this, he changes places with Charles and tries to get home with the man. Hawkeye asks Radar to use his rabbit for Margaret's pregnancy test. Radar resists until Hawkeye promises to save the rabbit's life. Margaret is ambivalent when the test reveals no pregnancy. Klinger valiantly tries to get his weakened captor to a waiting helicopter, only to have the man pass out.

Mail Call Three (2/6/78)

Written by Everett Greenbaum and Jim Fritzell. *Directed by* Charles S. Dubin. *Guest Stars:* Oliver Clark, Jack Grapes.

Mail for someone named Ben Pierce keeps getting mistakenly delivered to Hawkeye. Reading the latest letter, Hawkeye finds the man is quite popular with women. B.J.'s letter from Peg reports house troubles and passes from other men. Radar is upset to learn his mother is dating someone. Klinger has a letter from his wife saying she wants a divorce, but nobody believes him. B.J. gets drunk worrying about Peg, and Klinger decides to go AWOL. Hawkeye tells Radar his own jealousy prevented his father from remarrying. When the other Ben Pierce arrives to get his letters, Hawkeye is mystified at the man's lack of sex appeal. Klinger returns, having decided his wife isn't worth the risk of going AWOL.

Temporary Duty (2/13/78)

Written by Larry Balmagia. *Directed by* Burt Metcalfe. *Guest Stars:* George Lindsey, Marcia Rodd, Enid Kent.

Potter assigns Hawkeye and a nurse to the 8063 as part of medical exchange. Roy Dupree and Lorraine Anderson arrive at the 4077 in exchange. Charles is enchanted with the nurse, who inquires about her old friend Margaret. Dupree offends both B.J. and Charles, and Margaret doesn't like it when Lorraine flirts with Charles. They have a confrontation in which they discuss Margaret's emotional life. They hug and make up. When Dupree indicates he'd like to stay at the 4077, B.J. and Charles make sure he doesn't stay by goading him into angering Potter.

Potter's Retirement (2/20/78)

Written by Laurence Marks. *Directed by* William Jurgensen. *Guest Stars:* George Wyner, Peter Hobbs, Ken White, Johnny Haymer. *Note:* Potter says he has one year to retirement.

Potter is called to Seoul as the unit prepares for a Kentucky Derby party.

He returns in a bad mood, having learned there are bad reports about him coming from the unit. When he returns to the 4077, he lashes out at everyone, saying he will see that a spot inspection goes well and then he will return to the United States. B.J. and Hawkeye investigate and discover a spy was sent by HQ after a disgruntled colonel complained. Potter gets the inspection called off. When Hawkeye, B.J., and Radar plead with him to stay, he decides to.

Dr. Winchester and Mr. Hyde (2/27/78)

Written by Ken Levine, David Isaacs, and Ronny Graham. *Directed by* Charles S. Dubin. *Guest Stars:* Chris Murney, Joe Tornatore, Ron Max, Rod Gist.

Though he refuses Klinger's request for some "pep pills," Charles himself starts to take them to keep up with his work. In the meantime, Radar gets wind of marines sponsoring mouse races and decides to enter his. Charles, artificially energized, gets a lot done but he begins to have trouble sleeping. On the day of the race, he increases his bet after slipping the mouse some of his pills. Radar's mouse wins, but he notices she is hyperactive. When Charles starts having serious symptoms, Hawkeye and B.J. find his pills. They decide to give the marines their money back.

Major Topper (3/27/78)

Written by Allyn Freeman. *Directed by* Charles S. Dubin. *Guest Stars:* Hamilton Camp, Andrew Bloch, Donald Blackwell, Peter Zapp, Paul Linke, John Kirby, Michael Mann.

Charles begins telling tall tales in OR while Klinger works with Boots Miller, who seems to be in his own fantasy world—playing reporter and using a soup ladle as a microphone. They learn they are down to their last box of morphine and scramble to get some more. Potter decides they have to try placebos as pain killers. Meanwhile, Hawkeye and B.J. try to one-up Charles with their own tall tales. Klinger becomes convinced Boots is crazy and Potter has the man transferred. The placebos work, and Charles tops Hawkeye's story.

YEAR 7, 1978-1979

Cast and Crew

Regular Cast: Alan Alda as Hawkeye Pierce, Gary Burghoff as Radar O'Reilly, Mike Farrell as B.J. Hunnicutt, Harry Morgan as Sherman Potter, Loretta Swit as Margaret Houlihan, David Ogden Stiers as Charles Winchester, Jamie Farr as Max Klinger, and William Christopher as Father Mulcahy. *Executive Producer* Burt Metcalfe. *Produced by* Burt Metcalfe, David Lawrence.

Executive Script Consultants Ken Levine and David Isaacs. *Story Editor* Larry Balmagia. *Story Consultant* Ronny Graham. *Creative Consultants* Gene Reynolds and Alan Alda. *Developed for Television by* Larry Gelbart. *Associate Producer* Stanford Tischler. *Executive Production Manager* Mark Evans. *Unit Production Manager/Assistant Director* David Hawks. *Second Assistant Director* Michele Futrell. *Directors of Photography* William Cline, Dominick R. Palmer, Jr. *Film Editors* Stanford Tischler, Larry L. Mills. *Music Supervision* Lionel Newman. *Art Director* David Haber. *Set Decorator* Bert Allen. *Medical Advisor* Walter D. Dishell, M.D. *Post Production Supervisor* Joseph Silver. *Theme* Johnny Mandel. *Casting* Sam Christensen, Joyce Robinson.

Commander Pierce (9/18/78)

Written by Ronny Graham. *Directed by* Burt Metcalfe. *Guest Stars:* James Lough, Andrew Massett, Jan Jorden, Enid Kent, Kellye Nakahara.

When Potter is called away to Seoul for meetings, he leaves Hawkeye in charge. When a jeep arrives with a wounded soldier, B.J. learns a wounded doctor has been left at the aid station. He leaves to go get the man without telling Hawkeye, who has learned they are due to get a lot of casualties. When B.J. returns, Hawkeye chews him out for leaving without his permission. When Potter returns, he tries to get the doctors back on friendly terms.

Peace on Us (9/25/78)

Written by Ken Levine and David Isaacs. *Directed by* George Tyne. *Guest Stars:* Kevin Hagen, Hugh Gillan, Michael Payne, Michael LaGuardia, Don Cummins, Rollin Moriyama, Perren Page.

The whole unit takes it badly when Potter announces the peace talks have reached an impasse. Margaret looks forward to time in Tokyo with Donald, but is upset by news he's been transferred to the States. When Potter tells Hawkeye that the rotation points needed to get out of Korea have been increased, he decides to take off for Panmunjon to talk to the negotiators himself. While Margaret contemplates a divorce, Hawkeye tells the Americans and the Koreans at the peace talks to get moving on peace. When he returns to the 4077, the unit greets him with a party.

Lil (10/2/78)

Written by Sheldon Bull. *Directed by* Burt Metcalfe. *Guest Star:* Carmen Mathews. *Note:* Potter resists infidelity in this episode. In year ten's "Strange Bedfellows," he shares a youthful indiscretion with his son-in-law.

Col. Lillian Rayburn comes to the 4077 to inspect the nurses. Immediately, Potter is charmed by her presence, and they hit it off well. In the meantime, Hawkeye wonders what "B.J." really stands for and becomes obsessed with discovering his "real" name. Potter and Lil spend the next day on a long picnic. She makes a move on Potter, and he somewhat reluctantly tells her he wants to remain faithful to his wife. In the epilogue, B.J. tells Hawkeye he was named after his parents, Bea and Jay.

Our Finest Hour (10/9/78. One-hour episode)

Written by Ken Levine, David Isaacs, Larry Balmagia, and Ronny Graham. *Directed by* Burt Metcalfe. *Special Credits: Co-Producer* Phil Savenik. *Associate Producers:* Doug Bleeck, Bonnie Peterson, Susie F. Walker. *Production Coordinators:* Karen Lieberman, Ginny Olah. *Videotape Editor:* Bob Schneider. *Guest Star:* Clete Roberts. *Note:* This episode features Hawkeye's scathing criticism of bringing the American "way of life" to Korea.

This episode finds Clete Roberts returning to the 4077 to follow up on his work in year four's "The Interview." The ensemble cast is asked a series of questions. Their answers are interspersed with clips from previous years' shows and newsreel clips from the early 1950s. The interviews concern how the 4077 copes with the harshness of war, what they miss about home, what it's like to deal with army bureaucracy, and how the 4077 resembles a family.

The Billfold Syndrome (10/16/78)

Written by Ken Levine and David Isaacs. *Directed by* Alan Alda. *Nominated for* ACE Eddie Award, Editing (Stanford Tischler and Larry L Mills); Emmy, Outstanding Film Editing (Stanford Tischler and Larry L. Mills). *Guest Stars:* Kevin Geer, Allan Arbus.

Charles is in a bad mood because he has found out he will not be appointed chief of thoracic surgery in Boston. He tells Hawkeye and B.J. he wants to be left alone and decides not to talk to them. This they take as a challenge. Meanwhile, when a group of poorly treated casualties arrives, Hawkeye discovers the medic Jerry is experiencing shell shock. They decide to call Sidney Freedman, who uses hypnosis to recreate a battlefield scene and find out that Jerry's little brother died in combat.

None Like It Hot (10/23/78)

Written by Ken Levine, David Isaacs, and Johnny Bonaduce. *Directed by* Tony Mordente. *Guest Stars:* Ted Gehring, Johnny Haymer, Jan Jorden, Kellye Nakahara, Jeff Maxwell, Mic Rodgers.

The timely arrival of a portable bathtub for Hawkeye and B.J. during a heat wave brings a lot of problems when the rest of the camp finds out and demands they share the tub. In the meantime, Klinger decides to sweat his way out of the army and puts on a raccoon coat. Radar's tonsillitis flares up and the medical staff decides it's time for the tonsils to come out. When a supply sergeant comes to try to buy the tub from Hawkeye and B.J., they resist; but when Radar asks for ice cream after his surgery, they decide to trade the tub for ice cream.

They Call the Wind Korea (10/30/78)

Written by Ken Levine and David Isaacs. *Directed by* Charles S. Dubin. *Guest Stars:* Tom Dever, Paul Cavonis, Randy Stumpf, Enid Kent.

An imminent wind storm finds the unit preparing while Charles tries to find a way other than helicopter to get to Seoul for his R and R in Tokyo. He enlists Klinger to get him there by jeep. They try a shortcut and come across an overturned truck with injured Greek soldiers. Meanwhile, the 4077 water tower collapses and several are injured. Margaret feels responsible for an injured nurse and tries to comfort her. Charles and Klinger spend the night with the Greek soldiers. In the morning, Klinger sets out to find help, only to find the overturned truck is just over a hill from the 4077.

Major Ego (11/6/78)

Written by Larry Balmagia. *Directed by* Alan Alda. *Guest Stars:* Greg Mullavey, David Dean, Frank Pettinger, Phyllis Katz, Patricia Stevens, Roy Goldman.

In the OR, Charles performs cardiac massage to save a patient. Soon after, a reporter from *Stars and Stripes* arrives to do a story on Charles but also takes a liking to Margaret. When another patient Charles worked on has difficulty, Hawkeye thinks the man is hemorrhaging and decides to reopen him. This infuriates Charles, but he is chagrined when Hawkeye finds a suture leak. Margaret spends the night with the reporter. He wants a relationship, but she is content with one night. The newly humbled Charles rips up the article and refuses to let the reporter publish it.

Baby, It's Cold Outside (11/13/78)

Written by Gary David Goldberg. *Directed by* George Tyne. *Winner:* Writers Guild Award, Teleplay (Gary David Goldberg). *Guest Stars:* Terry Wills, Teck Murdock, David Cramer, Jan Jorden.

A cold spell finds Charles with long johns and a goose-down coat and everyone else jealous. Margaret gets Charles to trade gloves with her, but he later regrets the trade. The cold weather causes mines to explode; one explodes near Klinger and causes him temporary loss of his hearing. One of Hawkeye's patients has to be warmed up by immersing him in water. When Potter tells Klinger his hearing loss could have gotten him out of the army, he tries to fake losing it again. Charles tricks Margaret into giving up his gloves.

Point of View (11/20/78)

Written by Ken Levine and David Isaacs. *Directed by* Charles S. Dubin. *Nominated for* Emmy, Outstanding Directing in Comedy (Charles S. Dubin). Emmy, Outstanding Writing in Comedy (Ken Levine and David Isaacs); Directors Guild Award (Charles S. Dubin); Writers Guild Award (Ken Levine and David Isaacs). *Guest Stars:* Brad Gorman, Marc Baxley, Edward Gallardo, Jan Jorden, Hank Ross, David Stafford, Paul Tuerpe.

The audience follows this episode through the eyes of a soldier, Pvt. Rich, injured in the throat. He meets the 4077 and experiences some of its zaniness, especially Klinger. Meanwhile the staff wonders what's eating Potter, who's in a bad mood. Conversations between Potter and Rich reveal the colonel is upset at having missed his wedding anniversary. Rich tells Hawkeye and he sets out to help the situation. A fractured larynx causes Rich to go under the knife a second time. In the meantime, Radar calls Potter's wife and gets Potter on the phone with her.

Dear Comrade (11/27/78)

Written by Tom Reeder. *Directed by* Charles S. Dubin. *Guest Stars:* Sab Shimono, Larry Block, Robert Clotworthy, Todd Davis, David Dozer, Dennis Troy, Wayne Long, James Saito, Laurie Bates.

B.J. and Hawkeye arrive back from Tokyo to find Charles has hired a houseboy and the Swamp is extraordinarily clean. The audience learns the man is a Chinese spy who is at the 4077 to discover the secrets to their success. When the GIs in post-op come down with a strange rash, the Chinese spy cooks up a local potion for the rash and it works. Hawkeye wins a jeep in a card game, but it has an artillery gun attached to it, and Potter tells him to get rid of it. Hawkeye and B.J. fill the gun's shaft with cement. The spy tells his superiors the 4077 is too unorthodox to be imitated.

Out of Gas (12/4/78)

Written by Tom Reeder. *Directed by* Mel Damski. *Guest Stars:* Justin Lord, Byron Chung, Johnny Haymer, George Claiborne.

During a cold spell, the unit gets word there will be lot of casualties while they are short of anesthesia—sodium pentothal. They use ether instead and have to turn off the heat to prevent explosions. Mulcahy suggests they try to get pentothal through the black market and uses some of Charles's fine wine for collateral. Charles insists on going with Mulcahy, but he screws up the deal. When Charles and Mulcahy return to find the marketers have gotten drunk on the wine, they take the pentothal.

An Eye for a Tooth (12/11/78)

Written by Ronny Graham. *Directed by* Charles S. Dubin. *Guest Star:* Peter Palmer. *Note:* This episode was inspired by intra-cast practical joking which involved director Richard Attenborough in the studio cafeteria.

A food fight in the mess tent between Hawkeye and Margaret has Charles contriving a series of escalating practical jokes. Father Mulcahy, just turned down for promotion, gets upset when he hears about the rapid advancement of a chopper pilot. Later, one of the practical jokes results in the destruction of a special dummy that chopper pilots use as a counterweight when they have an unbalanced load. Mulcahy agrees to substitute for the dummy when a pilot needs to pick up a wounded man. When he returns, Potter promises to put him in for a commendation. The last practical joke is on Charles.

Dear Sis (12/18/78)

Written by Alan Alda. *Directed by* Alan Alda. *Guest Stars:* Lawraon Driscoll, Patrick Driscoll, Jo Ann Thompson, W. Perren Page, Jeff Maxwell.

Father Mulcahy writes a letter to his sister and tells her about life at the 4077 around Christmastime. During triage, he helps Margaret with a restless patient. The man punches him, and he returns with a knockout blow. Teasing from Hawkeye doesn't help as he feels guilty about a man of the cloth using violence. Everyone is rather low by the time Christmas comes, but Charles is lifted when he opens a present revealing his old toboggan cap—a gift arranged by Mulcahy. He's so touched, he praises Mulcahy and says, "You saved me, Father." Hawkeye toasts Mulcahy at the party for his work in making life bearable at the 4077.

B.J. Papa San (1/1/79)

Written by Larry Balmagia. *Directed by* James Sheldon. *Guest Stars:* Dick O'Neill, Mariel Aragon, Chao-Li Chi, Stephen Keep, Johnny Haymer, Shizuko Hoshi.

B.J., depressed at being away from home, starts looking after a Korean family whose father has pneumonia. Meanwhile, a general comes to the 4077 and gets repeatedly reinjured. B.J. gets supplies for the Korean family and has Radar try to track down the family's son. When Radar finds the man, Hawkeye and B.J. rush to the family's hut only to find them gone.

Inga (1/8/79)

Written by Alan Alda. *Directed by* Alan Alda. *Nominated for* Emmy, Outstanding Directing in a Comedy (Alan Alda). *Winner:* Emmy, Outstanding Writing in a Comedy (Alan Alda). *Guest Stars:* Mariette Hartley, Phyllis Katz, Mark Favara.

When a Swedish doctor named Inga arrives, both Hawkeye and Charles compete for her attention. In the OR, she shows up Hawkeye with a new surgical method. When he speaks of her resentfully, Margaret says he can't handle women as equals. Later, Charles resents her quick, effective action on one of his patients in post-op. When Hawkeye finally begins to woo her anew, it is time for her to leave.

The Price (1/15/79)

Written by Erik Tarloff. *Directed by* Charles S. Dubin. *Guest Stars:* Miko Mayama, Yuki Shimoda, Ken Mochizuki, Jeff Maxwell, Johnny Haymer, Dennis Sakamoto, Leigh Kim.

Potter is concerned about an elderly Korean man who does their laundry. The man used to be in the cavalry and is embarrassed by his current status. Hawkeye and B.J. hide a boy who is evading the South Korean "draft." Potter decides to give the elderly man his horse, but the man's daughter returns the horse the next day because her father has died. The Korean boy decides to enlist. Klinger tries to bribe his way out of the army but gives up the plan when Potter threatens a court-martial.

The Young and the Restless (1/22/79)

Written by Mitch Markowitz. *Directed by* William Jurgensen. *Nominated for* Writers Guild Award, Teleplay (Mitch Markowitz). *Guest Star:* James Canning.

The doctors get a visit from a young surgeon whose knowledge and skills Charles and Potter come to resent. Potter is limping with phlebitis and requires bedrest. Charles tries to critique the surgeon's techniques but is put in his place. In the meantime, Klinger's latest scam is to act like he's back in Toledo. Potter begins to feel like he's no longer needed, but another round of wounded brings him out of bed.

Hot Lips Is Back in Town (1/29/79)

Written by Larry Balmagia and Bernard Dilbert. *Directed by* Charles S. Dubin. *Guest Stars:* Peggy Lee Brennan, Walter Brooke, Jan Jorden, Enid Kent, Kellye Nakahara.

Mail brings the final divorce documents for Margaret, while Radar falls in love with a newly arrived nurse. Late at night, Margaret comes to Potter's tent to tell him she is going to make the army her career and has plans for the nurses to do most of the triage. She gets things going quickly and invites a general to inspect her new program. When the general arrives for inspection, Margaret is surprised to learn he's more interested in her than in her triage program. Dejected, she kicks him out of her tent. Radar finally gets up the nerve to ask the nurse out and is shocked when she accepts.

C*A*V*E (2/5/79)

Written by Larry Balmagia and Ronny Graham. *Directed by* William Jurgensen. *Guest Stars:* Basil Hoffman, Mark Taylor, Charles Jenkins, Enid Kent, Jennifer Davis.

When shells start falling near camp, Potter calls ICOR and learns the shelling is "friendly." They decide to bug out and find a cave that will serve them adequately. Hawkeye's objection is unclear until he tells Potter he is claustrophobic. When one of his patients worsens, he and Margaret take the patient back to camp and operate on him. Hawkeye learns of Margaret's aversion to loud noises. With the surgery successful, they wait for the return of the unit, which comes after the shelling ceases.

Rally Round the Flagg Boys (2/12/79)

Written by Mitch Markowitz. *Directed by* Harry Morgan. *Guest Stars:* Ed Winter, Neil Thompson, Bob Okazaki, Jerry Fujikawa, James Lough, Roy Goldman.

Charles and a wounded soldier object when Hawkeye gives a North Korean priority in OR. Colonel Flagg arrives to interrogate the North Korean, but Hawkeye refuses access to the man. Flagg is convinced Hawkeye is a communist sympathizer and blackmails Charles into spying on him. In the meantime, a wounded GI's buddy comes to the Swamp, argues with Hawkeye and hits him. B.J. shakes the man up himself. Flagg tries to cut off the North Korean's IV tubes and Radar objects. Charles decides to set Flagg up for a practical joke.

Preventative Medicine (2/19/79)

Written by Tom Reeder. *Directed by* Tony Mordente. *Guest Stars:* James Wainwright, Larry Flash Jenkins, Jeff Maxwell.

A long OR session has the doctors complaining about a Colonel Lacy, who has a high casualty rate. In post-op, they learn his men regard the colonel as a maniac. In the meantime, Klinger is threatening voodoo on Potter. When Lacy arrives to see his men, Potter confronts him and says he is careless with men's lives. Margaret's admiration turns to repulsion when she learns how many men he's willing to sacrifice to take a hill. When Hawkeye hears Lacy pleading with HQ for permission to take the hill, he concocts a plot to keep the man out of action, but B.J. tells Hawk the plan accomplished nothing since it didn't stop the war. Klinger gives his voodoo stuff to Mulcahy after he becomes convinced he jinxed Colonel Lacy.

A Night at Rosie's (2/26/79)

Written by Ken Levine and David Isaacs. *Directed by* Burt Metcalfe. *Guest Stars:* Keye Luke, Joshua Bryant, Joseph Di Reda, Eileen Saki, Richard Lee Sung, Kellye Nakahara, JoAnn Thompson, Jennifer Davis, Jim Burk.

After two days in surgery, Hawkeye strolls into Rosie's for breakfast and decides to stay. A GI named Scully walks in. He's left the front and is AWOL. When B.J. comes by to get Hawkeye, they decide they aren't going back to the camp and instead get drunk. Klinger arrives and heads for the craps game in the back room. Margaret comes by and meets Scully. Hawkeye and B.J. grab Charles when he arrives and tie him up. Potter is furious when he discovers the whole camp is at Rosie's. Margaret helps Scully escape when MPs come looking for him.

Ain't Love Grand (3/5/79)

Written by Ken Levine and David Isaacs. *Directed by* Mike Farrell. *Guest Stars:* Kit McDonough, Sylvia Chang, Eileen Saki, Michael Williams, Judy Farrell.

B.J. is worrying about a patient sent to Seoul, and Hawkeye is climbing the walls. Charles goes to Rosie's and is propositioned by a young Korean "business girl." In the meantime, Klinger meets a nurse from the 8063 who likes his dressing routine. Charles tries to reform and refine the business girl, who ultimately turns him down. Meanwhile, when Klinger thinks about a serious relationship, he finds the nurse is just in it for the kicks. B.J. and Hawkeye drive each other nuts until B.J. learns his patient has improved and will be okay.

The Party (3/12/79)

Written by Burt Metcalfe and Alan Alda. *Directed by* Burt Metcalfe. *Note:* In year three's "Bulletin Board," Margaret implies her father is dead; here, he's alive.

When mail call finds Potter, Radar, and B.J. trading addresses for their relatives back home, B.J. gets inspired to have all their families get together in New York. Once the families set a date, Klinger objects to a group picture because he never told his mother he was sent to Korea. Margaret is pleased to learn her separated parents will reunite for her sake. The party is a hit and all have a good time. Klinger learns he couldn't fool his mother, and Radar begins to anticipate taking up Charles's parents on their invitation to his family to visit Cape Cod.

YEAR 8, 1979-1980

Cast and Crew

Regular Cast: Alan Alda as Hawkeye Pierce, Mike Farrell as B.J. Hunnicutt, Harry Morgan as Sherman Potter, Loretta Swit as Margaret Houlihan, David Ogden Stiers as Charles Winchester, Jamie Farr as Max Klinger, and William Christopher as Father Mulcahy. *Executive Producer* Burt Metcalfe. *Produced by* Jim Mulligan and John Rappaport. *Executive Story Editors* Dan Wilcox and Thad Mumford. *Story Editor* Dennis Koenig. *Story Consultant* Ronny Graham. *Creative Consultants* Gene Reynolds and Alan Alda. *Developed for Television by* Larry Gelbart. *Associate Producer* Stanford Tischler. *Executive Production Manager* Mark Evans. *Unit Production Manager/Assistant Director* David Hawks. *Second Assistant Director* Cathy Kinsock. *Director of Photography* Dominick R. Palmer, Jr. *Film Editors* Stanford Tischler, Larry L. Mills. *Music Supervision* Lionel Newman. *Art Director* David Haber/Frank Smith. *Set Decorator* Bert Allen. *Medical Advisor* Walter D. Dishell, M.D. *Post Production Supervisor* Joseph Silver. *Theme* Johnny Mandel. *Casting* Sam Christensen, Joyce Robinson.

Too Many Cooks (9/17/79)

Written by Dennis Koenig. *Directed by* Charles S. Dubin. *Guest Stars:* Gary Burghoff, Ed Begley, Jr., John Randolph.

Hawkeye's patient with a knee injury turns out to be a cook with a talent for making army food enjoyable. Klinger, who's clerking for Radar while he's on R and R, turns the mess hall into a restaurant. When Potter learns the cook has been kept at the 4077 when he should have shipped out, he gets angry. Potter's also upset that his wife has written a letter saying she wants him home for a change. A general's visit to the 4077 brings the cook's talents to his attention and the general decides he will be his personal cook. When the man says he wants to cook for his unit at the front, the general relents. Potter gets another letter from his wife; she understands his work after meeting a GI who was injured in Korea.

Are You Now, Margaret (9/24/79)

Written by Thad Mumford and Dan Wilcox. *Directed by* Charles S. Dubin. *Winner:* Writers Guild Award (Thad Mumford and Dan Wilcox). *Guest Stars:* Lawrence Pressman, Jennifer Davis, Jeff Maxwell, Leland Sun.

A congressional aide comes to the 4077 and says he wants to investigate the war effort and the 4077's operation. Margaret fawns over the man—she's never been closer to congressional power. Mulcahy, and then Potter, get suspicious about the man's motives when he starts asking about deadbeats and malcontents. When Hawkeye, B.J., and Potter confront him, he admits he's come on a communist witch-hunt and is zeroing in on Margaret. They defend her vigorously and then decide to blackmail him. They refer to Margaret as Hot Lips, which prompts him to pay her a visit. As the man makes his move, Klinger pops out of Margaret's armoire and snaps a picture. The man leaves in a huff.

Guerrilla My Dreams (10/1/79)

Written by Bob Colleary. *Directed by* Alan Alda. *Guest Stars:* Mako, Gary Burghoff, Joshua Bryant, Huanani Minn, George Kee Cheung, Marcus Mukai, Connie Izay.

Wounded arrive, among them an injured Korean woman. When a South Korean officer comes by and claims she's an enemy guerrilla, Hawkeye gets defensive and tries to shield her. In the meantime, Scully is among the injured, and Margaret takes special care of him. Hawkeye has a confrontation with the Korean officer in post-op, and Scully tells Hawkeye the officer is known for torturing prisoners to death. Potter tries to transfer the woman to another MASH unit. The officer catches them trying to sneak her out of camp and decides to take her away, but not before she curses Hawkeye and the others as her enemies.

Goodbye Radar, Pt.1 (10/8/79)

Written by Ken Levine and David Isaacs. *Directed by* Charles S. Dubin. *Nominated for* Writers Guild Award, Teleplay (Ken Levine and David Isaacs— Pts. 1 and 2). *Guest Stars:* Gary Burghoff, Marylin Jones, Johnny Haymer, Michael O'Dwyer, Richard Lee-Sung, Tony Cristino, Arell Blanton, Sean Fallon Walsh, Jon St. Elwood.

Generator problems during an OR session cause Hawkeye to get his finger caught in a rib spreader. Klinger and Zale try to get the generator working. In the meantime, Radar, trying to return to the 4077, meets a nurse while waiting for a flight. He learns she's on her way home to a town not far from his hometown. When a place opens up on a flight to Seoul, he tells her he will look her up when he gets home. Back at the 4077, B.J. and Potter improvise a Wangenstein to help a patient's infection drain. When Radar arrives back, the office is a mess and he can't find a new generator. The episode closes with news of Radar's uncle's death, meaning he will be going home on a hardship discharge.

Goodbye Radar, Pt. 2 (10/15/79)

Written by Ken Levine and David Isaacs. *Directed by* Charles S. Dubin. *Nominated for* Emmy, Outstanding Writing in a Comedy (Ken Levine and David Isaacs); Writers Guild Award, Teleplay (Ken Levine and David Isaacs— Pts. 1 and 2). *Guest Stars:* Gary Burghoff, Lee de Broux, Whitney Rydbeck, David Dozer.

Klinger panics as he tries to learn Radar's job. The camp still has no generator, so when wounded arrive in the evening, Radar devises a scheme to provide lighting for operating on them. Afterward, Radar is reluctant to leave, since he feels he is indispensable to the unit. Klinger makes a trade for a generator in Seoul, which impresses Radar. The unit prepares for a farewell party only to have wounded arrive. As the rest of the unit scrambles to OR, Radar quickly says his goodbyes to everyone, and B.J. makes arrangements for Radar to meet his family in San Francisco. Radar leaves by jeep.

Period of Adjustment (10/22/79)

Written by Jim Mulligan and John Rappaport. *Directed by* Charles S. Dubin. *Nominated for* Writers Guild Award, Teleplay (John Rappaport and Jim Mulligan); Emmy, Outstanding Directing (Charles S. Dubin). *Winner:* Directors Guild Award (Charles S. Dubin). *Guest Stars:* Jeff Maxwell, Eileen Saki, Gwen Farrell, Jan Jorden.

Potter has to cover for Klinger, who has gotten far behind in his army paperwork. Potter keeps comparing him to Radar. Everyone gives him a hard time. A letter from B.J.'s wife brings news of Radar's visit and puts B.J. into a funk when he reads his daughter called Radar "Daddy." Mulcahy tells Potter about another company clerk who had a tough time learning his job—

Radar. B.J. gets very drunk, smashes the still, and punches Hawkeye. Potter talks to Klinger and tells him to make the job his. B.J. and Hawkeye make up.

Nurse Doctor (10/29/79)

Written by Sy Rosen, Thad Mumford, and Dan Wilcox. Story by Sy Rosen. Directed by Charles S. Dubin. Guest Stars: Alexandra Stoddart, Jeff Maxwell, Kellye Nakahara.

Father Mulcahy is helping a nurse study for medical exams. The nurses seem to resent her as a know-it-all. Meanwhile, the road to Seoul is closed, and the unit is forced to cope with a water shortage, but somehow Charles remains fresh as a daisy. During another study session, the nurse gives Mulcahy an enthusiastic hug, which makes him uncomfortable. He suggests she study with one of the doctors. Later, they learn the nurse has asked for a transfer. Margaret tells her to work hard studying and gives her encouragement. When Hawkeye and B.J. learn Charles has been using bottled water to keep clean, they give him a hard time.

Private Finance (11/5/79)

Written by Dennis Koenig. Directed by Charles S. Dubin. Guest Stars: Shizuko Hoshi, Denice Kumagai, Mark Kologi, Joey Pento, Philip Simms, Art Evans, Mark Harrison, James Emery.

While Klinger tries to stop a young girl from prostitution, her mother misinterprets his actions. A group of wounded arrive, among them a soldier who is carrying a substantial wad of cash. The doctors learn from his platoon that he has no friends because he became a wheeler-dealer in the army. When the soldier dies, they decide to send the money to his parents, but they have a hard time writing the accompanying letter. Meanwhile Potter and Margaret visit the Korean woman to get her off Klinger's back. The teenage girl tells her mother that Klinger was honorable. When the soldier's parents return the money to Hawkeye, the 4077 gives part of it to the woman and the girl so they can leave the war zone.

Mr. and Mrs. Who (11/12/79)

Written by Ronny Graham. Directed by Burt Metcalfe. Guest Stars: Claudette Nevins, James Keane.

Charles returns from R and R in a hangover haze, and his luggage contains articles of women's clothing. Even Charles is puzzled. Meanwhile, hemorrhagic fever is hitting some of the patients. The army issues new treatment guidelines that seem to put the men at greater risk. The staff decides to defy the guidelines and soon the patients begin to come out of the fever. Charles is shocked when pictures from his trip show he was the groom at a wedding. "Mrs. Winchester" visits and tells him it was all part of a wild party and the "wedding" was a hoax.

The Yalu Brick Road (11/19/79)

Written by Mike Farrell. *Directed by* Charles S. Dubin. *Nominated for* Emmy, Outstanding Achievement in Film Editing (Stanford Tischler and Larry E. Mills) *Winner:* ACE "Eddie," Editing (Stanford Tischler and Larry E. Mills). *Guest Stars:* Soon-Teck Oh, G.W. Bailey, Bob Okazaki, Roy Goldman, Kellye Nakahara, Jeff Maxwell, Byron Chung.

A turkey dinner for Thanksgiving results in salmonella poisoning for many at the 4077. B.J. and Hawkeye are returning to camp when an accident in the road causes them to swerve and tip over. As they begin to walk home, a North Korean surrenders to them, even though he's the one with a gun. Back at the 4077, Charles, Margaret, and Mulcahy are the only healthy ones left and are stuck taking care of the others. The North Korean, B.J. and Hawkeye treat another man and find a motorcycle to take them home.

Life Time (11/26/79)

Written by Alan Alda and Walter Dishell, M.D. *Directed by* Alan Alda. *Guest Stars:* Kevin Brophy, J.J. Johnston, Kellye Nakahara, Roy Goldman, JoAnn Thompson, Jeff Maxwell. *Notes:* This episode takes place in "real" time. Viewers see a clock in the lower right corner to emphasize how quickly the doctors must work before paralysis becomes likely. No laugh track is used in this episode.

A soldier arrives with a lacerated aorta. Hawkeye does an emergency procedure to quell the bleeding. They try to buy more time as they search for a graft. When more wounded arrive, the buddy of a nearly dead soldier objects to B.J. not trying to save him. The buddy gets more upset when he learns they want to use his friend's artery as a graft for the other man. B.J. works fast to take the graft when the man dies and Mulcahy suggests the buddy tell the injured man who gets the graft all about his buddy. The operation is successful.

Dear Uncle Abdul (12/3/79)

Written by John Rappaport and Jim Mulligan. *Directed by* William Jurgensen. *Guest Stars:* Kelly Ward, Richard Lineback, Alexander Petale.

This episode follows Klinger as he writes a letter to his uncle. During an OR session, Potter remarks that the Korean war has no rallying slogans or songs. This gets Mulcahy started on a song about the war. Klinger writes about all the weird things the officers make him do. Hawkeye and B.J. are concerned when a "slow" soldier comes looking for his injured buddy. Concerned he's not front-line material, his buddy makes sure other men in the unit will look after the man. After several attempts, Mulcahy comes up with a touching song about the pointlessness of war.

Captains Outrageous (12/10/79)

Written by Thad Mumford and Dan Wilcox. *Directed by* Burt Metcalfe. *Guest Stars:* Eileen Saki, John Orchard, Sirri Murad, G. W. Bailey, Paul Cavonis, Momo Yashima.

A glowing letter from Potter has Father Mulcahy hoping for a promotion. Meanwhile, when a fight at Rosie's results in broken ribs for her, the medical staff offers to run the bar during her recovery. She tells Hawkeye, B.J., and Margaret to take care of Muldoon, an MP she pays off to stay open. Potter learns Mulcahy's file has been lost at the Pentagon, and Mulcahy gets upset. An angry Potter gets the promotion back on track. Once Rosie comes back, the bar is shut down because Charles offended Muldoon.

Stars and Stripe (12/17/79)

Written by Dennis Koenig. *Directed by* Harry Morgan. *Nominated for* Emmy, Outstanding Directing in a Series (Harry Morgan). *Guest Stars:* Joshua Bryant, Jeff Maxwell.

Potter announces that Charles and B.J. have been asked to write up an operation they performed using new techniques. The two spat over who should get most of the credit. Hawkeye feels excluded and becomes jealous of both. Potter points out a lot of people were involved in the successful surgery. Scully comes to see Margaret, but she's disappointed to learn he's been demoted to private for fighting. He demeans her own rank and achievements. She tries to make up with him, but she objects when he wants to make her a "new woman." B.J. and Charles decide to submit their paper under the name of the 4077.

Yessir, That's Our Baby (12/31/79)

Written by Jim Mulligan. *Directed by* Alan Alda. *Guest Stars:* Howard Platt, William Bogert, Yuki Shimoda, Elizabeth Farley.

A baby left outside the Swamp brings joy to the 4077. Mulcahy is distressed to learn she is mixed race (her father was a GI) as this will cause her to be an outcast in Korean society. They try to send her to the United States for adoption but run into red tape and arrogance. When they visit the Korean government, they learn the United States is the only country that won't accept such children. They are forced to leave the girl with some monks where she will grow up isolated from the outside world.

Bottle Fatigue (1/7/80)

Written by Thad Mumford and Dan Wilcox. *Directed by* Burt Metcalfe. *Nominated for* Emmy, Outstanding Directing (Burt Metcalfe). *Guest Stars:* Shelley Long, David Hirokane, Shari Saba, Jeff Maxwell.

Hawkeye decides to quit drinking for a week, but soon he begins to drive everyone crazy with his self-righteousness. In the meantime, Charles is enraged to learn his sister is marrying an Italian. B.J. gets tired of listening to both Hawkeye and Charles and leaves the Swamp. Charles's tirades about his sister's beau offend Klinger and Mulcahy, but then he gets a letter from her announcing the wedding is off because his family won't let him marry outside their faith. A chastened Charles writes his sister and apologizes. After a frightening incident in the OR, Hawkeye feels he needs a drink, but he decides instead to have one only when he *wants* one—not *needs* one.

Heal Thyself (1/14/80)

Written by Dennis Koenig. *Story by* Dennis Koenig and Gene Reynolds. *Directed by* Mike Farrell. *Guest Star:* Edward Herrman.

Potter comes down with mumps after a visit by the orphans. Klinger avoids him because he hasn't had them. While others fuss over him, Potter gets cranky—even more so when Charles gets the mumps and is brought over to share Potter's tent. A replacement surgeon with lots of combat experience immediately impresses Hawkeye and B.J. When casualties begin to stack up, however, the surgeon breaks down, ending up in Potter's tent in shock.

Old Soldiers (1/21/80)

Written by Dennis Koenig. *Directed by* Charles S. Dubin. *Guest Stars:* Jane Connell, Sally Imamura, Jason Autajay. *Note:* This is Harry Morgan's favorite episode.

Potter takes a call late at night and leaves to visit a friend. The unit cares for local orphans when they take refuge from the shelling. When Potter returns, he is not in a talking mood. The rest of the staff begins to speculate wildly when a package from a law firm arrives. Then they get invitations to join the colonel in his tent. There he tells them about four World War I buddies who made a pledge that whoever is the last surviving member of the group would drink in the others' memory. Potter is that survivor, and he invites his friends at the 4077 to share the cognac with him.

Morale Victory (1/28/80)

Written by John Rappaport. *Directed by* Charles S. Dubin. *Guest Stars:* James Stephens, G. W. Bailey, Jeff Maxwell.

Potter challenges B.J. and Hawkeye by naming them morale officers. Meanwhile, Charles goes to see a patient whose leg he was able to save from amputation, but the man is more concerned about his injured hand—he's a classical concert pianist. Charles tries to get the man to appreciate that his talent is in his head and heart. The morale officers are on the verge of being lynched when Hawkeye dreams up an outdoor seafood party.

Lend a Hand (2/4/80)

Written by Alan Alda. *Directed by* Alan Alda. *Guest Stars:* Robert Alda, Anthony Alda, Daren Kelly, Shari Saba. *Notes:* Alan Alda's father Robert and son Anthony make guest appearances in this episode. It is Robert Alda's second appearance as Dr. Borelli.

Hawkeye learns B.J. has fabricated a birthday for Hawkeye to give the unit something to get excited about. Dr. Borelli returns to the 4077 with a new nerve grafting technique. Borelli irritates Hawkeye by insisting everything be done his way. When Potter gets a call for a surgeon to go to an aid station, Hawkeye volunteers to get out of the birthday party and tells the others its B.J.'s wedding anniversary. Borelli volunteers to go with Hawkeye, and they argue heatedly at the aid station. When shells start falling, Borelli and Hawkeye injure their left and right hands respectively. They finish the surgery with each using his one good hand to make a pair.

Goodbye Cruel World (2/11/80)

Written by Thad Mumford and Dan Wilcox. *Directed by* Charles S. Dubin. *Guest Stars:* Alan Arbus, Clyde Kusatsu, Philip Bruns, James Lough, David Cramer, Kellye Nakahara.

Klinger's attempts to make his office homey bring only ridicule from the medical staff. He resents it because they have their own homey touches. He decides to forge a Section Eight and works on forging Potter's signature. Hawkeye works on a heroic soldier who's been wounded many times. The man attempts suicide when he learns he is going home. Sidney Freedman learns that his Chinese American ancestry is causing him to have conflicting feelings—he can't be a "good American" and a "good Chinese" at the same time. His previous wounds are other attempts at suicide. When Potter offers to let Klinger have one memento of home in the office, he feels guilty and goes all the way to Tokyo to retrieve the forged Section Eight papers.

Dreams (2/18/80)

Written by Alan Alda. *Story by* Alan Alda and James Jay Rubinfier. *Directed by* Alan Alda. *Nominated for* Emmy, Outstanding Directing in a Series (Alan Alda). *Guest Stars:* Ford Rainey, Robin Haynes, Catherine Bergstrom, Fred Stuthman, Kurtis Sanders, Ray Lynch, Connie Izay, Rick Waln, Kellye Nakahara, Dennis Troy. *Notes:* No laugh track is used in this episode. This episode received a lot of positive fan mail.

The staff is already exhausted when the PA announces more wounded. The episode follows the dreams Margaret, Potter, B.J., Charles, Mulcahy, Klinger and Hawkeye have during short nap breaks—dreams that start out pleasant but wind up being nightmares. At the end of it all, they have treated 211 patients in 33 hours. When surgery is finally done, someone mentions sleep, and everyone decides to avoid it.

War Co-Respondent (3/3/80)

Written by Mike Farrell. *Directed by* Mike Farrell. *Guest Stars:* Susan St. James, Brad Wilkin, Calvin Levels, Kellye Nakahara. *Note:* According to the production staff, the only joke ever repeated on the show is "When did this line start using stewardesses?" It is first heard in this episode and is repeated in year ten's "That's Show Biz."

A bus full of wounded finds a woman among them—newspaper cartoonist Aggie O'Shea. Hawkeye immediately has eyes for her, but she has eyes for B.J. Everyone notices her interest in him, and he finally admits to Hawkeye he is very attracted to her. When she confronts him directly with her desires, he tells her his lifeline is to California and his family.

Back Pay (3/10/80)

Written by Thad Mumford, Dan Wilcox, and Dennis Koenig. *Directed by* Burt Metcalfe. *Guest Stars:* Sab Shimono, Peter Kim, Jerry Fujikawa, G. W. Bailey, Richard Herd.

Potter puts Charles in charge of showing three Korean doctors around the 4077. When Klinger delivers the mail, Hawkeye is outraged to learn a doctor back home is making lots of money doing x-rays for Selective Service. He sends a bill to the surgeon general's office to compensate him for all the work he's done. An investigator arrives and tears the bill up. While Charles disdains his guests, they help fix his bad back with some acupuncture. Hawkeye clashes with the investigator, who breaks his foot kicking a bag of x-rays.

April Fools (3/24/80)

Written by Dennis Koenig. *Directed by* Charles S. Dubin. *Guest Stars:* Pat Hingle, G. W. Bailey, Roy Goldman, Jennifer Davis.

A series of April Fools jokes gets Potter on edge when he learns a tough colonel is coming to inspect the 4077. Supposedly on "good behavior," the medical staff is caught having a pillow fight when the man pulls up. Klinger decides to go straight military and hams it up for the colonel. The colonel criticizes the staff during surgery but is impressed with Klinger. The staff confronts the colonel, but he threatens them with court-martial for gross insubordination. When Klinger flips back into Section Eight mode, the colonel declares him a broken man and offers to discharge him. Hawkeye, Charles, B.J., and Margaret decide to go for broke and arrange to have a bucket of beer dumped on the colonel. When they pull it off, it looks as if their joke has had terrible consequences—until the colonel reveals that he and Potter set up their own little joke.

YEAR 9, 1980-1981

Cast and Crew

Regular Cast: Alan Alda as Hawkeye Pierce, Mike Farrell as B.J. Hunnicutt, Harry Morgan as Sherman Potter, Loretta Swit as Margaret Houlihan, David Ogden Stiers as Charles Winchester, Jamie Farr as Max Klinger, and William Christopher as Father Mulcahy. *Executive Producer* Burt Metcalfe.

Produced by John Rappaport. *Executive Script Consultants* Dan Wilcox and Thad Mumford. *Executive Story Editor* Dennis Koenig. *Creative Consultants* Gene Reynolds and Alan Alda. *Developed for Television by* Larry Gelbart. *Associate Producer* Stanford Tischler. *Executive Production Manager* Mark Evans. *Unit Production Manager/Assistant Director* David Hawks. *Second Assistant Director* Cathy Kinsock. *Director of Photography* Dominick R. Palmer, Jr. *Film Editors* Stanford Tischler, Larry L. Mills. *Music Supervision* Lionel Newman. *Art Director* Frank Taylor Smith, Duane R. Alt. *Set Decorator* Bert Allen. *Medical Advisor* Walter D. Dishell, M.D. *Post Production Supervisor* Joseph Silver. *Theme* Johnny Mandel. *Casting* Joyce Robinson and Associates.

The Best of Enemies (11/17/80)

Written by Sheldon Bull. *Directed by* Charles S. Dubin. *Guest Star:* Mako.

Hawkeye is excited as he leaves for Seoul. Charles brags about his bridge skills, which causes Potter to challenge him to a game. Potter recruits Margaret, and Charles cajoles B.J. into being his partner. Meanwhile, Hawkeye never makes it to Seoul; he wrecks when he swerves to avoid falling shells. A North Korean with a gun takes Hawkeye to a wounded buddy. He works valiantly to save the man, but the man dies. Hawkeye and the North Korean bury the man together. The bridge match sees changes in partners, and B.J. and Margaret win.

Letters (11/24/80)

Written by Dennis Koenig. *Directed by* Charles S. Dubin. *Guest Stars:* Richard Paul, Eileen Saki, Larry Cedar, Michael Currie. *Note:* Klinger refers to B.J. as "Captain Big Boots."

The unit answers a bunch of letters from a fourth grade class in Hawkeye's hometown, Crabapple Cove, Maine. Hawkeye ends up with a tough letter to respond to—he hears from a boy whose brother was injured in Korea and was put back on the line only to be killed. Mulcahy suggests that answering the letter will help Hawkeye clarify his own conflicted feelings about what he's doing in Korea. Meanwhile, Klinger gathers a crowd to watch Potter try to break the camp's consecutive free throw record.

Cementing Relationships (12/1/80)

Written by Davis Pollock and Elias Davis. *Directed by* Charles S. Dubin. *Guest Stars:* Joel Brooks, Alan Toy, Mel Harris.

Frustrated at the number of post-operative infections, Hawkeye determines the OR floor may be responsible. Meanwhile, a jilted Italian soldier falls for Margaret and rabidly pursues her. When the Corps of Engineers refuses to pour a concrete floor because MASH is mobile, the members of the 4077 decide to do the job themselves. The Italian soldier leaves but soon returns. Desperately, Margaret says she loves Charles.

Father's Day (12/8/80)

Written by Karen L. Hall. *Directed by* Alan Alda. *Guest Stars:* Andrew Duggan, Jeffrey Kramer, Art LaFleur. *Note:* In year three's "Bulletin Board," Margaret implies her father is dead; in year seven's "The Party," both her parents are alive but separated from one another. In "Father's Day," they are divorced.

Margaret gets word that her father will be visiting and starts whipping everyone into shape to impress him. Meanwhile, a grateful GI pledges he will divert a general's side of beef to the 4077 in thanks. Margaret's visit with her father doesn't go well. Potter tries to console her and confronts her father about his coolness to his daughter. When he leaves, he tells Margaret he loves her. MP's arrive looking for the beef but are bribed with some of the steak.

Death Takes a Holiday (12/15/80)

Written by Mike Farrell. *Directed by* Mike Farrell. *Guest Stars:* G.W. Bailey, Keye Luke, Yoshiki Hoover, Kellye Nakahara, Jeff Maxwell, Sally Imamura, Perren Page.

During a truce on Christmas Eve, Klinger delivers Christmas packages. Charles, who has received many packages, fails to share when they learn supplies have been cut and the Christmas party for the orphans will be meager. Later, however, he takes the orphans some candy. Sniper fire brings a wounded soldier in late Christmas night. He cannot be saved, but B.J. decides that the man should not die on Christmas. Hawkeye, B.J., and Margaret try to keep the man alive until midnight. In the meantime, Charles gets angry when he hears from the kids that they received no candy. The man who runs the orphanage tells him he sold it on the black market so that he could buy food for the orphans for the next month. A chastened Charles apologizes to the man.

A War for All Seasons (12/29/80)

Written by Dan Wilcox and Thad Mumford. *Directed by* Burt Metcalfe. *Nominated for* Writers Guild Award (Dan Wilcox and Thad Mumford). *Guest Stars:* Carl Freed, Laurie Bates, Jeff Maxwell.

The camp celebrates New Year's Eve and rings in 1951 with the hope that they won't be there next year. The episode follows the seasons of the year with lots of talk about catalog orders, the year's pennant race, and the corn Father Mulcahy is growing. The next New Year's Eve finds Potter toasting to a return home in the next year.

Your Retention Please (1/5/81)

Written by Erik Tarloff. *Directed by* Charles S. Dubin. *Guest Stars:* Barry Corbin, Sam Weisman, Jeff Maxwell.

Klinger is excited to get a letter from his ex-wife, thinking she wants to get back together, but instead he learns she is marrying his best friend.

Meanwhile, the retention officer makes his annual visit. He tries to reenlist a male nurse who reacts harshly because the army refuses to promote male nurses. When the retention officer sees a despondent Klinger, he takes advantage of his depression and gets him to reenlist. A savvy Potter arranges things so that the reenlistment won't be official, and Klinger is saved from his hasty decision. A ceremony makes the male nurse an honorary lieutenant.

Tell It to the Marines (1/12/81)

Written by Hank Bradford. *Directed by* Harry Morgan. *Guest Stars:* Stan Wells, Michael McGuire, Denny Miller, James Gallery.

When left in charge, Charles uses Klinger as his personal servant. Meanwhile, an injured marine faces a perplexing problem. He is a Dutch citizen who joined the military when his mother moved to the United States after marrying an American. A divorce means she will be deported before he returns home in three weeks. Hawkeye uses the media to aid the man's cause, and the Dutch government comes up with an embassy job for the man's mother.

Taking the Fifth (1/19/81)

Written by Elias Davis and David Pollock. *Directed by* Charles S. Dubin. *Guest Stars:* Charles Hallahan, Judy Farrell, Margie Impert, Jan Jorden.

The doctors are frustrated because the army has banned the use of curare, an anesthesia. When Hawkeye asks Klinger to repay a loan, he does so with some fine wine. Hawkeye decides to parlay this coup into a date and posts an ad on the bulletin board, announcing that he and his wine would like some company. One nurse accepts the offer. Difficulty getting a patient anesthetized makes Potter curse the army's rules on curare. When he hears the Canadians have plenty, he makes a trade. Hawkeye meets his date only to learn he will share his wine with all the nurses as they get back at him for his sexism.

Operation Friendship (1/26/81)

Written by Dennis Koenig. *Directed by* Rena Down. *Guest Star:* Tim O'Connor.

Klinger is injured after pushing Charles out of harm's way when an autoclave explodes. Charles dotes on Klinger and pledges his service for saving his life. Klinger proceeds to milk the situation for all he can. B.J. won't let anyone look at his injured arm, but when he can't operate, they call a specialist who quickly turns Hawkeye off with his air of superiority. The specialist finds B.J. needs surgery. A resentful Charles continues to wait on Klinger.

No Sweat (2/2/81)

Written by John Rappaport. *Directed by* Burt Metcalfe. *Nominated for* Writers Guild Award, Teleplay (John Rappaport). *Guest Stars:* W. Perren Page, Jeff Maxwell, Kellye Nakahara.

A hot spell has everyone miserable and up late into the evening. Klinger is trying to fix the PA. B.J. is worried that Peg needs him at home. Charles is in the mess tent sorting through documents sent by his family as they face an IRS audit. Margaret is struggling with a case of prickly heat rash on her bottom that she doesn't want the doctors to know about. Hawkeye scolds B.J. when he wonders if Peg is having an affair. Margaret finally pleads with Potter to get her calamine lotion. She doesn't know that Klinger has just finished fixing the PA. The camp has a good laugh as she talks about her rash.

Depressing News (2/9/81)

Written by Dan Wilcox and Thad Mumford. *Directed by* Alan Alda. *Guest Stars:* William Bogert, David Dozer, Rodney Saulsberry.

The enterprising Klinger starts a camp paper and recruits writers and subscribers. The supply truck brings a truck full of tongue depressors. Hawkeye decides to put the tongue depressors to use by building a replica of the Washington monument. Klinger publicizes Hawkeye's "monument to stupidity" and it attracts the attention of *Stars and Stripes*. The "reporter" also serves as an army information man and wants to put a patriotic angle on the story by using it for recruitment back home. This causes Hawkeye to rig the structure to blow up as the photo is shot.

No Laughing Matter (2/16/81)

Written by Elias Davis and David Pollock. *Directed by* Burt Metcalfe. *Guest Stars:* Robert Symonds, Mae Hi, Nathan Jung, Eileen Saki, Jeff Maxwell, Kellye Nakahara.

B.J. gives Hawkeye a hard time about making fun of everything. Hawkeye decides to go 24 hours without telling a joke to prove him wrong. The colonel who sent Charles to the 4077 comes for a visit, and Potter fears Charles may seek retribution. Klinger suggests Charles try the opposite by indulging the colonel's ego and whims. When the colonel arrives, he asks Charles to find him some companionship for the evening. Margaret goes to drop off reports for the colonel who thinks she is his "companion" and assaults her. All of this drives Hawkeye nuts as he resists making sarcastic comments. The colonel tells Charles that if he lies for him, he will get transferred to Tokyo. Charles preserves Margaret's honor instead.

Oh, How We Danced (2/23/81)

Written by John Rappaport. *Directed by* Burt Metcalfe. *Guest Stars:* Yuki Shimoda, Arlen Dean Snyder, Catherine Bergstrom, Michael Choe, Jennifer Davis, Shari Saba.

B.J. gets homesick as his wedding anniversary approaches. Margaret suggests they do something for the date, and Hawkeye begins to execute a plan. Meanwhile, a Korean grandfather arrives with his injured grandson. Potter

assigns Charles to do a sanitation inspection for a unit at the front. His negative report results in a punch from the offending officer. Hawkeye promises
to drop the report if the officer will replace the Korean boy's lost harmonica.
Hawkeye and the rest of the staff surprise B.J. with a home movie from Peg.
Using B.J.'s own words, she acts out how they would spend their anniversary
together if they could.

Bottoms Up (3/2/81)

Written by Dennis Koenig. *Directed by* Alan Alda. *Guest Stars:* Gail Strick-
land, Shari Saba, Kellye Nakahara, Jeff Maxwell, Laurie Bates, Bill Snider,
Jimmy Baron.

An old friend of Margaret's is spending her last few weeks at the 4077
before returning home. When a past drinking problem resurfaces, Margaret
pulls her friend out of the OR. Meanwhile, a series of practical jokes causes
the unit to turn against Hawkeye and sympathize with Charles, the target of
the jokes. Hawkeye tries to redeem himself but B.J. makes him look bad.
Hawkeye and Charles turn the tables by putting a naked sleeping B.J. in the
nurses' tent. When he wakes up, the whole camp greets him. When Margaret's
friend starts hallucinating in the mess tent, the 4077 helps her dry out.

The Red/White Blues (3/9/81)

Written by David Pollock and Elias Davis. *Directed by* Gabriel Beaumont.
Guest Stars: Roy Goldman, Jeff Maxwell, Kellye Nakahara, Frank Pettinger,
JoAnn Thompson.

When Hawkeye gives Potter his last annual physical before retirement,
he discovers the colonel has high blood pressure. Potter asks Hawkeye to keep
it quiet and give him two weeks to bring it down. Soon, the whole unit is trying to help him but instead they drive him crazy. Meanwhile, when some cases
of malaria crop up, they seek to administer chloroquine, the preventative, but
they discover all they have is primaquine. After taking his pill, Klinger gets
sick, but everyone thinks he's faking it. When a second soldier has similar
symptoms, they realize its a reaction to the drug. After two weeks, Potter's
blood pressure is down.

Bless You, Hawkeye (3/16/81)

Written by Dan Wilcox and Thad Mumford. *Directed by* Nell Cox. *Nominated for* Writers Guild Award (Thad Mumford and Dan Wilcox). *Guest
Stars:* Alan Arbus, Barry Schwartz, Dennis Troy, Pamela Coleman.

An ambulance arrives with soaking wet wounded. That night Hawkeye
starts having sneezing spells. When Hawkeye starts itching and the symptoms intensify, Potter calls Sidney Freedman. Freedman investigates the
clothing the injured soldiers wore and asks Hawkeye a series of questions
about his childhood and experiences with water. More questions bring out a

frightening incident from childhood when Hawkeye was pushed into water. Freedman deduces the smell of the soldiers evoked the smells from Hawkeye's childhood trauma. The sneezing spells cease.

Blood Brothers (4/6/81)

Written by Elias Davis and David Pollock. *Directed by* Harry Morgan. *Nominated for* Directors Guild Award (Harry Morgan). *Guest Stars:* Patrick Swayze, Ray Middleton, G.W. Bailey, Jeff Maxwell, Tom Kindle, Robert Baldwin, Roy Goldman, Dennis Troy.

A GI worries about his more seriously injured buddy and donates blood for him. Hawkeye discovers the donor GI has leukemia. He struggles to tell him, and when he does, the GI wants to defer his own treatment so that he can be evacuated with his buddy. Meanwhile, Father Mulcahy worries about an upcoming visit from a cardinal. But Mulcahy spends all night with the GI, missing the crucial Sunday service he is supposed to lead with the cardinal in attendance. When he finally gets to the service, Mulcahy tells the touching story of the man as a contrast to his own desires to impress the cardinal.

The Foresight Saga (4/13/81)

Written by David Pollock and Elias Davis. *Directed by* Charles S. Dubin. *Guest Stars:* Rummel Mor, Philip Sterling, Jeff Maxwell.

The staff is eager to read their first letter from Radar back in Iowa. It's an upbeat letter that says things are going well. A phone call to Radar reveals his letter was a put-on and things are tough for them. In the meantime, the unit is ecstatic when a Korean family donates fresh cabbage to them. An eye doctor has come for a visit after Klinger breaks both pairs of Potter's glasses. Potter gets new glasses, and the staff gets a pair for the Korean family's son as well. Later, the boy returns, wounded and without his family. The staff realizes his farm skills can help Radar's family, so they arrange for the boy to go back to the States to join Radar and farm in Iowa.

The Life You Save (5/4/81)

Written by John Rappaport and Alan Alda. *Directed by* Alan Alda. *Winner:* Directors Guild Award (Alan Alda). *Guest Stars:* G.W. Bailey, Val Bisoglio, Andrew Parks, Jim Knaub, Arthur Taxier, Jim Boeke, Jack Kearney, Paul Ventura, Wayne Morton, Meshach Taylor, Shari Saba, Roy Goldman, Gwen Farrell, Dennis Troy.

During triage outside, sniper fire breaks out, and the staff scrambles to get the wounded into the OR. Charles discovers after surgery that a sniper's bullet passed through his cap, and he becomes contemplative as a result. Meanwhile, Hawkeye draws KP supervision. He signs for trays that Klinger later tells him don't exist. They "procure" trays from the 8063, which leads to further complications. Charles by now is obsessed with what death is like. He tries to get answers from a man whose heart stopped and was restarted. Later, he goes to the front, where his encounter with a dying man seems to bring resolution.

YEAR 10, 1981-1982

Cast and Crew

Regular Cast: Alan Alda as Hawkeye Pierce, Mike Farrell as B.J. Hunnicutt, Harry Morgan as Sherman Potter, Loretta Swit as Margaret Houlihan, David Ogden Stiers as Charles Winchester, Jamie Farr as Max Klinger, and William Christopher as Father Mulcahy. *Executive Producer* Burt Metcalfe. *Supervising Producer* John Rappaport. *Producers* Dan Wilcox, Thad Mumford, Dennis Koenig. *Executive Script Consultants* Dan Wilcox and Thad Mumford/Elias Davis and David Pollock. *Executive Story Editor* Dennis Koenig, Karen Hall. *Creative Consultants* Gene Reynolds and Alan Alda. *Developed for Television by* Larry Gelbart. *Associate Producer* Stanford Tischler. *Executive Production Manager* Mark Evans. *Unit Production Manager/Assistant Director* David Hawks. *Second Assistant Director* Cathy Kinsock. *Director of Photography* Dominick R. Palmer, Jr. *Film Editors* Stanford Tischler, Larry L. Mills. *Music Supervision* Lionel Newman. *Art Director* Frank Taylor Smith, John Leimanis. *Set Decorator* Bert Allen. *Medical Advisor* Walter D. Dishell, M.D. *Post Production Supervisor* Joseph Silver. *Theme* Johnny Mandel. *Casting* Joyce Robinson and Associates.

That's Show Biz (10/26/81. One-hour episode)

Written by Elias Davis and David Pollock. *Directed by* Charles S. Dubin. *Guest Stars:* Gwen Verdon, Gail Edwards, Danny Dayton, Karen Landry, Amanda McBroom, Kellye Nakahara, Freddie Dawson, Brian Byers, Richard Molnar, Joshua Grenrock, Martin Ferrero, Paul Tuerpe. *Note:* This episode contains the only repeated joke of the entire series: "When did this line start using stewardesses?" It was used in year eight's "War Co-Respondent."

A USO troupe comes to the 4077 when one of the performers has an emergency appendectomy. The 4077 staff convinces the troupe to put a show on in post-op. Before they leave the next day, the troupe impresses the 4077 both with their talents and with the care they show for the patients.

Identity Crisis (11/2/81)

Written by Dan Wilcox and Thad Mumford. *Directed by* David Ogden Stiers. *Guest Stars:* Dirk Blocker, Squire Fridell, Joe Pantoliano, Jeff Maxwell, Kellye Nakahara, JoAnn Thompson, Shari Saba, Bill Snider.

A group of wounded men presents some dilemmas for the 4077 staff. One man is depressed after learning his girlfriend is marrying a wealthy boy. Another man is concerned about his black bag; they soon discover he is a stock salesman when he begins to make his pitch to the other wounded. A transfusion reaction in one patient results in a confession to Father Mulcahy that he has switched dog tags with a dead soldier as a way to get home. When Mulcahy confronts the man with the letters of the dead soldier whose identity he has assumed, he decides to become himself again.

Rumor at the Top (11/9/81)

Written by David Pollock and Elias Davis. *Directed by* Charles S. Dubin. *Guest Stars:* Nicholas Pryor, Jeff Maxwell, Roy Goldman.

Speculation and rumors about an upcoming inspection of the 4077 convince the unit they will be broken up. When the unit exhibits crazy behavior, the inspector starts packing to leave, thinking the whole unit has flipped out. When wounded arrive and the 4077 springs into action, the man sees why they are a crack unit. He tells them he was looking at their operation with an eye toward replicating their success, not to break up the unit.

Give 'em Hell, Hawkeye (11/16/81)

Written by Dennis Koenig. *Directed by* Charles S. Dubin. *Guest Stars:* Stefan Gierasch, Ed Vasgersian, Lance Toyoshima, John Lavachielli, Xander Berkeley, Kellye Nakahara, Mae Hi.

The slow pace of truce talks provokes Hawkeye to write a letter to President Truman telling him to get the war settled. When a colonel arrives to ask about their equipment needs, he makes a deal to give them a water heater if they beautify the camp. Klinger helps Margaret create a little park along with a boy who tells B.J. he wants an operation on his eyes so he can look more like an American. Margaret convinces the boy he will be attractive to women just as he is. Shortly after the major approves of the park, an ambulance pulls into camp out of control and destroys it.

Wheelers and Dealers (11/23/81)

Written by Dan Wilcox and Thad Mumford. *Directed by* Charles S. Dubin. *Guest Stars:* Anthony Charnota, Tony Becker, Chris Petersen, G.W. Bailey, Shari Saba, Jeff Maxwell.

A letter from Peg finds B.J. fretting over her taking a job. Col. Potter gets a traffic ticket and goes to driving safety classes. B.J. begins to bet on everything to make enough money so Peg doesn't have to work. When Potter flunks his driver safety exam, he makes Klinger stay up and help him study. Margaret and Hawkeye confront B.J. on his obnoxious betting and help him realize he's gotten out of hand. Potter passes the written test but nearly runs Klinger over when he takes his road test.

Communication Breakdown (11/30/81)

Written by Karen L. Hall. *Directed by* Alan Alda. *Guest Stars:* James Saito, Byron Chung, Abigail Nelson, JoAnn Thompson, Jeff Maxwell, Kwang Ho Baek, Roy Goldman, Kellye Nakahara. *Note:* No laugh track is used in this episode.

A lack of second class mail has stopped newspapers from getting to the 4077. When Charles gets a box of newspapers from his family he exhibits his usual selfishness and tightly controls others' access to them. Hawkeye discovers a South Korean MP is the brother of a North Korean prisoner. Hawkeye arranges for the brothers to talk by staging a blood transfusion. In the meantime, Charles gets very angry and refuses to share his papers when he decides one has been stolen. His attempt at retribution backfires on him.

Snap Judgment (12/7/81)

Written by Paul Perlove. *Directed by* Hy Averback. *Guest Stars:* Peter Hobbs, Peter Jurasik, Richard Winters, Mickey Jones, Jeff Maxwell, George Chung, Richard Lee-Sung, Monty Bane, Eileen Saki. *Note:* First part of a two-part story concluding with "Snappier Judgment," below.

A rash of thefts plagues the camp. When a Polaroid camera is stolen, Klinger writes up a report but fails to send it. Trying to make amends, he buys a camera on the black market but is arrested by MPs. He faces the possibility of six months at hard labor.

Snappier Judgment (12/14/81)

Written by Paul Perlove. *Directed by* Hy Averback. *Guest Stars:* Peter Hobbs, Jack Blessing, Jim Boeke, Monty Bane.

Klinger faces trial and is pressured by the army to name others involved in the black market as way to avoid punishment. Since he doesn't know anyone, it won't help. Charles offers to be his defense lawyer but shows he is way out of his league when he goes up against a young prosecutor. Hawkeye and B.J. hatch a plot to catch a real thief using Charles's tape recorder as bait. An MP is caught (by the Polaroid) taking the recorder. They take the evidence to the trial and arrive just in time to get Klinger off the hook.

'Twas the Day After Christmas (12/28/81)

Written by David Pollock and Elias Davis. *Directed by* Burt Metcalfe. *Guest Stars:* Michael Ensign, Leo Lewis, Val Bisoglio, Kellye Nakahara, Jeff Maxwell, Roy Goldman, Bill Snider. *Note:* No laugh track is used in this episode.

After celebrating Christmas with British soldiers, the unit decides to adopt their traditional "Boxing Day," the day after Christmas, when subordinates and superiors switch roles. Klinger becomes CO and assigns the roles for the day. All the officers find their new jobs more difficult and frustrating than they imagine. Temporary officers find their bosses' jobs aren't all that easy either.

Follies of the Living/Concerns of the Dead (1/4/82)

Written by Alan Alda. *Directed by* Alan Alda. *Nominated for* Emmy, Outstanding Writing in a Comedy (Alan Alda). *Guest Stars:* Kario Salem, Randall Patrick, Jeff Tyler, Perren Page. *Note:* No laugh track is used in this episode.

Klinger is sick and having delusions. The doctors can't determine what is wrong. In his condition he "sees" a young GI named Westin die and talks to him about what is happening. The episode follows Klinger's delusions of Westin, in which the dead man at first denies and then realizes he is dead. The doctors decide Klinger has a kidney stone and try to lower his temperature with ice (after earlier having ignored Margaret's suggestions to that effect). Klinger talks with Westin, but the others don't understand who Klinger is talking to. When Klinger awakes, he asks everyone about Westin, and they just don't get it.

The Birthday Girls (1/11/82)

Written by Karen L. Hall. *Directed by* Charles S. Dubin. *Guest Stars:* Jerry Fujikawa, Kellye Nakahara. *Note:* This episode talks about the introduction of Levophed, which was used casually in earlier episodes. No laugh track is used in this episode.

While the doctors at the 4077 deal with a Korean farmer's pregnant cow, Margaret enlists Klinger to take her to Seoul so she can rendezvous with a general in Tokyo. She insists he take a short cut, but the bumpy road causes the jeep to break down. As Margaret and Klinger prepare to spend the night in a jeep, Klinger learns it's Margaret's birthday. She shares whiskey and her frustrations with him. When they return to camp the next day, Margaret learns she has won the pool on the timing of the calf's birth.

Blood and Guts (1/18/82)

Written by Lee H. Grant. *Directed by* Charles S. Dubin. *Guest Stars:* Gene Evans, Brett Cullen, Rita Wilson. *Note:* No laugh track is used in this episode.

The camp eagerly awaits the arrival of famed journalist Clayton Kibbee. He brings six pints of blood and intends to write about the injured who receive the blood. He immediately begins to woo the women of the 4077, much to the concern of Hawkeye, who sees his dates get stolen by Kibbee. B.J. inherits a motorcycle when a GI comes in injured from an accident. When the injured man gets some of the blood, Kibbee fabricates a story about the man's heroic deeds. When Hawkeye hears him call the story in, he objects to Kibbee's glorification of war. Later, Kibbee gets drunk and takes B.J.'s motorcycle to the front and crashes it on the way. When Hawkeye and B.J. find him, Hawkeye informs him he will need some of the blood he brought and suggests he tell the truth this time.

A Holy Mess (2/1/82)

Written by Elias Davis and David Pollock. *Directed by* Burt Metcalfe. *Guest Stars:* Cyril O'Reilly, David Graf, Val Bisoglio, Ray Goldman, Ed Ramirez, Bill Snider, Dennis Troy, Leland Sun, Kip Curtis.

The 4077 is thrilled when Potter announces a local farmer has donated real eggs in gratitude for saving his farm. A GI arrives AWOL from the front, and MPs soon follow. When the man requests sanctuary, Mulcahy obliges and asserts the laws of God take precedence over the army's rules. The egg breakfast is relocated outside as Mulcahy keeps the man in the mess tent. When Mulcahy tries to talk him into giving up, the man threatens him with a gun. Mulcahy disarms the man, who is then sent to Sidney Freedman for treatment.

The Tooth Shall Set You Free (2/8/82)

Written by Elias Davis and David Pollock. *Directed by* Charles S. Dubin. *Guest Stars:* Tom Atkins, Jason Bernard, John Fujioka, Larry Fishburne, Bill Snider, Kellye Nakahara. *Note:* No laugh track is used in this episode.

Charles is exhibiting all the signs of a bad tooth but refuses to admit it. Wounded combat engineers arrive, and soon afterward their CO comes to visit them. The fact that he wants to send a black soldier home while keeping a white man confuses Hawkeye, who tries to uncover the CO's motives. In the meantime, Margaret confronts Charles on his use of codeine and learns he is afraid of the dentist. Potter tells him the tooth must be pulled. Hawkeye, B.J., and Potter set up the CO to admit he doesn't like blacks and opposes an integrated army.

Pressure Points (2/15/82)

Written by David Pollock. *Directed by* Charles S. Dubin. *Nominated for* Emmy, Outstanding Directing in Comedy (Charles S. Dubin). *Guest Stars:* Alan Arbus, John O'Connell, Gene Pietragallo, William Rogers, Roy Goldman.

Potter is very bothered when he learns Hawkeye had to open up one of his patients to remove some fragments that caused an infection. When Potter loses his cool during a guest lecture, he calls upon Sidney Freedman to help him deal with his crisis of confidence. He tells Freedman he feels his skills are slipping and doesn't feel comfortable about performing surgery. In the meantime, Charles decides to retaliate against his sloppy roommates by becoming a slob himself. When the rivalry nearly destroys the Swamp, Potter reacts calmly. Freedman asks why he was easy on them. Potter says they were just blowing off steam. Freedman suggests Potter needs to do the same.

Where There's a Will, There's a War (2/22/82)

Written by Elias Davis and David Pollock. *Directed by* Alan Alda. *Nominated for* Emmy, Outstanding Directing in a Comedy (Alan Alda). *Guest*

Stars: Dennis Howard, Larry Ward, Jim Borelli, James Emery, Jeff Maxwell, Kellye Nakahara, Brian Fuld, Ned Bellamy, Dennis Flood, Tom Valentine, Corkey Ford. *Note:* No laugh track is used in this episode.

Hawkeye is sent when a battalion aid station calls for a replacement surgeon. B.J. returns from Seoul and feels guilty having seen his buddy head into danger. Hawkeye arrives at the aid station and works under harrowing conditions. When he learns the surgeon he is replacing was killed the night before, he begins to write a will and ponders what he will leave his companions at the 4077. In the meantime, the whole unit is concerned and B.J. panics when he hears from a wounded soldier that a surgeon at the aid station has been killed. When the fighting stops, Hawkeye is allowed to return.

Promotion Commotion (3/1/82)

Written by Dennis Koenig. *Directed by* Charles S. Dubin. *Guest Stars:* G.W. Bailey, John Matuszak, Jim Reid Boycem, Deborah Harmon, Cameron Dye, Richard Fullerton, Jeff Maxwell, Kellye Nakahara, Roy Goldman, Bill Snider.

The promotion season finds Charles, Hawkeye, and B.J. the object of brown-nosing and unusual military decorum—especially from Klinger. But Charles's biggest worry is about a big GI with a record who threatens to harm him if he doesn't get a promotion. Potter takes an interest in a young GI because the man gets harassed by his unit buddies. Potter learns they give him a hard time about being a virgin and faithful to his girlfriend. The teasing causes the man to volunteer for a transfer to explosive ordnance detail, but he later reconsiders. Klinger is the only soldier promoted. Hawkeye and B.J. help Charles deal with the big GI by tricking the man and transferring him out of the unit.

Heroes (3/15/82)

Written by Thad Mumford and Dan Wilcox. *Directed by* Nell Cox. *Guest Stars:* Pat McNamara, Earl Boen, Britt Leach, Matthew Faison, Gerard Castillo, Jay Gerber, Al Rossi, Tierre Turner, Hennen Chambers, Eddie Frescas, David Orr, Richard Cummings.

When Father Mulcahy learns a retired boxing champion is going to visit the 4077, he gets excited about meeting this boyhood hero. When the army advance man tells Klinger to order steaks for the champ's dinner, Klinger tries to get other special treats for himself and the unit. The champ arrives and proves to be a complainer. At the dinner, he suffers a massive stroke, bringing a slew of reporters who hang on Hawkeye's word. He resents the attention but can't seem to convince the others that he does. Mulcahy stays with the boxer until he dies.

Sons and Bowlers (3/22/82)

Written by Elias Davis and David Pollack. *Directed by* Hy Averback. *Nominated for* Emmy, Outstanding Directing (Hy Averback). *Guest Stars:*

Dick O'Neill, William Lucking, Roger Hampton, Kellye Nakahara. *Note:* Hawkeye reveals his mother died when he was 10—but in year one's "Dear Dad... Again," he asked his father in a letter "to give Mom and Sis a kiss."

The 4077 is frustrated at always losing to a marine unit in sports tournaments, and Klinger suggests a bowling match may be the answer. Potter, who blames Margaret for the losses, continually rejects her as a bowling partner. In the meantime, Hawkeye gets a letter from his father telling him he is going into the hospital for unidentified surgery. Hawkeye assumes the worst because of the way his father kept him in the dark when his mother died. He sweats it out until he is able to talk to him and learns things will be okay. When B.J. is called to the hospital, Potter has no choice but to put Margaret in the bowling lineup. She helps win the match.

Picture This (4/5/82)

Written by Karen L. Hall. *Directed by* Burt Metcalfe. *Nominated for* Emmy, Outstanding Directing (Burt Metcalfe). *Guest Stars:* John Fujioka, Jeff Maxwell. *Note:* No laugh track is used in this episode.

Hawkeye alienates the others when he objects, with fanatical intensity, to B.J. wearing one of his socks. Potter, searching for a birthday present for his wife, comes up with the idea of painting a portrait of the medical staff. But the Swampmates are feuding, making the portrait sitting difficult. Hawkeye takes residence in a hut and learns life can be lonely. Margaret, Father Mulcahy and Klinger all take it on themselves to get the doctors back on speaking terms. Potter manages to complete a painting showing them as a happy family.

That Darn Kid (4/12/82)

Written by Karen L. Hall. *Directed by* David Ogden Stiers. *Guest Stars:* G.W. Bailey, John P. Ryan, Tom Kindle, Jeff Maxwell, Richard Lee Sung, Kellye Nakahara.

When a local merchant decides to sell his wares and move south, Klinger buys a goat from him with the hope of making money selling fresh milk. Hawkeye, who has been named paymaster, has just begun to distribute scrip when wounded arrive. Charles takes a loan from Rizzo to buy what he has decided is a rare vase from an ancient dynasty. Klinger's goat manages to eat all the scrip. An investigator assigned to look at the case refuses to believe the story and Hawkeye faces owing the army. The delayed pay makes Charles unable to pay Rizzo for the loan. Charles gets further angered when he learns his vase isn't rare at all—merely a cheap copy. Potter, Hawkeye, and Klinger set the investigator up when they have the goat enter his tent and consume his reports.

YEAR 11, 1982-1983

Cast and Crew

Regular Cast: Alan Alda as Hawkeye Pierce, Mike Farrell as B.J. Hunnicutt, Harry Morgan as Sherman Potter, Loretta Swit as Margaret Houlihan, David Ogden Stiers as Charles Winchester, Jamie Farr as Max Klinger, and William Christopher as Father Mulcahy. *Executive Producer* Burt Metcalfe. *Supervising Producer* John Rappaport. *Producers* Dan Wilcox, Thad Mumford, Dennis Koenig *Executive Script Consultants* Elias Davis and David Pollock/Karen Hall. *Story Editor* Karen Hall. *Creative Consultants* Gene Reynolds and Alan Alda. *Developed for Television by* Larry Gelbart. *Associate Producer* Stanford Tischler. *Executive Production Manager* Mark Evans. *Unit Production Manager/Assistant Director* David Hawks. *First/Second Assistant Director* Cathy Kinsock. *Second Assistant Director* Barbara Gelman. *Director of Photography* Dominick R. Palmer, Jr. *Film Editors* Stanford Tischler, Larry L. Mills. *Music Supervision* Lionel Newman. *Art Director* John Leimanis. *Set Decorator* Bert Allen. *Medical Advisor* Walter D. Dishell, M.D. *Post Production Supervisor* Joseph Silver. *Theme* Johnny Mandel. *Casting* Joyce Robinson and Associates.

Hey, Look Me Over (10/25/82)
Written by Alan Alda. *Directed by* Susan Oliver. *Guest Stars:* Kellye Nakahara, Peggy Feury, Perry Lang, Deborah Harmon, Gary Grubbs, Shari Saba, Jeff Maxwell, Rita Wilson.

Just as the nurses return to a shambles after a bug out, Margaret learns that a very tough inspector is on her way to the 4077. Hawkeye tries to hit on the nurses during cleanup but is put off and rebuffed by everyone but Kellye, who is not as pretty as some of the others but would like to be teased by him. They dance at the officers' club, but when the music gets slow, Hawkeye breaks things off and checks out the other women, ignoring her. When the inspector arrives, she is tough on Margaret. Kellye confronts Hawkeye in the scrub room. Margaret, embarrassed at the commotion, becomes furious with Hawkeye and Kellye for arguing loudly. Hawkeye later sees Kellye confront a patient and learns a lesson about inner beauty. Margaret is ecstatic to learn she's been given a satisfactory rating.

Trick or Treatment (11/1/82)
Written by Dennis Koenig. *Directed by* Charles S. Dubin. *Guest Stars:* George Wendt, Richard Lineback, Andrew Clay, James Lough, Herman Poppe, R.J. Miller, Arnold Turner, Arlee Reed, Terry Brannon, John Otrin.

It's Halloween and the 4077 is in costume when some marines arrive injured from a brawl. Wounded arrive and break up the party. One among the wounded arrives and is declared dead, but viewers see his fingers move. Hawk-eye has a tough case who refuses to eat. He lost his buddies in a foxhole when they were eating an early Thanksgiving dinner and he went to get seconds. When he returned he found them all dead from a shell. When Mulcahy returns, he rushes to give last rites to the "dead" man, only to see the man shed a tear. An amazed medical staff congratulates Mulcahy for saving the man's life.

Foreign Affairs (11/8/82)

Written by David Pollock and Elias Davis. *Directed by* Charles S. Dubin. *Guest Stars:* Melinda Mullins, Jeffrey Tambor, Soon-Teck Oh, Byron Chung, Buddy Farmer, Patrick Romano, JoAnn Thompson, Dennis Troy.

A wounded North Korean pilot arrives at the 4077. An army PR man arrives claiming the man has defected in response to a flyer drop. He's anxious to boost flagging support for the war back home. The PR man promises the pilot citizenship and hero treatment in the States, but the man says he did not defect and wants to be treated as a prisoner. A French International Red Cross volunteer arrives and is charmed by Charles. They talk all night and fall for each other, but he soon backs off when he learns the woman has an "unacceptable" past. In the meantime, Hawkeye and B.J. hatch a plot to send their South Korean translator home as the pilot.

The Joker Is Wild (11/15/82)

Written by John Rappaport and Dennis Koenig. *Directed by* Burt Metcalfe. *Guest Stars:* Clyde Kusatsu, David Haid, Jeff Maxwell, Jin-Taek Yi, Terry Mayer. *Note:* No laugh track is used in this episode.

A series of practical jokes by B.J. produces complaints that his jokes aren't original. B.J. decides to challenge the others to a joke-out and promises to get each of them in the next 24 hours. B.J. seemingly "zings" everybody but Hawkeye. The next morning Hawkeye walks into the mess tent claiming to have bested B.J. The others disagree, and he soon learns that all the other jokes were staged and the only one "gotten" was him.

Who Knew? (11/22/82)

Written by David Pollock and Elias Davis. *Directed by* Harry Morgan. *Guest Stars:* Kellye Nakahara, Enid Kent, Shari Saba, JoAnn Thompson. *Note:* No laugh track is used in this episode.

Hawkeye returns late at night from a date with Millie Carpenter in a great mood. The next morning, Potter announces Carpenter has been killed when she went for a walk and stepped on a land mine. Hawkeye volunteers to eulogize her but struggles when he realizes how little he knew about her. When Mulcahy finds her diary, he gives it to Hawkeye, who learns he meant a great deal to her. In the meantime, Klinger is trying to get Charles to invest in his "invention"—hula hoops. Hawkeye gives a touching eulogy in which he tells all the others at the 4077 how much he loves them and criticizes himself for keeping his distance from others.

Bombshells (11/28/82)

Written by Dan Wilcox and Thad Mumford. *Directed by* Charles S. Dubin. *Guest Stars:* Gerald O'Laughlin, Allen Williams, Stu Charno, Michael Bond, Michael Carmine, Robert Townsend, Ken Neumeyer, Paul Tuerpe, Bill Snider, Natasha Bauman.

A series of rumors prompts Hawkeye to say some people will believe everything they hear. He then starts a rumor about Marilyn Monroe coming to the 4077 in gratitude for working on her cousin. Soon after, Potter gets a call from a general who has heard about the Marilyn visit and insists he come see her. The hoax is in full motion until Hawkeye manages to send the 4077 a fake telegram canceling her visit due to complications on the movie set. In the meantime, B.J. and a chopper pilot go fishing only to find a wounded man. B.J. tries to save the man, but they have to leave him behind when sniper fire starts hitting the chopper. B.J. is given a bronze star but gives the medal to a wounded GI who says hearing Marilyn was coming for a visit kept him alive.

Settling Debts (12/6/82)

Written by Dan Wilcox and Thad Mumford. *Directed by* Mike Switzer. *Guest Stars:* Guy Boyd, Jeff East, Michael Lamont, Jack McCulloch, Jennifer Davis Westmore.

Potter is suspicious when he sees a letter in his wife's handwriting addressed to Hawkeye. It turns out she has paid off their home's mortgage early and has sent the mortgage to them to have a burning party for Potter. The staff plans the party while he becomes convinced his wife has bought a houseboat in Florida—something he is fiercely opposed to. A wounded young lieutenant arrives and tells B.J. he's paralyzed from the waist down. The North Korean sniper who shot the lieutenant later comes in wounded and his sergeant threatens to shoot him until the lieutenant tells him not to. Potter finally walks into his tent and realizes his fears were unfounded.

The Moon Is Not Blue (12/13/82)

Written by Larry Balmagia. *Directed by* Charles S. Dubin. *Guest Stars:* Hamilton Camp, Sandy Helberg, Jan Jorden, Larry Ward, Jeff Maxwell, Jan Jorden.

Hawkeye and B.J. decide to try to get better movies for the unit but discover it's almost impossible. Meanwhile, a wounded general arrives and objects to the 4077's unofficial officers' club and orders it closed. Then the medical staff learns ICOR has sent placebos instead of codeine. When Klinger complains to Hawkeye the heat is getting to him, Hawkeye gives him one of the placebos and tells him it will make him cool and comfortable. When B.J. reads about a new "racy" movie, they try to work the bureaucracy to get it, but a double switch results in another rerun. In the meantime, the medical staff is forced to try the placebos as painkillers when the army won't send more codeine. They work. When Klinger learns the placebos were the source of his cure, he immediately begins sweating.

Run for the Money (12/20/82)

Written by Mike Farrell, David Pollock, and Elias Davis. *Directed by* Nell Cox. *Guest Stars:* Thomas Calloway, Mark Anderson, Phil Brock, William Schilling, Robert Alan Browne, Barbara Tarbuck, Kellye Nakahara, Michael Conn, Ken Wright, Juney Smith, Ron Kapra.

While he runs to keep in shape, Father Mulcahy frets over the condition of the orphanage. When Klinger thinks a track star has been assigned to the 4077, he hatches a plot to challenge the 8063 to a race. The unit bets on its man only to learn he is the track star's *father*. They recruit Mulcahy for the run. In the meantime, a stuttering soldier is taken under the wing of Charles, who tries to convince him his stuttering has nothing to do with his level of intelligence. Viewers learn the reason for his compassion when it is revealed Charles's sister also stutters. When race day comes, Mulcahy comes from behind to win—but not before insisting all winnings get donated to the orphanage.

UN, the Night and the Music (1/3/83)

Written by David Pollock and Elias Davis. *Directed by* Harry Morgan. *Guest Stars:* George Innes, Kavi Raz, Dennis Holahan, David Packer, Kellye Nakahara, Bill Snider, Shari Saba, Jeff Maxwell. *Note:* Loretta Swit and guest star Dennis Holahan met during this episode and eventually married.

A UN delegation arrives at the 4077 to observe their work for 24 hours. Margaret becomes enchanted by a Swedish officer while Charles welcomes a British officer who shares his penchant for the finer things in life. B.J. has a tough leg case but tells the man he will be okay. Later, he has to amputate the man's leg and feels guilty because of his earlier assurances. B.J. is amazed when the man jokes about his condition. The Swede reveals to Hawkeye he must avoid Margaret because an old injury has left him impotent, but when Margaret finds out, she does not reject him. Charles and the British officer compete to be the more knowledgeable snob, and the man has the last laugh on Charles.

Strange Bedfellows (1/10/83)

Written by Mike Farrell. *Directed by* Karen L. Hall. *Guest Star:* Dennis Dugan. *Note:* Dugan appeared as a GI in year three's "Love and Marriage."

Charles is snoring at night and keeping Hawkeye and B.J. awake, but he refuses to admit it, even when they use his tape recorder to get evidence. Meanwhile, Potter is happy to get a visit from his son-in-law, but distressed when he gets a call from a Tokyo hotel about a woman's nightgown left in his son-in-law's room. After a talk with Father Mulcahy, Potter confronts his son-in-law, who admits to his indiscretion. Potter tells him about his own infidelity long ago. When B.J. and Hawkeye gather the whole unit near the tent to witness the snoring and convince Charles, he relents.

Say No More (1/24/83)

Written by John Rappaport. *Directed by* Charles S. Dubin. *Guest Stars:* John Anderson, Michael Horton, Chip Johnson, James Karen, Jeff Maxwell, Kellye Nakahara, Jeff Chapman, Norman Garrett, Dennis Troy.

Margaret's plans to attend a lecture in Seoul by an expert on emergency care get complicated when she comes down with laryngitis. Later, the lecture gets canceled because the man has to return to the United States. A general comes to visit his son while at the same time planning for a new offensive. The son dies rather suddenly after seeming to be okay. The general seems truly grieved, but Hawk is shocked when the general quickly resumes his war planning. Margaret gets to meet the expert after all.

Friends and Enemies (2/7/83)

Written by Karen L. Hall. *Directed by* Jamie Farr. *Guest Stars:* John McLiam, Jim LeFebvre, Kellye Nakahara, Matthew Price, Jeff Maxwell, Jack Yates, Roy Goldman, Bill Snider, JoAnn Thompson, Jennifer Davis.

Margaret gets a record player but no records and proceeds to get friendly with Charles to get some of his. Meanwhile, Woody, an old friend of Potter's, arrives at the 4077 as part of a group of wounded. Hawkeye learns from another man that Woody wandered in during fighting and started giving orders to stay, which caused more injuries. Potter reacts defensively but determines the men are right and confronts Woody on his behavior, telling him he will report him. B.J. tries to manipulate both Charles and Margaret so he won't have to hear any more of Charles's records, but they get back at him.

Give and Take (2/14/83)

Written by Dennis Koenig. *Directed by* Charles S. Dubin. *Guest Stars:* Craig Wasson, G.W. Bailey, Derek Wong, Jeff Maxwell, Kellye Nakahara, Sagan Lewis, Alberta Jay.

Potter returns from Seoul to learn Charles did not fulfill his charity officer duties on payday. The duty gets traded and bartered among the medical staff and is finally given back to Charles. In the meantime, a wounded North Korean comes in, soon followed by the GI who shot him. The two men are placed next to each other, making the American uncomfortable. The North Korean shows generosity to him but later dies and the GI feels remorse. He talks to

Potter who suggests it should be a rule of war to know your enemy before you can kill them. Charles solves his charity collection problem by contributing for everyone.

As Time Goes By (2/21/83)

Written by Dan Wilcox and Thad Mumford. *Directed by* Burt Metcalfe. *Guest Stars:* Rosalind Chao, G.W. Bailey, Michael Swan, Mark Herrier, Jeff Maxwell, Kellye Nakahara, Wesley Thompson, Chao Li Chi, Oksun Kim, JoAnn Thompson, Brigitte Chandler.

Charles reads about a time capsule being buried under a Los Angeles skyscraper and Margaret gets inspired to do one for the 4077. Hawkeye volunteers to help but Margaret is skeptical he will treat it as a joke. In the meantime, B.J. plays a joke on Rizzo, who gets retribution when he brings a fake grenade into the showers when B.J. is showering. A young Korean woman is accused of firing at GIs, but she denies it and is later proved innocent. Margaret and Hawkeye end up doing separate time capsule solicitations and conflict with each other. When the unit gathers for the time capsule burying, Margaret learns Hawkeye has selected some very appropriate items. Best of all, Margaret and Hawkeye decide to bury the hatchet.

Goodbye, Farewell and Amen (2/28/83)

Written by Alan Alda, Burt Metcalfe, John Rappaport, Thad Mumford, Dan Wilcox, David Pollock, Elias Davis, and Karen Hall. *Directed by* Alan Alda. *Guest Stars:* Allan Arbus, Rosalind Chao, G.W. Bailey, Shari Saba, Jeff Maxwell, Gwen Farrell, Kellye Nakahara, Roy Goldman.

See text (Chapter 8) for a summary of this 2½-hour final episode.

Notes

Chapter 1. The Situation Comedy as Social History

1. The material for this section is drawn and synthesized from: Darrell Y. Hamamoto, *Nervous Laughter: Television Situation Comedy and Liberal Democratic Ideology* (New York: Praeger, 1989); Hal Himmelstein, *Television Myth and the American Mind*, 2nd ed. (Westport, CT: Praeger, 1994); and David Marc, *Comic Visions: Television Comedy and American Culture* (Boston: Unwin Hyman, 1989). Other program information comes from Tim Brooks and Earle Marsh, *The Complete Directory to Prime Time Network and Cable TV Shows, 1946–Present*, 6th ed. (New York: Ballantine, 1995).

2. Hamamoto, *Nervous Laughter*, p. 112.

3. Himmelstein, *Television Myth*, p. 122–159.

4. Richard Adler, *All in the Family: A Critical Appraisal* (New York: Praeger, 1979).

5. Neil Vidmar and Milton Rokeach, "Archie Bunker's Bigotry: A Study in Selective Perception and Exposure," p. 123–138; John C. Brigham and Linda W. Giesbrecht, "All in the Family: Racial Attitudes," p. 139–145; G. Cleveland Wilhoit and Harrold de Bock, "All in the Family in Holland," p. 146–158 in Adler, ed., *All in the Family*.

6. Marc, *Comic Visions*, p. 16.

7. Himmelstein, *Television Myth*, p. 113–114.

8. Himmelstein, *Television Myth*, p. 113.

9. Himmelstein, *Television Myth*, p. 115.

Chapter 2. From Novel to Film to Television

1. David Marc, *Comic Visions: Television Comedy and American Culture* (Boston: Unwin Hyman, 1989).

2. Todd Gitlin, *Inside Prime Time* (New York: Pantheon, 1983).

3. Marc, *Comic Visions*, p. 19.

4. The information presented here is drawn from Michael Harris, Carl H. Steele, and Elsa M. Bruton, *M*A*S*H: Binding Up the Wounds* (New York: George Fenmore, 1983); Suzy Kalter, *The Complete Book of M*A*S*H* (New York: H.N. Abrams, 1988); and David S. Reiss, *M*A*S*H: The Exclusive, Inside Story of TV's Most Popular Show* (Indianapolis: Bobbs-Merrill, 1980).

5. Kalter, *Complete Book of M*A*S*H*; Reiss, *M*A*S*H*.

6. Kalter, *Complete Book of M*A*S*H*.

7. Gitlin, *Inside Prime Time*, p. 217.

8. Gorton Carruth, *The Encyclopedia of American Facts and Dates*, 8th ed. (New York: Harper and Row, 1987).

9. "The troubled U.S. Army in Vietnam." *Newsweek*, January 11, 1971, p. 29–37.

10. "My Lai: A question of orders." *Time*, January 25, 1971, p. 24; "Who is responsible for My Lai?" *Time*, March 8, 1971, p. 18–19.

11. "The clamor over Calley: who shares the guilt?" *Time*, April 12, 1971, p. 14–21; "Judgment at Fort Benning." *Newsweek*, April 12, 1971, p. 27–29.

12. "More atrocities?" *Time*, March 22, 1971, p. 26; "And now a general." *Newsweek*, June 14, 1971, p. 29; "A second My Lai?" *Newsweek*, January 31, 1972, p. 13–14.

13. "Who else is guilty?" *Newsweek*, April 12, 1971, p. 30–32; "End of the affair." *Newsweek*, October 4, 1971, p. 22; "Closing the My Lai case." *Time*, November 25, 1974, p. 19–20.

14. "The government vs. the press." *Newsweek*, July 5, 1971, p. 17–22; "Ellsberg: the battle over the right to know." *Time*, July 5, 1971, p. 7–12.

15. "The cooling of America." *Time*, February 22, 1971, p. 10.

16. "The campus mood, '71: A Newsweek poll." *Newsweek*, February 22, 1971, p. 61–63.

17. "Indochina: the new optimism." *Newsweek*, March 1, 1971, p. 18–19; "Indochina: Nixon's strategy of withdrawal." *Time*, March 1, 1971, p. 19; "Assessing the Laos invasion." *Newsweek*, April 5, 1971, p. 25–29.

18. "Vietnamization: the reality and the myth." *Newsweek*, August 2, 1971, p. 38–39.

19. "Trashing the Capitol." *Newsweek*, March 15, 1971, p. 28–29; "A bomb in the Senate." *Time*, March 15, 1971, p. 25.

20. "The chess of ending a war." *Time*, May 10, 1971, p. 12–15; "Self defeat for the 'army of peace.'" *Time*, May 17, 1971, p. 13–15; "The war on two fronts." *Newsweek*, May 1, 1971, p. 22–23; "Once more a time for protest." *Newsweek*, May 3, 1971, p. 24–29; "What price protest?" *Newsweek*, May 10, 1971, p. 25–27; "The biggest bust." *Newsweek*, May 17, 1971, p. 24–29.

Chapter 3. It's a Man's War—Year 1

1. Suzy Kalter, *The Complete Book of M*A*S*H* (New York: H.N. Abrams, 1988).

2. Kalter, *Complete Book of M*A*S*H*, p. 27.

3. Kalter, *Complete Book of M*A*S*H*, p. 37.

4. "Teen age sex: letting the pendulum swing." *Time*, August 21, 1972, p. 34–40.

5. "Single motherhood." *Time*, September 6, 1971, p. 48.

6. "Abortion: how it's working." *Newsweek*, July 19, 1971, p. 50–52.

7. "Legal abortion: who, why and where." *Time*, September 27, 1971, p. 67–70.

8. "The abortion revolution." *Newsweek*, February 5, 1973, p. 27+; "Abortion: what happens now." *Newsweek*, February 5, 1973, p. 66–67.

9. "First no to sex bias." *Time*, December 6, 1971, p. 71.

10. "Never underestimate...." *Newsweek*, July 26, 1971, p. 29–30.

11. "Women's lib: beyond sexual politics." *Time*, July 26, 1971, p. 36–37; Gorton Carruth, *The Encyclopedia of American Facts and Dates*, 8th ed. (New York: Harper and Row, 1987).

12. "The year of the woman." *Newsweek*, November 4, 1974, p. 20–27; "Womenpower at the polls." *Newsweek*, November 18, 1974, p. 39.

13. "The new woman, 1972." *Time*, March 20, 1972, p. 25.

14. "One giant leap for womankind." *Time*, April 3, 1972, p. 16–17; "Woman power." *Newsweek*, April 3, 1972, p. 27–28.

15. "Some like it not." *Newsweek*, January 15, 1973, p. 17–18; "Trouble for ERA." *Time*, February 19, 1973, p. 22–25

16. Ruth Byne, "Women's lib: beyond sexual politics." *Time*, July 26, 1971, p. 36–37; "A woman's place is on the job." *Time*, July 26, 1971, p. 56.

17. "Facing equality for women." *Time*, October 4, 1971, p. 58–59.

18. "The new campus rebels: women." *Newsweek*, December 10, 1973, p. 120–125.

19. "Situation report." *Time*, March 20, 1972, p. 63; "The new woman, 1972." *Time*, March 20, 1972, p. 25.

20. "Gloria Steinem: A liberated woman despite beauty, chic and success." *Newsweek*, August 16, 1971, p. 51–52.

21. Carruth, *Encyclopedia*.

22. "Not for women only." *Time*, February 21, 1972, p. 66.

23. "The new breed." *Newsweek*, August 30, 1971, p. 62.

24. "The women vs. ABC." *Newsweek*, May 15, 1972, p. 57.

25. Carruth, *Encyclopedia*.

26. "The militant homosexual." *Newsweek*, August 23, 1971, p. 45–48; "Gay liberation." *Newsweek*, November 27, 1972, p. 34; "The gay church." *Time*, August 23, 1971, p. 39.

27. "Gay power." *Newsweek*, February 26, 1973, p. 32.

28. "The militant homosexual." *Newsweek*, August 23, 1971, p. 47.

29. "A different Fourth." *Time*, July 5, 1971, p. 6.

30. "The government vs. the press." *Newsweek*, July 5, 1971, p. 17–22; "The secret history of the war (cont'd.)." *Newsweek*, July 12, 1971, p. 21; "Round three: more Pentagon disclosures." *Time*, July 12, 1971, p. 12–13; "Again the Pentagon Papers." *Time*, July 19, 1971, p. 30.

31. "The government vs. the press." *Newsweek*, July 5, 1971, p. 18.

32. "Setting a date." *Newsweek*, July 5, 1971, p. 25.

33. "A different Fourth." *Time*, July 5, 1971, p. 6; "The old glory." *Newsweek*, July 26, 1971, p. 26.

34. "Nixon's coup: to Peking for peace." *Time*, July 26, 1971, p. 11–17.

35. "A vote for youth." *Time*, July 12, 1971, p. 8; "How will the young vote?" *Time*, August 23, 1971, p. 9–10.

36. "How will youth vote?" *Newsweek*, October 25, 1971, p. 28–38; "A profile of the new voter." *Newsweek*, October 25, 1971, p. 38–49.

37. "Week of a thousand sorties." *Newsweek*, January 10, 1972, p. 22–23.

38. "Vietnamization: is it working?" *Time*, February 7, 1972, p. 34+; "Mr. Nixon's new Vietnam offensive." *Newsweek*, February 21, 1972, p. 18–20.

39. "The air war resumes." *Time*, January 3, 1972, p. 34–39; "Statue of liberty play." *Newsweek*, January 10, 1972, p. 20+; "Strategies for '72." *Newsweek*, January 17, 1972, p. 45; "Squeezing the balloon." *Newsweek*, April 3, 1972, p. 31; "Vietnamization: a policy under the gun?" *Time*, April 17, 1972, p. 35–39; "The president battles at three fronts." *Time*, May 1, 1972, p. 11–13; "Nixon at the brink over Vietnam." *Time*, May 22, 1972, p. 11–15.

40. "The war that won't go away." *Newsweek*, April 17, 1972, p. 16–21; "Mr. Nixon strikes back." *Newsweek*, April 24, 1972, p. 21–22.

41. "The president battles on three fronts." *Time*, May 1, 1972, p. 13; "In furious battle." *Newsweek*, April 24, 1972, p. 31–33.

42. "Hanoi's high-risk drive for victory." *Time*, May 15, 1972, p. 24–32; "Vietnam: The specter of defeat." *Newsweek*, May 15, 1972, p. 20–22; "What went wrong in Vietnam: The fallacies in U.S. policy." *Newsweek*, May 15, 1972, p. 24–25.

43. "Vietnam: an issue that won't go away." *Newsweek*, August 28, 1972, p. 11–13; "The battle of the POW's." *Newsweek*, October 9, 1972, p. 24–28; "At last, the shape of a settlement." *Time*, October 30, 1972, p. 13–17; "A deal with Hanoi, a deal with Thieu." *Newsweek*, October 30, 1972, p. 24–25; "The shape of peace." *Time*, November 6, 1972, p. 14–18.

44. "Could it have been settled sooner?" *Time*, November 6, 1972 p. 18; "The Vietnam deal: why now?" *Newsweek*, November 6, 1972 p. 36–39; "Another pause in the pursuit of peace." *Time*, November 13, 1972, p. 17–18.

45. "How Henry did it in Vietnam." *Time*, June 10, 1974, p. 41–42.

46. "Diplomacy by terror." *Newsweek*, January 1, 1973, p. 10; "More bombs than ever." *Time*, January 1, 1973, p. 10–12; "What the bombing did." *Newsweek*, January 8, 1973, p. 11–12.

47. "Paris peace in nine chapters." *Time*, February 5, 1973, p. 12–14; "At last, the Vietnam peace." *Time*, February 5, 1973, p. 18–24; "No calm after the storm?" *Newsweek*, February 12, 1973, p. 18–20; "Waging the cease-fire in Vietnam." *Newsweek*, February 26, 1973, p. 35–36.

48. Carruth, *Encyclopedia*. "Amnesty for war exiles?" *Newsweek*, Janu-

ary 17, 1972, p. 19–26; "Amnesty: a peace not at hand." *Newsweek*, February 12, 1973, p. 23.

49. Seymour Hersh, "The decline and near fall of the U.S. Army." *Saturday Review*, November 18, 1972, p. 58–65.

50. Kalter, *Complete Book of M*A*S*H*, p. 29–31.

51. Kalter, *Complete Book of M*A*S*H*, p. 29.

52. Kalter, *Complete Book of M*A*S*H*, p. 115.

53. Kalter, *Complete Book of M*A*S*H*, p. 53.

54. Gerald Clarke, "M*A*S*H." *Time*, October 16, 1972, p. 95; "Oneliners behind the lines." *Life*, October 27, 1972, p. 16.

55. Allene Tamley, "Get away from anything." *Vogue*, March 1973, p. 64–66.

56. "Mashed morality." *Newsweek*, April 23, 1973, p. 53.

57. Harry Waters, "Rated PG." *Newsweek*, September 11, 1972, p. 76.

Chapter 4. War Is Hell... —Years 2–3

1. Suzy Kalter, *The Complete Book of M*A*S*H* (New York: H.N. Abrams, 1988), p. 53.

2. Kalter, *Complete Book of M*A*S*H*, p. 65.

3. Kalter, *Complete Book of M*A*S*H*, p. 29

4. Joseph Heller, *Catch-22* (New York: Simon and Schuster, 1961). Milo Minderbender was a lieutenant who built up an enterprise in the army that could accomplish or acquire almost anything.

5. "Fuel: button up your overcoat." *Newsweek*, November 12, 1973, p. 91–92; "Cold comfort for a long, hard winter." *Time*, December 19, 1973, p. 33–34.

6. "And now, the chillout." *Time*, January 22, 1973, p. 69; "America's energy crisis." *Newsweek*, January 22, 1973, p. 52–60; "The energy crisis (contd.)." *Newsweek*, February 12, 1973, p. 74; "The energy crisis: time for action." *Time*, May 7, 1973, p. 41–42.

7. "The Arab oil squeeze." *Newsweek*, September 17, 1973, p. 33–35; "Stepping on the gas to meet a threat." *Time*, November 26, 1973, p. 24–26; "Energy: how high is up?" *Newsweek*, January 7, 1974, p. 18–22; "Oil: paying the price, pulling together." *Newsweek*, January 14, 1974, p. 27; "Oil: playing the numbers game." *Newsweek*, January 21, 1974, p. 78; "The times they are a-changin'." February 18, 1974, p. 19–21.

8. "From crisis to political issue." *Time*, March 11, 1974, p. 30–31; "Results of a lifted embargo." *Time*, March 18, 1974, p. 22+; "The embargo's hazy finish." *Time*, March 25, 1974, p. 26+.

9. "The book banners." *Newsweek*, March 26, 1973, p. 64; "The book banners." *Newsweek*, September 30, 1974, p. 94–95.

10. "And now, a third Vietnam." *Newsweek*, July 16, 1973, p. 36–37.

11. "Countdown in Cambodia." *Newsweek*, July 16, 1973, p. 34–35;

"Cambodia: inside story." *Newsweek*, August 6, 1973, p. 32–33; "The odd pause that wasn't." *Time*, August 13, 1973, p. 27–28; "Desperate days for besieged Phnom Penh." *Time*, August 20, 1973, p. 27+; "When bombs fall by mistake." *Newsweek*, August 20, 1973, p. 34–35.

12. "The agony of Cambodia." *Newsweek*, March 10, 1975, p. 22–30; "Who are the Khmer Rouge?" *Newsweek*, March 10, 1975, p. 26; "The noose gets tighter." *Newsweek*, March 17, 1975, p. 35–36.

13. "And still the war…" *Newsweek*, February 10, 1975, p. 24–25; "Indochina: how much longer?" *Time*, March 24, 1975, p. 12–25.

14. "The great retreat." *Newsweek*, March 31, 1975, p. 16–20; "Biting the bullet." *Newsweek*, March 31, 1975, p. 20; "Thieu's risky retreat." *Time*, March 31, 1975, p. 30–39; "Why did the ARVN break?" *Newsweek*, April 7, 1975, p. 41–44; "Now, trying to pick up the pieces." *Time*, April 14, 1975, p. 6–8; "Toward the final agony." *Time*, April 14, 1975, p. 8–12.

15. "Striking the colors." *Newsweek*, April 21, 1975, p. 20–22; "Seeking the last exit from Vietnam." *Time*, April 21, 1975, p. 6–10; "Last chopper out of Saigon." *Time*, May 12, 1975, p. 11–12.

16. "Where they go." *Time*, April 14, 1975, p. 14–15; "The orphans: saved or lost?" *Time*, April 21, 1975, p. 10–11; "Orphans of the storm." *Newsweek*, April 14, 1975, p. 28–30; "Clouds over the airlift." *Time*, April 28, 1975, p. 20; "The bitter legacy of the babylift." *Time*, May 24, 1976, p. 17.

17. "The end of a thirty years' war." *Time*, May 12, 1975, p. 8–10; "Saigon: a calm week under communism." *Time*, May 19, 1975, p. 23+.

18. "The ITT affair: politics and justice." *Newsweek*, March 20, 1972, p. 24–26; "How the U.S. settled with ITT." *Newsweek*, March 20, 1972, p. 26–28.

19. "The ITT controversy revisited." *Time*, August 13, 1973, p. 18–19.

20. "ITT: Another cover up." *Newsweek*, July 29, 1974, p. 36–38.

21. "Chile under Marxism: does it work?" *Newsweek*, November 15, 1981, p. 43–47; "ITT: now, the Chile papers." *Newsweek*, April 3, 1972, p. 18–19; "The worse things get, the better." *Time*, April 9, 1973, p. 18; "…and more on ITT." *Newsweek*, April 2, 1973, p. 18.

22. "The bugs at the Watergate." *Time*, July 3, 1972, p. 10+; "The spies who came in from the heat." *Newsweek*, September 18, 1972, p. 40–45; "Watergate: plenty to probe." *Newsweek*, February 12, 1973, p. 25-26; "A point for Ellsberg." *Newsweek*, February 12, 1973, p. 26.

23. Gorton Carruth, *The Encyclopedia of American Facts and Dates*, 8th ed. (New York: Harper and Row, 1987), p. 726; "Watergate: A sneak preview." *Newsweek*, March 19, 1973, p. 21–22; "The growing Watergate mess." *Newsweek*, April 2, 1973, p. 14–18; "Watergate's widening waves of scandal." *Time*, April 2, 1973, p. 11–13.

24. "Ellsberg: case dismissed." *Newsweek*, May 21, 1973, p. 25–26+; "Practicing on Ellsberg." *Time*, May 7, 1973, p. 20–21; "Pentagon Papers: case dismissed." *Time*, May 21, 1973, p. 28–30.

25. "The fight over the future of the FBI." *Time*, March 26, 1973, p. 17–27.

26. "Defying Nixon's reach for power." *Time*, April 16, 1973, p. 10–15; "The crowded blotter of Watergate suspects." *Time*, May 14, 1973, p. 22–23; "Exposing the big cover-up." *Newsweek*, May 28, 1973, p. 26–31; "Thinking the unthinkable." *Newsweek*, May 28, 1973, p. 31–33.

27. "They had a little list." *Newsweek*, July 9, 1973, p. 14–15; "The Nixon tapes." *Newsweek*, July 30, 1973, p. 12–17; "Watergate I: the evidence to date." *Time*, August 20, 1973, p. 16–18; "Three men of high principle." *Time*, October 29, 1973; "The great tapes crisis." *Newsweek*, October 29, 1973, p. 22–30; "Seven tumultuous days." *Time*, November 5, 1973, p. 13–18; "The president: 'I'm not a crook.'" *Newsweek*, November 19, 1973, p. 26; "How the public feels about Nixon and Watergate now." *Time*, November 19, 1973, p. 25–26.

28. "Operation friendly persuasion." *Newsweek*, March 25, 1974, p. 22–27; "The president gambles on going public." *Time*, May 13, 1974, p. 10–14; "The voters: Nixon should go." *Time*, May 13, 1974, p. 19; "The public: disillusioned." *Time*, May 20, 1974, p. 18–22.

29. "Damaging deletions from the tapes." *Time*, June 24, 1974, p. 31–32; "An encyclopedia of evidence." *Newsweek*, July 22, 1974, p. 21–25; "The fateful vote to impeach." *Time*, August 5, 1974, p. 10–18.

30. "The fateful vote." *Newsweek*, August 5, 1974, p. 18–22; "A unanimous no to Nixon." *Time*, August 5, 1974, p. 20–25.

31. "The specter in the dock." *Newsweek*, October 28, 1974, p. 26–27; "The verdict on Watergate." *Newsweek*, January 13, 1975, p. 16–18; "Was justice finally done?" *Newsweek*, January 13, 1975, p. 19–24.

32. "Operating at home." *Time*, May 28, 1973, p. 27–28.

33. "The CIA's new bay of bucks." *Newsweek*, September 23, 1974, p. 51+; "One year later: absolute order." *Time*, September 23, 1974, p. 46–47; "The CIA: time to come in from the cold." *Time*, September 30, 1974, p. 17+.

34. "More than civil war?" *Time*, September 3, 1973, p. 36.

35. "The bloody end of a Marxist dream." *Time*, September 24, 1973, p. 35–46; "Chile: the brutal death of an idea." *Newsweek*, September 24, 1973, p. 42–48.

36. "The military and its master." *Time*, September 24, 1973, p. 38; "The generals consolidate their coup." *Time*, October 1, 1973, p. 26–29; "Slaughterhouse in Santiago." *Newsweek*, October 8, 1973, p. 53–54; "Strangelovian scenario." *Time*, October 15, 1973, p. 48–50.

37. "In a shadow country." *Time*, April 22, 1974, p. 44; "The year of the generals." *Newsweek*, September 16, 1974, p. 49; "The war over secret warfare." *Newsweek*, September 30, 1974, p. 37–39; "The exorcists." *Newsweek*, April 28, 1975, p. 42–47.

38. David Reiss, *M*A*S*H: The Exclusive, Inside Story of TV's Most Popular Show* (Indianapolis: Bobbs-Merrill, 1980), p. 109.

39. Reiss, *M*A*S*H*, p. 98.

40. Jerome H. Jaffe, ed., *Encyclopedia of Drugs and Alcohol*, Vol. 2 (New York: Macmillan, 1995), p. 688–692.

41. Carruth, *Encyclopedia*; "The no. 1 drug problem." *Newsweek*, February 28, 1972, p. 54; "The new teen fad: booze." *Newsweek*, March 5, 1973, p. 68.

42. "A firecracker explodes." *Newsweek*, October 21, 1974, p. 42; "The fall of chairman Wilbur Mills." *Time*, December 16, 1974, p. 22–26; "Wilbur's repentance." *Newsweek*, January 13, 1975, p. 26–27.

43. "The pot report: still inconclusive." *Time*, February 15, 1971, p. 46.

44. "The AMA: switch on pot." *Newsweek*, July 3, 1972, p. 50.

45. "Grass grows more acceptable." *Time*, September 10, 1973, p. 67–68.

46. "Tyrannical king coke." *Time*, April 16, 1973, p. 69.

47. Kalter, *Complete Book of M*A*S*H*, p. 179.

48. "Goals that look like quotas." *Time*, January 29, 1973, p. 77; "Racism in reverse." *Newsweek*, March 11, 1974, p. 61–62; "Affirmative action: the negative side." *Time*, July 15, 1974, p. 86.

49. "Echoes of Little Rock." *Newsweek*, September 23, 1974, p. 48.

50. "Raid at Wounded Knee." *Time*, March 12, 1973, p. 21; "Return to Wounded Knee." *Newsweek*, March 12, 1973, p. 27–29; "Verdict on Wounded Knee." *Newsweek*, September 30, 1974, p. 54–55; "Over the brink." *Time*, September 30, 1974, p. 32.

51. Carruth, *Encyclopedia*.

52. "Out of the closet." *Time*, March 5, 1973, p. 80.

53. "Gay power." *Newsweek*, February 26, 1973, p. 32; "The lesbian as mother." *Newsweek*, September 24, 1973, p. 75–76; "Homosexual rights." *Newsweek*, May 20, 1974, p. 76–77.

54. "The gay church." *Time*, August 23, 1971, p. 38–39; "Gay manifesto." *Time*, June 25, 1973, p. 80.

55. "The boys in the band." *Newsweek*, April 1, 1973, p. 108.

56. Kalter, *Complete Book of M*A*S*H*, p. 83; Reiss, *M*A*S*H*, p. 84; Michael Harris, Carl H. Scheele, and Elsa Bruton, *M*A*S*H: Binding Up the Wounds* (New York: George Fenmore, 1983), p. 9.

57. Kalter, *Complete Book of M*A*S*H*, p. 33, notes that the army had abandoned the points system for rotation after World War II and that it was never applied to doctors. This is one of the few historical inaccuracies in the show.

58. Harris, Sheele, and Burton, *M*A*S*H*, p. 9; Reiss, *M*A*S*H*, p. 151.

Chapter 5. Hearts and Minds—Years 4–5

1. "Why they come." *Time*, April 14, 1975, p. 13–14; "Turning off the last lights." *Time*, May 5, 1975, p. 19–21; "The privileged exiles." *Time*,

May 12, 1975, p. 13; "Bitter debate on who got out." *Time*, May 19, 1975, p. 24–25.

2. "An irony of history." *Newsweek*, April 28, 1975, p. 16–17; "Last exit from Saigon." *Newsweek*, May 5, 1975, p. 30–33; "Now on to 'camp fortuitous.'" *Time*, May 12, 1975, p. 14+; "A warmer welcome for the homeless." *Time*, May 19, 1975, p. 9–10; "Journey to 'freedom land.'" *Time*, May 19, 1975, p. 10–14.

3. "The new Americans." *Newsweek*, May 12, 1975, p. 32+; "A cool and wary reception." *Time*, May 12, 1975, p. 24–26; "The final commitment: people." *Time*, May 12, 1975, p. 26.

4. "Blunders, breakdowns—and action." *Time*, July 21, 1975, p. 18–19.

5. Wilbur J. Scott, "PTSD and Agent Orange: implications for a sociology of veteran's issues." *Armed Forces and Society*, Summer 1992, p. 592–612; Roger J. Spiller, "Shell shock." *American Heritage*, May/June 1990, p. 75–87.

6. "Dear Sigmund" won an Emmy Award for Outstanding Directing and a Writers Guild Award for Alan Alda. He also got an Emmy nomination for writing, and the show received nominations for cinematography and film editing. A key part—Radar's letter to a dead GI's parents—was written at the end of a long night after Alda's house had been burglarized (David Reiss, *M*A*S*H: The Exclusive, Inside Story of TV's Most Popular Show* [Indianapolis: Bobbs-Merrill, 1980] p. 24).

7. Dane Archer and Rosemary Gartner, "The myth of the violent veteran." *Psychology Today*, December 1978, p. 94–96+.

8. "Scars of Vietnam." *Commonweal*, February 20, 1970, p. 554–556; "The Vietnam vet: 'no one gives a damn.'" *Newsweek*, March 29, 1971, p. 27–30; "Why Vietnam veterans feel like forgotten men." *U.S. News and World Report*, March 29, 1971, p. 42–44.

9. "Heroin: a plaything?" *Time*, May 7, 1973, p. 90.

10. "The vets: heroes as orphans." *Newsweek*, March 5, 1973, p. 22–24; "Forgotten warriors?" *Time*, March 12, 1973, p. 17–18.

11. Robert Jay Lifton, "The 'gook syndrome' and 'numbed warfare.'" *Saturday Review*, November 18, 1972, p. 66–72; Lifton also wrote a book on Vietnam veterans: *Home from the War: Vietnam Veterans, Neither Victims nor Executioners* (New York: Simon and Schuster, 1973).

12. "Postwar wounds." *Time*, September 2, 1974, p. 63; *CBS Evening News*, September 4, 1974.

13. "Home from Vietnam." *U.S. News and World Report*, February 12, 1973, p. 21–23; "Vietnam veterans: shocking report on damaged lives." *Redbook*, May 1973, p. 94+; "Permanent war prisoners." *Newsweek*, March 5, 1973, p. 23; *CBS Evening News*, August 22, 1977, and October 24, 1977.

14. "If the draft dodgers come home." *U.S. News and World Report*, December 6, 1971, p. 34; "Pros and cons of granting amnesty." *Time*, January 10, 1972, p. 16–17; "How the courts are treating draft dodgers." *U.S. News*

and World Report, January 15, 1973, p. 26–27; "Just desserts for deserters and dodgers." *Nation's Business*, July 1973, p. 24; "Acrimony over amnesty." *Time*, March 24, 1974, p. 24–25; "Amnesty." *Newsweek*, April 8, 1974, p. 29.

15. "The amnesty issue." *Time*, September 9, 1974, p. 14; "Amnesty at last." *Newsweek*, September 30, 1974, p. 30–32; "Amnesty failure." *Time*, September 22, 1975, p. 6; "Deserter interview." *Newsweek*, July 4, 1976, p. 61–62.

16. "The pardon that brought no peace." *Time*, September 16, 1974, p. 10–12; "Next, a Vietnam amnesty." *Newsweek*, September 16, 1974, p. 26–33.

17. "Citizen Reagan." *Time*, January 6, 1975, p. 21; "Ready on the right." *Newsweek*, March 24, 1975, p. 20–24; "The growing challenge of Reagan." *Time*, October 27, 1975, p. 13–14; "Can Reagan stop Ford?" *Newsweek*, November 24, 1975, p. 30–34.

18. *NBC Nightly News*, January 12, 1977; *ABC Evening News*, January 26, 1977; *ABC Evening News*, June 24, 1977; *CBS Evening News*, August 24, 1977; "Pardon: how broad a blanket?" *Time*, January 17, 1977, p. 22+; "After the pardon." *Newsweek*, January 31, 1977, p. 28–29; "Carter's first act touches off storm." *U.S. News and World Report*, January 31, 1977, p. 22.

19. "The war over secret warfare." *Newsweek*, September 30, 1974, p. 37–39; "What the CIA knew." *Newsweek*, July 15, 1974, p. 29–30.

20. "A true-blue-ribbon panel." *Newsweek*, January 20, 1975, p. 20–22.

21. "The directors defend themselves." *Time*, January 27, 1975, p. 29; "A peek in the CIA's closet." *Newsweek*, January 27, 1975, p. 29–30.

22. "Now you see it, now you don't." *Newsweek*, June 16, 1975, p. 18–20; "Leaving murky murders to the Senate." *Time*, June 16, 1975, p. 9–10; "The cloak comes off." *Newsweek*, June 23, 1975, p. 16–18; "Who's watching whom." *Newsweek*, June 23, 1975, p. 19–27.

23. "The casualty." *Newsweek*, July 21, 1975, p. 17–19; "Tantalizing bits of evidence." *Time*, August 4, 1975, p. 8.

24. "The Pandora's box at the FBI." *Newsweek*, February 3, 1975, p. 11–12; "The FBI's turn." *Newsweek*, February 17, 1975, p. 21; "J. Edgar Hoover's secret files." *Newsweek*, March 10, 1975, p. 16–17; "The FBI's 'black bag boys.'" *Newsweek*, July 28, 1975, p. 18–21; "Tales of the FBI." *Newsweek*, December 1, 1975, p. 35–36; "It all began with FDR." *Newsweek*, December 15, 1975, p. 27–28.

25. "The CIA's hit list." *Newsweek*, December 1, 1975, p. 28–32; "How the CIA does business." *Newsweek*, May 1, 1975, p. 25–28; "Inquest on intelligence." *Newsweek*, May 10, 1976, p. 40–44.

26. "Not guilty." *Newsweek*, December 15, 1975, p. 27.

27. "Vietnam: a year later." *Newsweek*, May 5, 1976, p. 40–45.

28. "An agonizing reappraisal." *Time*, April 7, 1975, p. 11; "Asphyxiating the capital." *Time*, March 17, 1975, p. 34+; "The captain's log: a tale of terror." *Time*, May 26, 1975, p. 11.

29. "Independence—but for whom?" *Time*, November 17, 1975, p. 42–44;

"The battle over Angola." *Time*, December 29, 1975, p. 7–9; "Angola—from the home front." *Newsweek*, January 5, 1976, p. 33–34; "Angola: detente under fire." *Newsweek*, January 19, 1976, p. 20–29; "How much has Angola hurt the U.S.?" *Time*, February 23, 1976, p. 22; "An easy rout—and an olive branch." *Time*, February 23, 1976, p. 18–21.

Chapter 6. This War Just Isn't Working Out for Me—Years 6–7

1. "Women versus women." *Newsweek*, November 3, 1975, p. 25; "Setback for feminists." *Newsweek*, November 17, 1975, p. 53.
2. "Women: A new ERA." *Newsweek*, October 16, 1978, p. 38–39.
3. "Wait till next year." *Newsweek*, March 17, 1975, p. 23; "Saying no to NOW." *Time*, April 28, 1975, p. 75–76.
4. "Abortion: who pays?" *Newsweek*, July 4, 1977, p. 12–13.
5. "Reverse discrimination." *Newsweek*, March 3, 1977, p. 66; "The landmark Bakke ruling." *Newsweek*, July 10, 1978, p. 19–31; "Bakke wins, quotas lose." *Time*, July 10, 1978, p. 8–16.
6. "Women move toward credit equality." *Time*, October 25, 1975, p. 63–64.
7. "Lib in a land of macho." *Newsweek*, July 7, 1975, p. 28–29.
8. "Sportswomanlike conduct." *Newsweek*, June 3, 1974, p. 50–55; "Equal play, equal pay." *Newsweek*, September 5, 1977, p. 83; "Comes the revolution." *Time*, June 26, 1978, p. 54–59.
9. "This woman's army." *Newsweek*, October 20, 1975, p. 41; "Bring me people." *Newsweek*, July 12, 1976, p. 24–27; "Women warriors." *Newsweek*, September 19, 1977, p. 12.
10. "Rookie of the year." *Newsweek*, January 19, 1976, p. 49.
11. "The new New York Times." *Newsweek*, November 20, 1978, p. 133.
12. "Barbara Walters—star of the morning." *Newsweek*, May 6, 1974, p. 56–63; "The $5 million woman." *Newsweek*, May 3, 1976, p. 78–80.
13. "How to succeed: fail, lose or die." *Newsweek*, March 4, 1974, p. 50–51.
14. "Divided over women." *Time*, October 4, 1976, p. 74–75; "Women priests at last." *Newsweek*, September 27, 1976, p. 62; "Women ordained." *Newsweek*, January 17, 1977, p. 85; "Father, make her a priest." *Time*, January 17, 1977, p. 41.
15. "Episcopal split." *Time*, February 13, 1979, p. 60.
16. "Women march on Houston." *Time*, November 28, 1977, p. 12–14; "A women's agenda." *Newsweek*, November 28, 1977, p. 57–59.
17. "Rape alert." *Newsweek*, November 10, 1975, p. 70–79.
18. "The new housewife blues." *Time*, March 14, 1977, p. 63–70.
19. "How men are changing." *Newsweek*, January 16, 1978, p. 52–61.
20. "The me decade and the third great awakening." In Tom Wolfe, *The*

Purple Decades (New York: Berkley Books, 1983), p. 265–293. Originally published in *New York Magazine*, August 23, 1976.

21. "Getting it." *Newsweek*, February 17, 1975, p. 46.

22. "est: there is nothing to get." *Time*, June 7, 1976, p. 53–54.

23. "The power of positive eyewash." *Forbes*, December 1, 1975, p. 22–23.

24. "I am the cause of my world." *Psychology Today*, August 1975, p. 38; "We're gonna tear you down and put you back together again." *Psychology Today*, August 1975, p. 35–40+; "Pay attention you turkeys." The *New York Times Magazine*, May 2, 1976, p. 44–50+.

25. "Food for thought." *Newsweek*, August 28, 1978, p. 78.

26. Ralph Keyes, "I'm ok, you're probably ok." *Newsweek*, October 13, 1975, p. 20; Margaret Halsey, "What's wrong with 'me, me, me.'" *Newsweek*, April 17, 1978, p. 25.

27. "The new narcissism." *Harper's*, October 1975, p. 45–50+; "The new narcissism." *Newsweek*, January 30, 1978, p. 70.

28. "Getting your head together." *Newsweek*, September 6, 1976, p. 56–62.

29. "Coming on strong." *Newsweek*, October 13, 1975, p. 64.

30. "Another Ringer." *Newsweek*, July 25, 1977, p. 78.

31. "The Jesus revolution." *Time*, September 24, 1973, p. 80–81; "A challenge from evangelicals." *Time*, August 5, 1974, p. 48–50; "Religion: return to conservatism." *U.S. News and World Report*, January 5, 1976, p. 52; "Comeback for seminaries in the U.S." *U.S. News and World Report*, January 5, 1976, p. 53–55; "Life with father Moon." *Newsweek*, June 14, 1976, p. 60–66.

32. "Counting souls." *Time*, October 4, 1976, p. 75.

33. "Politics from the pulpit." *Newsweek*, September 6, 1976, p. 49–51; "Born again." *Newsweek*, October 25, 1976, p. 68–78.

34. "Homosexuals: Anita Bryant's crusade." *Newsweek*, April 11, 1977, p. 39.

35. "Back to that old time religion." *Time*, December 26, 1977, p. 52–58.

36. *NBC Nightly News*, September 6, 1977.

37. *ABC World News Tonight*, September 20, 1977.

38. *NBC Nightly News*, October 19–21, 1977.

39. *CBS Evening News*, January 27, 1978.

40. "Bump in the night." *Newsweek*, March 24, 1975, p. 89.

41. "Get up and boogie." *Newsweek*, November 8, 1976, p. 94–98.

42. "Hotspots of the urban night." *Time*, June 27, 1977, p. 56–57.

43. "Discomania: Saturday Night Fever." *Time*, December 19, 1977, p. 69–70; "Polyester dreams." *Harper's*, May 1978, p. 88–89; "The Travolta hustle." *Newsweek*, May 29, 1978, p. 97.

44. "The feverish hustle for big disco profits." *Business Week*, June 26, 1978, p. 42; "The disco scene." *Forbes*, July 10, 1978, p. 14; "Disco takes over." *Newsweek*, April 2, 1979, p. 56–60.

45. "The growling on Ford's right." *Time*, March 17, 1975, p. 11–13; "Ready on the right." *Newsweek*, March 24, 1975, p. 20–24.

46. "Right they are." *Newsweek*, August 23, 1976, p. 20–22; "A conservative drive aimed against the G.O.P." *U.S. News and World Report*, September 6, 1976, p. 15; "The conservatives' drive for a stronger voice." *U.S. News and World Report*, July 11, 1977, p. 47.

47. "Keeping the canal pacts afloat." *Time*, October 24, 1977, p. 35+; Dewitt C. Armstrong III, "Why we should leave Panama." *Newsweek*, November 28, 1977, p. 32–33; "Panama: more than just a ditch." *New York*, January 23, 1978, p. 6+; "A world of woes." *Newsweek*, September 28, 1978, p. 59.

48. "What is a liberal? A conservative?" *U.S. News and World Report*, October 4, 1976, p. 25; "Pop, what's a populist?" *Time*, October 4, 1976, p. 71; "An elegy for the new left." *Time*, August 15, 1977, p. 67–68

49. "The big tax revolt." *Newsweek*, June 19, 1978, p. 20–30; "Revolt over taxes." *Time*, June 5, 1978, p. 12–14.

50. "Is America turning right?" *Newsweek*, November 7, 1977, p. 34–44.

51. "Why the shift to conservatism?" *U.S. News and World Report*, January 23, 1978, p. 24–25.

52. "The 'conservative' myth." *The Nation*, July 17, 1976, p. 39–40.

53. "How real is that trend toward conservatism?" *Nation's Business*, April 1978, p. 13–14.

54. "Right on for the new right." *Time*, October 3, 1977, p. 24–25; "King Midas of 'the new right.'" *Atlantic*, November 1978, p. 52–61.

55. "Why the new right isn't doing well at the polls." *Business Week*, October 30, 1978, p. 158–160.

56. "The Senate's new right." *Newsweek*, April 2, 1979, p. 32–34.

57. "A world of woes." *Newsweek*, September 28, 1978, p. 59; "When Persians collide." *Newsweek*, November 28, 1977, p. 65; "Bloody Nicaragua." *Newsweek*, September 25, 1978, p. 46–48; "Iran: carrot and stick." *Newsweek*, September 25, 1978, p. 48–49; "Nicaragua: Cuba all over again?" *U.S. News and World Report*, September 11, 1978, p. 37; "The Shah's divided land." *Time*, September 18, 1978, p. 32–40.

58. Norman Podhoretz, "The culture of appeasement." *Harper's*, October 1977, p. 25–32.

59. "U.S. arms: Are our defenses down?" *Newsweek*, March 17, 1975, p. 45–53; "Is America No. 2?" *Newsweek*, March 1, 1976, p. 38–40.

60. "The Kremlin's unending quest for world domination." *U.S. News and World Report*, October 24, 1977, p. 54+; "How Russia and U.S. match up in output, living standards." *U.S. News and World Report*, October 24, 1977, p. 52–53; "Russia closing technology gap with U.S." *U.S. News and World Report*, March 27, 1978, p. 89.

61. "A new cold war?" *Newsweek*, June 12, 1978, p. 26–37.

62. "New alarm over Russian threat." *U.S. News and World Report*, October 30, 1978, p. 47–49.

Chapter 7. The Party's Over... — Years 8–9

1. "Alcohol: the #1 drug problem among teenagers today." *Parents Magazine*, January 1975, p. 42+.

2. "School-age drunks—a fresh worry." *U.S. News and World Report*, April 14, 1975, p. 40; "Alcohol and marijuana: spreading menace among teenagers." *U.S. News and World Report*, November 24, 1975, p. 28–30.

3. "The most dangerous drug." *Harper's Bazaar*, June 1976, p. 67–69; *NBC Nightly News*, July 8, 1976.

4. *NBC Nightly News*, August 18, 1975.

5. "Can alcoholics drink?" *Newsweek*, June 21, 1976, p. 58; "Booze for alcoholics?" *Time*, June 21, 1976, p. 45; *ABC World News Tonight*, July 1, 1976; *NBC Nightly News*, August 8, 1976.

6. *CBS Evening News*, March 8, 1976; "Mounting a counterattack against child alcoholism." *U.S. News and World Report*, July 11, 1977, p. 33–34.

7. "Mounting a counterattack against child alcoholism." *U.S. News and World Report*, July 11, 1977, p. 33–34; "As states crack down on teen-age drinking." *U.S. News and World Report*, September 18, 1978, p. 64.

8. *NBC Nightly News*, March 24, 1977; *CBS Evening News*, March 25, 1977, and December 4, 1977.

9. "As states crack down on teen-age drinking." *U.S. News and World Report*, September 18, 1978, p. 64; "The latest teen drug." *Newsweek*, January 8, 1979, p. 43–44; "A new prohibition for teen-agers." *Newsweek*, April 2, 1979, p. 38; "National minimum drinking age." Subcommittee Hearing on Alcoholism and Drug Abuse, Committee on Labor and Human Resources, United States Senate, June 19, 1984, p. 44–49.

10. "The ERA runs into a roadblock." *Time*, February 26, 1979, p. 19.

11. "Sisterhood at city hall." *Newsweek*, April 16, 1979, p. 48.

12. "Women in the armed forces." *Newsweek*, February 18, 1980, p. 34–42.

13. "Legal battle of the sexes." *Newsweek*, April 30, 1979, p. 68–75.

14. "Politics from the pulpit." *Time*, October 13, 1980, p. 28+.

15. *NBC Nightly News*, August 19, 1980; *ABC World News Tonight*, September 23–26, 1980; *CBS Evening News*, September 29, 1980; *NBC Nightly News*, September 29, 1980; *CBS Evening News*, October 3, 1980; *NBC Nightly News*, October 3, 1980.

16. "A fanatical abortion fight." *Time*, July 9, 1979, p. 26–27; *ABC World News Tonight*, April 30, 1981; *CBS Evening News*, June 17, 1981; *NBC Nightly News*, June 7, 1981.

17. *CBS Evening News*, March 11, 1981; *NBC Nightly News*, March 23, 1981; *ABC World News Tonight*, April 30, 1981.

18. "Refugees: seeking safe harbor." *Time*, July 4, 1977, p. 24+; "Vietnam's legacy." *Newsweek*, July 18, 1977, p. 18; "A cruise to nowhere." *Newsweek*, November 27, 1978, p. 58; "Flood tide of refugees." *Newsweek*, December 11, 1978, p. 51–52.

19. "Yearning to breathe free." *Time*, May 14, 1979, p. 14–15; "Boat people backlash." *Newsweek*, June 25, 1979, p. 55; "Facing a liquid Auschwitz." *Time*, July 2, 1979, p. 38–39; "Agony of the boat people." *Newsweek*, July 2, 1979, p. 45–50; "A rescue plan at last." *Time*, July 30, 1979, p. 36–37.

20. "A rescue plan at last." *Time*, July 30, 1979, p. 36–37+.

21. John Rappaport, "Yearnotes Year 9." P. 181 in Suzy Kalter, *The Complete Book of M*A*S*H* (New York: H.N. Abrams, 1988).

22. "Iran at the brink." *Newsweek*, January 8, 1979, p. 14–19; "A helpless giant in Iran." *Newsweek*, November 19, 1979, p. 61–75; "We're going to kick your butts." *Time*, November 19, 1979, p. 30.

23. "Finally, fire in his eyes." *Time*, April 21, 1980, p. 14–17; "The wavering allies." *Newsweek*, April 21, 1980, p. 36; "Debacle in the desert." *Time*, May 5, 1980, p. 12–25.

24. "Hostage breakthrough." *Time*, January 26, 1981, p. 13–19; "The hostages return." *Newsweek*, February 2, 1981, p. 22–32.

25. "The neutron bomb furor." *Time*, April 17, 1978 p. 10–14; "Furor over the neutron bomb." *Newsweek*, April 17, 1978, p. 34–39+.

26. "Fit for active duty?" *Newsweek*, March 26, 1979, p. 43–44+.

27. "Has Carter saved SALT?" *Newsweek*, October 15, 1979, p. 63–67; "Carter's widening crisis." *Newsweek*, January 7, 1980, p. 16–17; "My opinion of the Russians has changed most dramatically." *Time*, January 14, 1980, p. 10–17; "Afghanistan takeover—why Russians acted." *U.S. News and World Report*, January 14, 1980, p. 24–26; "The chill of a new cold war." *Newsweek*, January 14, 1980, p. 24–27; "The grain cutback." *Newsweek*, January 14, 1980, p. 27.

28. "Shootout over the Med." *Time*, August 31, 1981, p. 24–26; "To the shores of Tripoli." *Newsweek*, August 31, 1981, p. 14–18; "Candles in the night." *Time*, January 4, 1982, p. 52+; "Poland: the resistance." *Newsweek*, January 4, 1982, p. 12–19.

29. "A pacifist wave in Europe." *Newsweek*, August 24, 1981, p. 28–31.

30. "A looser leash for the CIA." *Newsweek*, December 14, 1981, p. 38; "Defense: new muscle for America?" *U.S. News and World Report*, December 29, 1980 and January 5, 1981, p. 27–30; "Putting up a tougher front to the world," *U.S. News and World Report*, December 29, 1980, and January 5, 1981, p. 31.

31. "Reagan: 'peace through strength.'" *The Washington Post*, August 19, 1980, p. A1; "Reagan, in speech to legion, says Carter has falsified military statistics." *The New York Times*, August 21, 1980, p. B8.

Chapter 8. Goodbye, Farewell
and Amen—Years 10–11

1. Suzy Kalter, *The Complete Book of M*A*S*H* (New York: H.N. Abrams, 1988), p. 157.
2. Kalter, *Complete Book of M*A*S*H*, p. 199.
3. "Reagan's high-risk budget." *Newsweek*, February 15, 1982, p. 22–25; "Taking aim at the Pentagon." *Newsweek*, February 15, 1982, p. 24–25; "Challenge to change." *Time*, March 2, 1981, p. 10–15.
4. "Politics in post ERA era." *Newsweek*, July 12, 1982, p. 33; "Women's issues of the '80's." *Newsweek*, June 22, 1981, p. 58–59; "How long till equality?" *Time*, July 12, 1982, p. 20–29.
5. "A woman for the court." *Newsweek*, July 20, 1981, p. 16–18+; "The brethren's first sister." *Time*, July 20, 1981, p. 8–12+; *CBS Evening News*, July 7, 1981; *NBC Nightly News*, July 8, 1981.
6. "How long till equality?" *Time*, July 12, 1982, p. 20–29.
7. "A secret war for Nicaragua." *Newsweek*, November 8, 1982, p. 42–46+.
8. "The peekaboo offensive." *Newsweek*, March 15, 1982, p. 35–36.
9. "Poland: the resistance." *Newsweek*, January 4, 1982, p. 12–19; "Candles in the night." *Time*, January 4, 1982, p. 52–57.
10. "A case of pipeline politics." *Newsweek*, March 15, 1982, p. 36–37.
11. "A pacifist wave in Europe." *Newsweek*, August 24, 1981, p. 28–29+; "A vision of the apocalypse." *Newsweek*, April 19, 1982, p. 97–98; "Freeze march." *Time*, June 14, 1982, p. 24; "Giving peace a chance." *Newsweek*, June 21, 1982, p. 40–41; "A movement gathers force." *Time*, June 21, 1982, p. 39.
12. "Reagan's high-risk budget." *Newsweek*, February 15, 1982, p. 22–25.
13. "The U.S. Marines go ashore." *Newsweek*, September 6, 1982, p. 30–32; "The marines have landed." *Time*, September 6, 1982, p. 26–28; "A time of reckoning." *Newsweek*, October 4, 1982, p. 20–24; "'God—Oh, my God.'" *Time*, October 4, 1983, p. 20–23; "The troubled soul of Israel." *Newsweek*, October 4, 1982, p. 30–34+.
14. The information and statistics on the final episode, "Goodbye, Farewell and Amen," come from Kalter, *Complete Book of M*A*S*H*, p. 34.
15. Joe Saltzman, "The legacy of 'M*A*S*H.'" *USA Today*, July 1983, p. 61; "MASH hysteria." *Newsweek*, February 28, 1983, p. 49.
16. "Farewell to the M*A*S*H gang." *Newsweek*, February 28, 1983, p. 45; "M*A*S*H, you were a smash." *Time*, February 28, 1983, p. 65.
17. "Farewell to the M*A*S*H gang." *Newsweek*, February 28, 1983, p. 46.
18. "Farewell to the gang at the front." *Macleans*, February 28, 1983, p. 46.

19. "Farewell to the M*A*S*H gang." *Newsweek*, February 28, 1983, p. 44+.

20. Joe Saltzman, "The legacy of 'M*A*S*H.'" *USA Today*, July 1983, p. 61.

21. "In the midst of death, a festival of life." *The Christian Century*, March 23–30, 1983, p. 260–261.

22. "Farewell to the M*A*S*H gang." *Newsweek*, February 28, 1983, p. 48.

23. "The memorial that healed our wounds." *U.S. News and World Report*, November 21, 1983, p. 68–70; "The Vietnam War Memorial." *America*, January 22, 1983, p. 54–55.

24. "The marines pay the price." *Newsweek*, September 12, 1983, p. 40–45; "The marine massacre." *Newsweek*, October 31, 1983, p. 20–25; "Carnage in Lebanon." *Time*, October 31, 1983, p. 14–25.

25. "Days of shock." *Time*, November 7, 1983, p. 20–34+; "Americans at war." *Newsweek*, November 7, 1983, p. 52–58+; "After the troops pull out." *U.S. News and World Report*, November 14, 1983, p. 22–25; "Not all sugar and spice." *Time*, November 28, 1983, p. 20–22.

26. "Keeping the press from the action." *Time*, November 7, 1983, p. 46–50; "Angry allies." *Time*, November 7, 1983, p. 47.

27. "Weighing the proper role." *Time*, November 7, 1983, p. 42+.

28. "Green grow the green berets." *Newsweek*, October 10, 1983, p. 46.

29. "America's secret warriors." *Newsweek*, October 10, 1983, p. 38–45.

Index